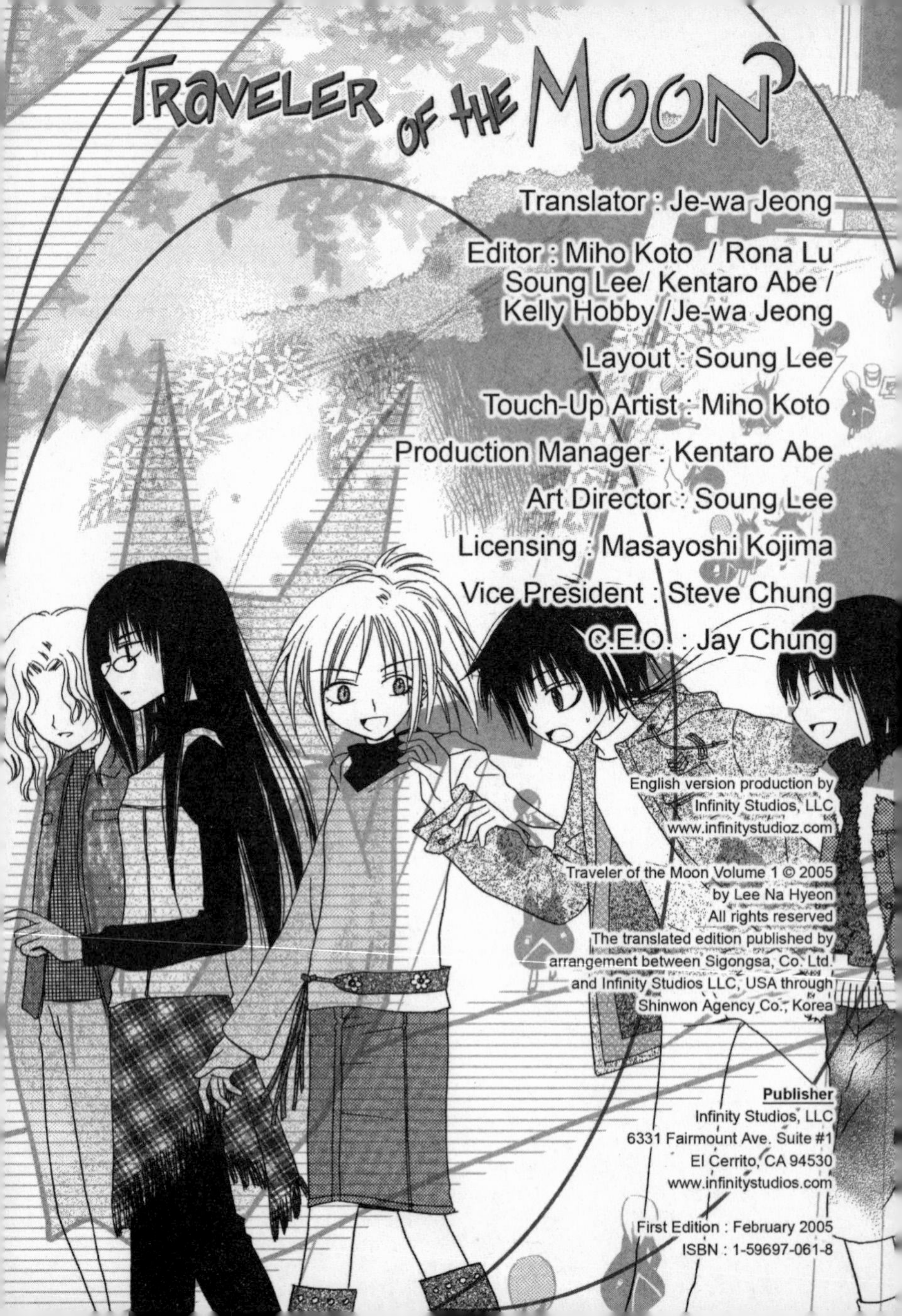

Traveler of the Moon

Translator : Je-wa Jeong

Editor : Miho Koto / Rona Lu
Soung Lee/ Kentaro Abe /
Kelly Hobby /Je-wa Jeong

Layout : Soung Lee

Touch-Up Artist : Miho Koto

Production Manager : Kentaro Abe

Art Director : Soung Lee

Licensing : Masayoshi Kojima

Vice President : Steve Chung

C.E.O. : Jay Chung

English version production by
Infinity Studios, LLC
www.infinitystudioz.com

The translated edition published by
arrangement between Sigongsa, Co. Ltd.
and Infinity Studios LLC, USA through
Shinwon Agency Co., Korea

Publisher
Infinity Studios, LLC
6331 Fairmount Ave. Suite #1
El Cerrito, CA 94530
www.infinitystudios.com

First Edition : February 2005
ISBN : 1-59697-061-8

TRAVELER OF THE MOON

1

Lee Na Hyeon

Infinity Studios
www.infinitystudioz.com

AUTHOR'S NOTE

If I only knew back then what I know now before all this started… it would have been so nice!! But then again, that would be an impossibility. On top of that, I'm guessing that I'll never get over this embarrassing feeling whenever I see my own book sitting there on a bookshelf. And who knows… maybe in 1 or 10 years I'll figure out how I can confidently draw comics, but later be so embarrassed whenever I see my own work around. ^^;;

July 2003, Lee Na Hyeon

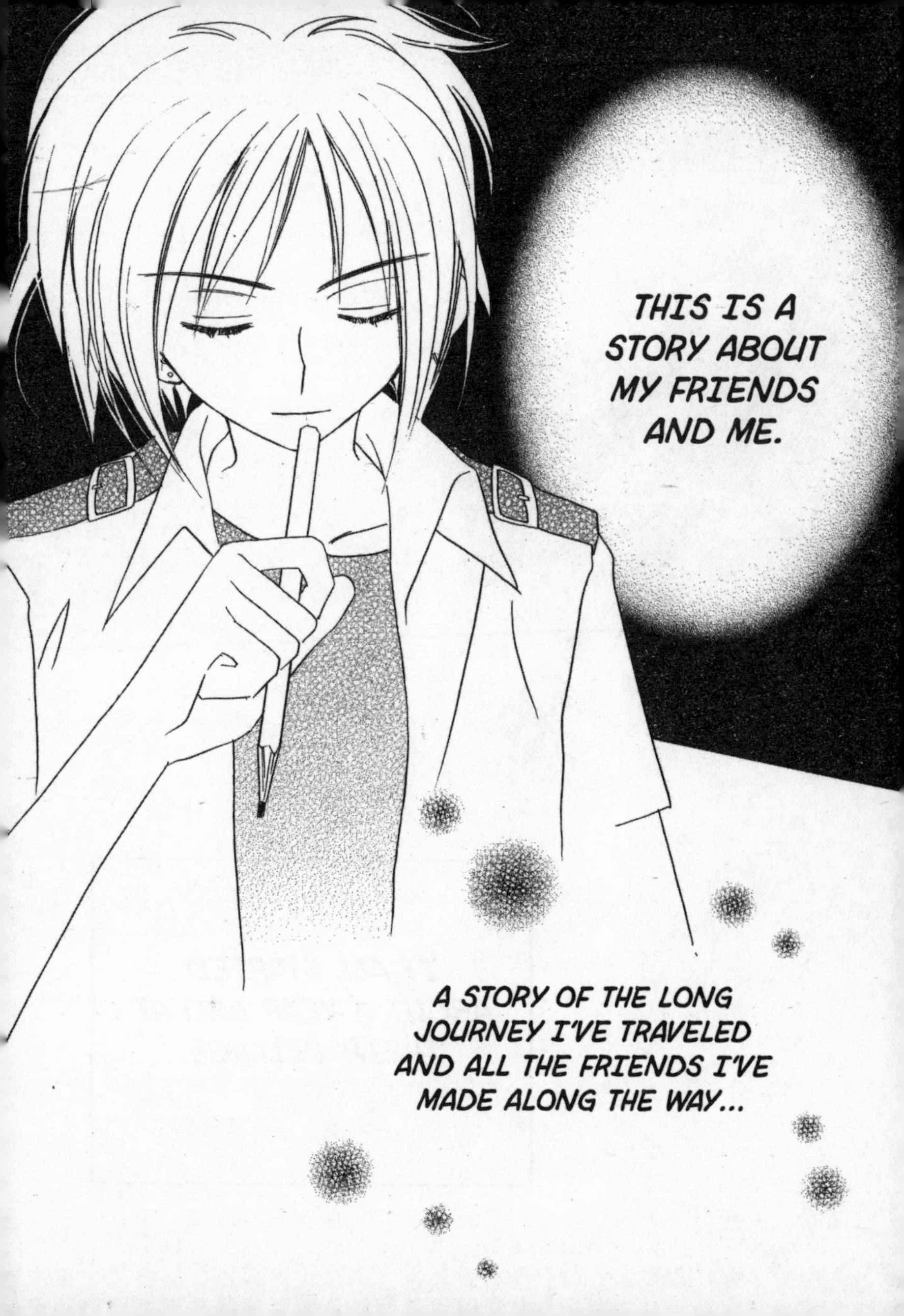
THIS IS A STORY ABOUT MY FRIENDS AND ME.
A STORY OF THE LONG JOURNEY I'VE TRAVELED AND ALL THE FRIENDS I'VE MADE ALONG THE WAY...

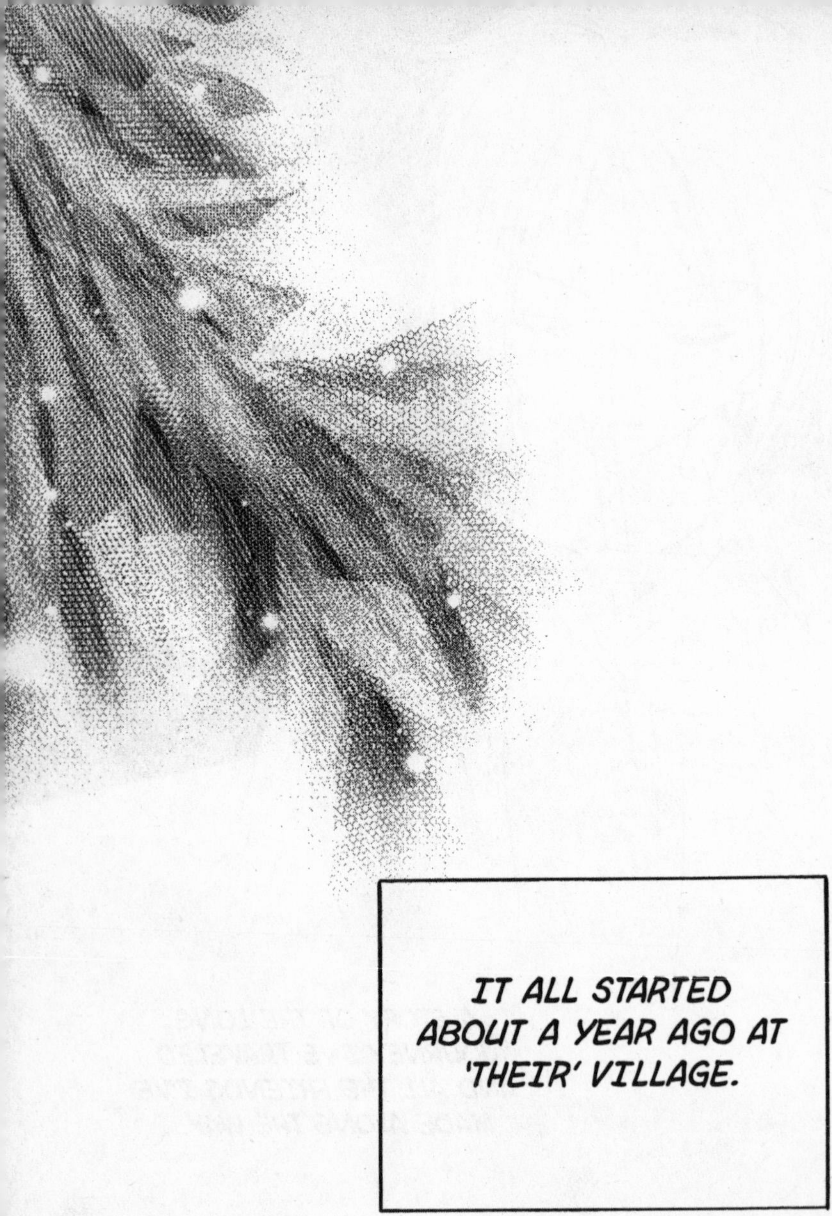
IT ALL STARTED ABOUT A YEAR AGO AT 'THEIR' VILLAGE.

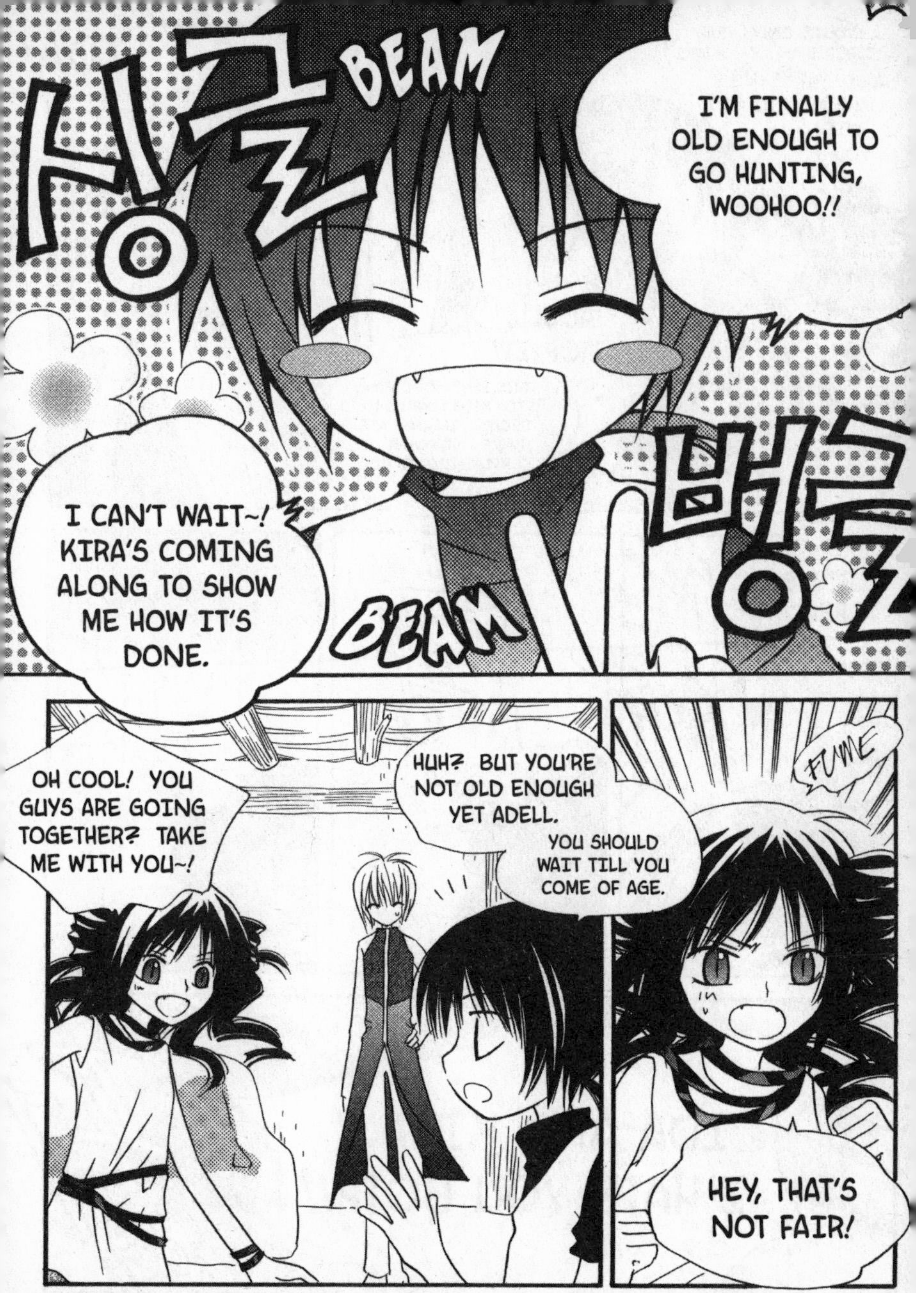
BEAM
I'M FINALLY OLD ENOUGH TO GO HUNTING, WOOHOO!!
I CAN'T WAIT~! KIRA'S COMING ALONG TO SHOW ME HOW IT'S DONE.
BEAM
OH COOL! YOU GUYS ARE GOING TOGETHER? TAKE ME WITH YOU~!
HUH? BUT YOU'RE NOT OLD ENOUGH YET ADELL.
YOU SHOULD WAIT TILL YOU COME OF AGE.
FUME
HEY, THAT'S NOT FAIR!

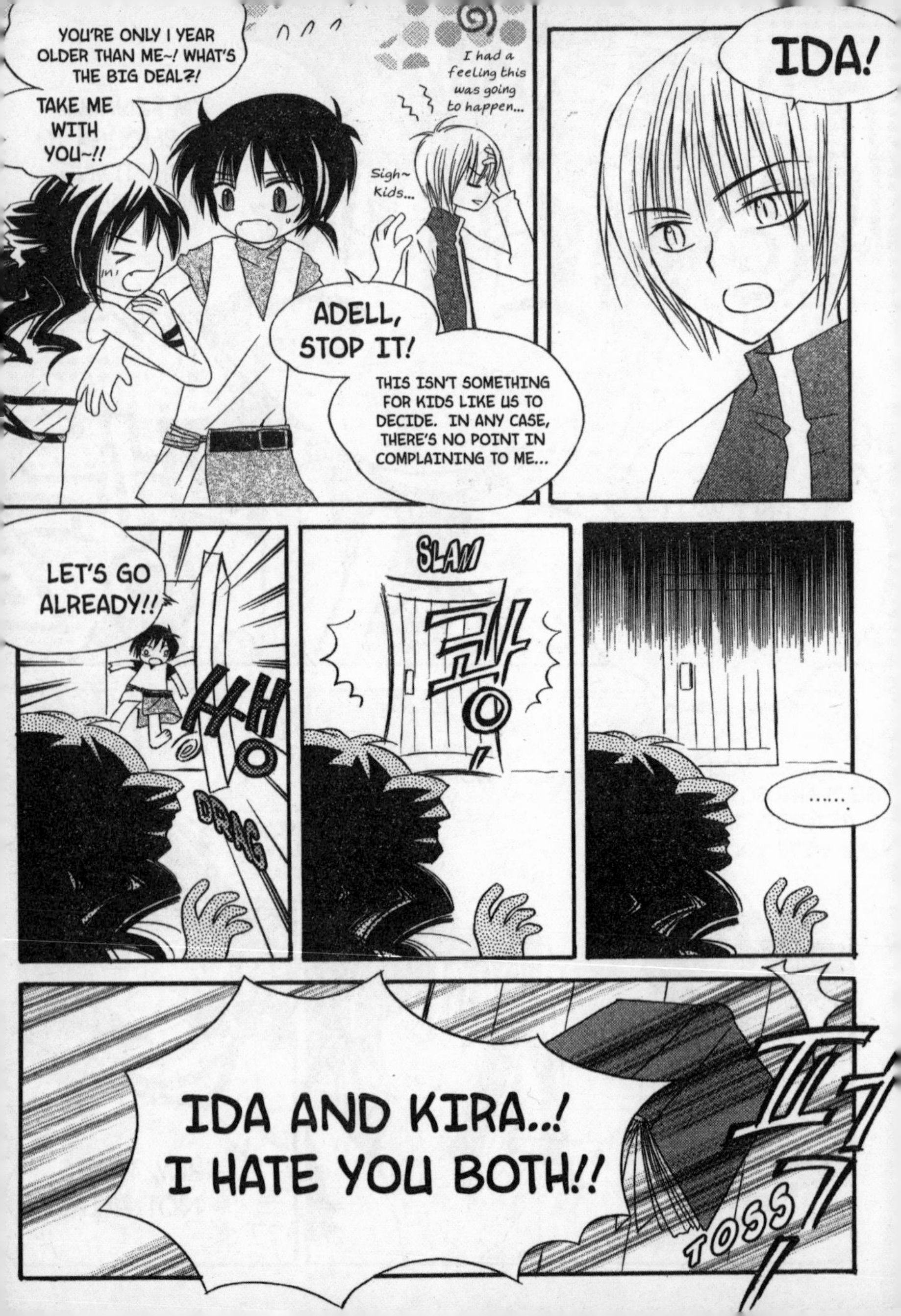
YOU'RE ONLY 1 YEAR OLDER THAN ME~! WHAT'S THE BIG DEAL?!
TAKE ME WITH YOU~!!
I had a feeling this was going to happen...
Sigh~ Kids...
ADELL, STOP IT!
THIS ISN'T SOMETHING FOR KIDS LIKE US TO DECIDE. IN ANY CASE, THERE'S NO POINT IN COMPLAINING TO ME...
IDA!
LET'S GO ALREADY!!
DRAG
SLAM
쾅
......
IDA AND KIRA..! I HATE YOU BOTH!!
TOSS

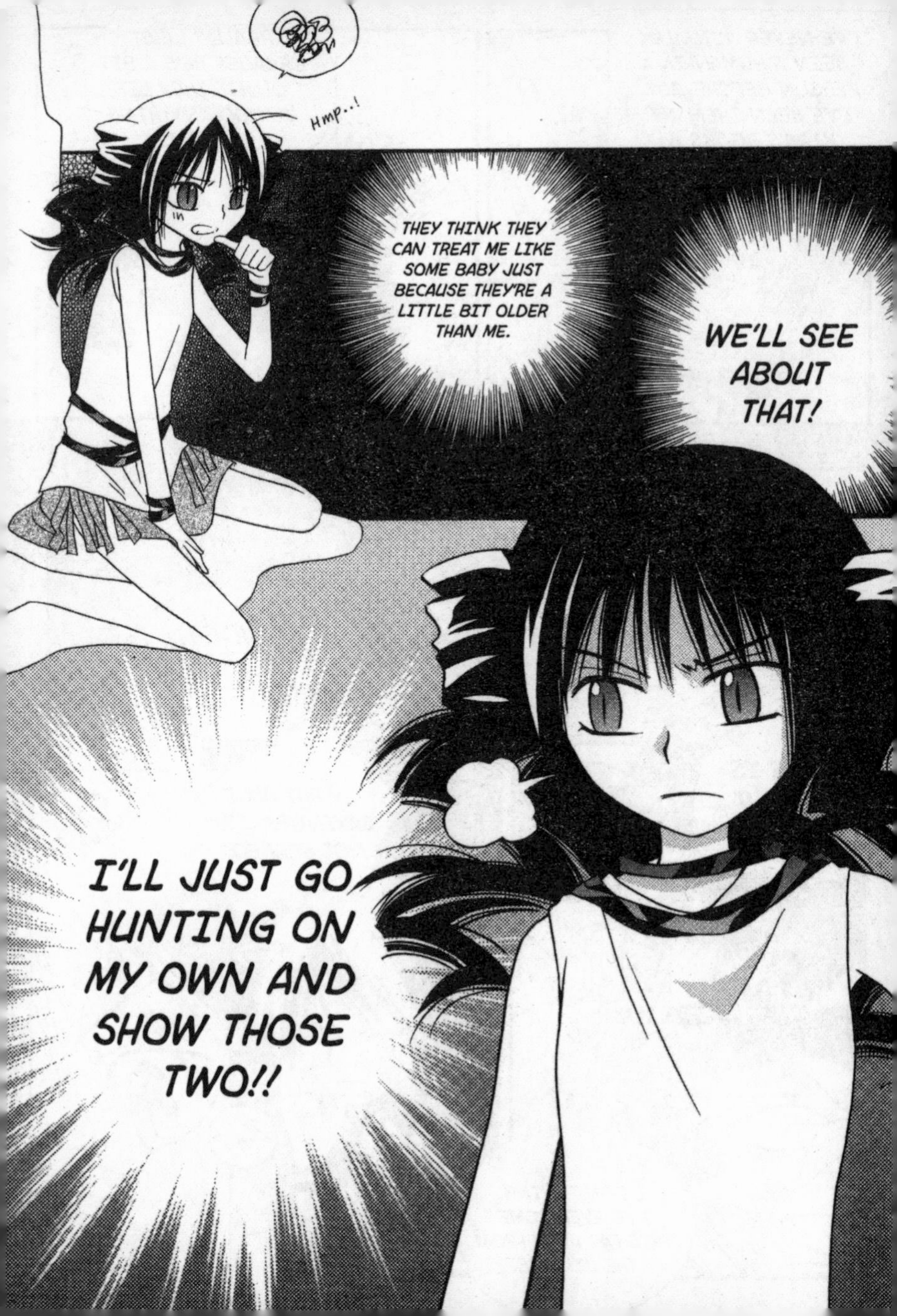
Hmp..!
THEY THINK THEY CAN TREAT ME LIKE SOME BABY JUST BECAUSE THEY'RE A LITTLE BIT OLDER THAN ME.
WE'LL SEE ABOUT THAT!
I'LL JUST GO HUNTING ON MY OWN AND SHOW THOSE TWO!!

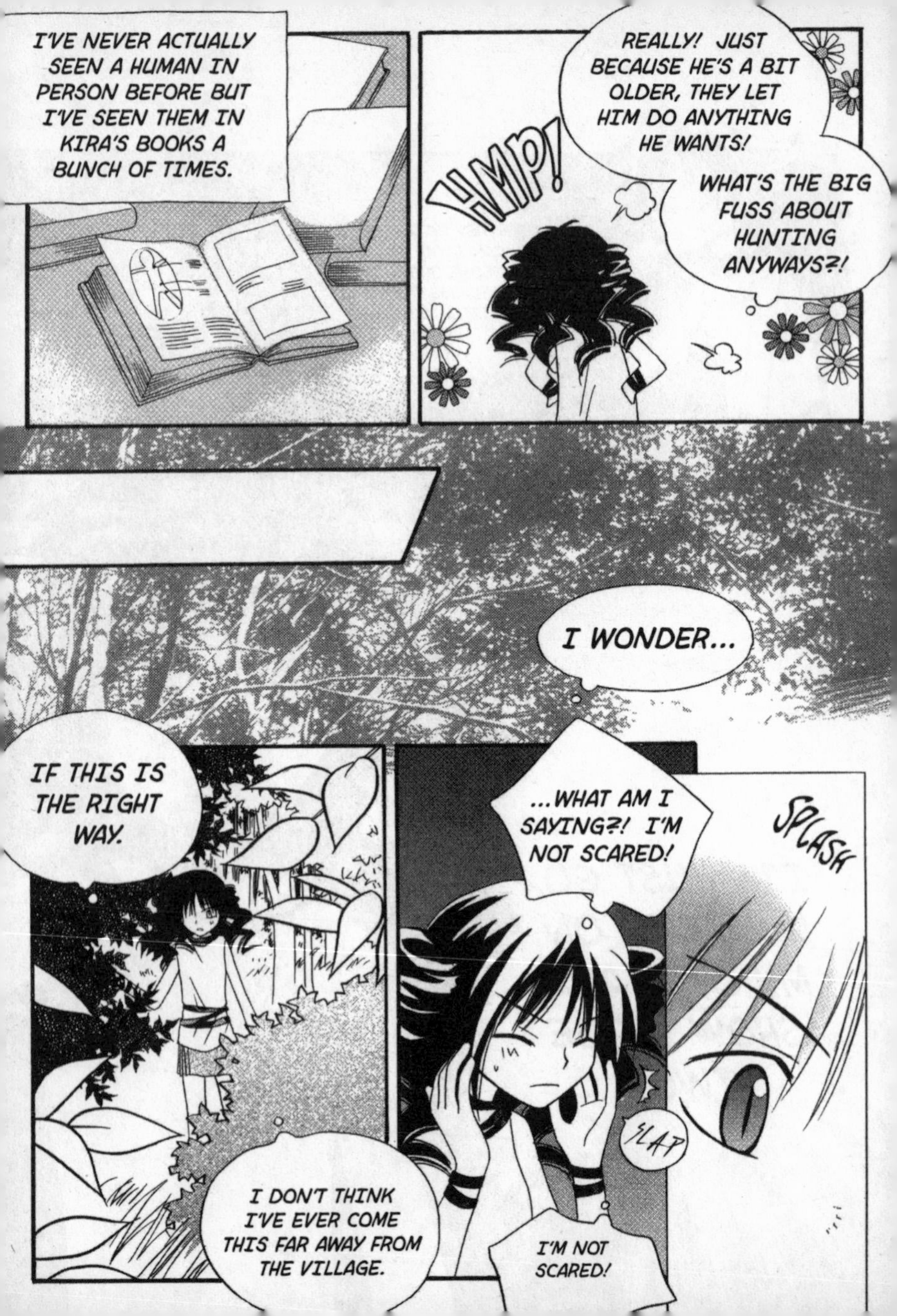
I'VE NEVER ACTUALLY SEEN A HUMAN IN PERSON BEFORE BUT I'VE SEEN THEM IN KIRA'S BOOKS A BUNCH OF TIMES.
REALLY! JUST BECAUSE HE'S A BIT OLDER, THEY LET HIM DO ANYTHING HE WANTS!
HMP!
WHAT'S THE BIG FUSS ABOUT HUNTING ANYWAYS?!
I WONDER...
IF THIS IS THE RIGHT WAY.
I DON'T THINK I'VE EVER COME THIS FAR AWAY FROM THE VILLAGE.
...WHAT AM I SAYING?! I'M NOT SCARED!
SLAP
I'M NOT SCARED!
SPLASH

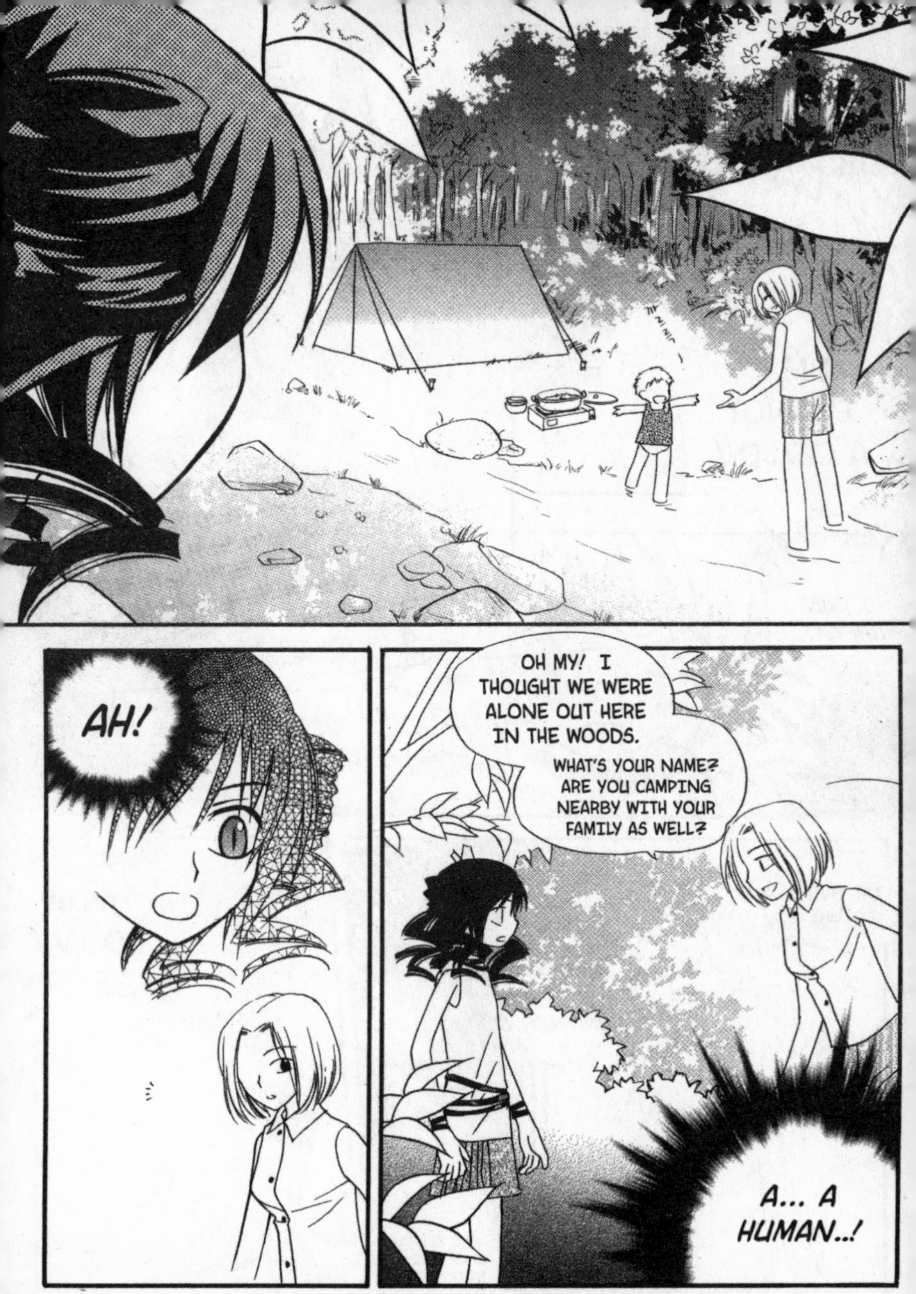
AH!
OH MY! I THOUGHT WE WERE ALONE OUT HERE IN THE WOODS.
WHAT'S YOUR NAME? ARE YOU CAMPING NEARBY WITH YOUR FAMILY AS WELL?
A... A HUMAN..!

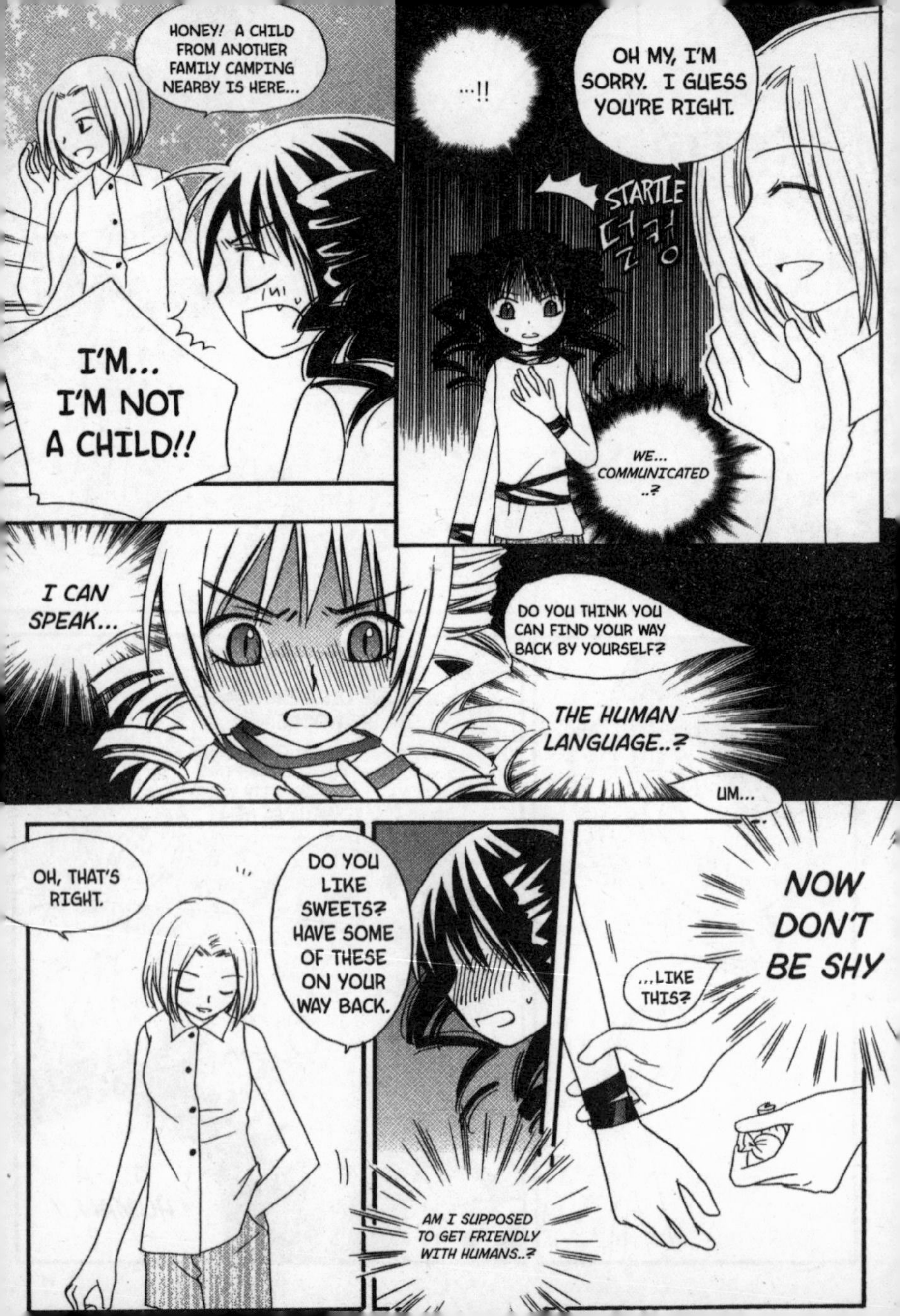
HONEY! A CHILD FROM ANOTHER FAMILY CAMPING NEARBY IS HERE...
I'M... I'M NOT A CHILD!!
...!!
OH MY, I'M SORRY. I GUESS YOU'RE RIGHT.
STARTLE
덜컹
WE... COMMUNICATED ..?
I CAN SPEAK...
DO YOU THINK YOU CAN FIND YOUR WAY BACK BY YOURSELF?
THE HUMAN LANGUAGE..?
UM...
OH, THAT'S RIGHT.
DO YOU LIKE SWEETS? HAVE SOME OF THESE ON YOUR WAY BACK.
AM I SUPPOSED TO GET FRIENDLY WITH HUMANS..?
NOW DON'T BE SHY
...LIKE THIS?

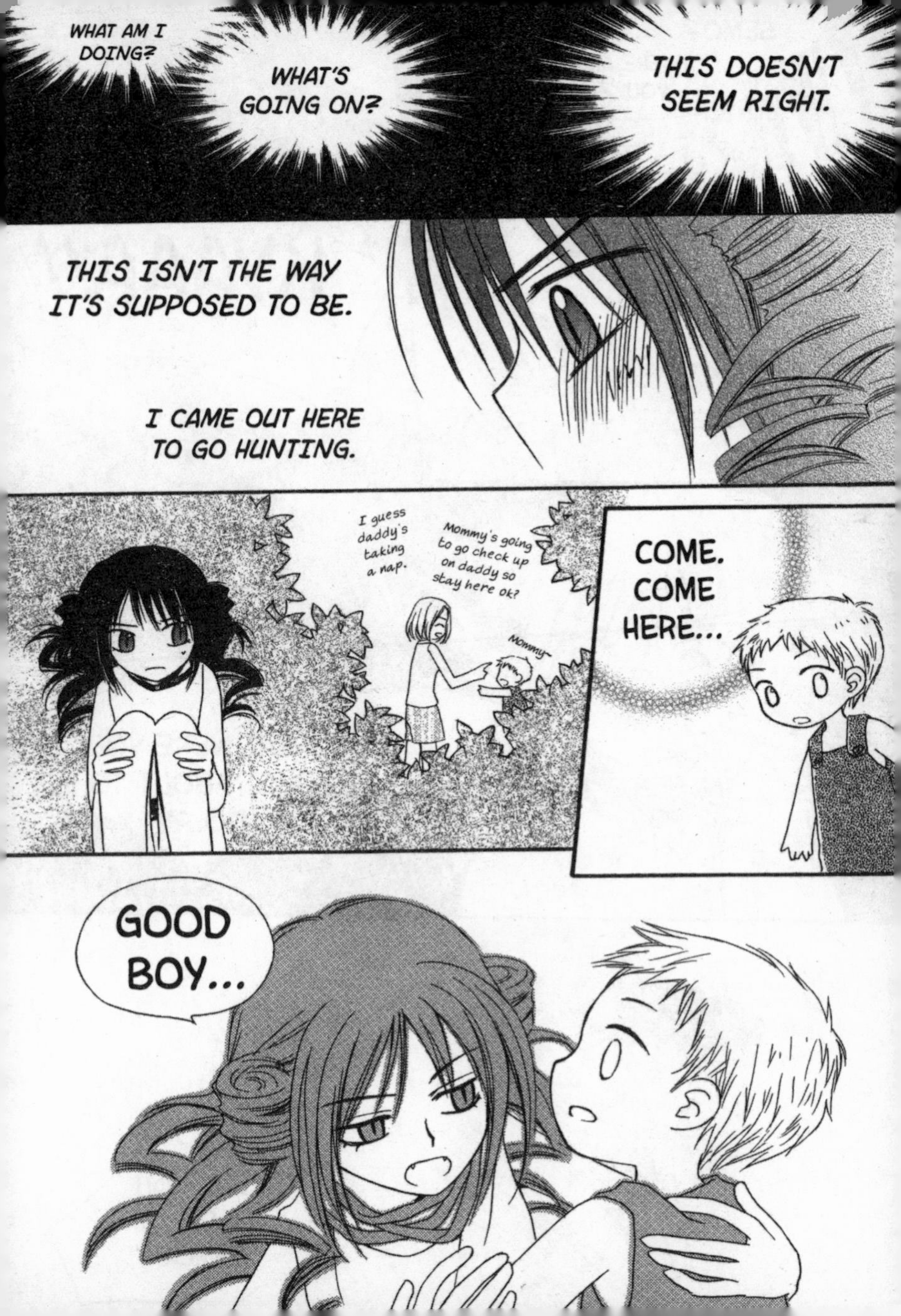
WHAT AM I DOING?
WHAT'S GOING ON?
THIS DOESN'T SEEM RIGHT.
THIS ISN'T THE WAY IT'S SUPPOSED TO BE.
I CAME OUT HERE TO GO HUNTING.
I guess daddy's taking a nap.
Mommy's going to go check up on daddy so stay here ok?
Mommy~
COME. COME HERE...
GOOD BOY...

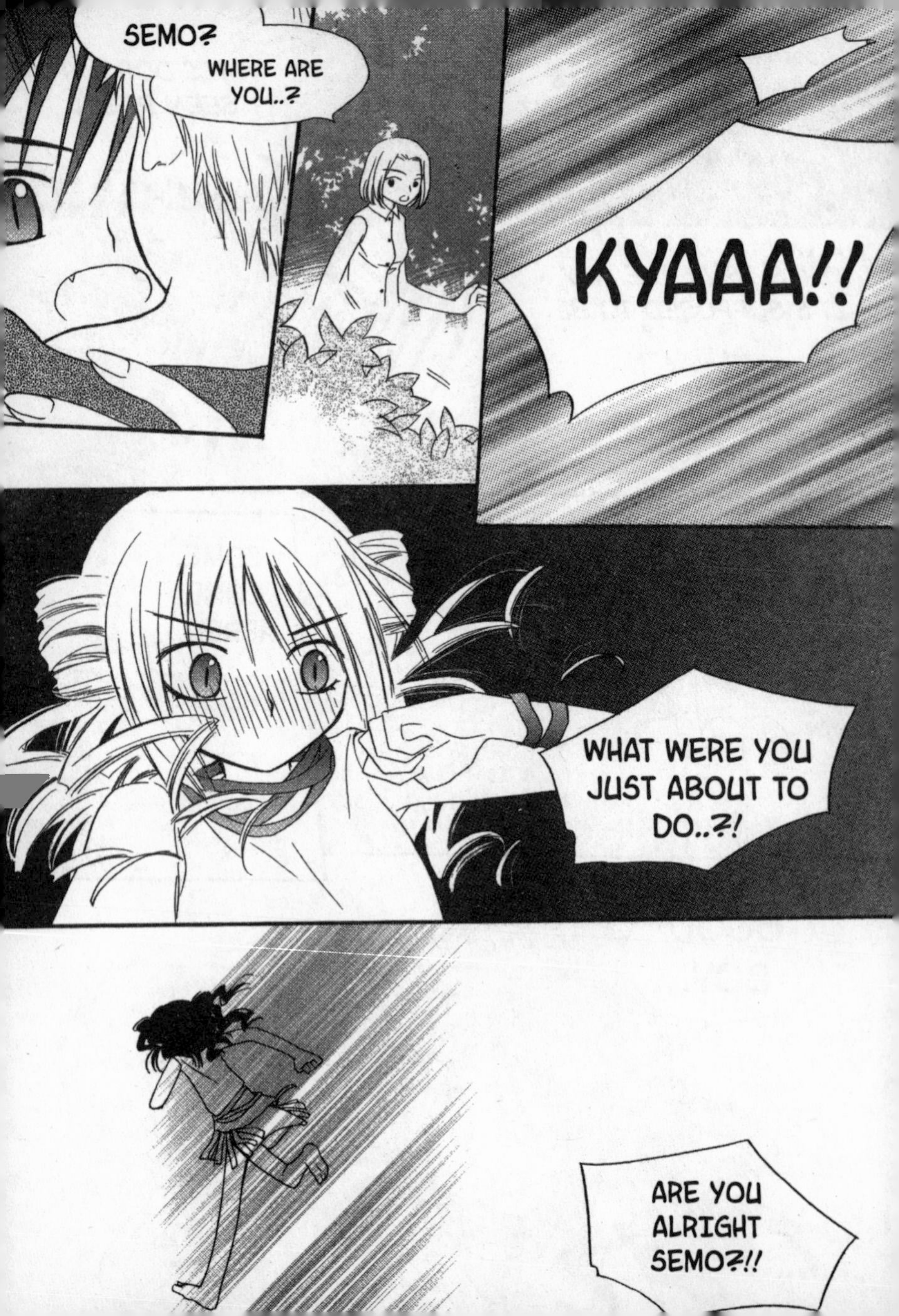
SEMO?
WHERE ARE YOU..?
KYAAA!!
WHAT WERE YOU JUST ABOUT TO DO..?!
ARE YOU ALRIGHT SEMO?!!

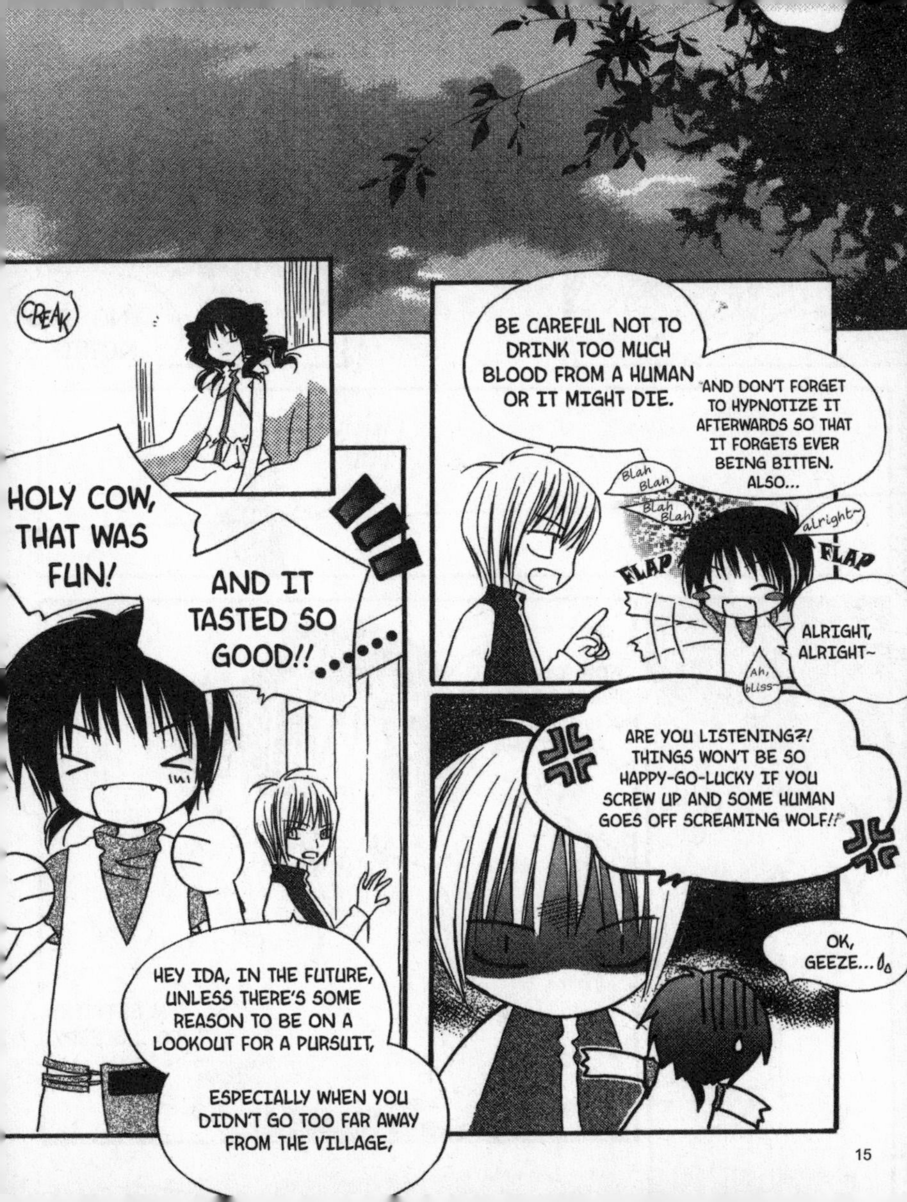
CREAK
HOLY COW, THAT WAS FUN!
AND IT TASTED SO GOOD!! ......
HEY IDA, IN THE FUTURE, UNLESS THERE'S SOME REASON TO BE ON A LOOKOUT FOR A PURSUIT,
ESPECIALLY WHEN YOU DIDN'T GO TOO FAR AWAY FROM THE VILLAGE,
BE CAREFUL NOT TO DRINK TOO MUCH BLOOD FROM A HUMAN OR IT MIGHT DIE.
AND DON'T FORGET TO HYPNOTIZE IT AFTERWARDS SO THAT IT FORGETS EVER BEING BITTEN. ALSO...
Blah Blah
Blah Blah
alright~
FLAP
FLAP
ALRIGHT, ALRIGHT~
Ah, bliss~
ARE YOU LISTENING?! THINGS WON'T BE SO HAPPY-GO-LUCKY IF YOU SCREW UP AND SOME HUMAN GOES OFF SCREAMING WOLF!!
OK, GEEZE...

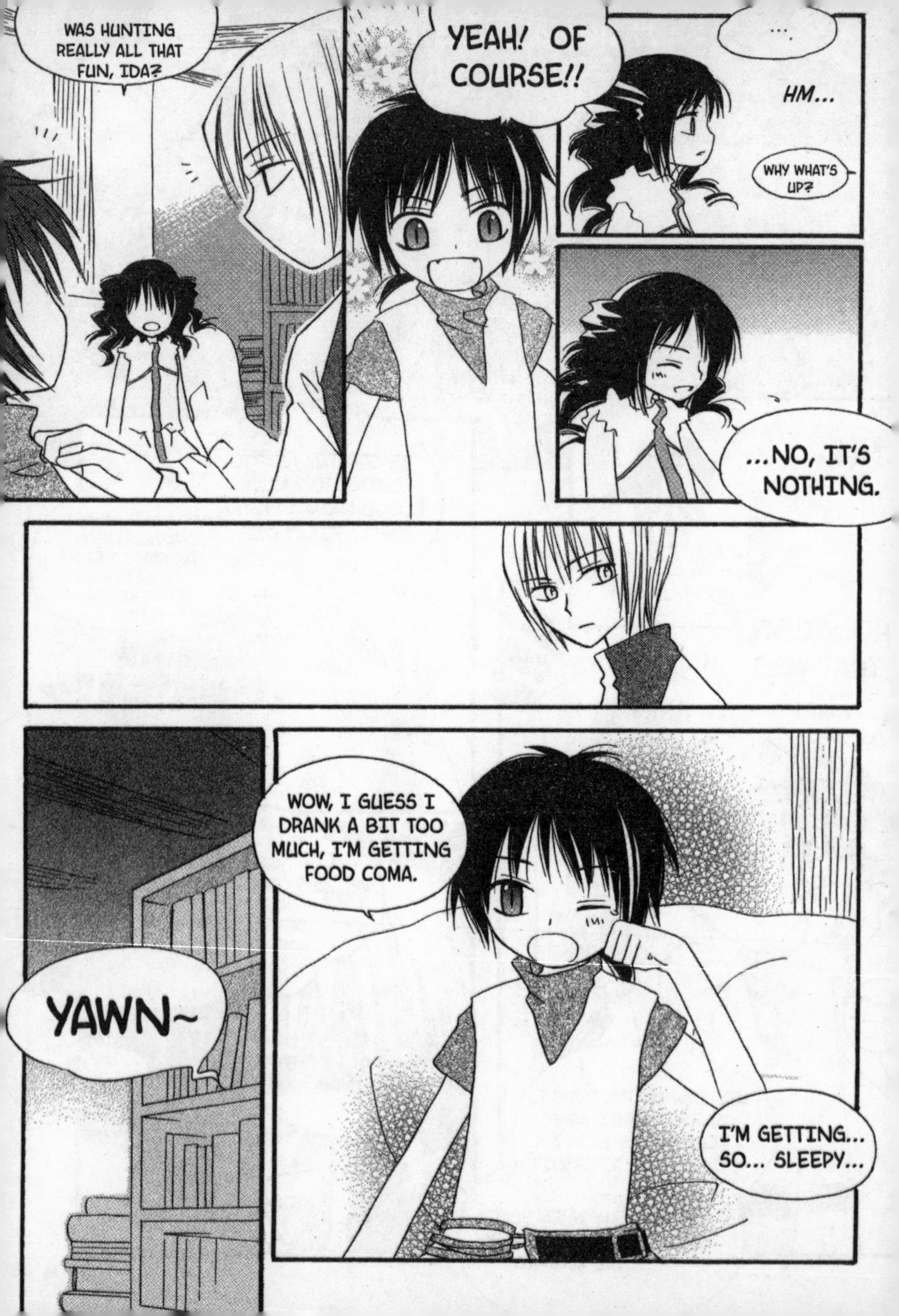
WAS HUNTING REALLY ALL THAT FUN, IDA?
YEAH! OF COURSE!!
...
HM...
WHY WHAT'S UP?
...NO, IT'S NOTHING.
WOW, I GUESS I DRANK A BIT TOO MUCH, I'M GETTING FOOD COMA.
YAWN~
I'M GETTING... SO... SLEEPY...

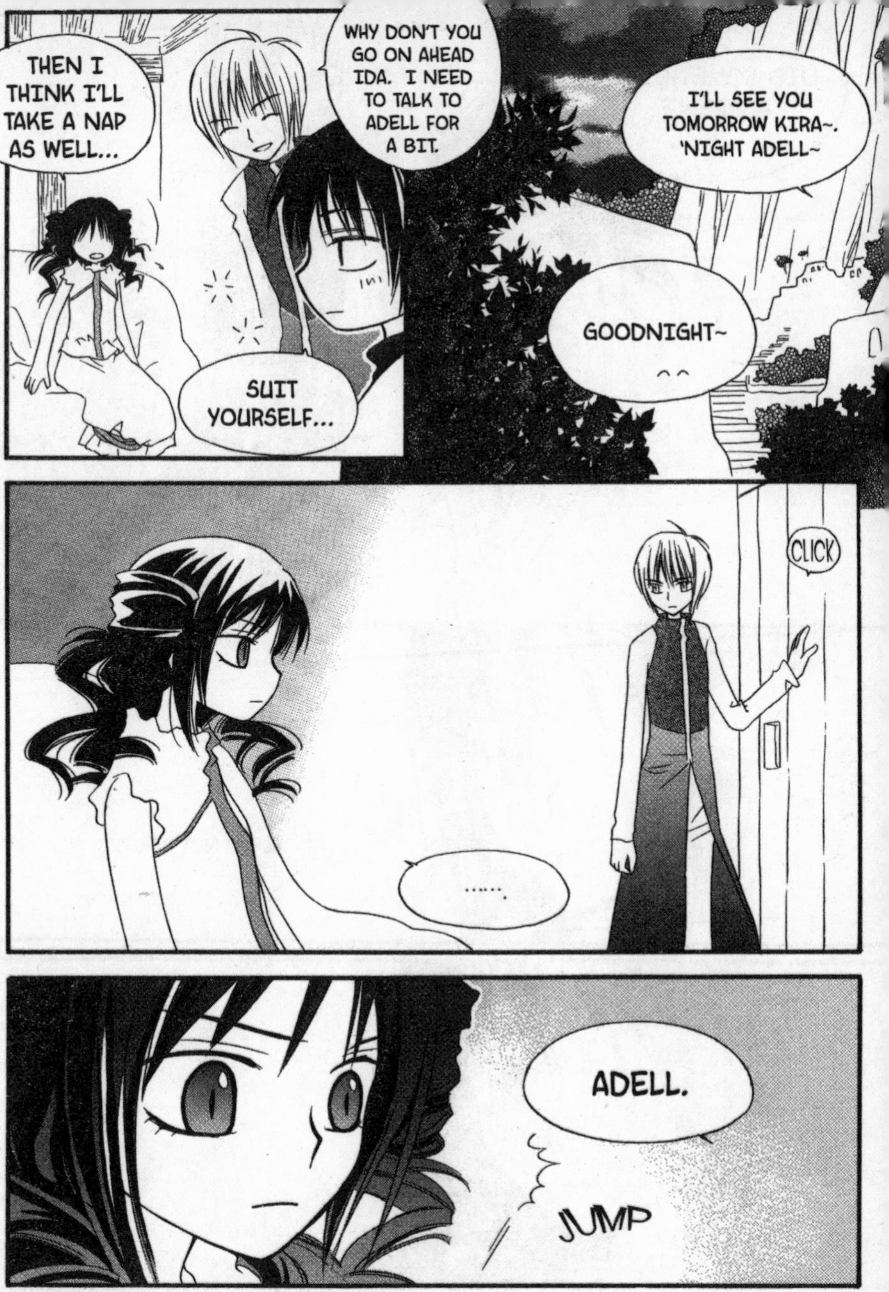
THEN I THINK I'LL TAKE A NAP AS WELL...
WHY DON'T YOU GO ON AHEAD IDA. I NEED TO TALK TO ADELL FOR A BIT.
SUIT YOURSELF...
I'LL SEE YOU TOMORROW KIRA~. 'NIGHT ADELL~
GOODNIGHT~
^^
CLICK
....
ADELL.
JUMP

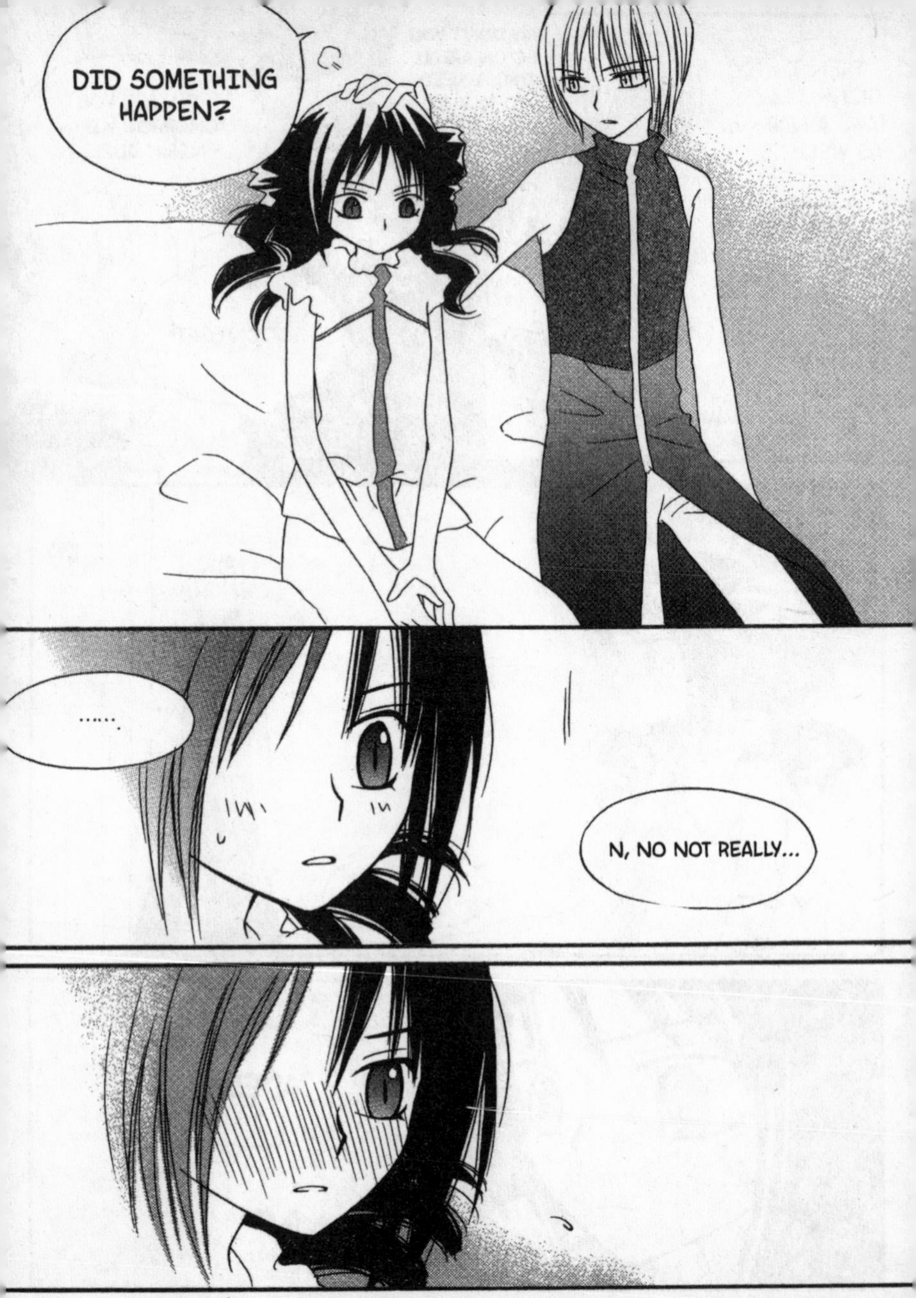
DID SOMETHING HAPPEN?
....
N, NO NOT REALLY...

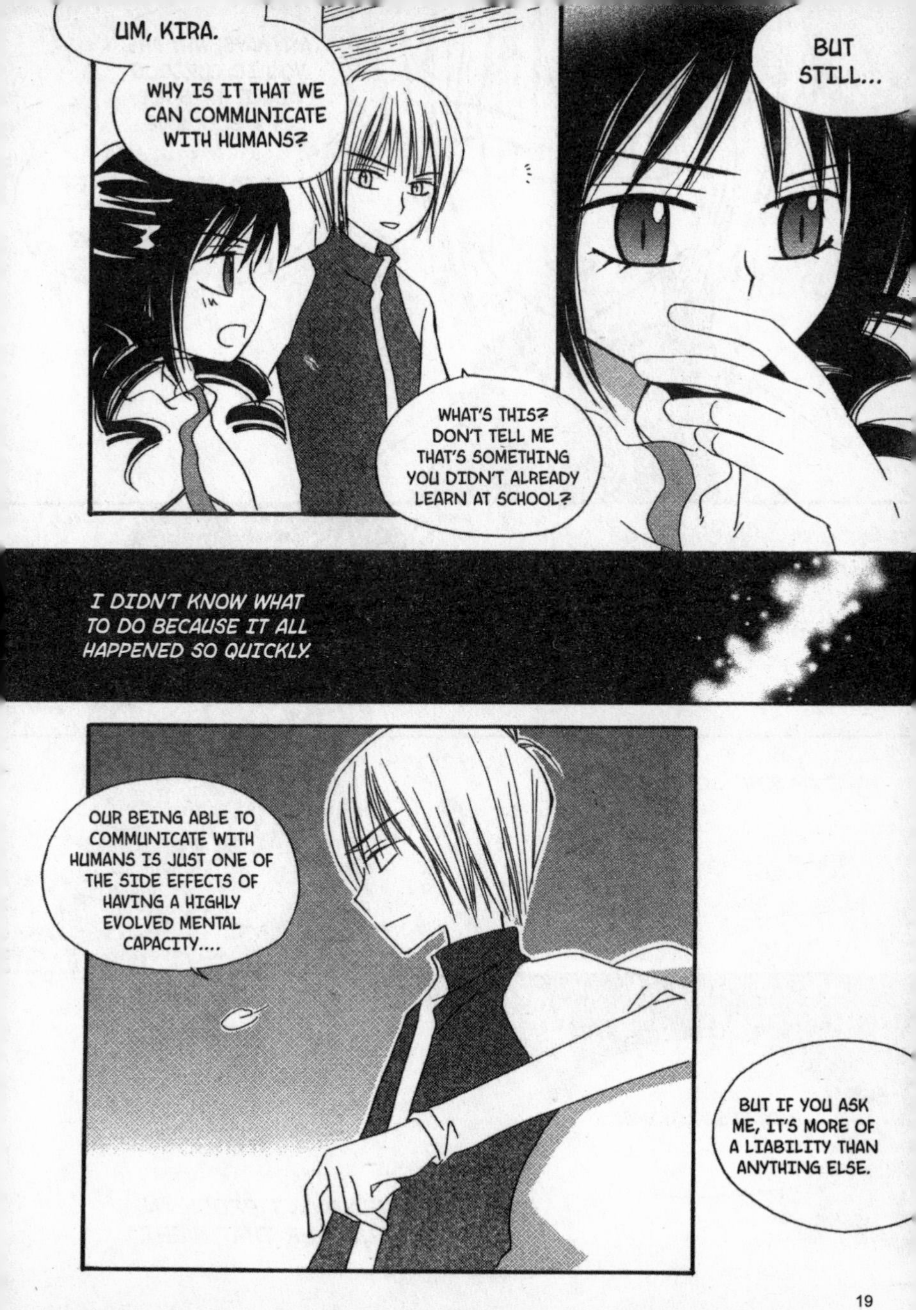
UM, KIRA.
WHY IS IT THAT WE CAN COMMUNICATE WITH HUMANS?
WHAT'S THIS? DON'T TELL ME THAT'S SOMETHING YOU DIDN'T ALREADY LEARN AT SCHOOL?
BUT STILL...
I DIDN'T KNOW WHAT TO DO BECAUSE IT ALL HAPPENED SO QUICKLY.
OUR BEING ABLE TO COMMUNICATE WITH HUMANS IS JUST ONE OF THE SIDE EFFECTS OF HAVING A HIGHLY EVOLVED MENTAL CAPACITY....
BUT IF YOU ASK ME, IT'S MORE OF A LIABILITY THAN ANYTHING ELSE.

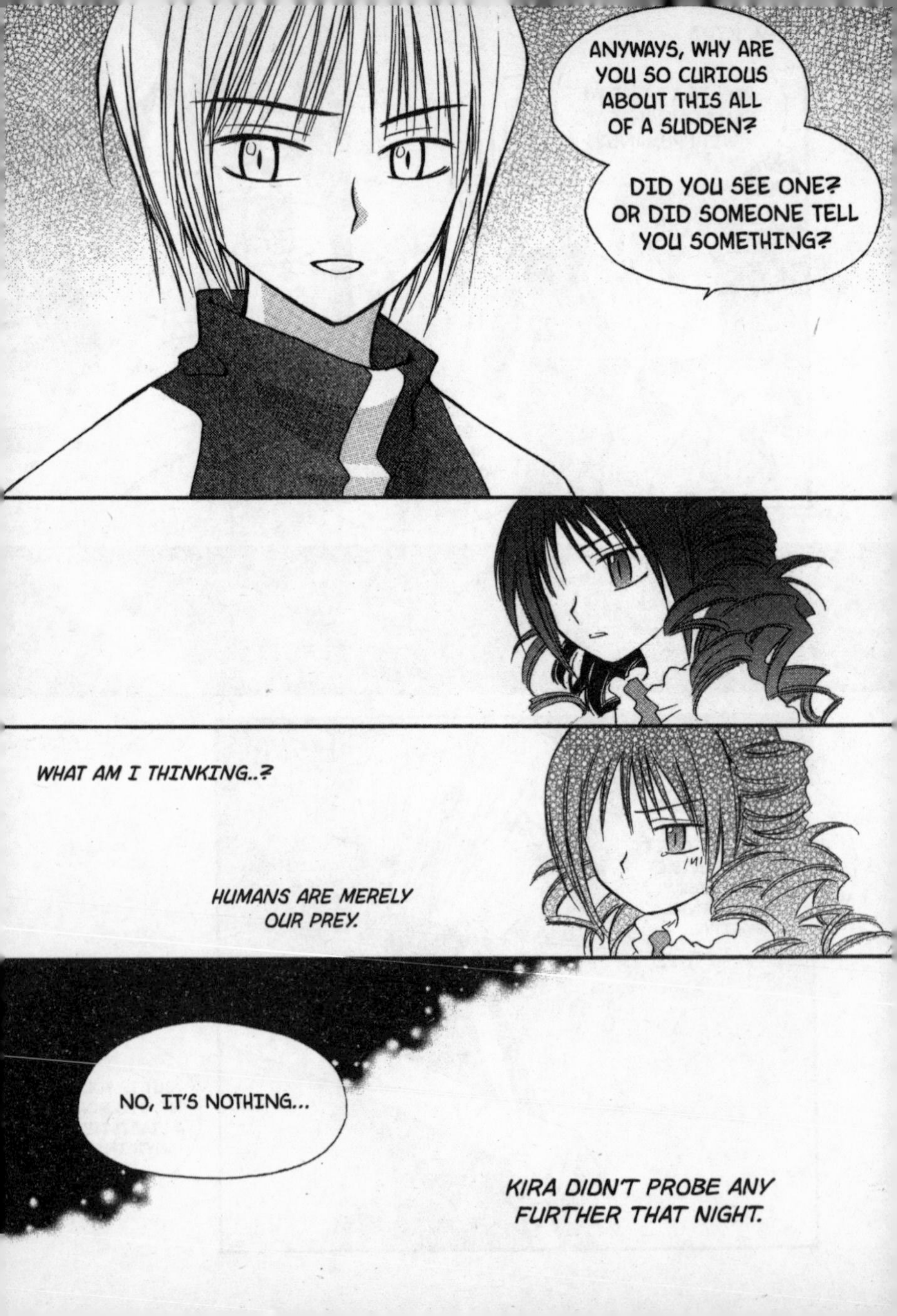
ANYWAYS, WHY ARE YOU SO CURIOUS ABOUT THIS ALL OF A SUDDEN?
DID YOU SEE ONE? OR DID SOMEONE TELL YOU SOMETHING?
WHAT AM I THINKING..?
HUMANS ARE MERELY OUR PREY.
NO, IT'S NOTHING...
KIRA DIDN'T PROBE ANY FURTHER THAT NIGHT.

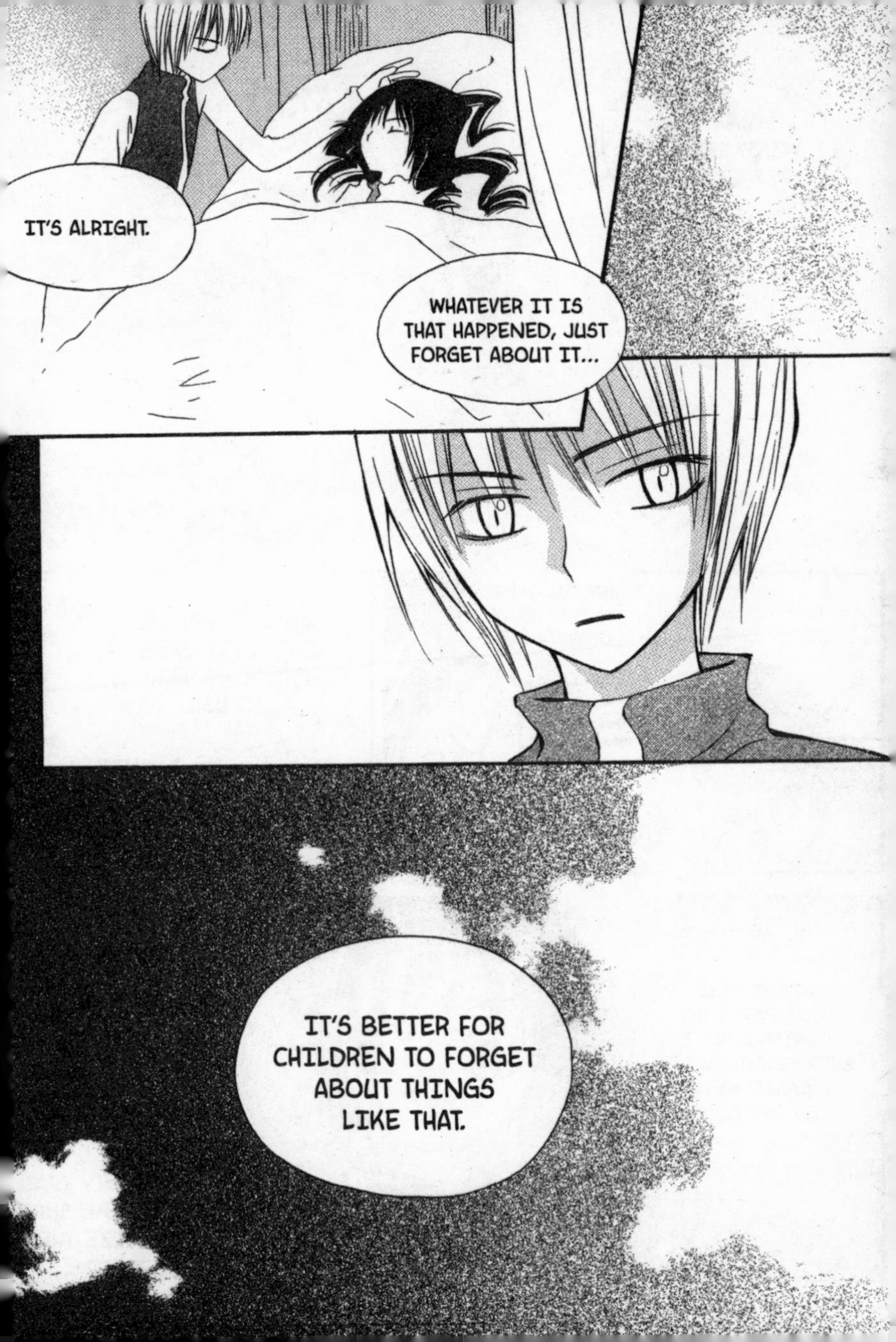
IT'S ALRIGHT.
WHATEVER IT IS THAT HAPPENED, JUST FORGET ABOUT IT...
IT'S BETTER FOR CHILDREN TO FORGET ABOUT THINGS LIKE THAT.

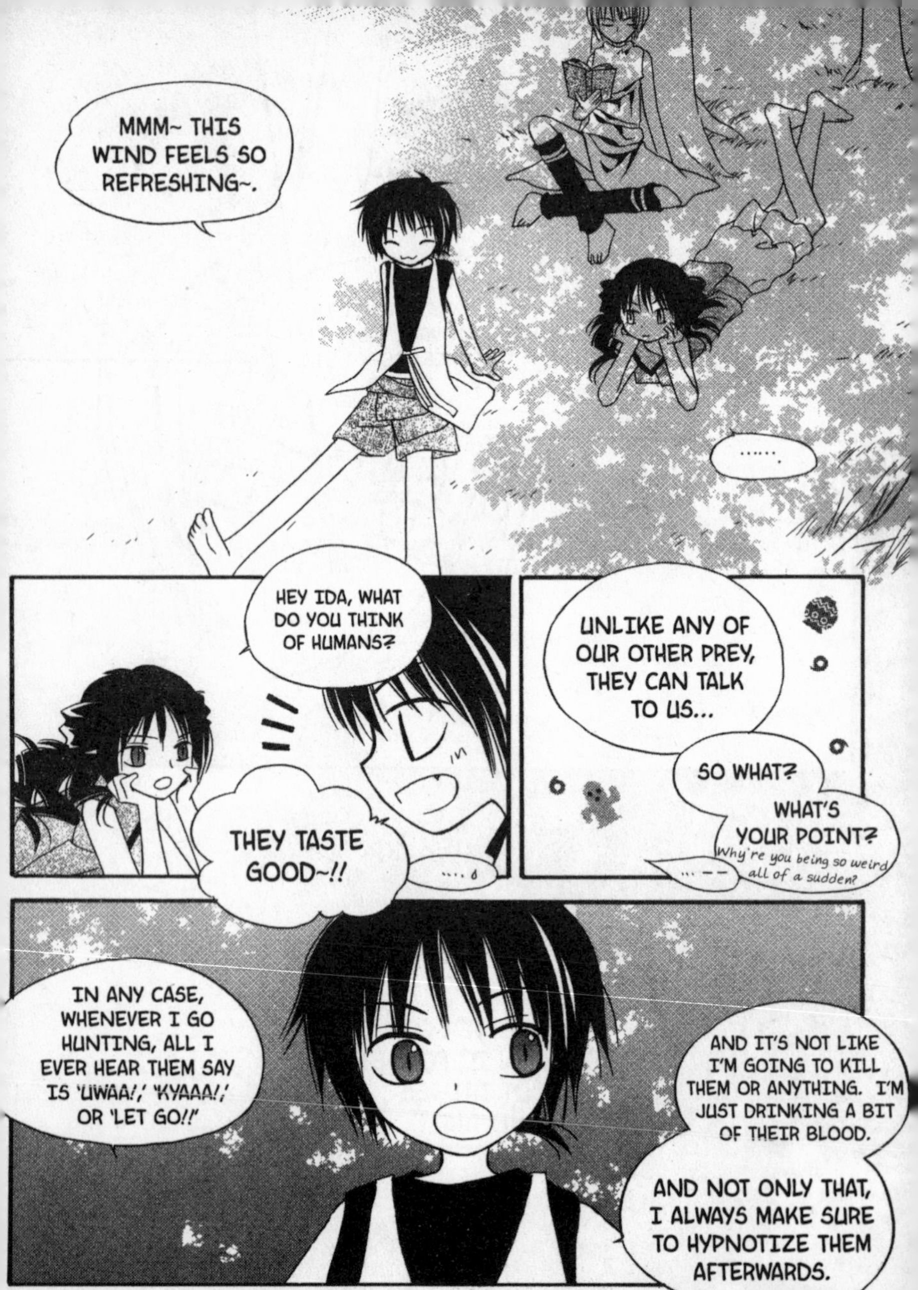
MMM~ THIS WIND FEELS SO REFRESHING~.
......
HEY IDA, WHAT DO YOU THINK OF HUMANS?
THEY TASTE GOOD~!!
....
UNLIKE ANY OF OUR OTHER PREY, THEY CAN TALK TO US...
SO WHAT?
WHAT'S YOUR POINT?
Why're you being so weird all of a sudden?
... --
IN ANY CASE, WHENEVER I GO HUNTING, ALL I EVER HEAR THEM SAY IS 'UWAA!,' 'KYAAA!,' OR 'LET GO!!'
AND IT'S NOT LIKE I'M GOING TO KILL THEM OR ANYTHING. I'M JUST DRINKING A BIT OF THEIR BLOOD.
AND NOT ONLY THAT, I ALWAYS MAKE SURE TO HYPNOTIZE THEM AFTERWARDS.

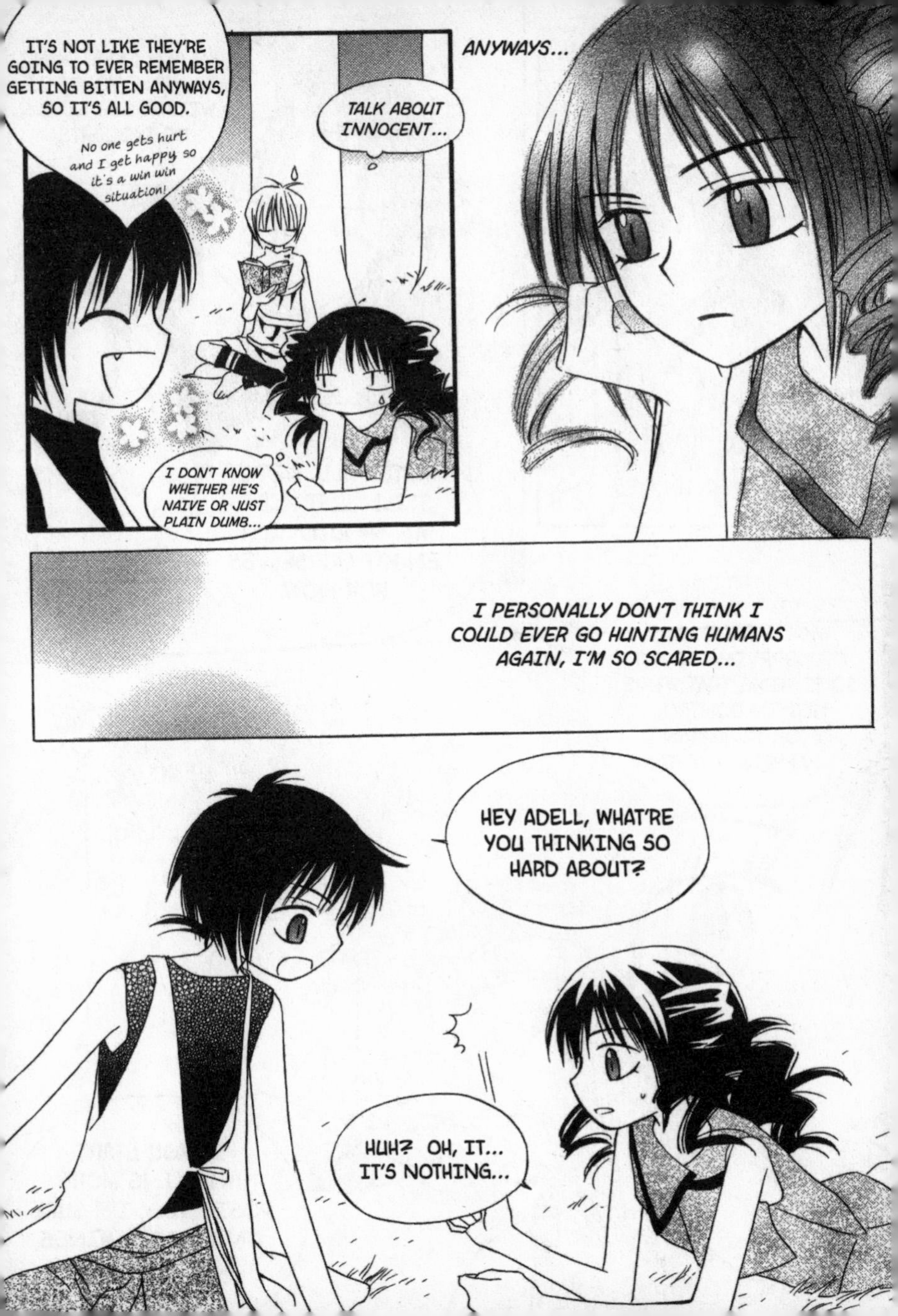
IT'S NOT LIKE THEY'RE GOING TO EVER REMEMBER GETTING BITTEN ANYWAYS, SO IT'S ALL GOOD.
No one gets hurt and I get happy so it's a win win situation!
TALK ABOUT INNOCENT...
I DON'T KNOW WHETHER HE'S NAIVE OR JUST PLAIN DUMB...
ANYWAYS...
I PERSONALLY DON'T THINK I COULD EVER GO HUNTING HUMANS AGAIN, I'M SO SCARED...
HEY ADELL, WHAT'RE YOU THINKING SO HARD ABOUT?
HUH? OH, IT... IT'S NOTHING...

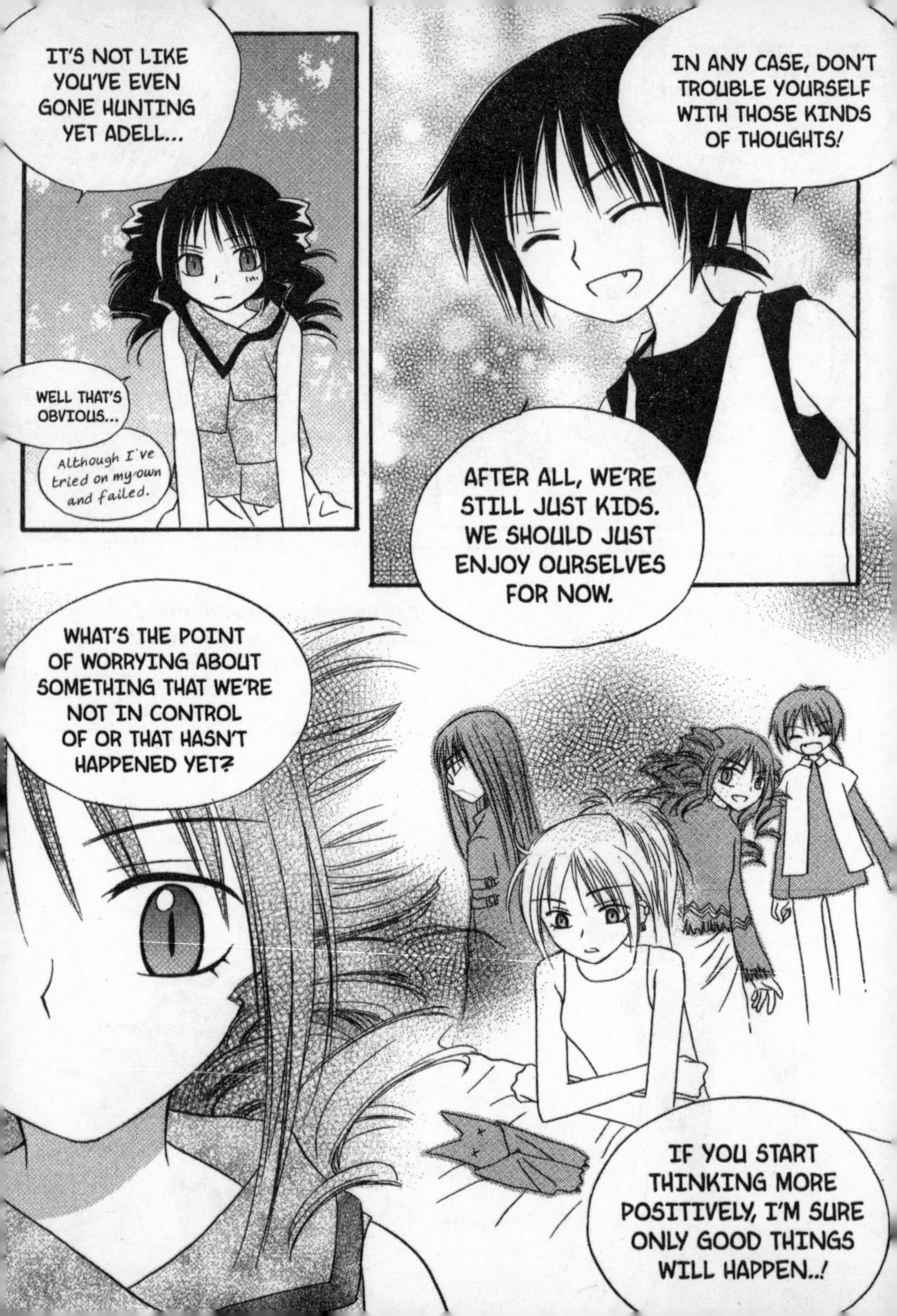
IT'S NOT LIKE YOU'VE EVEN GONE HUNTING YET ADELL...
WELL THAT'S OBVIOUS...
Although I've tried on my own and failed.
IN ANY CASE, DON'T TROUBLE YOURSELF WITH THOSE KINDS OF THOUGHTS!
AFTER ALL, WE'RE STILL JUST KIDS. WE SHOULD JUST ENJOY OURSELVES FOR NOW.
WHAT'S THE POINT OF WORRYING ABOUT SOMETHING THAT WE'RE NOT IN CONTROL OF OR THAT HASN'T HAPPENED YET?
IF YOU START THINKING MORE POSITIVELY, I'M SURE ONLY GOOD THINGS WILL HAPPEN..!

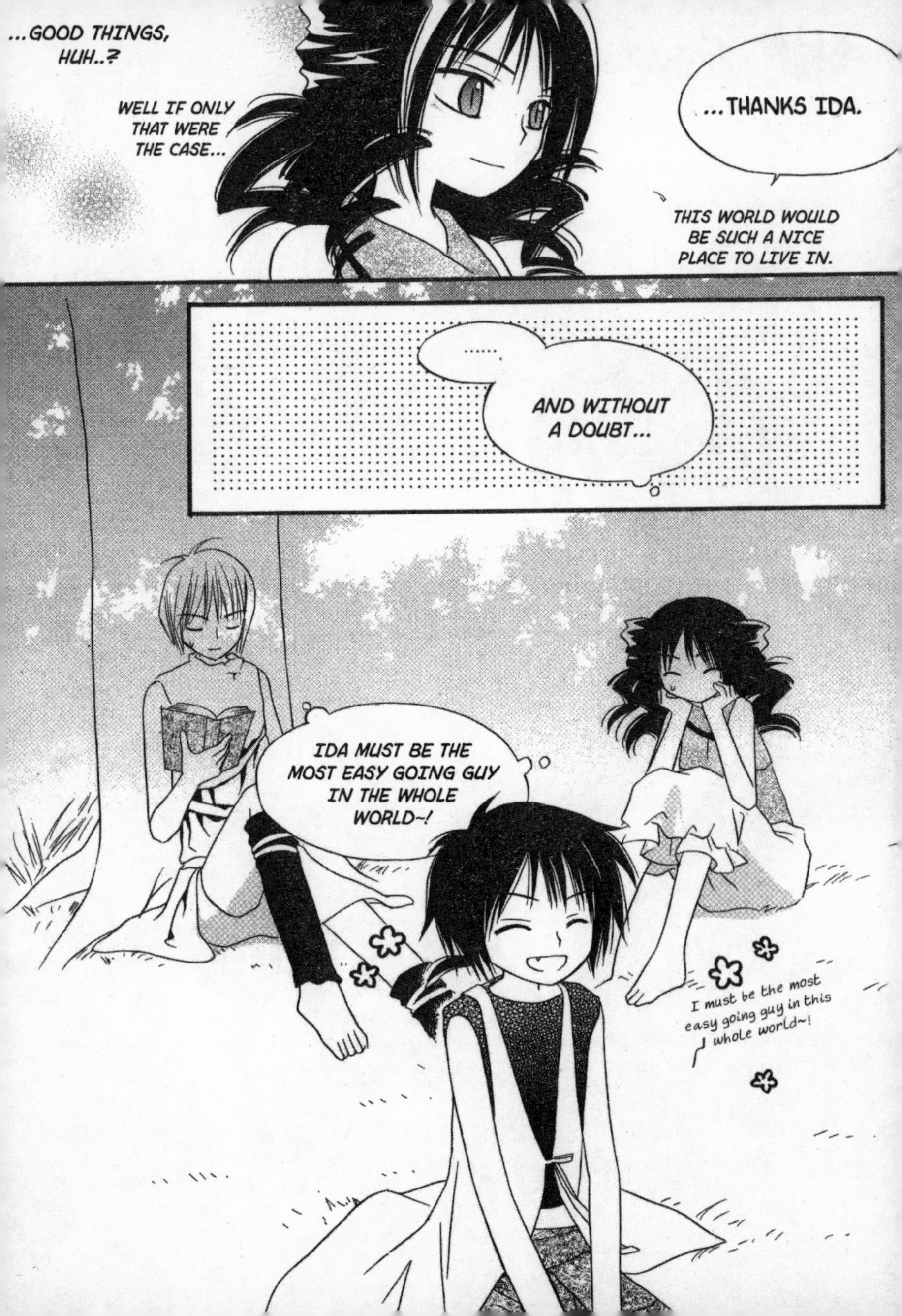
...GOOD THINGS, HUH..?
WELL IF ONLY THAT WERE THE CASE...
...THANKS IDA.
THIS WORLD WOULD BE SUCH A NICE PLACE TO LIVE IN.
......
AND WITHOUT A DOUBT...
IDA MUST BE THE MOST EASY GOING GUY IN THE WHOLE WORLD~!
I must be the most easy going guy in this whole world~!

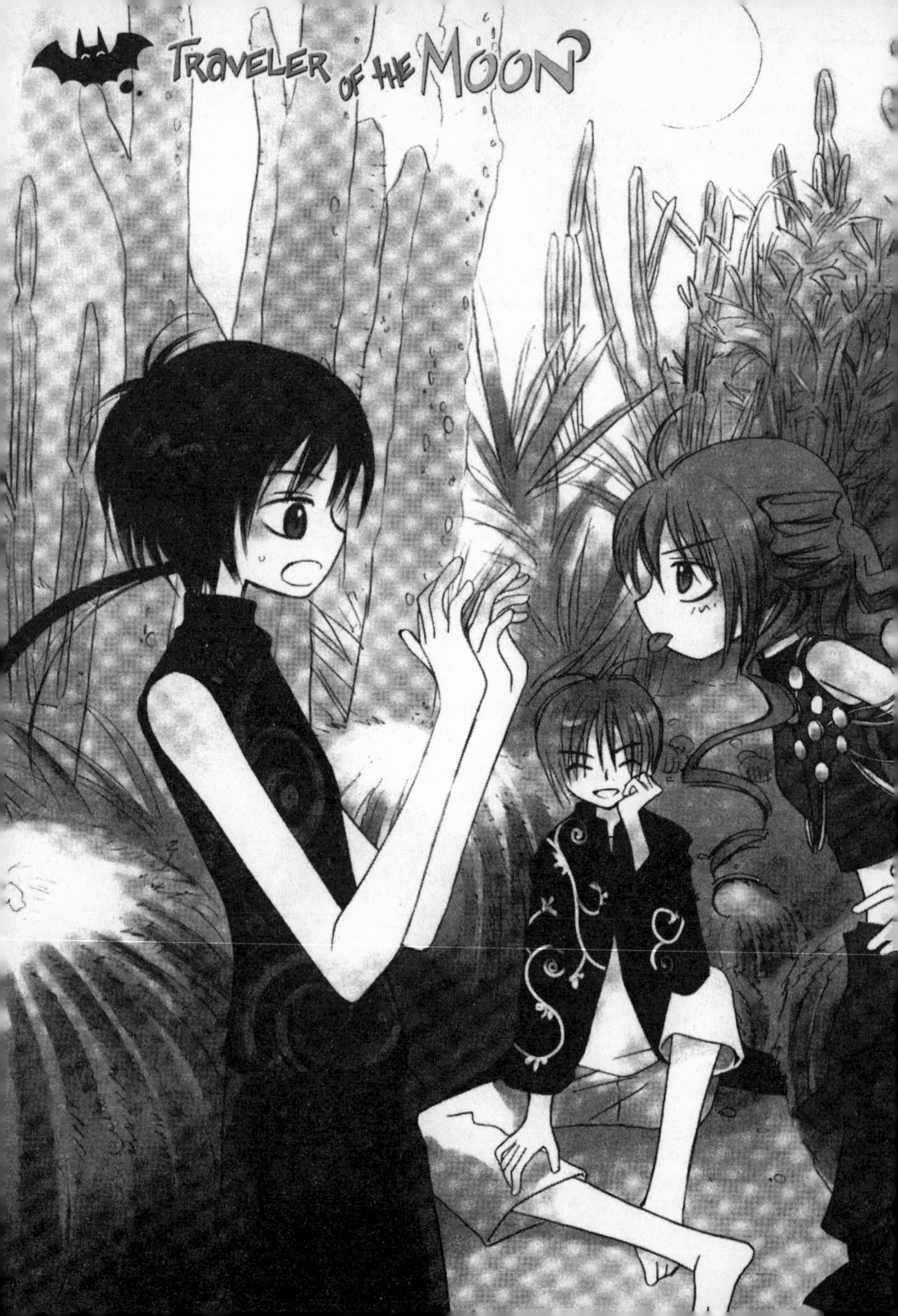
Traveler of the Moon

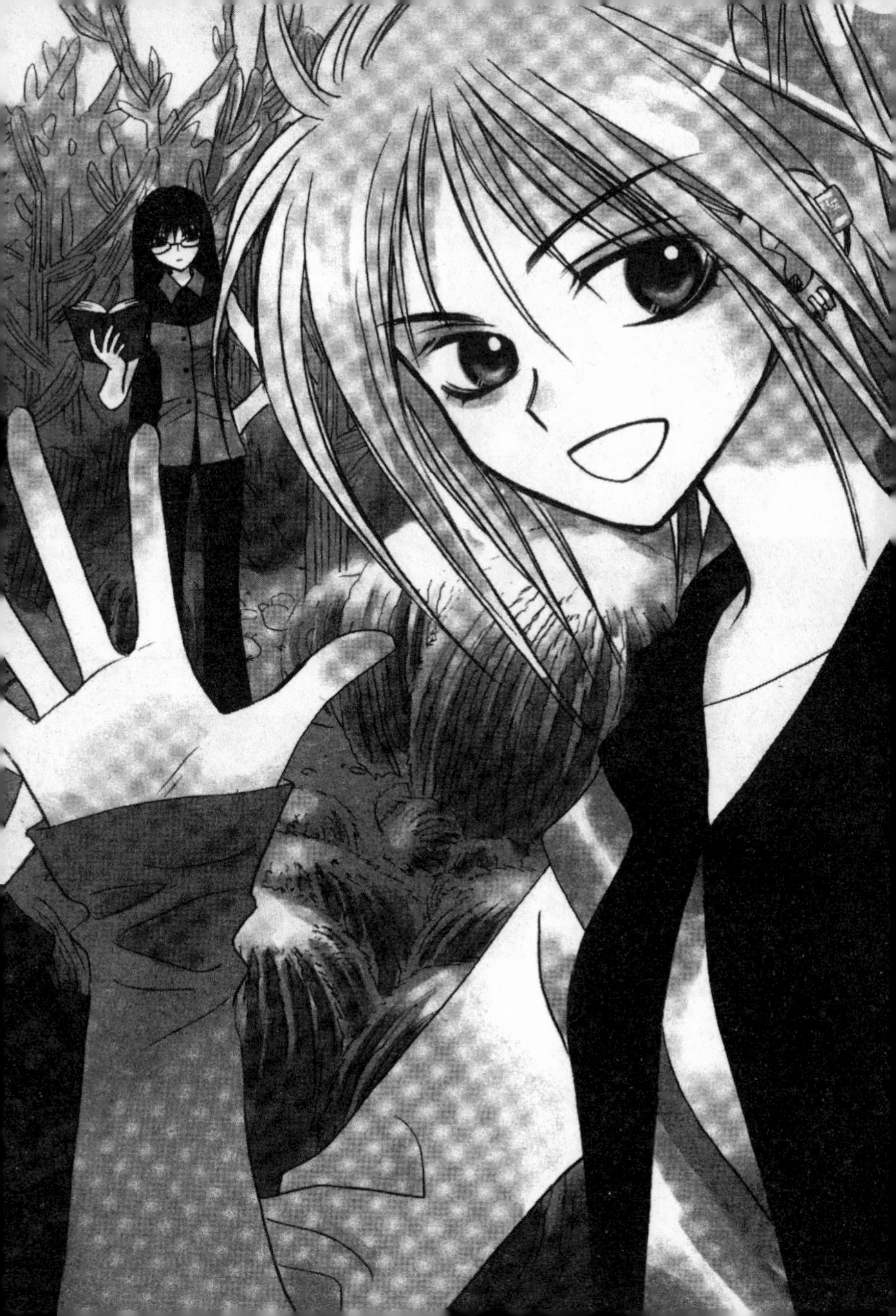

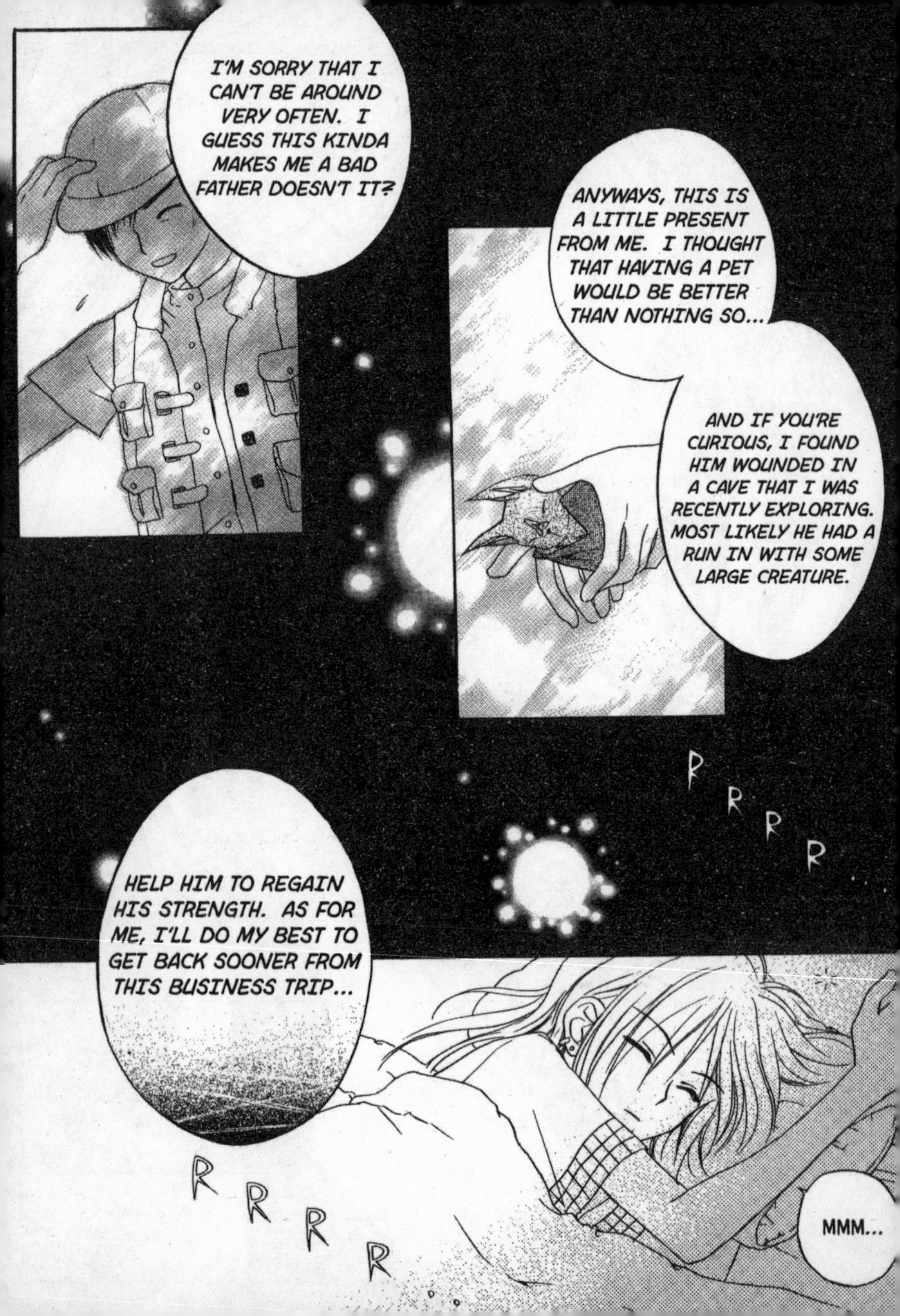
I'M SORRY THAT I CAN'T BE AROUND VERY OFTEN. I GUESS THIS KINDA MAKES ME A BAD FATHER DOESN'T IT?
ANYWAYS, THIS IS A LITTLE PRESENT FROM ME. I THOUGHT THAT HAVING A PET WOULD BE BETTER THAN NOTHING SO...
AND IF YOU'RE CURIOUS, I FOUND HIM WOUNDED IN A CAVE THAT I WAS RECENTLY EXPLORING. MOST LIKELY HE HAD A RUN IN WITH SOME LARGE CREATURE.
R R R R
HELP HIM TO REGAIN HIS STRENGTH. AS FOR ME, I'LL DO MY BEST TO GET BACK SOONER FROM THIS BUSINESS TRIP...
R R R R
MMM...

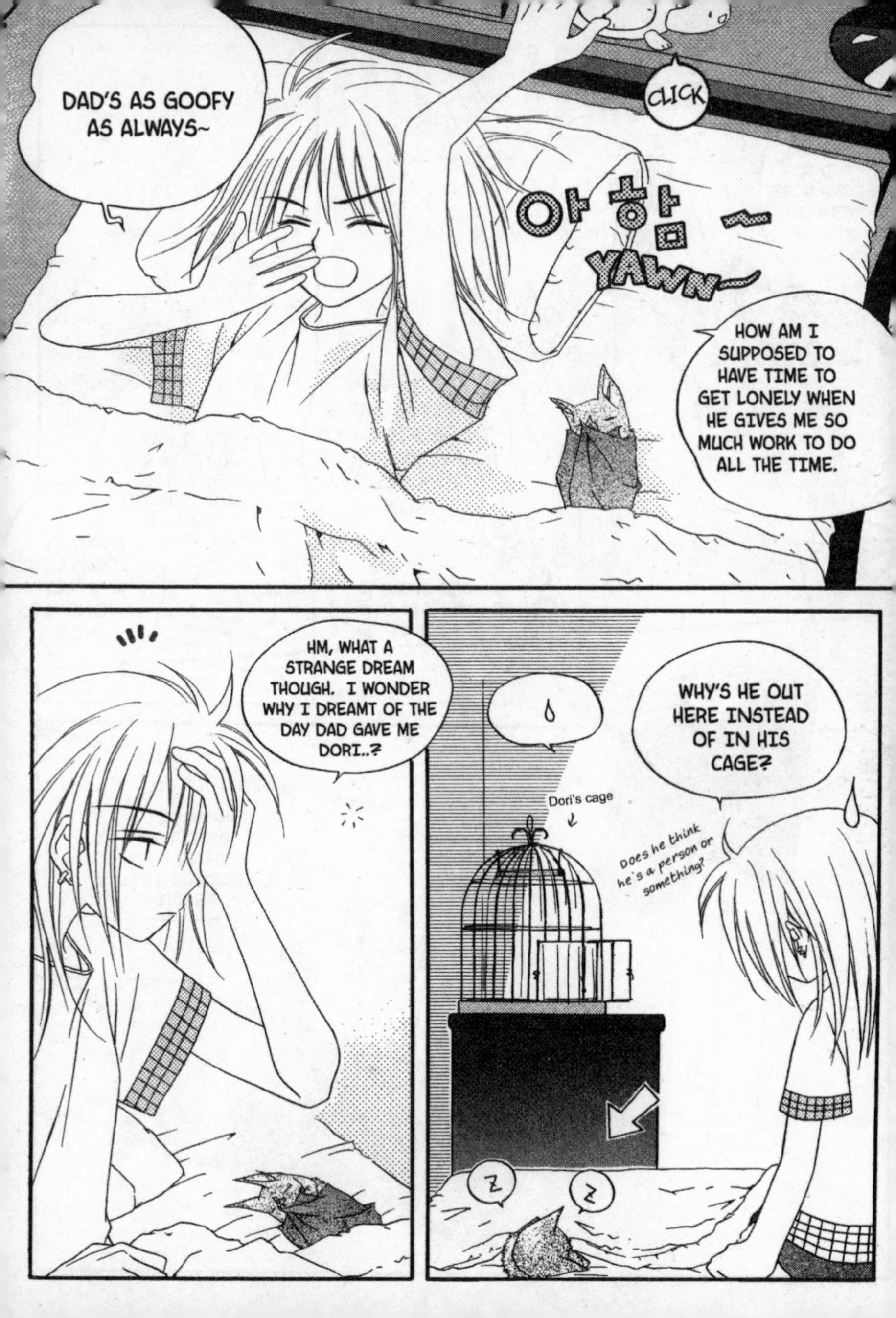
DAD'S AS GOOFY AS ALWAYS~
CLICK
아함~
YAWN~
HOW AM I SUPPOSED TO HAVE TIME TO GET LONELY WHEN HE GIVES ME SO MUCH WORK TO DO ALL THE TIME.
HM, WHAT A STRANGE DREAM THOUGH. I WONDER WHY I DREAMT OF THE DAY DAD GAVE ME DORI..?
WHY'S HE OUT HERE INSTEAD OF IN HIS CAGE?
Dori's cage
Does he think he's a person or something?
Z
Z

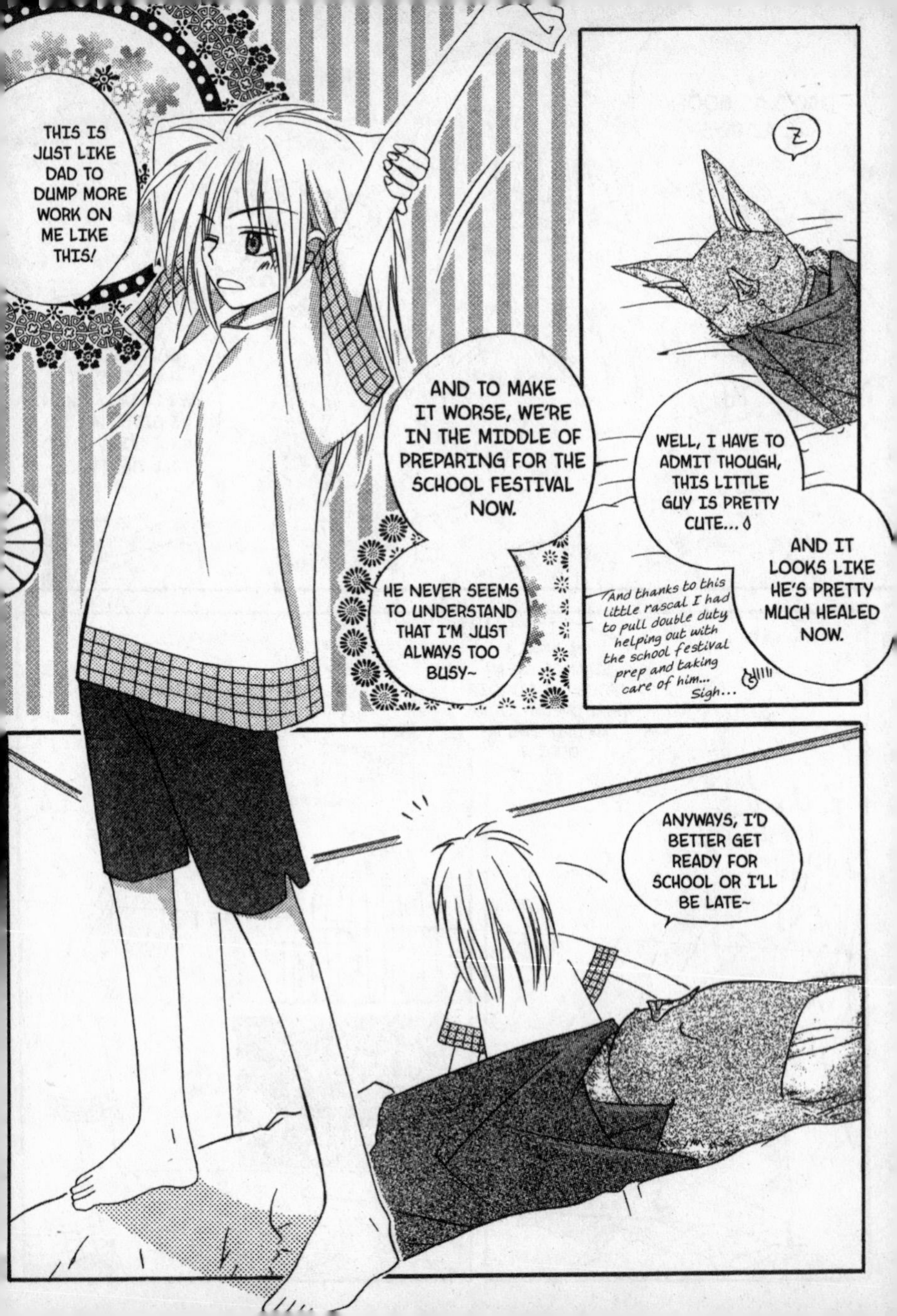
THIS IS JUST LIKE DAD TO DUMP MORE WORK ON ME LIKE THIS!
AND TO MAKE IT WORSE, WE'RE IN THE MIDDLE OF PREPARING FOR THE SCHOOL FESTIVAL NOW.
HE NEVER SEEMS TO UNDERSTAND THAT I'M JUST ALWAYS TOO BUSY~
Z
WELL, I HAVE TO ADMIT THOUGH, THIS LITTLE GUY IS PRETTY CUTE...
AND IT LOOKS LIKE HE'S PRETTY MUCH HEALED NOW.
And thanks to this little rascal I had to pull double duty helping out with the school festival prep and taking care of him... Sigh...
ANYWAYS, I'D BETTER GET READY FOR SCHOOL OR I'LL BE LATE~

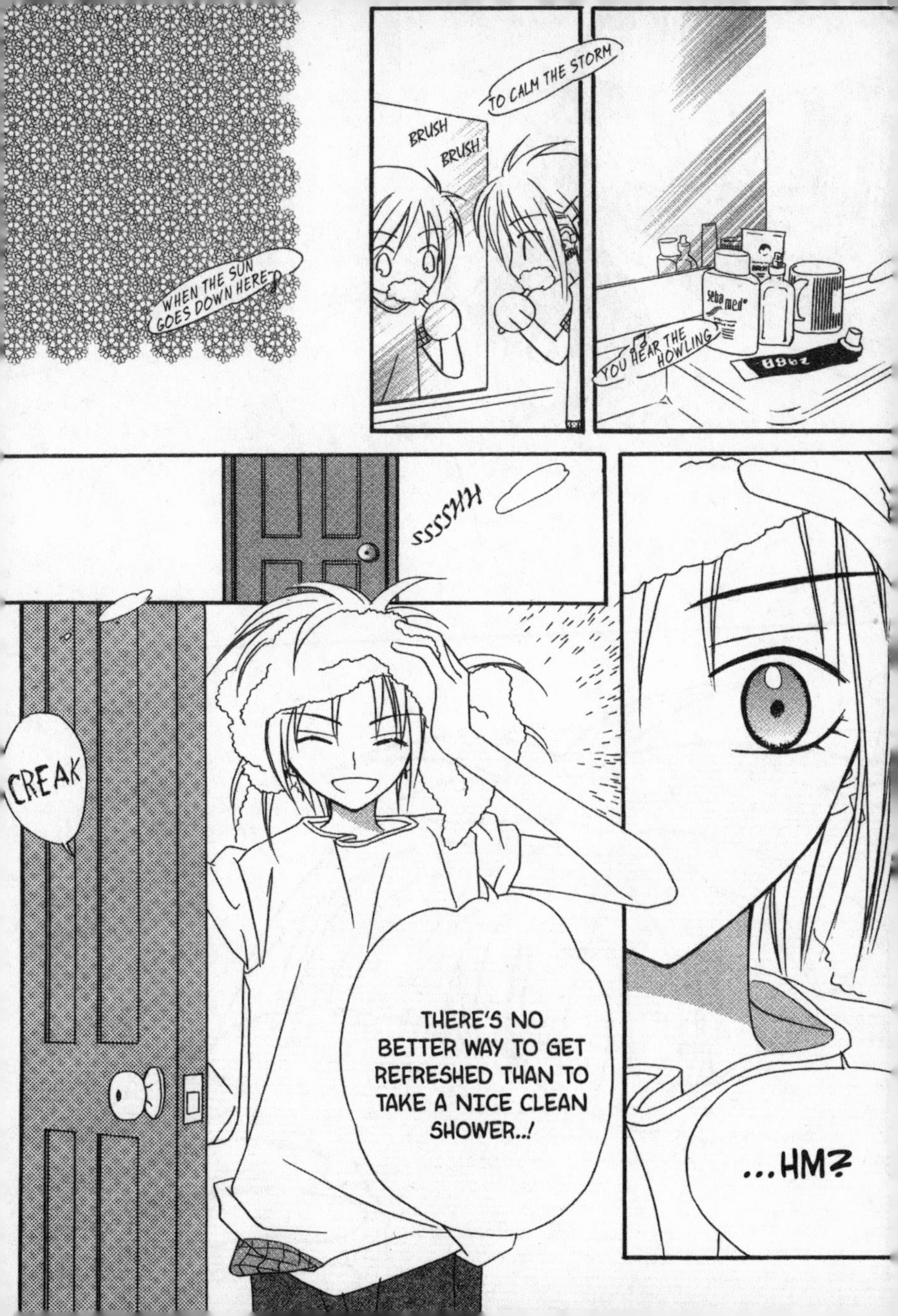
WHEN THE SUN GOES DOWN HERE
TO CALM THE STORM
BRUSH
BRUSH
YOU HEAR THE HOWLING
seba med
SSSSHH
CREAK
THERE'S NO BETTER WAY TO GET REFRESHED THAN TO TAKE A NICE CLEAN SHOWER..!
...HM?

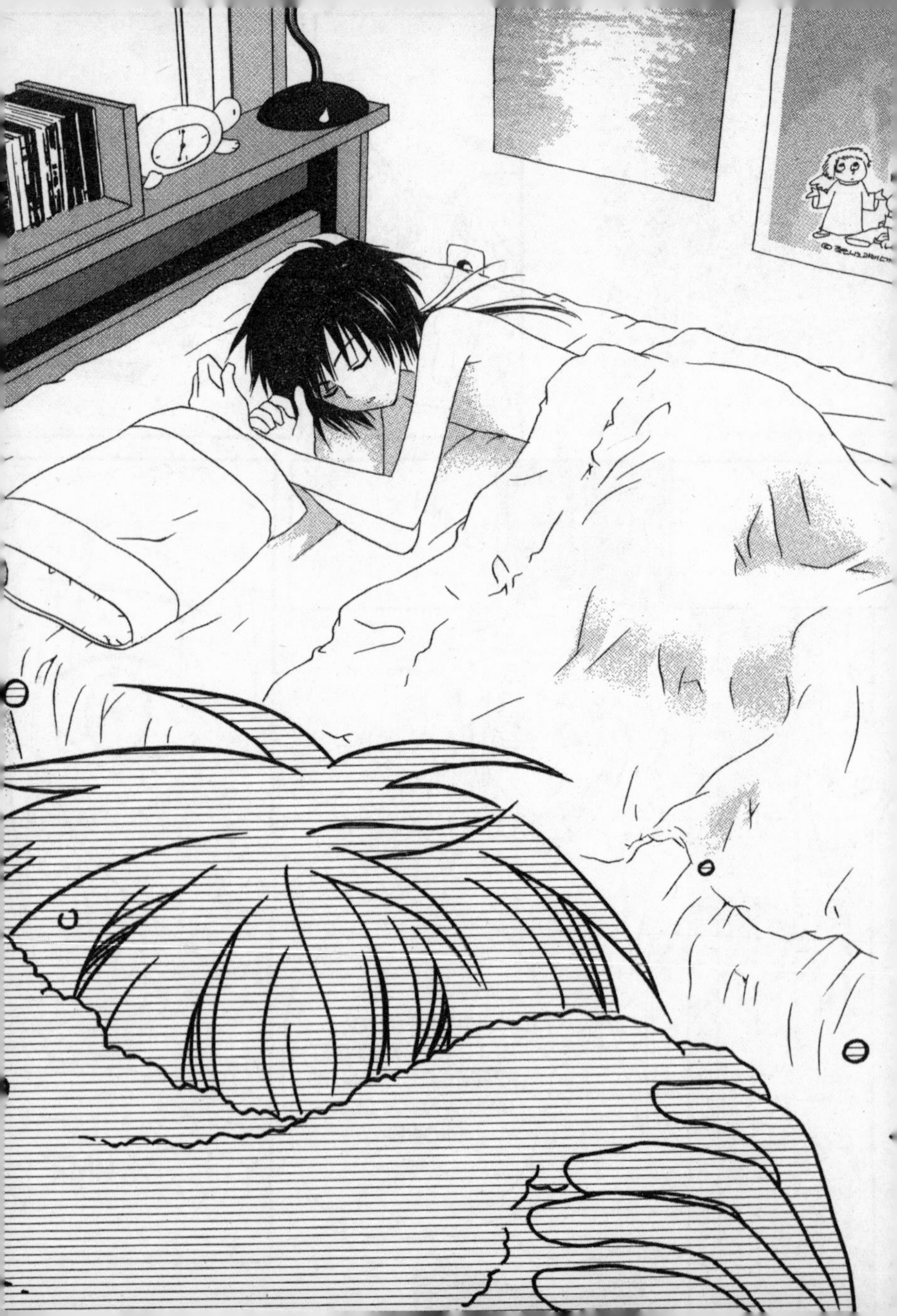

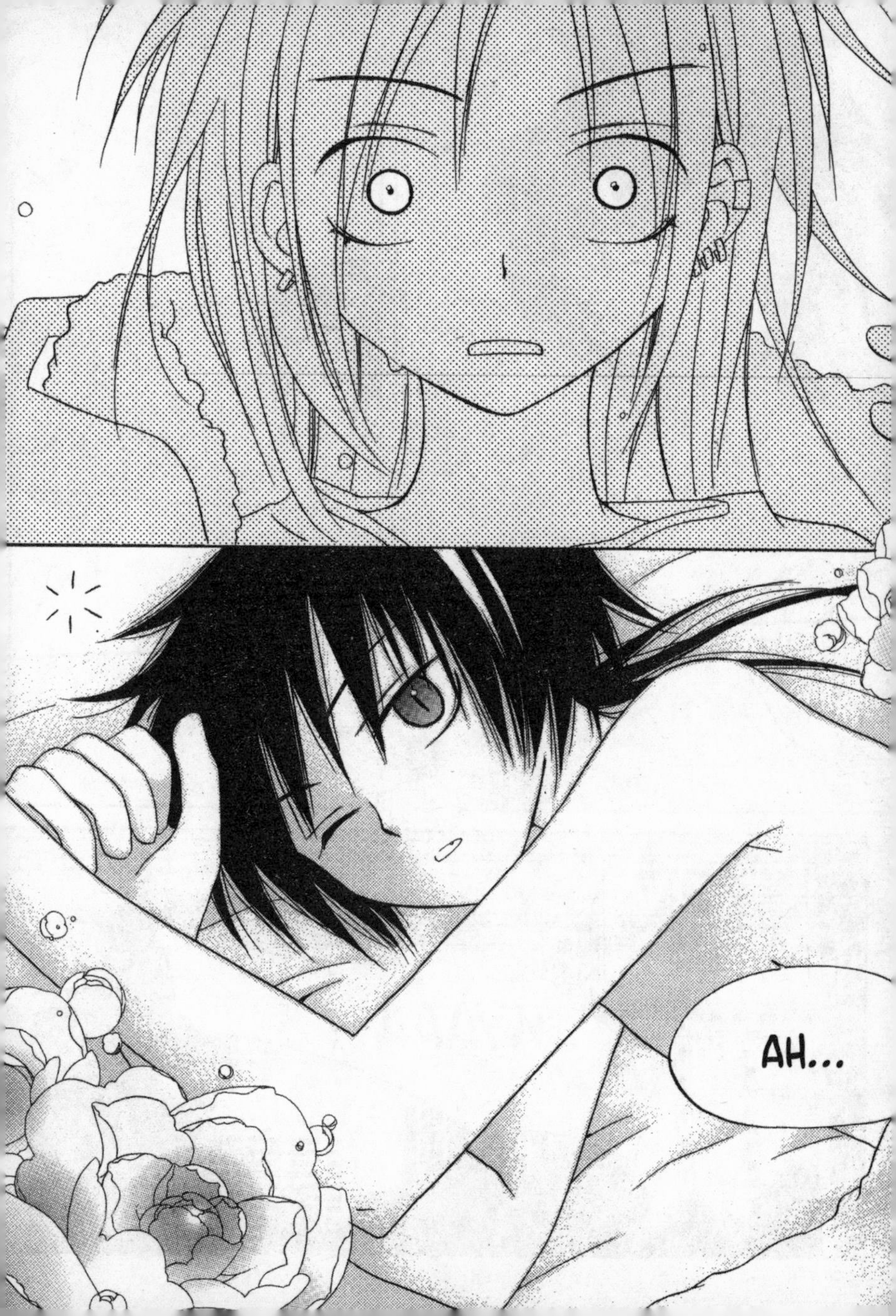
AH...

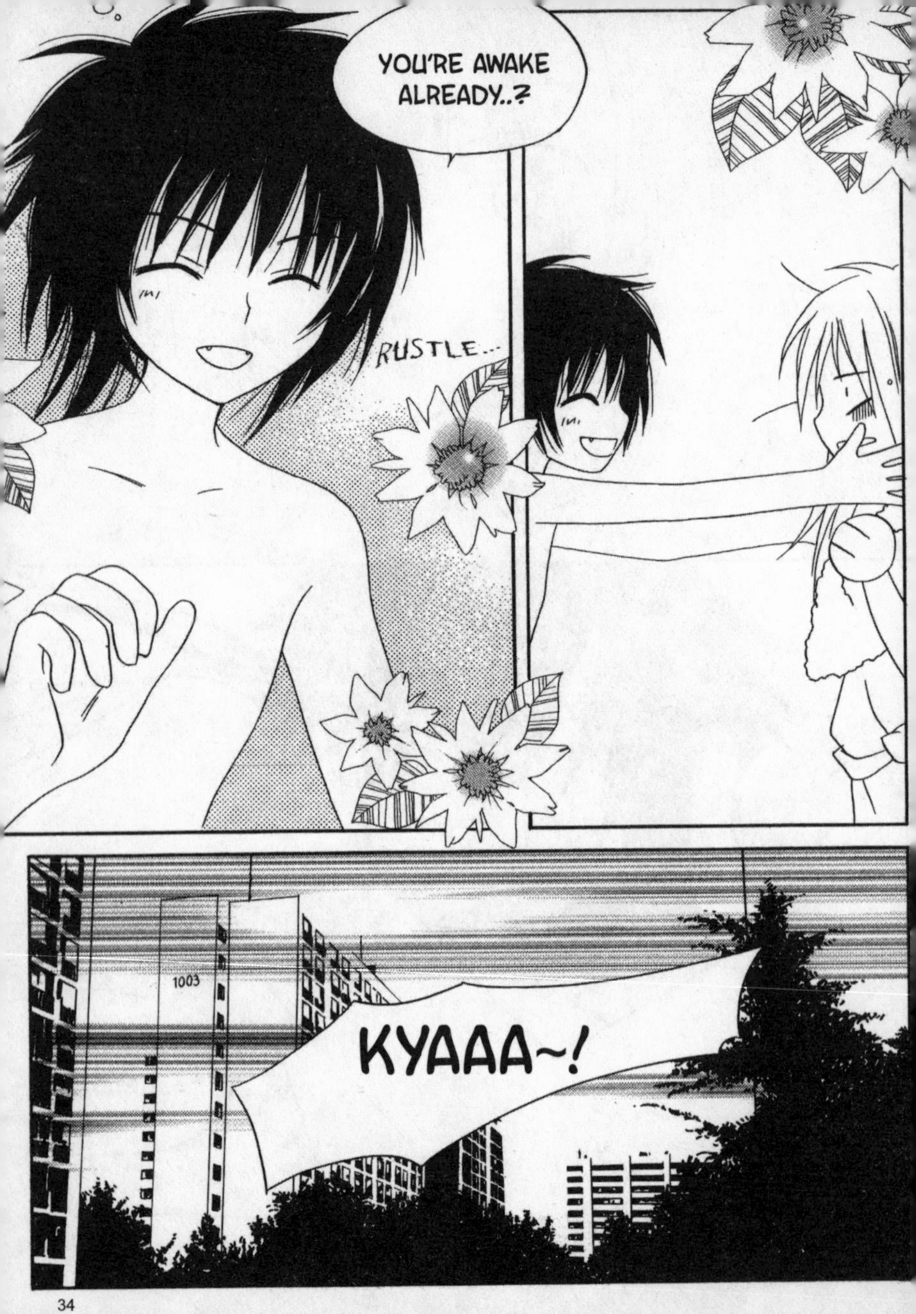
YOU'RE AWAKE ALREADY..?
RUSTLE...
1003
KYAAA~!

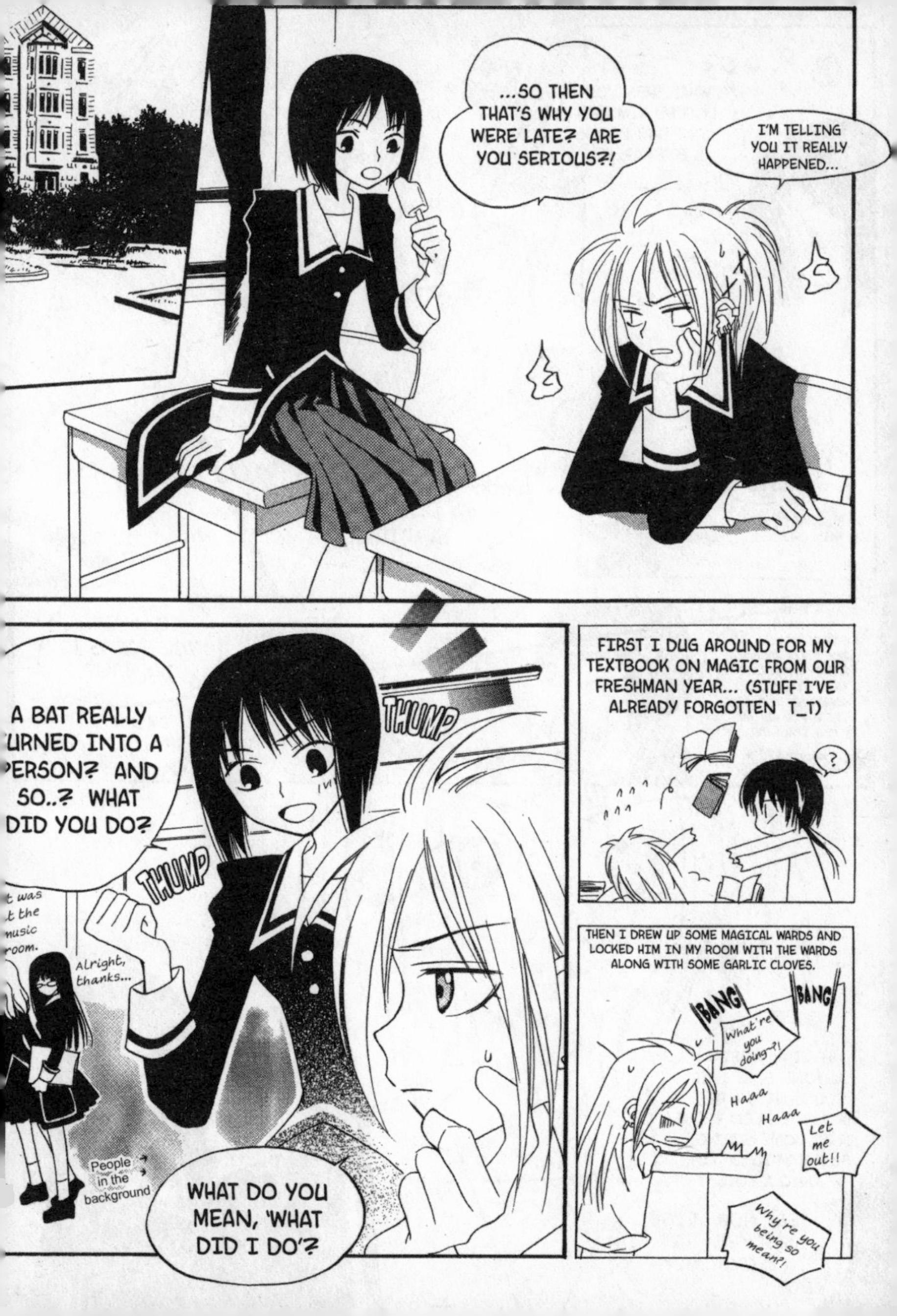
...SO THEN THAT'S WHY YOU WERE LATE? ARE YOU SERIOUS?!
I'M TELLING YOU IT REALLY HAPPENED...
A BAT REALLY URNED INTO A ERSON? AND SO..? WHAT DID YOU DO?
THUMP
THUMP
t was t the music room.
Alright, thanks...
People in the background
WHAT DO YOU MEAN, 'WHAT DID I DO'?
FIRST I DUG AROUND FOR MY TEXTBOOK ON MAGIC FROM OUR FRESHMAN YEAR... (STUFF I'VE ALREADY FORGOTTEN T_T)
?
THEN I DREW UP SOME MAGICAL WARDS AND LOCKED HIM IN MY ROOM WITH THE WARDS ALONG WITH SOME GARLIC CLOVES.
BANG
BANG
What're you doing-?!
Haaa
Haaa
Let me out!!
Why're you being so mean?!

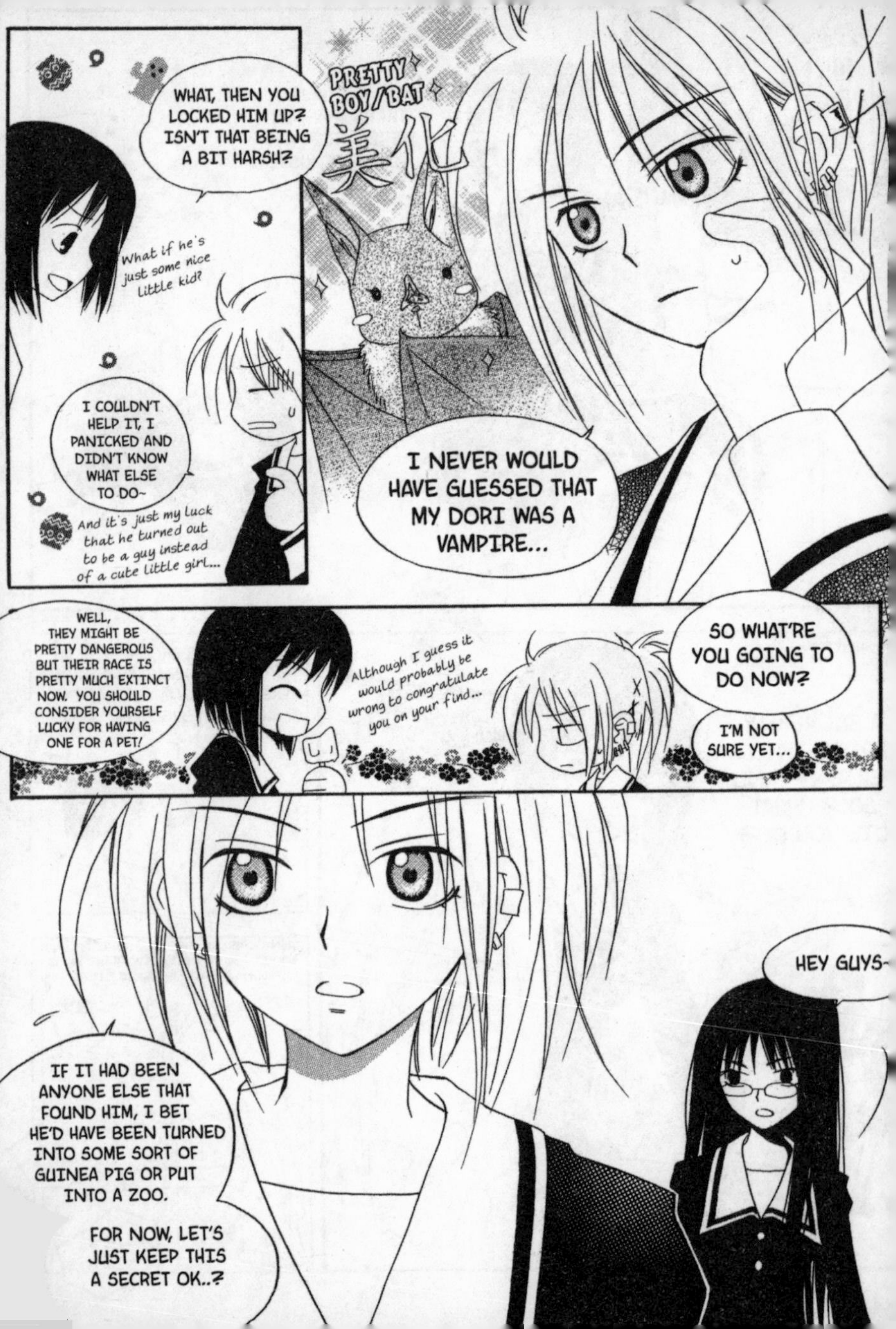
WHAT, THEN YOU LOCKED HIM UP? ISN'T THAT BEING A BIT HARSH?
What if he's just some nice little kid?
I COULDN'T HELP IT, I PANICKED AND DIDN'T KNOW WHAT ELSE TO DO~
And it's just my luck that he turned out to be a guy instead of a cute little girl...
PRETTY BOY/BAT
美化
I NEVER WOULD HAVE GUESSED THAT MY DORI WAS A VAMPIRE...
WELL, THEY MIGHT BE PRETTY DANGEROUS BUT THEIR RACE IS PRETTY MUCH EXTINCT NOW. YOU SHOULD CONSIDER YOURSELF LUCKY FOR HAVING ONE FOR A PET!
Although I guess it would probably be wrong to congratulate you on your find...
SO WHAT'RE YOU GOING TO DO NOW?
I'M NOT SURE YET...
IF IT HAD BEEN ANYONE ELSE THAT FOUND HIM, I BET HE'D HAVE BEEN TURNED INTO SOME SORT OF GUINEA PIG OR PUT INTO A ZOO.
FOR NOW, LET'S JUST KEEP THIS A SECRET OK..?
HEY GUYS-

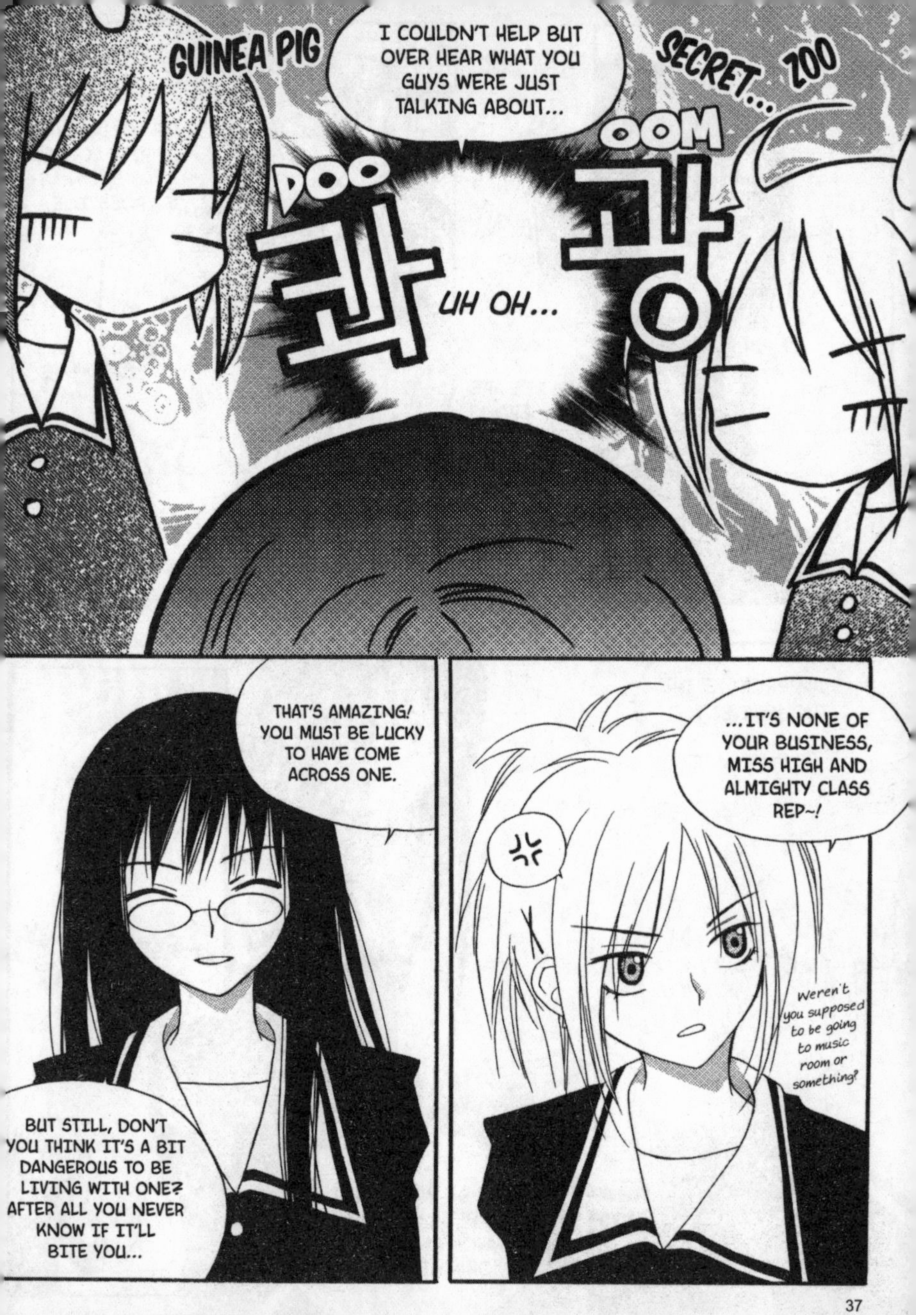
GUINEA PIG
I COULDN'T HELP BUT OVER HEAR WHAT YOU GUYS WERE JUST TALKING ABOUT...
SECRET... ZOO
DOO
쾅
UH OH...
OOM
광
THAT'S AMAZING! YOU MUST BE LUCKY TO HAVE COME ACROSS ONE.
BUT STILL, DON'T YOU THINK IT'S A BIT DANGEROUS TO BE LIVING WITH ONE? AFTER ALL YOU NEVER KNOW IF IT'LL BITE YOU...
...IT'S NONE OF YOUR BUSINESS, MISS HIGH AND ALMIGHTY CLASS REP~!
Weren't you supposed to be going to music room or something?

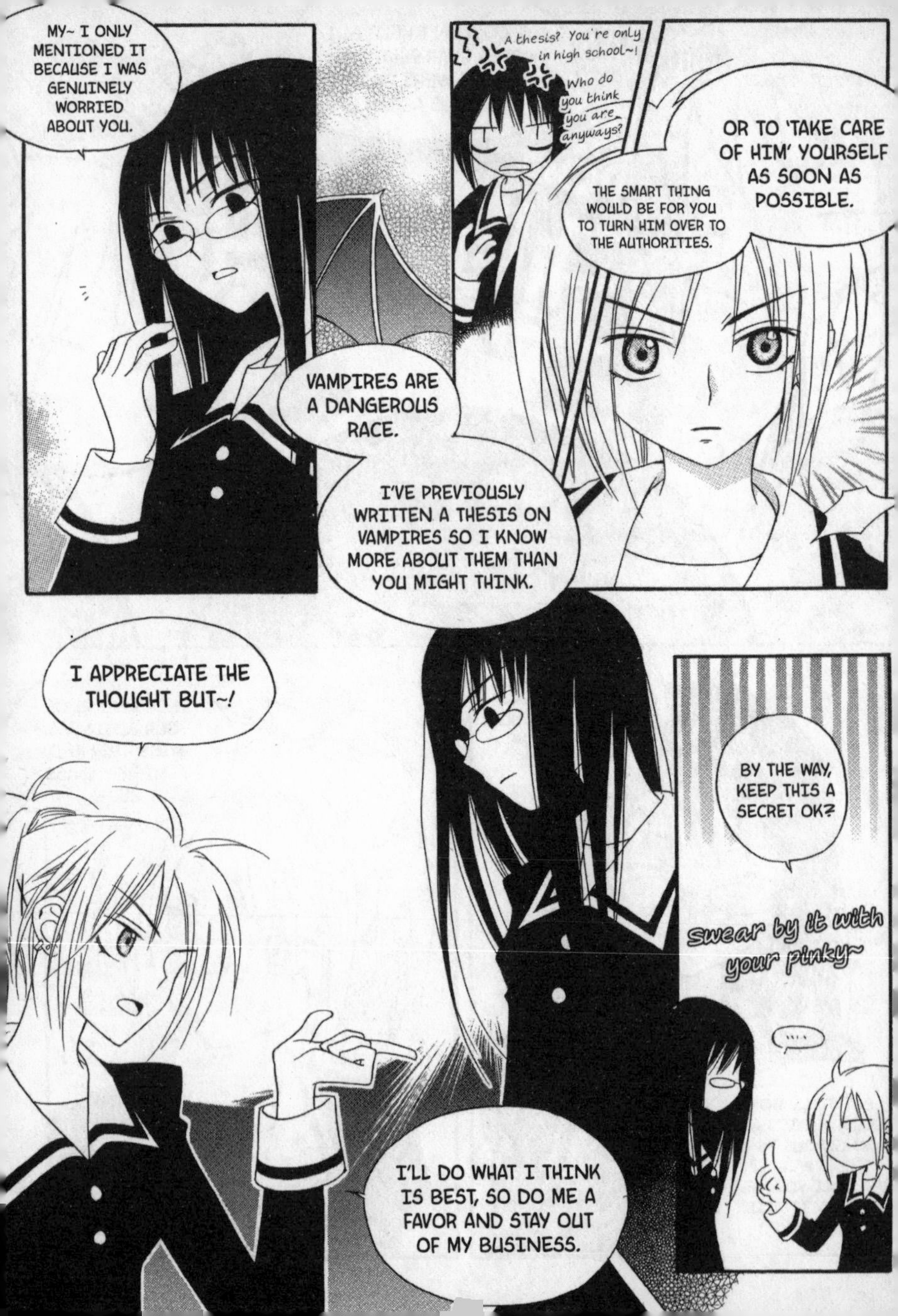

MY~ I ONLY MENTIONED IT BECAUSE I WAS GENUINELY WORRIED ABOUT YOU.
VAMPIRES ARE A DANGEROUS RACE.
I'VE PREVIOUSLY WRITTEN A THESIS ON VAMPIRES SO I KNOW MORE ABOUT THEM THAN YOU MIGHT THINK.
A thesis? You're only in high school~!
Who do you think you are anyways?
THE SMART THING WOULD BE FOR YOU TO TURN HIM OVER TO THE AUTHORITIES.
OR TO 'TAKE CARE OF HIM' YOURSELF AS SOON AS POSSIBLE.
I APPRECIATE THE THOUGHT BUT~!
I'LL DO WHAT I THINK IS BEST, SO DO ME A FAVOR AND STAY OUT OF MY BUSINESS.
BY THE WAY, KEEP THIS A SECRET OK?
Swear by it with your pinky~
...

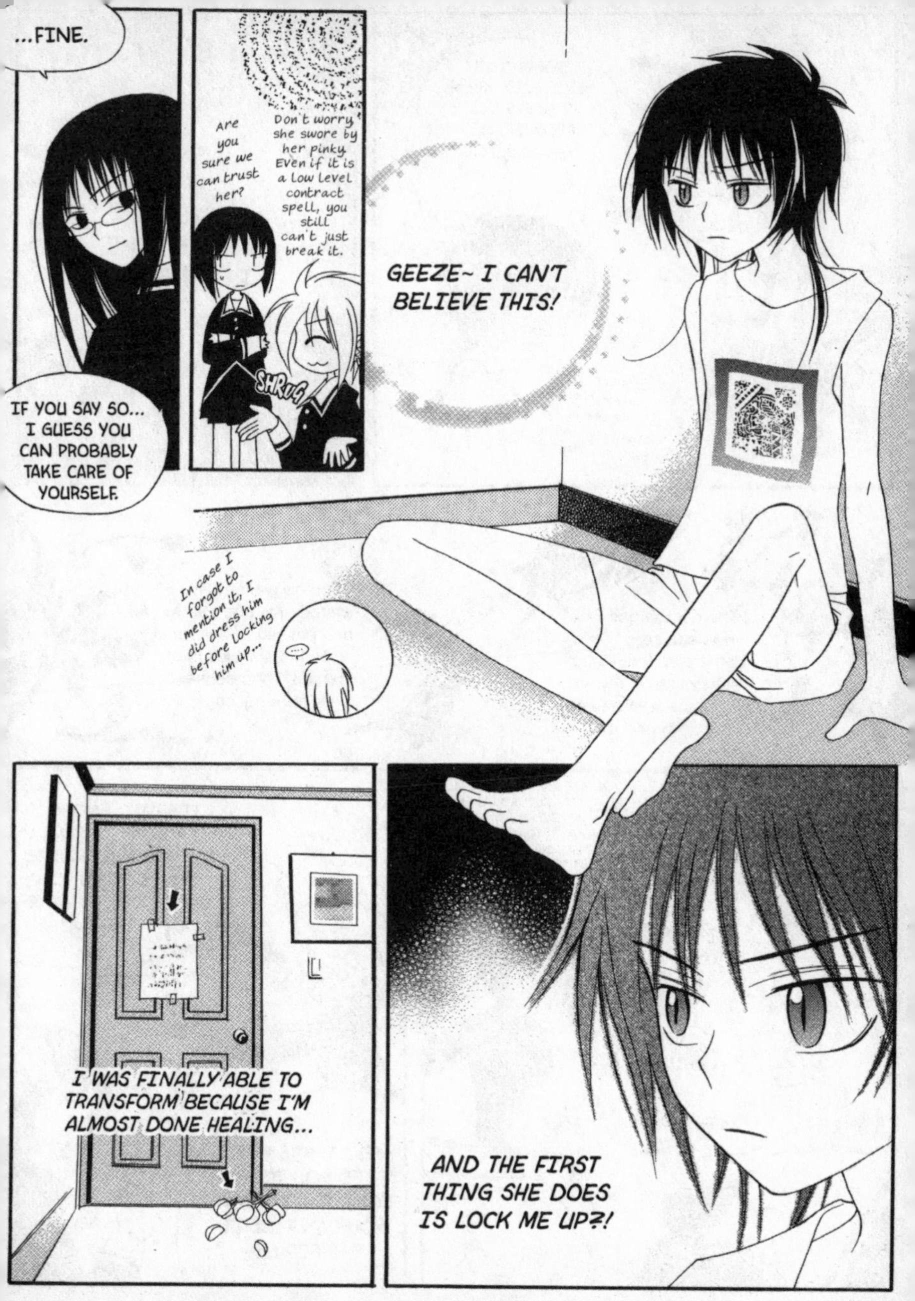
...FINE.
IF YOU SAY SO... I GUESS YOU CAN PROBABLY TAKE CARE OF YOURSELF.
Are you sure we can trust her?
Don't worry she swore by her pinky. Even if it is a low level contract spell, you still can't just break it.
SHRUG
GEEZE~ I CAN'T BELIEVE THIS!
In case I forgot to mention it, I did dress him before locking him up...
...
I WAS FINALLY ABLE TO TRANSFORM BECAUSE I'M ALMOST DONE HEALING...
AND THE FIRST THING SHE DOES IS LOCK ME UP?!

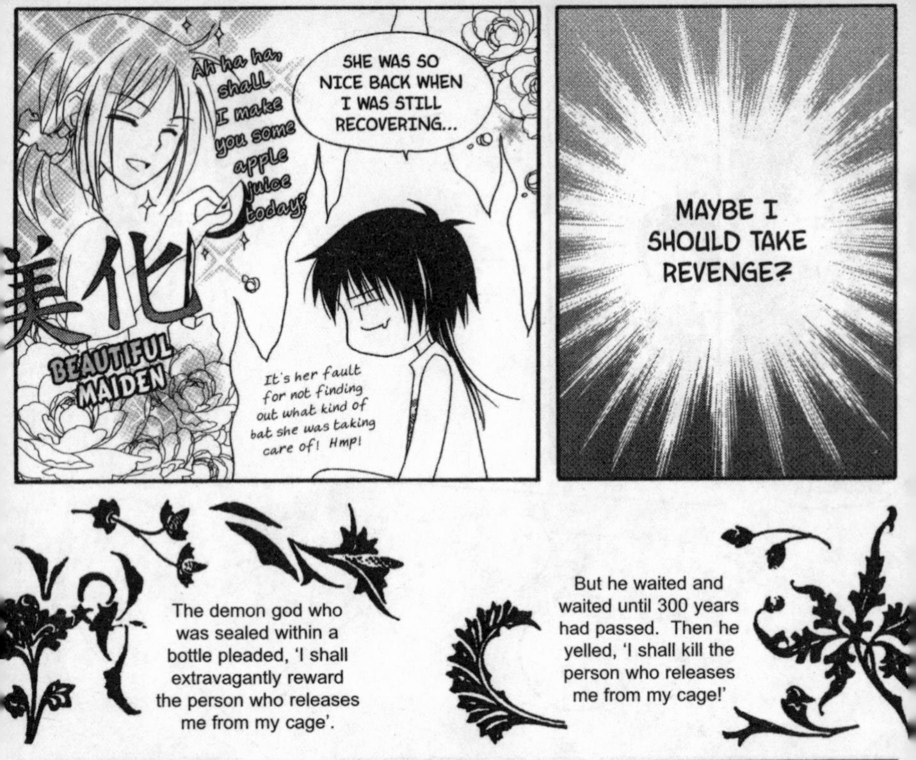
Ah ha ha, shall I make you some apple juice today?
SHE WAS SO NICE BACK WHEN I WAS STILL RECOVERING...
美化
BEAUTIFUL MAIDEN
It's her fault for not finding out what kind of bat she was taking care of! Hmp!
MAYBE I SHOULD TAKE REVENGE?

The demon god who was sealed within a bottle pleaded, 'I shall extravagantly reward the person who releases me from my cage'.

But he waited and waited until 300 years had passed. Then he yelled, 'I shall kill the person who releases me from my cage!'

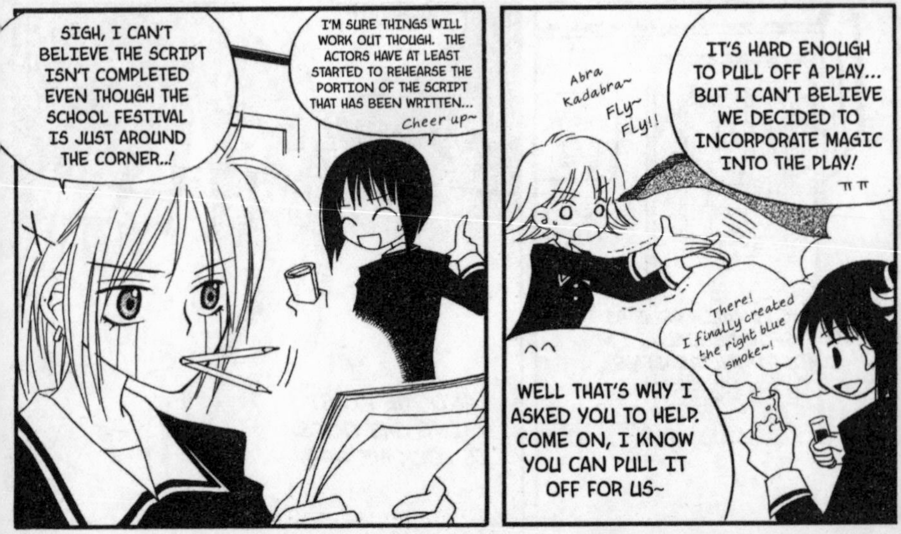
SIGH, I CAN'T BELIEVE THE SCRIPT ISN'T COMPLETED EVEN THOUGH THE SCHOOL FESTIVAL IS JUST AROUND THE CORNER..!
I'M SURE THINGS WILL WORK OUT THOUGH. THE ACTORS HAVE AT LEAST STARTED TO REHEARSE THE PORTION OF THE SCRIPT THAT HAS BEEN WRITTEN...
Cheer up~
Abra Kadabra~
Fly~ Fly!!
IT'S HARD ENOUGH TO PULL OFF A PLAY... BUT I CAN'T BELIEVE WE DECIDED TO INCORPORATE MAGIC INTO THE PLAY!
ㅠㅠ
There! I finally created the right blue smoke~!
^^
WELL THAT'S WHY I ASKED YOU TO HELP. COME ON, I KNOW YOU CAN PULL IT OFF FOR US~

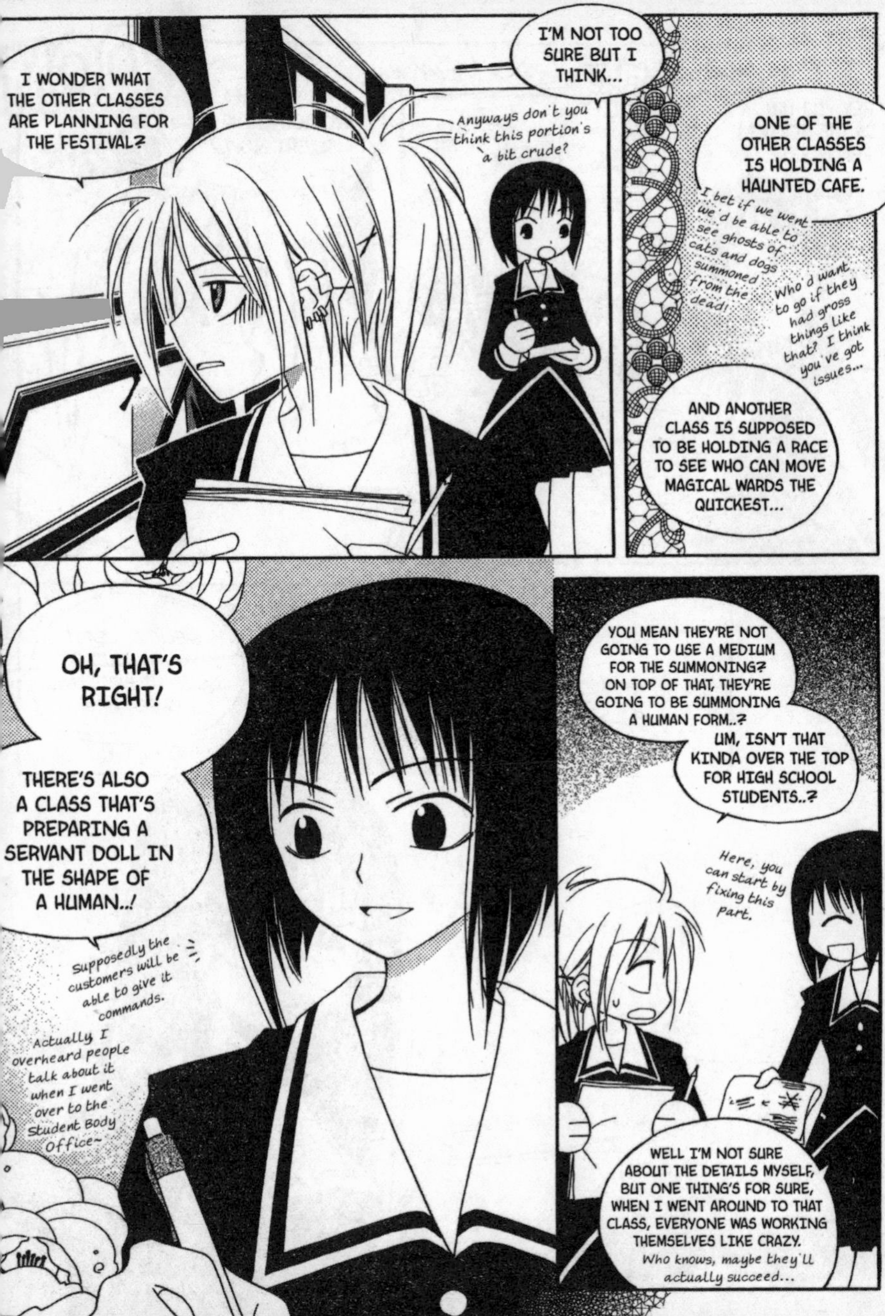

I WONDER WHAT THE OTHER CLASSES ARE PLANNING FOR THE FESTIVAL?
I'M NOT TOO SURE BUT I THINK...
Anyways don't you think this portion's a bit crude?
ONE OF THE OTHER CLASSES IS HOLDING A HAUNTED CAFE.
I bet if we went we'd be able to see ghosts of cats and dogs summoned from the dead!
Who'd want to go if they had gross things like that? I think you've got issues...
AND ANOTHER CLASS IS SUPPOSED TO BE HOLDING A RACE TO SEE WHO CAN MOVE MAGICAL WARDS THE QUICKEST...
OH, THAT'S RIGHT!
THERE'S ALSO A CLASS THAT'S PREPARING A SERVANT DOLL IN THE SHAPE OF A HUMAN..!
Supposedly the customers will be able to give it commands.
Actually I overheard people talk about it when I went over to the Student Body Office~
YOU MEAN THEY'RE NOT GOING TO USE A MEDIUM FOR THE SUMMONING? ON TOP OF THAT, THEY'RE GOING TO BE SUMMONING A HUMAN FORM..?
UM, ISN'T THAT KINDA OVER THE TOP FOR HIGH SCHOOL STUDENTS..?
Here, you can start by fixing this part.
WELL I'M NOT SURE ABOUT THE DETAILS MYSELF, BUT ONE THING'S FOR SURE, WHEN I WENT AROUND TO THAT CLASS, EVERYONE WAS WORKING THEMSELVES LIKE CRAZY.
Who knows, maybe they'll actually succeed...

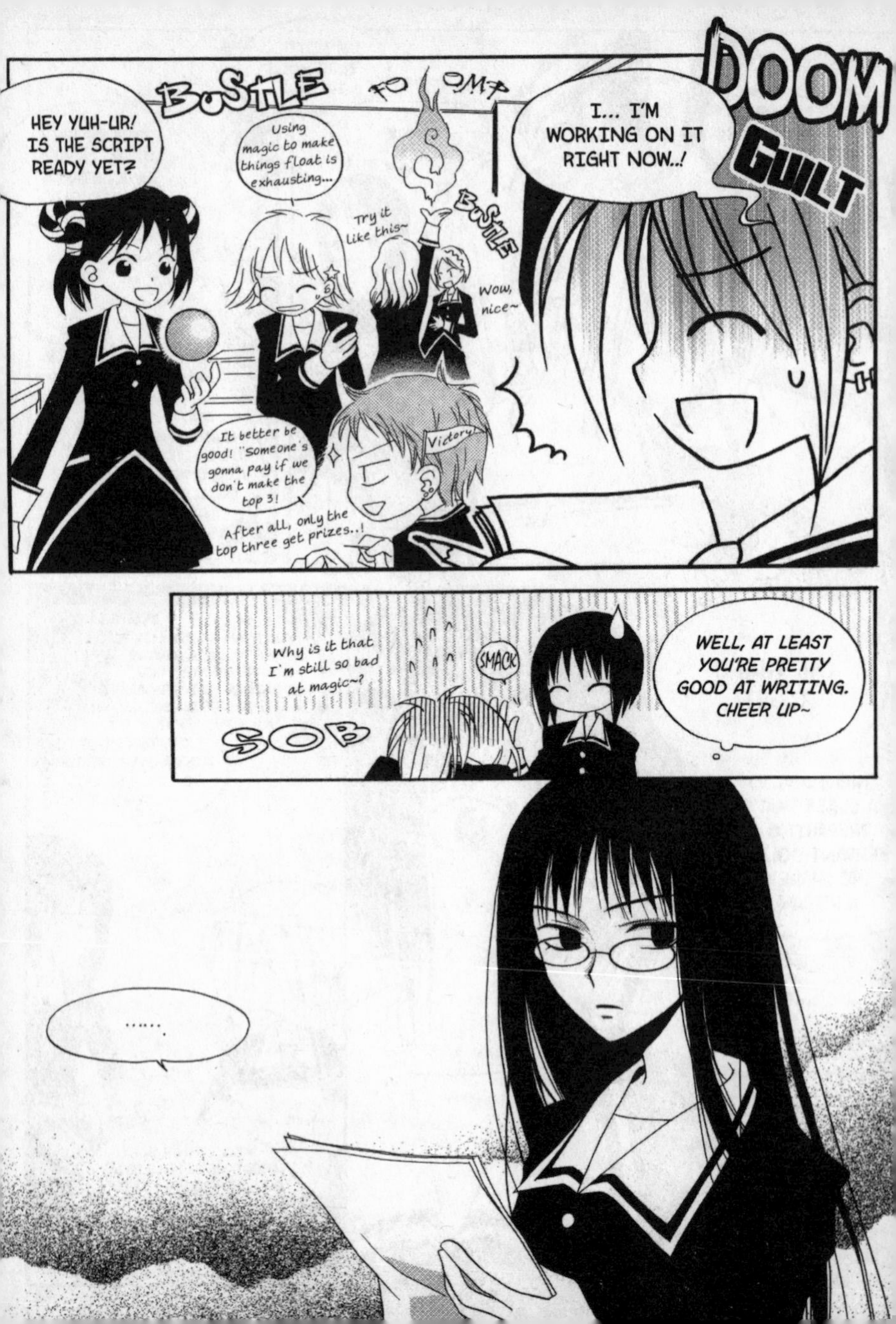
HEY YUH-UR! IS THE SCRIPT READY YET?
BUSTLE
Using magic to make things float is exhausting...
Try it like this~
BUSTLE
Wow, nice~
It better be good! Someone's gonna pay if we don't make the top 3!
Victory
After all, only the top three get prizes..!
I... I'M WORKING ON IT RIGHT NOW..!
DOOM
GUILT
Why is it that I'm still so bad at magic~?
SMACK
SOB
WELL, AT LEAST YOU'RE PRETTY GOOD AT WRITING. CHEER UP~
....

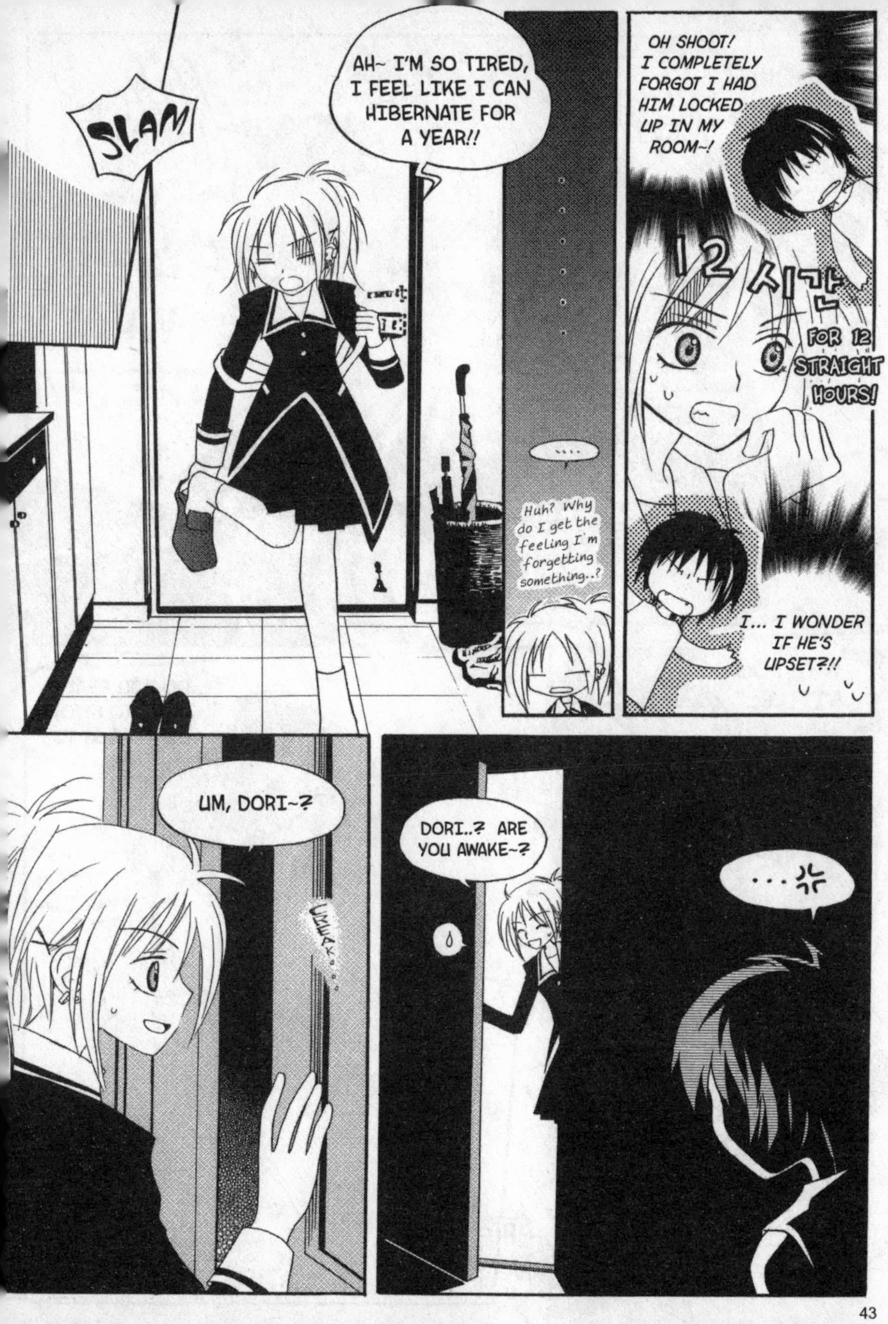
SLAM
AH~ I'M SO TIRED, I FEEL LIKE I CAN HIBERNATE FOR A YEAR!!
....
Huh? Why do I get the feeling I'm forgetting something..?
OH SHOOT! I COMPLETELY FORGOT I HAD HIM LOCKED UP IN MY ROOM~!
12 시간
FOR 12 STRAIGHT HOURS!
I... I WONDER IF HE'S UPSET?!!
UM, DORI~?
CREAK...
DORI..? ARE YOU AWAKE~?
...

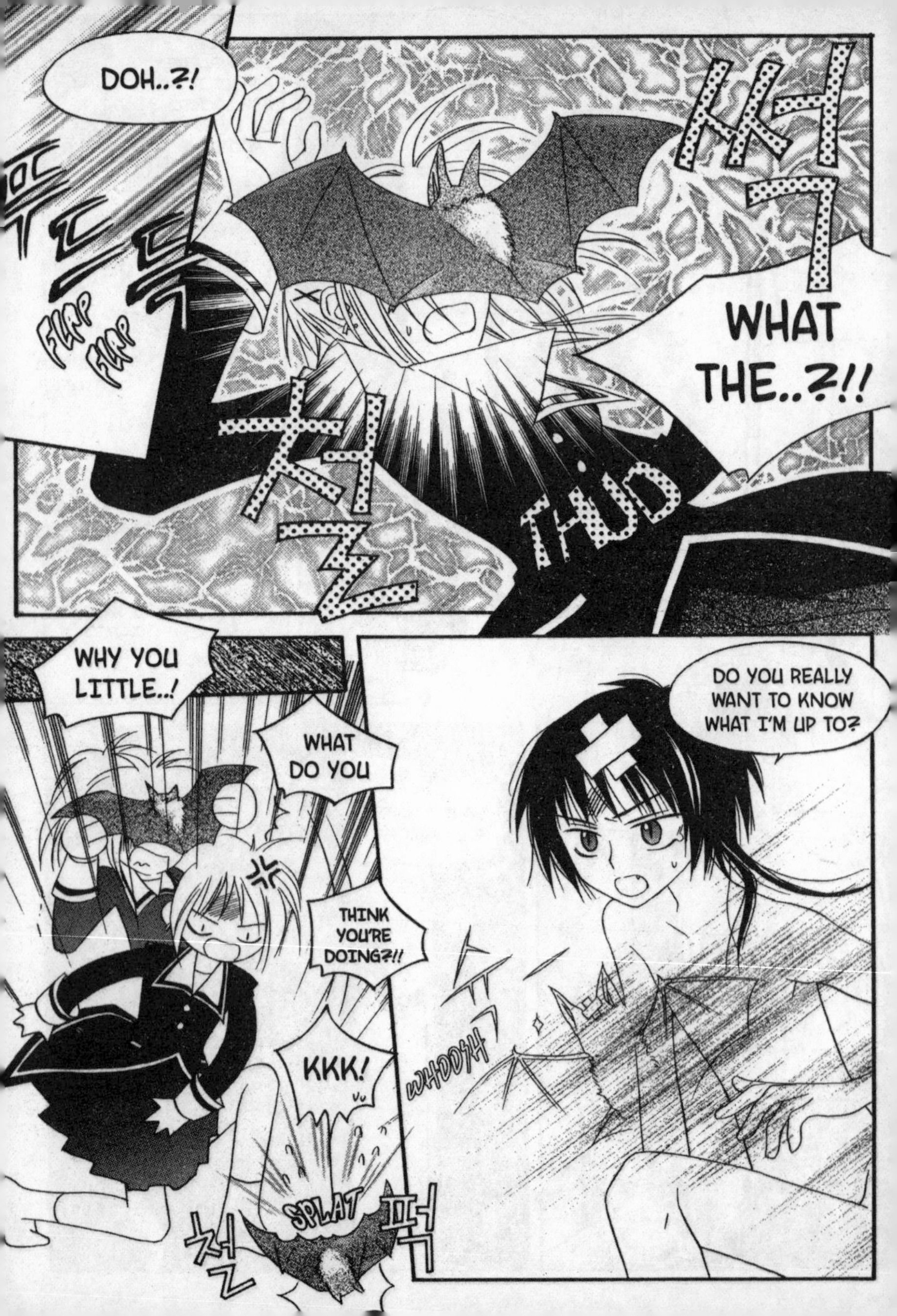

DOH..?!
FLAP FLAP
WHAT THE..?!!
THUD
WHY YOU LITTLE..!
WHAT DO YOU
THINK YOU'RE DOING?!!
KKK!
SPLAT
WHOOSH
DO YOU REALLY WANT TO KNOW WHAT I'M UP TO?

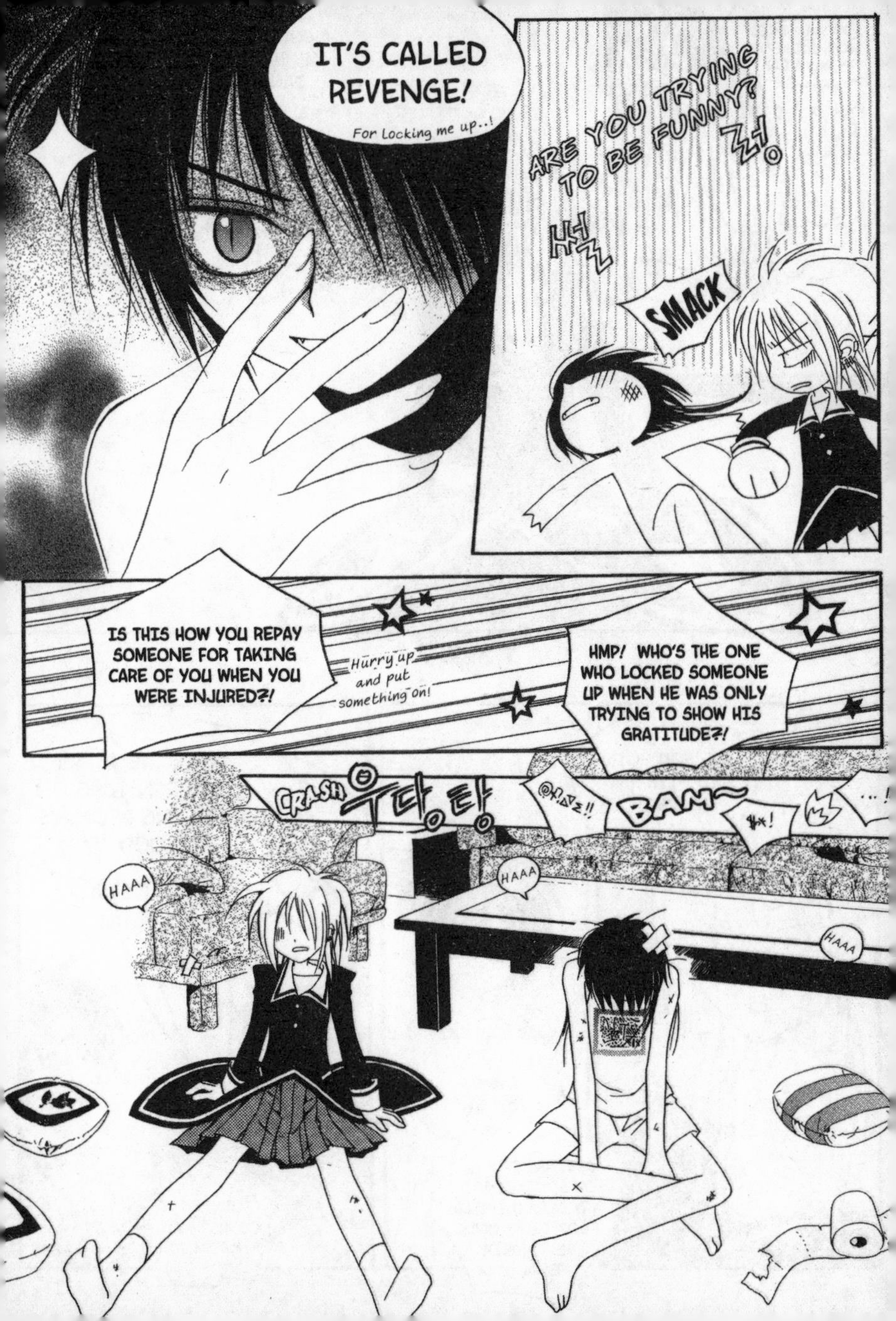
IT'S CALLED REVENGE!
For Locking me up..!
ARE YOU TRYING TO BE FUNNY?
SMACK
IS THIS HOW YOU REPAY SOMEONE FOR TAKING CARE OF YOU WHEN YOU WERE INJURED?!
Hurry up and put something on!
HMP! WHO'S THE ONE WHO LOCKED SOMEONE UP WHEN HE WAS ONLY TRYING TO SHOW HIS GRATITUDE?!
CRASH
BAM~
...!
HAAA
HAAA
HAAA

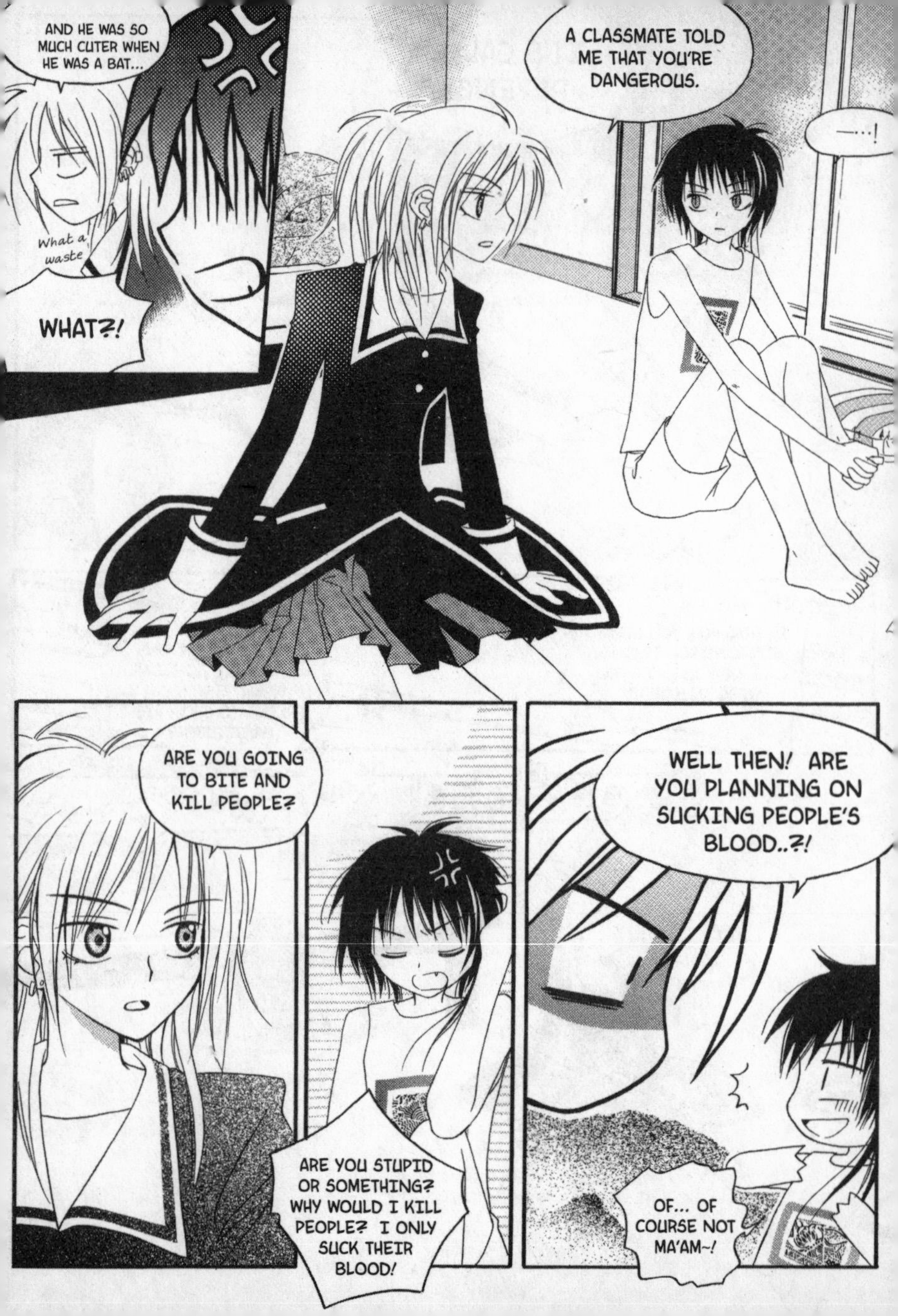
AND HE WAS SO MUCH CUTER WHEN HE WAS A BAT...
What a waste
WHAT?!
A CLASSMATE TOLD ME THAT YOU'RE DANGEROUS.
—...!
ARE YOU GOING TO BITE AND KILL PEOPLE?
ARE YOU STUPID OR SOMETHING? WHY WOULD I KILL PEOPLE? I ONLY SUCK THEIR BLOOD!
WELL THEN! ARE YOU PLANNING ON SUCKING PEOPLE'S BLOOD..?!
OF... OF COURSE NOT MA'AM~!

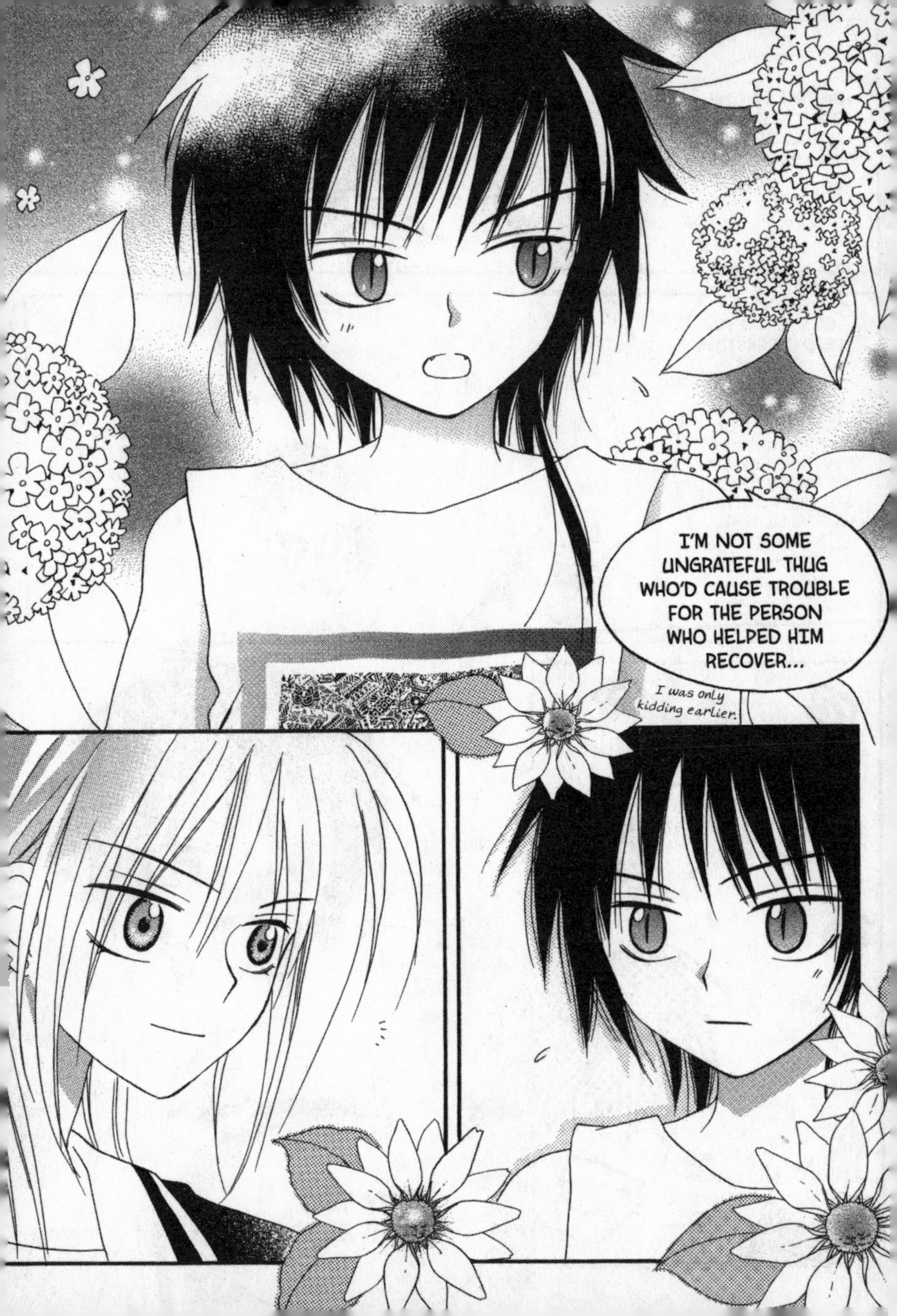
I'M NOT SOME UNGRATEFUL THUG WHO'D CAUSE TROUBLE FOR THE PERSON WHO HELPED HIM RECOVER...
I was only kidding earlier.

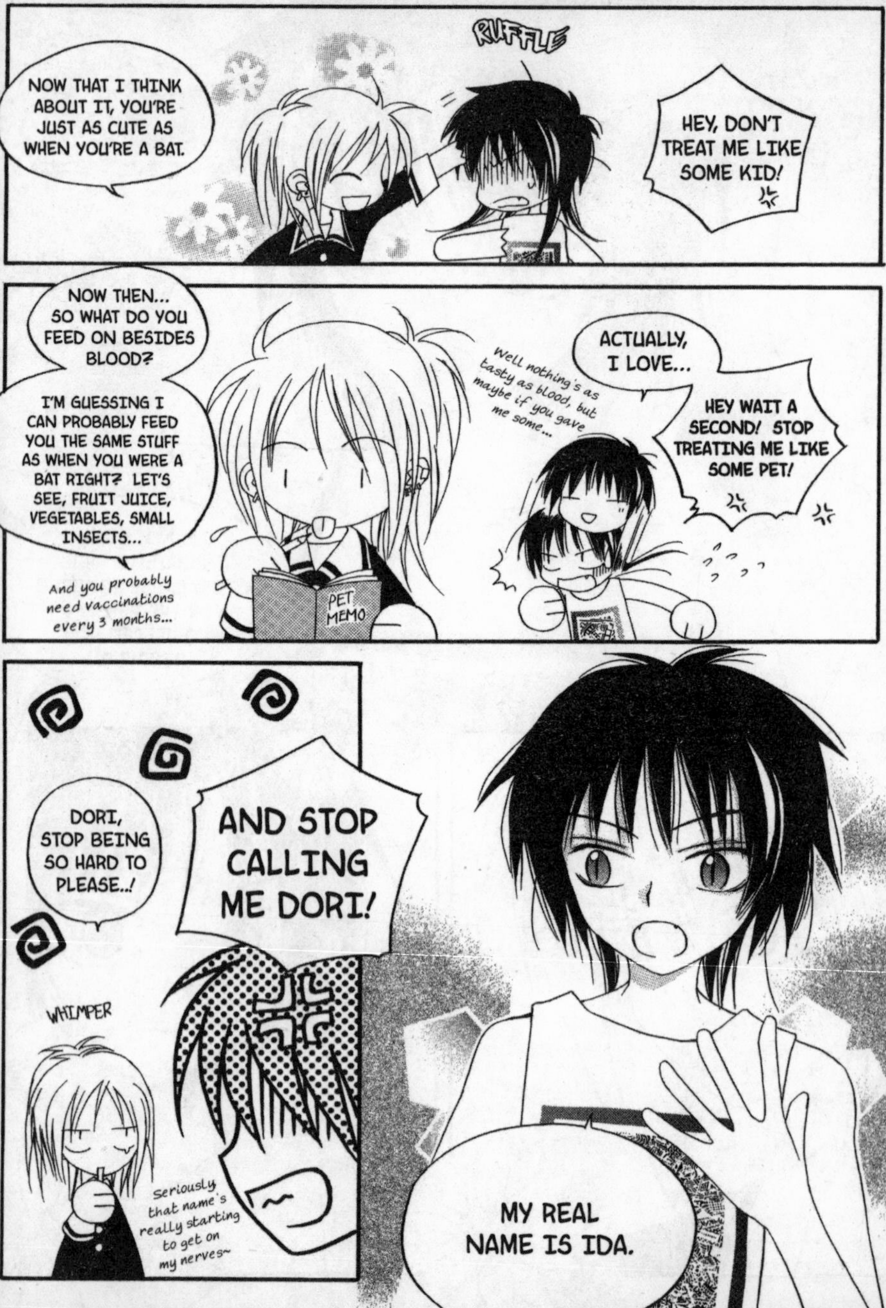

RUFFLE
NOW THAT I THINK ABOUT IT, YOU'RE JUST AS CUTE AS WHEN YOU'RE A BAT.
HEY, DON'T TREAT ME LIKE SOME KID!
NOW THEN... SO WHAT DO YOU FEED ON BESIDES BLOOD?
I'M GUESSING I CAN PROBABLY FEED YOU THE SAME STUFF AS WHEN YOU WERE A BAT RIGHT? LET'S SEE, FRUIT JUICE, VEGETABLES, SMALL INSECTS...
And you probably need vaccinations every 3 months...
PET MEMO
Well nothing's as tasty as blood, but maybe if you gave me some...
ACTUALLY, I LOVE...
HEY WAIT A SECOND! STOP TREATING ME LIKE SOME PET!
DORI, STOP BEING SO HARD TO PLEASE..!
AND STOP CALLING ME DORI!
WHIMPER
Seriously that name's really starting to get on my nerves~
MY REAL NAME IS IDA.

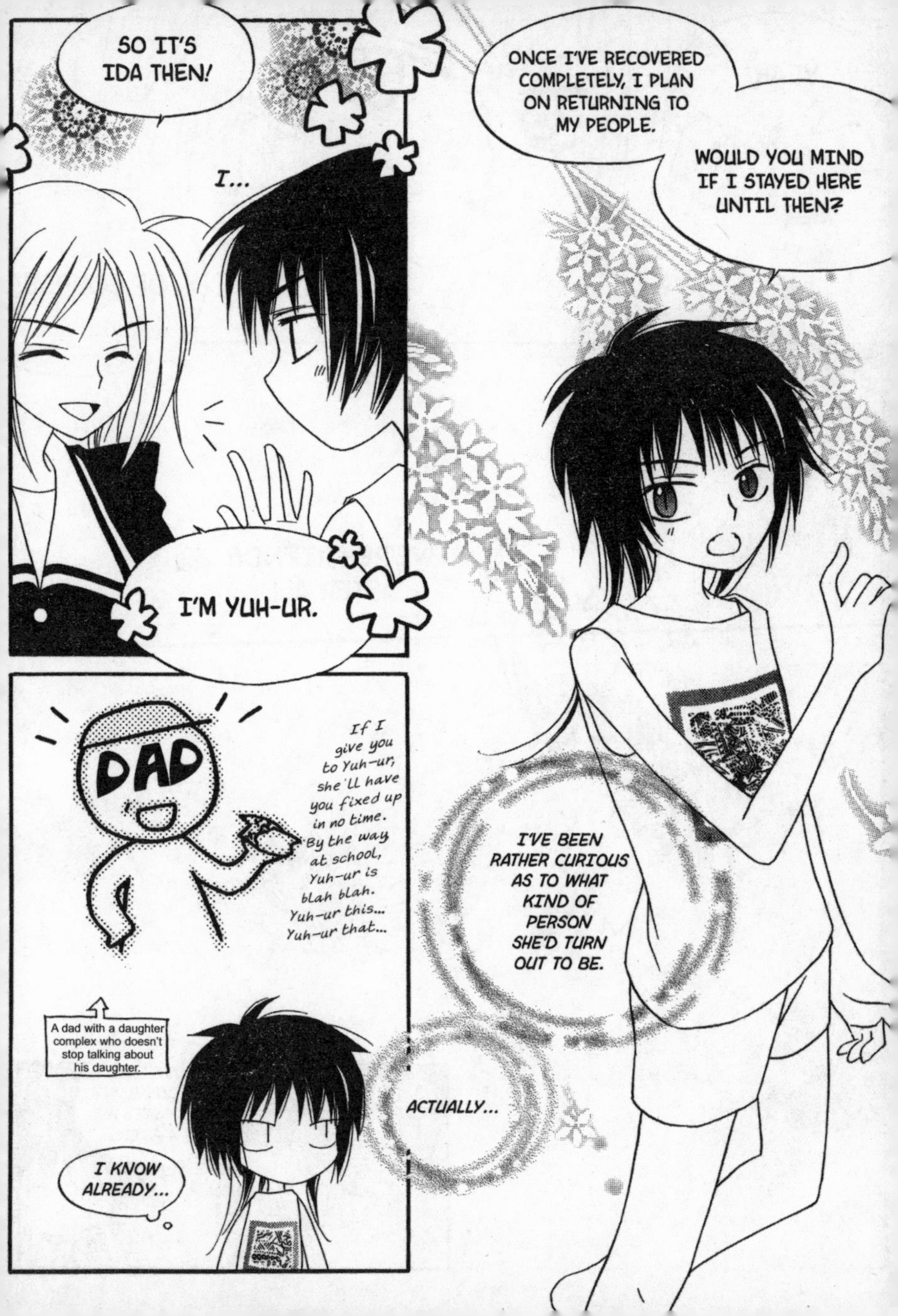
SO IT'S IDA THEN!
I...
I'M YUH-UR.
DAD
If I give you to Yuh-ur, she'll have you fixed up in no time. By the way at school, Yuh-ur is blah blah. Yuh-ur this... Yuh-ur that...
A dad with a daughter complex who doesn't stop talking about his daughter.
I KNOW ALREADY...
ONCE I'VE RECOVERED COMPLETELY, I PLAN ON RETURNING TO MY PEOPLE.
WOULD YOU MIND IF I STAYED HERE UNTIL THEN?
I'VE BEEN RATHER CURIOUS AS TO WHAT KIND OF PERSON SHE'D TURN OUT TO BE.
ACTUALLY...

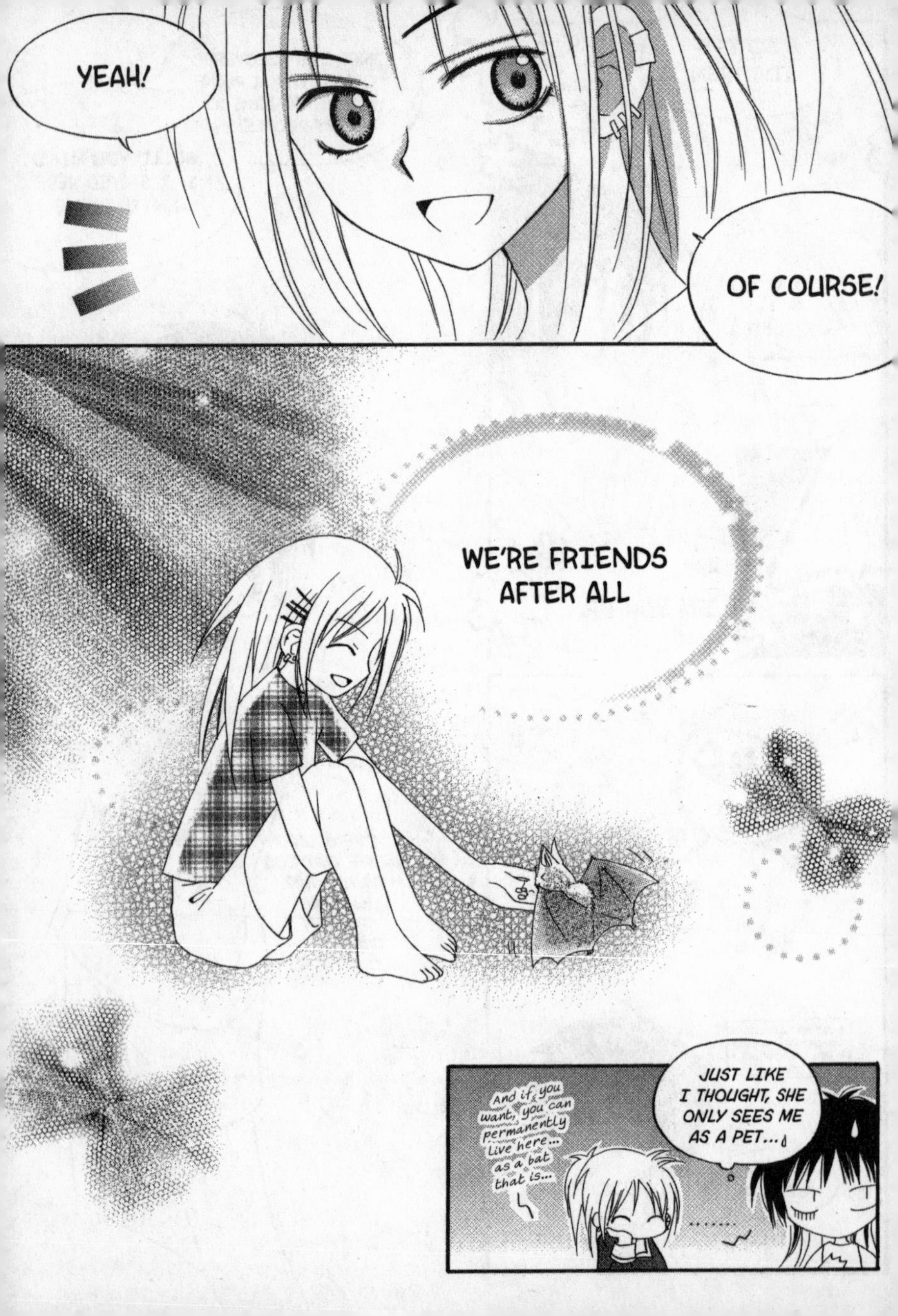
YEAH!
OF COURSE!
WE'RE FRIENDS AFTER ALL
And if you want, you can permanently live here... as a bat that is...
JUST LIKE I THOUGHT, SHE ONLY SEES ME AS A PET...
....

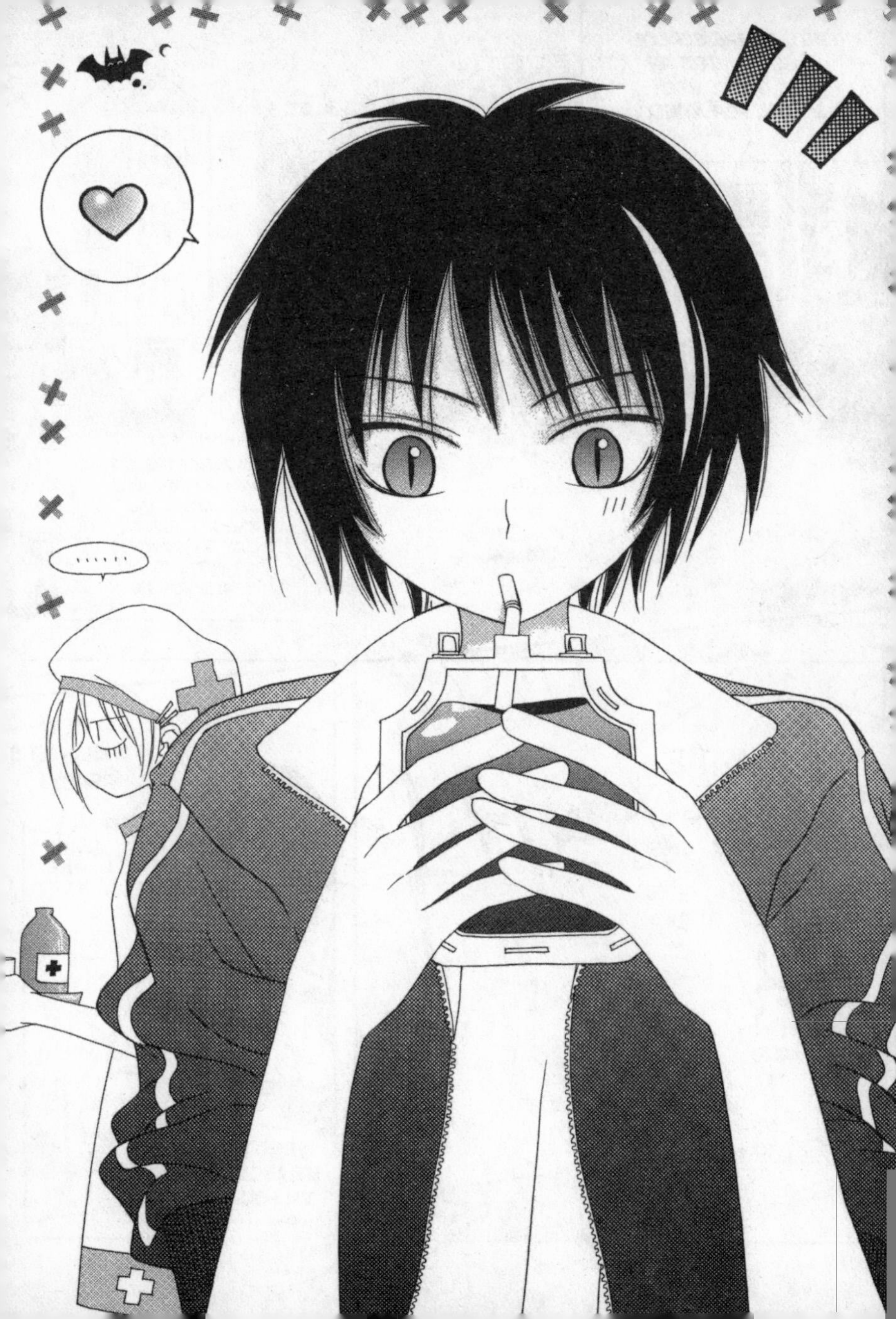
......

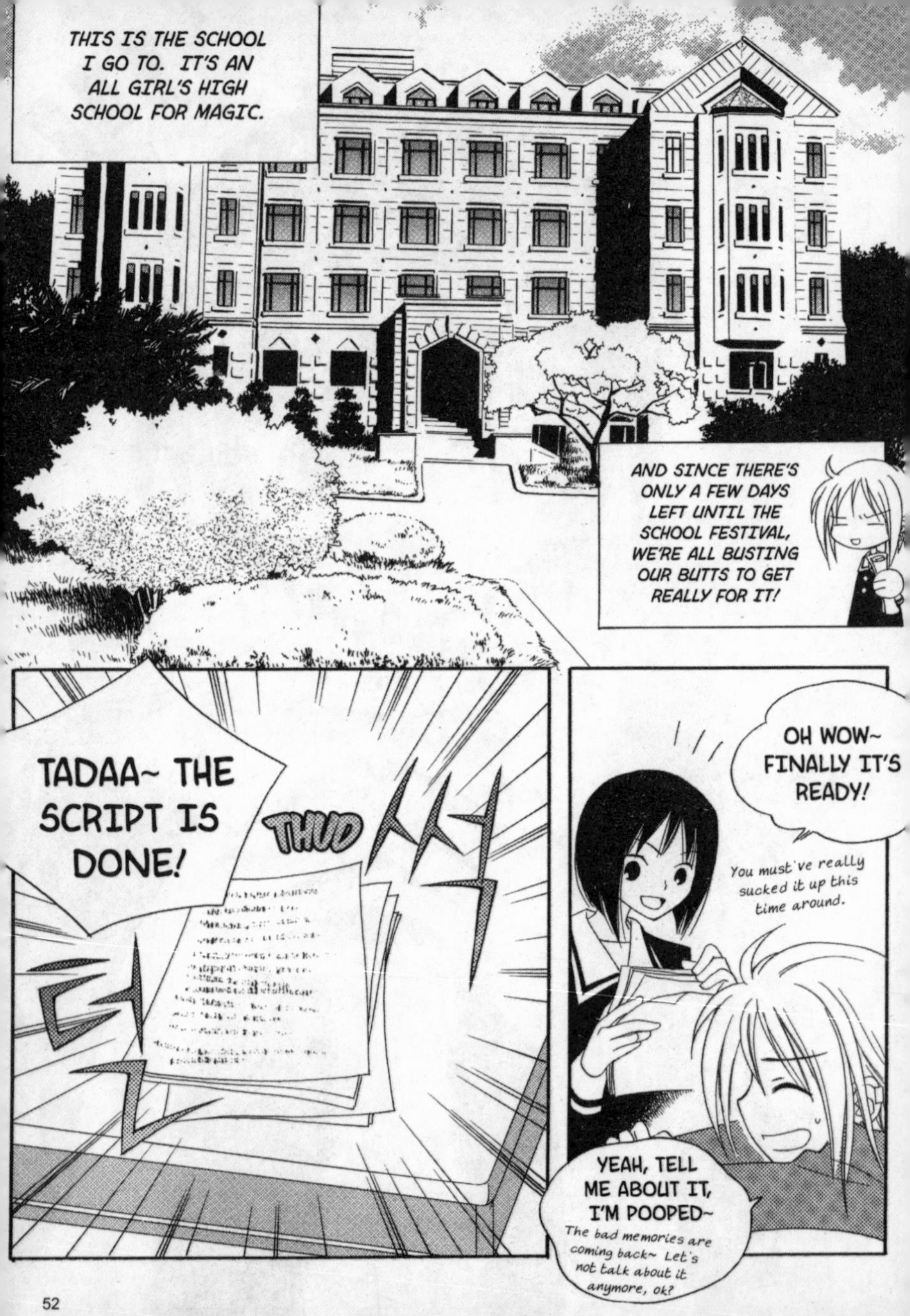
THIS IS THE SCHOOL I GO TO. IT'S AN ALL GIRL'S HIGH SCHOOL FOR MAGIC.
AND SINCE THERE'S ONLY A FEW DAYS LEFT UNTIL THE SCHOOL FESTIVAL, WE'RE ALL BUSTING OUR BUTTS TO GET REALLY FOR IT!
TADAA~ THE SCRIPT IS DONE!
THUD
OH WOW~ FINALLY IT'S READY!
You must've really sucked it up this time around.
YEAH, TELL ME ABOUT IT, I'M POOPED~
The bad memories are coming back~ Let's not talk about it anymore, ok?

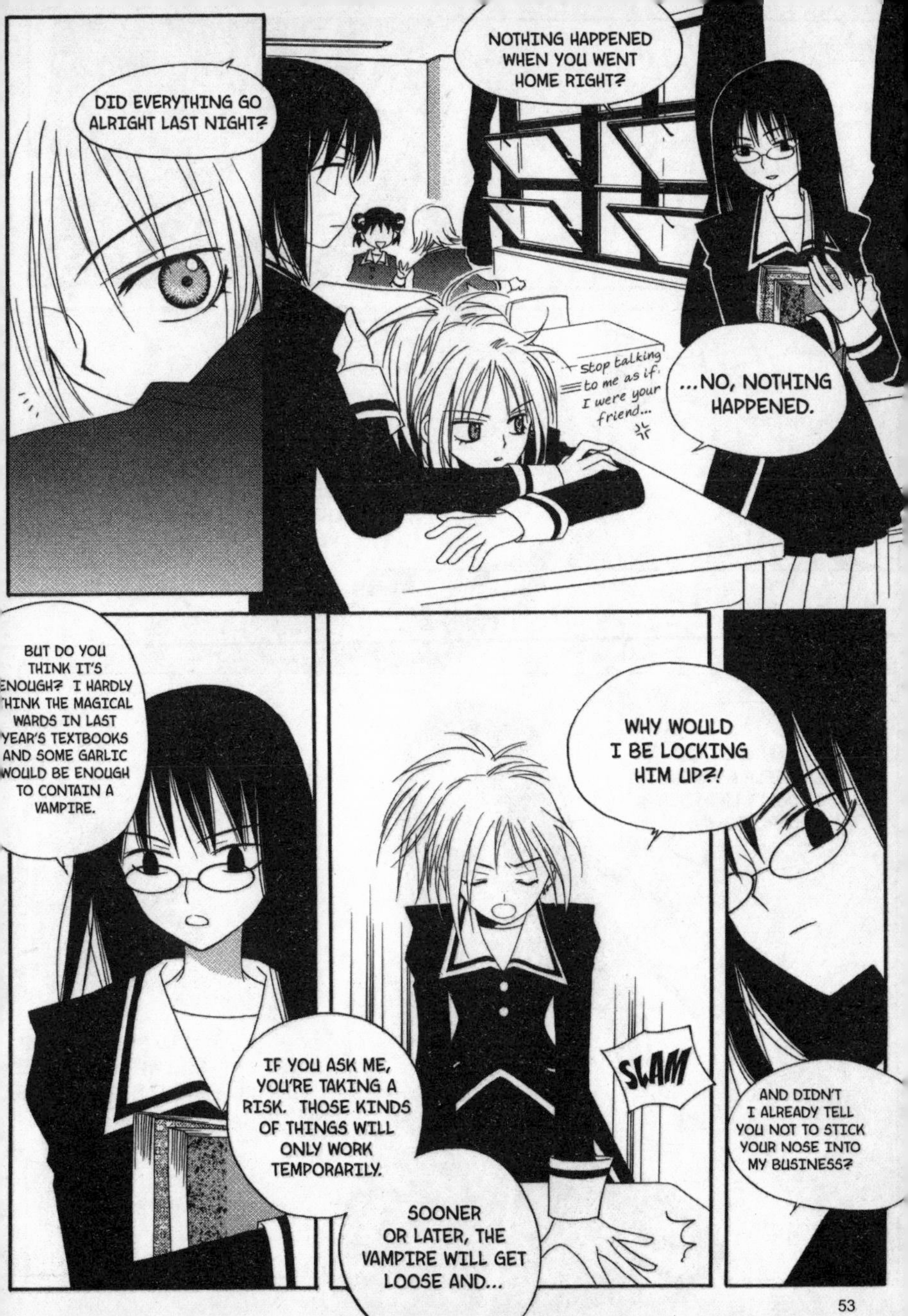
DID EVERYTHING GO ALRIGHT LAST NIGHT?
NOTHING HAPPENED WHEN YOU WENT HOME RIGHT?
Stop talking to me as if I were your friend...
...NO, NOTHING HAPPENED.
BUT DO YOU THINK IT'S ENOUGH? I HARDLY THINK THE MAGICAL WARDS IN LAST YEAR'S TEXTBOOKS AND SOME GARLIC WOULD BE ENOUGH TO CONTAIN A VAMPIRE.
IF YOU ASK ME, YOU'RE TAKING A RISK. THOSE KINDS OF THINGS WILL ONLY WORK TEMPORARILY.
SOONER OR LATER, THE VAMPIRE WILL GET LOOSE AND...
WHY WOULD I BE LOCKING HIM UP?!
SLAM
AND DIDN'T I ALREADY TELL YOU NOT TO STICK YOUR NOSE INTO MY BUSINESS?

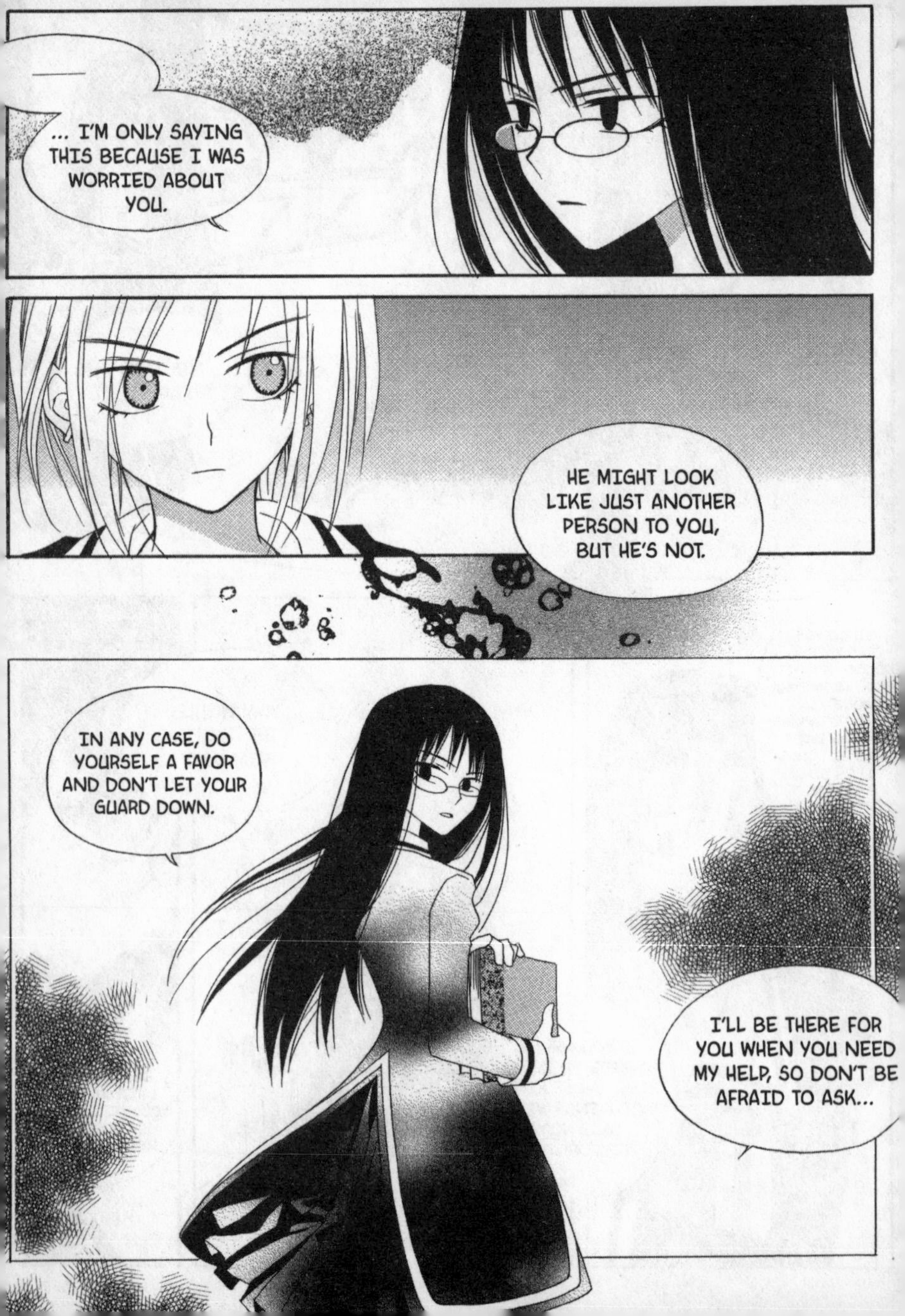
... I'M ONLY SAYING THIS BECAUSE I WAS WORRIED ABOUT YOU.
HE MIGHT LOOK LIKE JUST ANOTHER PERSON TO YOU, BUT HE'S NOT.
IN ANY CASE, DO YOURSELF A FAVOR AND DON'T LET YOUR GUARD DOWN.
I'LL BE THERE FOR YOU WHEN YOU NEED MY HELP, SO DON'T BE AFRAID TO ASK...

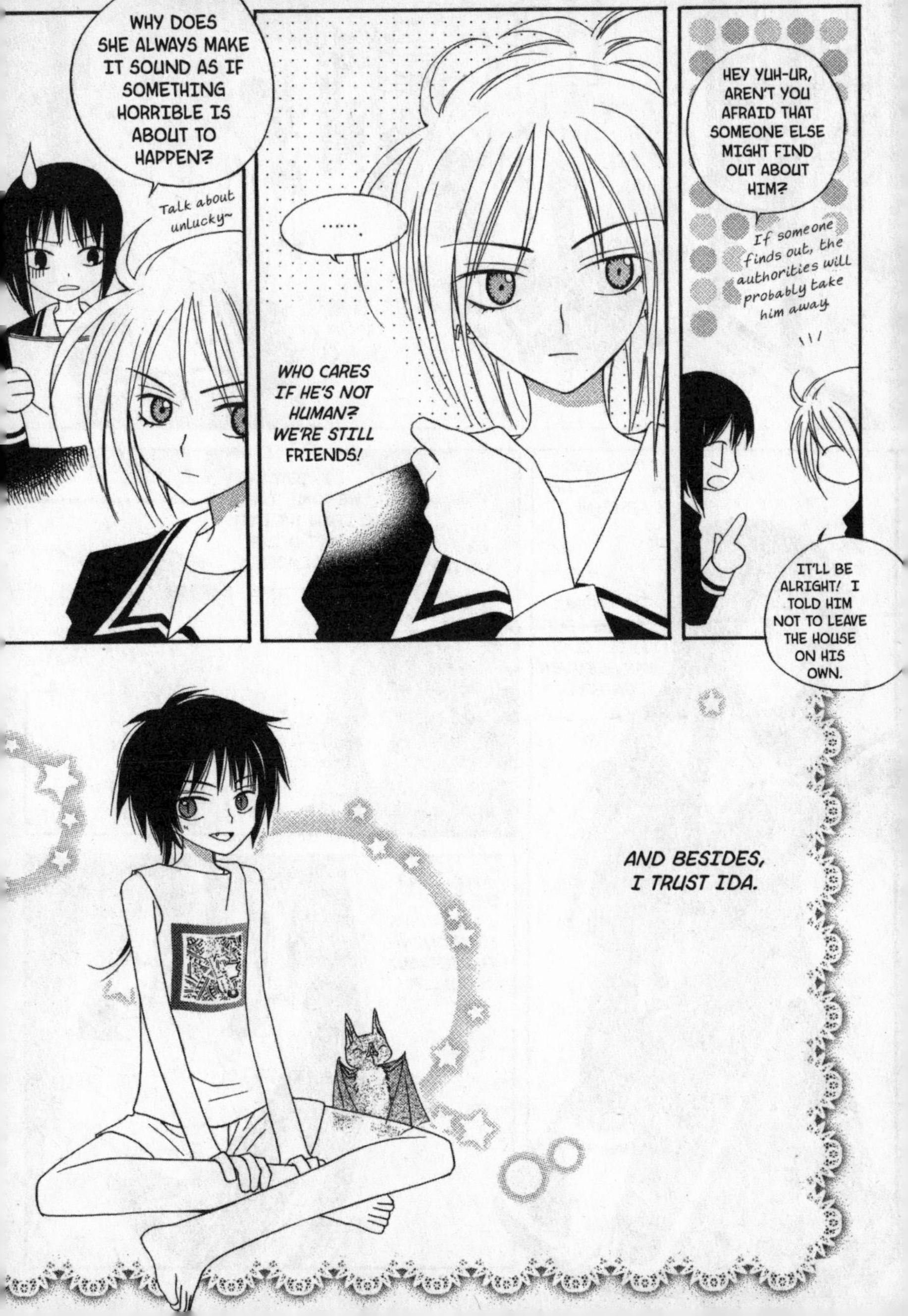
WHY DOES SHE ALWAYS MAKE IT SOUND AS IF SOMETHING HORRIBLE IS ABOUT TO HAPPEN?
Talk about unlucky~
......
WHO CARES IF HE'S NOT HUMAN? WE'RE STILL FRIENDS!
HEY YUH-UR, AREN'T YOU AFRAID THAT SOMEONE ELSE MIGHT FIND OUT ABOUT HIM?
If someone finds out, the authorities will probably take him away
IT'LL BE ALRIGHT! I TOLD HIM NOT TO LEAVE THE HOUSE ON HIS OWN.
AND BESIDES, I TRUST IDA.

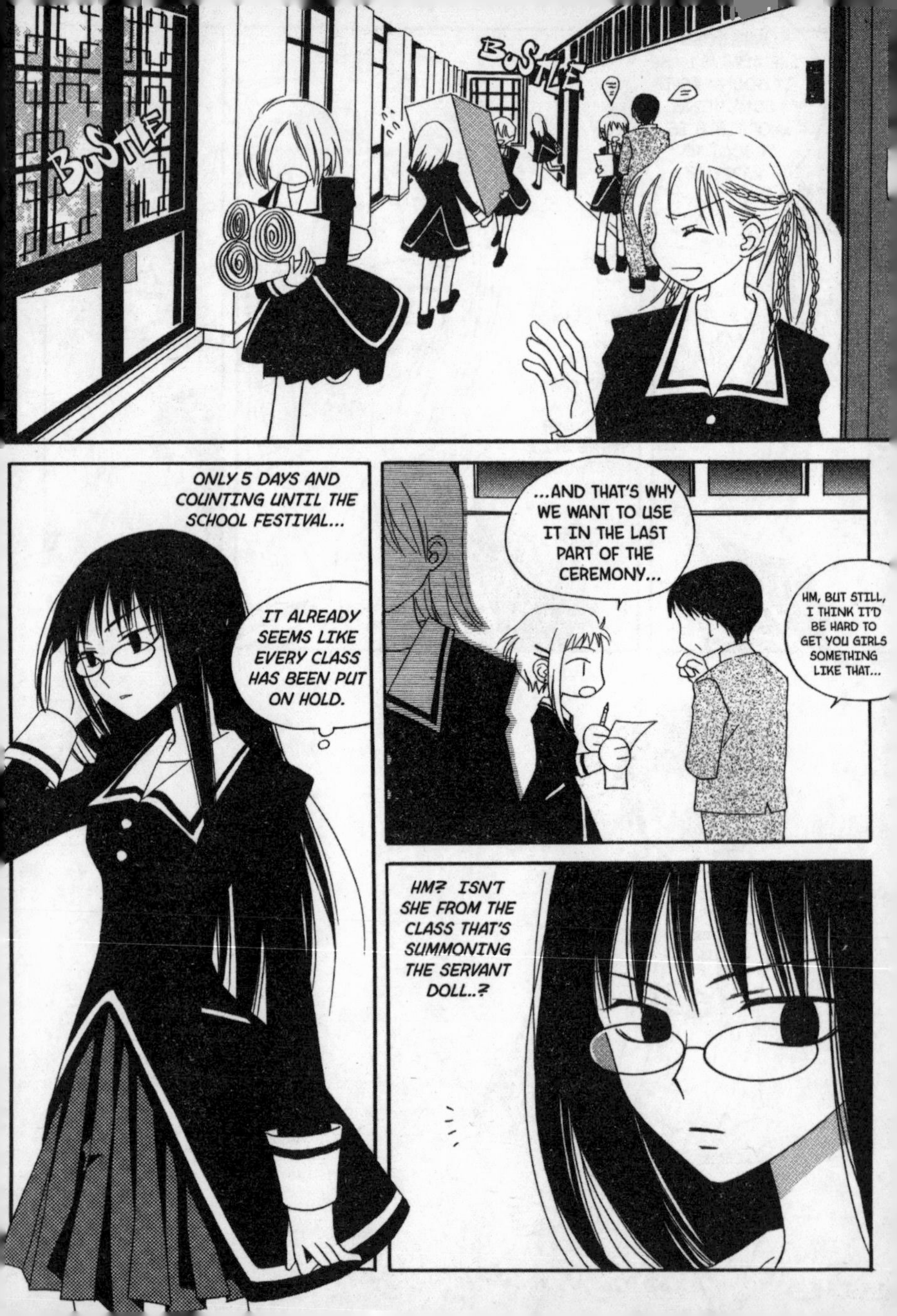
BUSTLE
BUSTLE
ONLY 5 DAYS AND COUNTING UNTIL THE SCHOOL FESTIVAL...
IT ALREADY SEEMS LIKE EVERY CLASS HAS BEEN PUT ON HOLD.
...AND THAT'S WHY WE WANT TO USE IT IN THE LAST PART OF THE CEREMONY...
HM, BUT STILL, I THINK IT'D BE HARD TO GET YOU GIRLS SOMETHING LIKE THAT...
HM? ISN'T SHE FROM THE CLASS THAT'S SUMMONING THE SERVANT DOLL..?

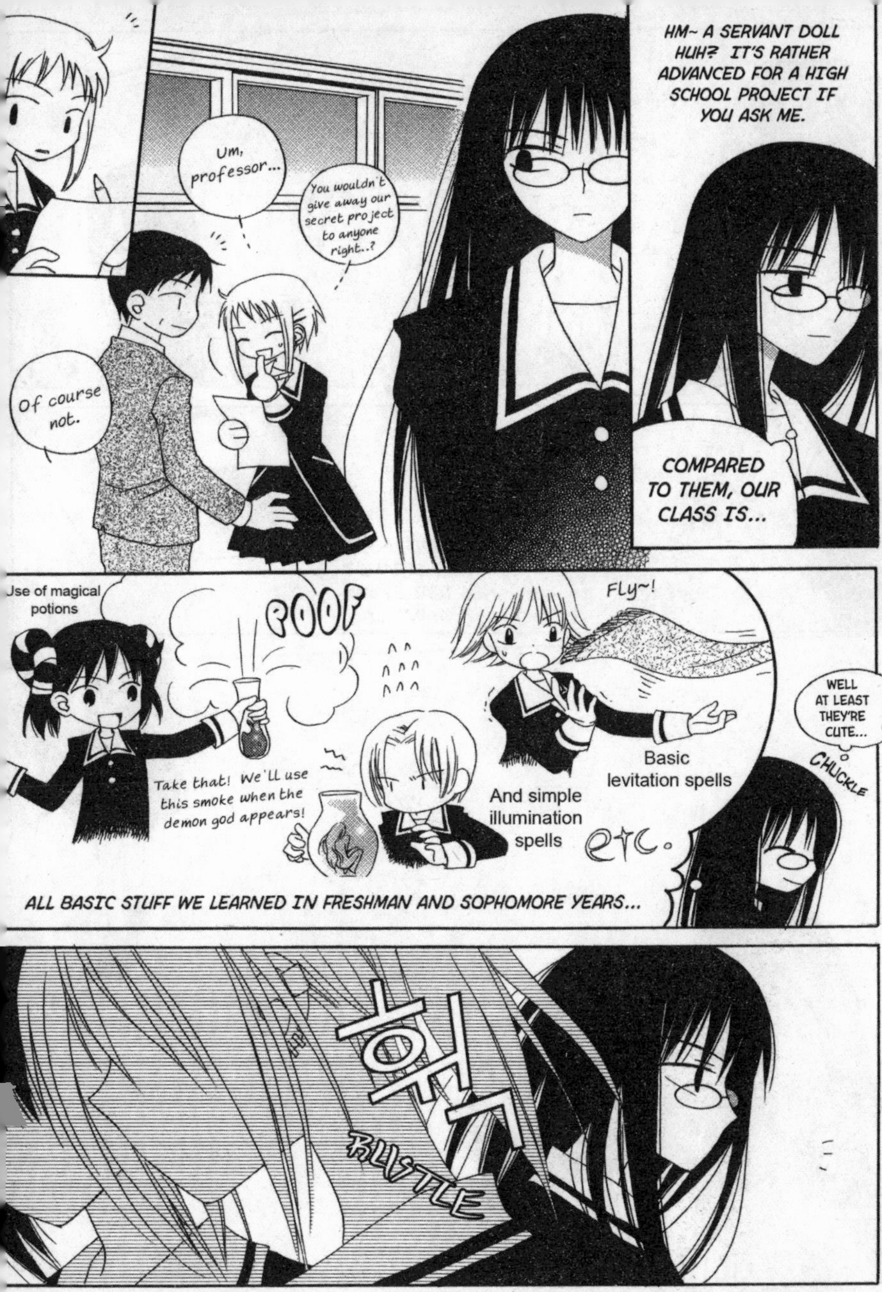
Um, professor...
You wouldn't give away our secret project to anyone right..?
Of course not.
HM~ A SERVANT DOLL HUH? IT'S RATHER ADVANCED FOR A HIGH SCHOOL PROJECT IF YOU ASK ME.
COMPARED TO THEM, OUR CLASS IS...
Jse of magical potions
POOF
Take that! We'll use this smoke when the demon god appears!
Fly~!
And simple illumination spells
Basic levitation spells
etc.
WELL AT LEAST THEY'RE CUTE...
CHUCKLE
ALL BASIC STUFF WE LEARNED IN FRESHMAN AND SOPHOMORE YEARS...
RUSTLE

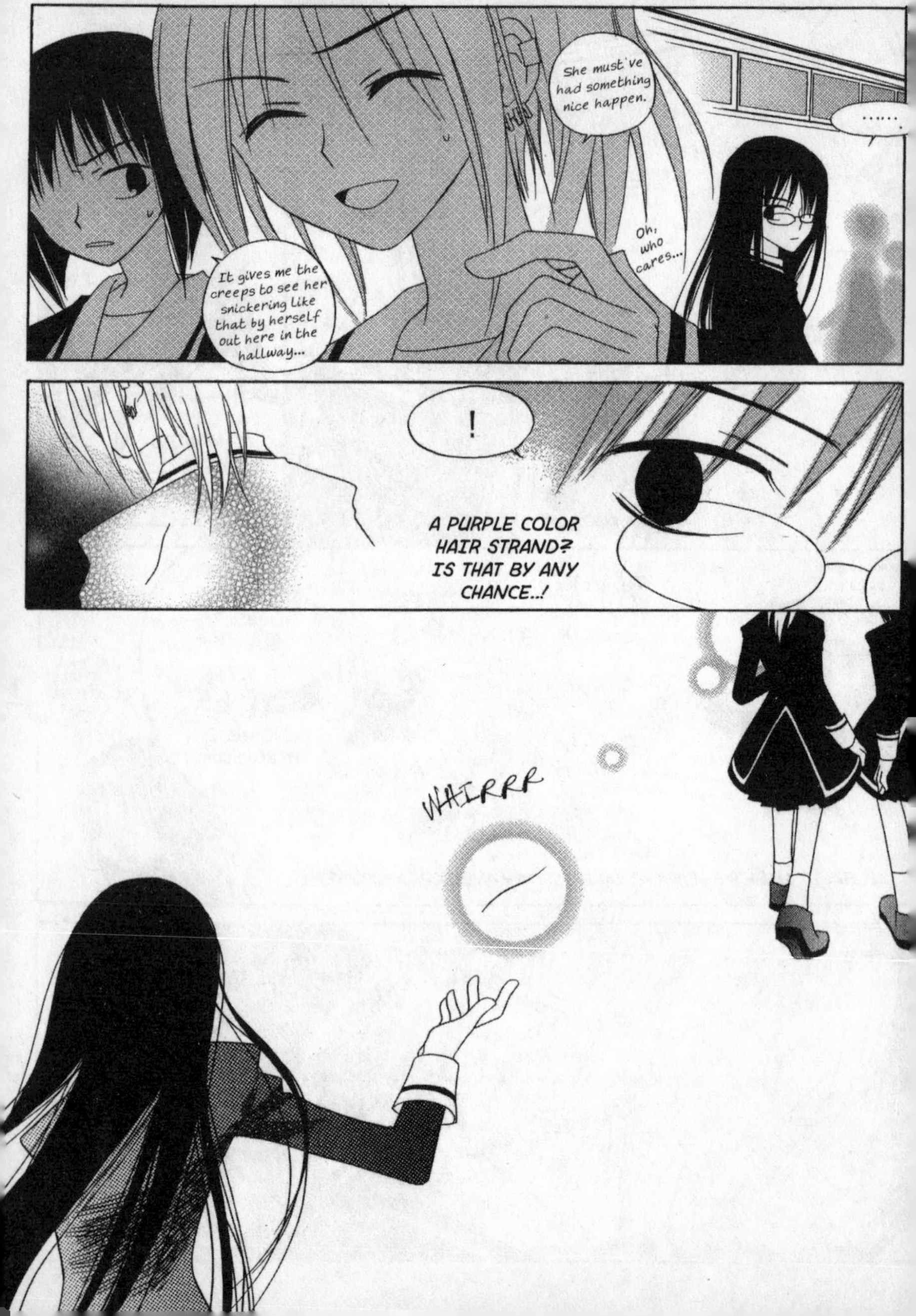
It gives me the creeps to see her snickering like that by herself out here in the hallway...
She must've had something nice happen.
Oh, who cares...
......
!
A PURPLE COLOR HAIR STRAND? IS THAT BY ANY CHANCE..!
WHIRRR

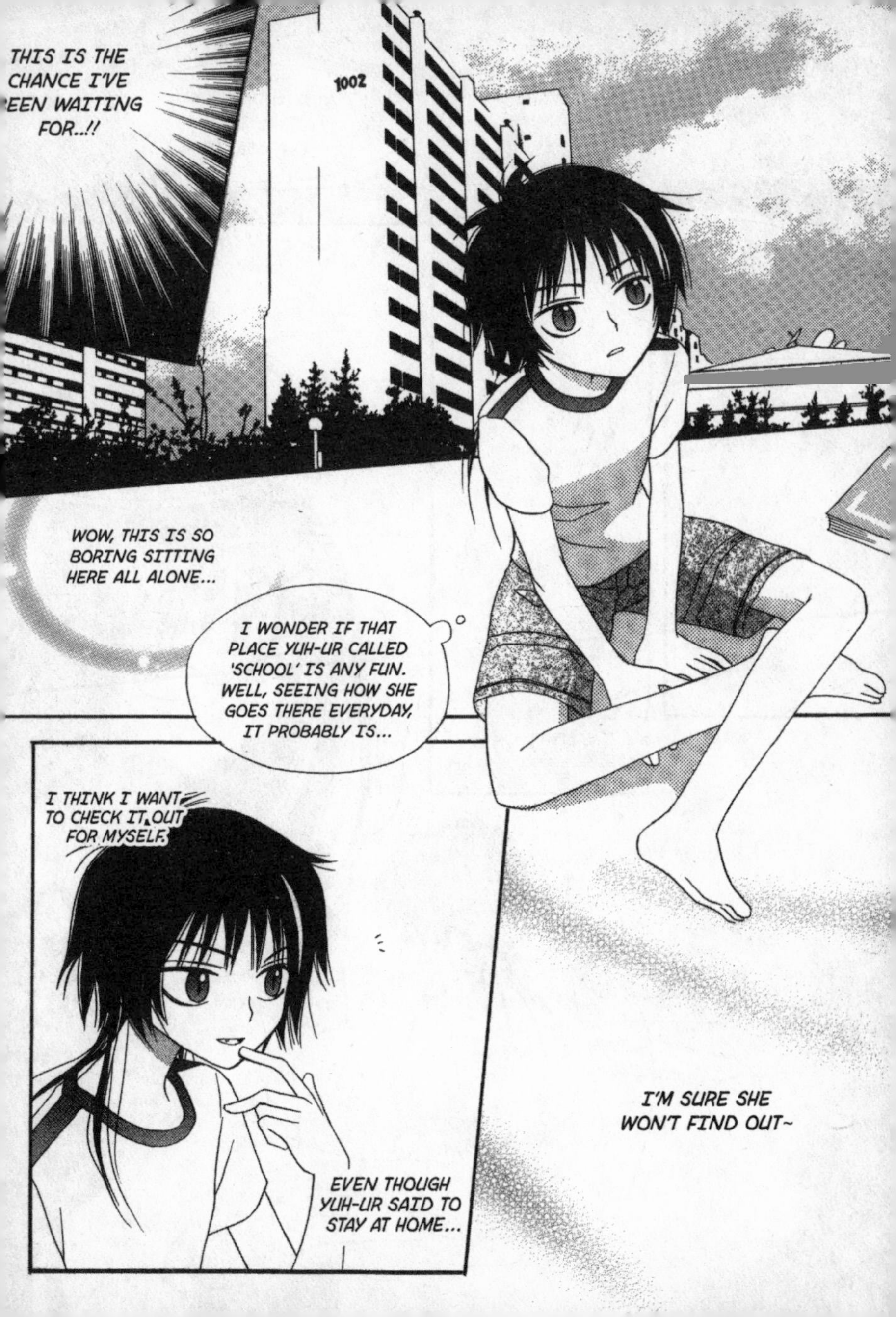
THIS IS THE CHANCE I'VE EEN WAITING FOR..!!
1002
WOW, THIS IS SO BORING SITTING HERE ALL ALONE...
I WONDER IF THAT PLACE YUH-UR CALLED 'SCHOOL' IS ANY FUN. WELL, SEEING HOW SHE GOES THERE EVERYDAY, IT PROBABLY IS...
I THINK I WANT TO CHECK IT OUT FOR MYSELF.
EVEN THOUGH YUH-UR SAID TO STAY AT HOME...
I'M SURE SHE WON'T FIND OUT~

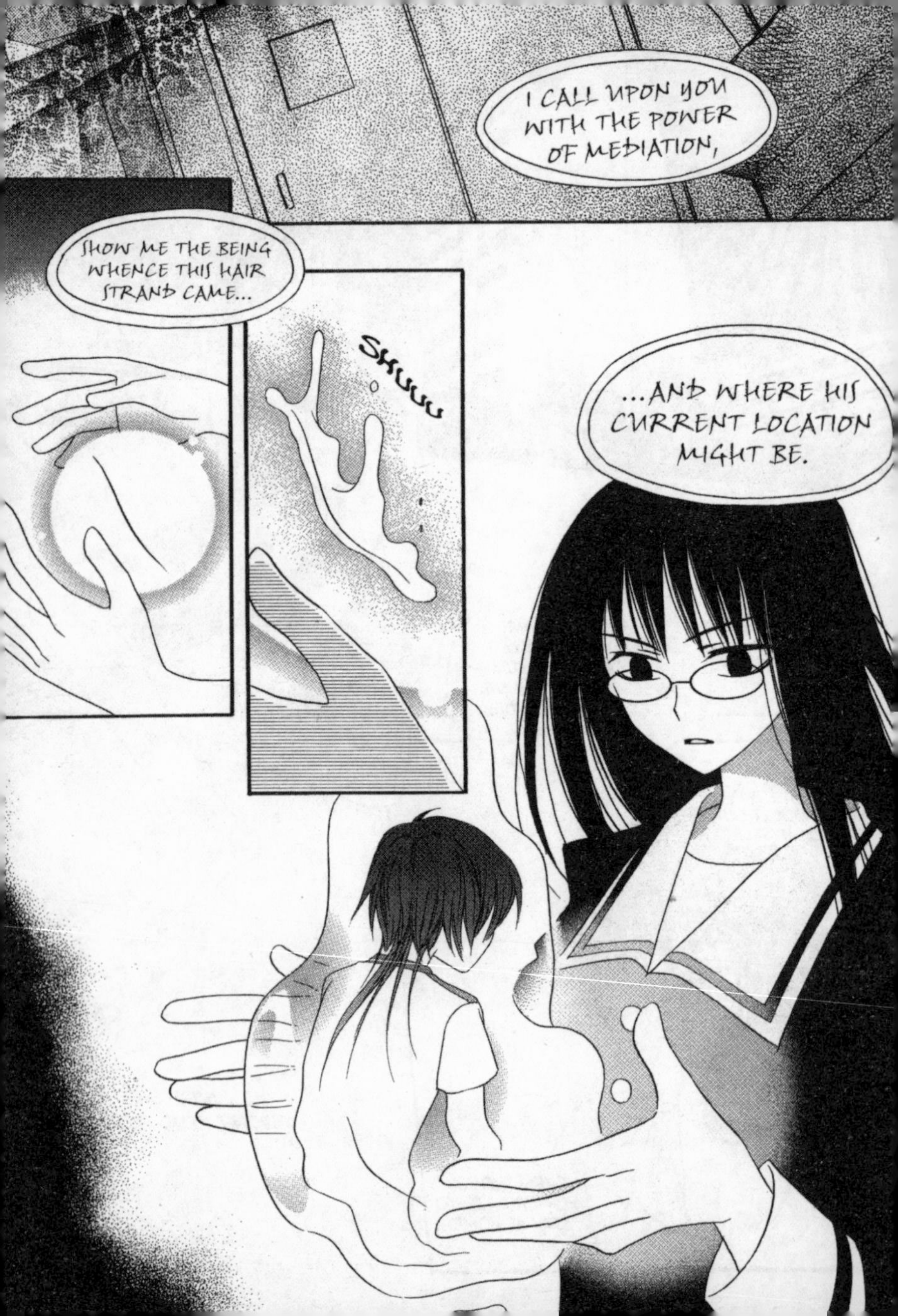
I CALL UPON YOU WITH THE POWER OF MEDIATION,
SHOW ME THE BEING WHENCE THIS HAIR STRAND CAME...
SHUUU
...AND WHERE HIS CURRENT LOCATION MIGHT BE.

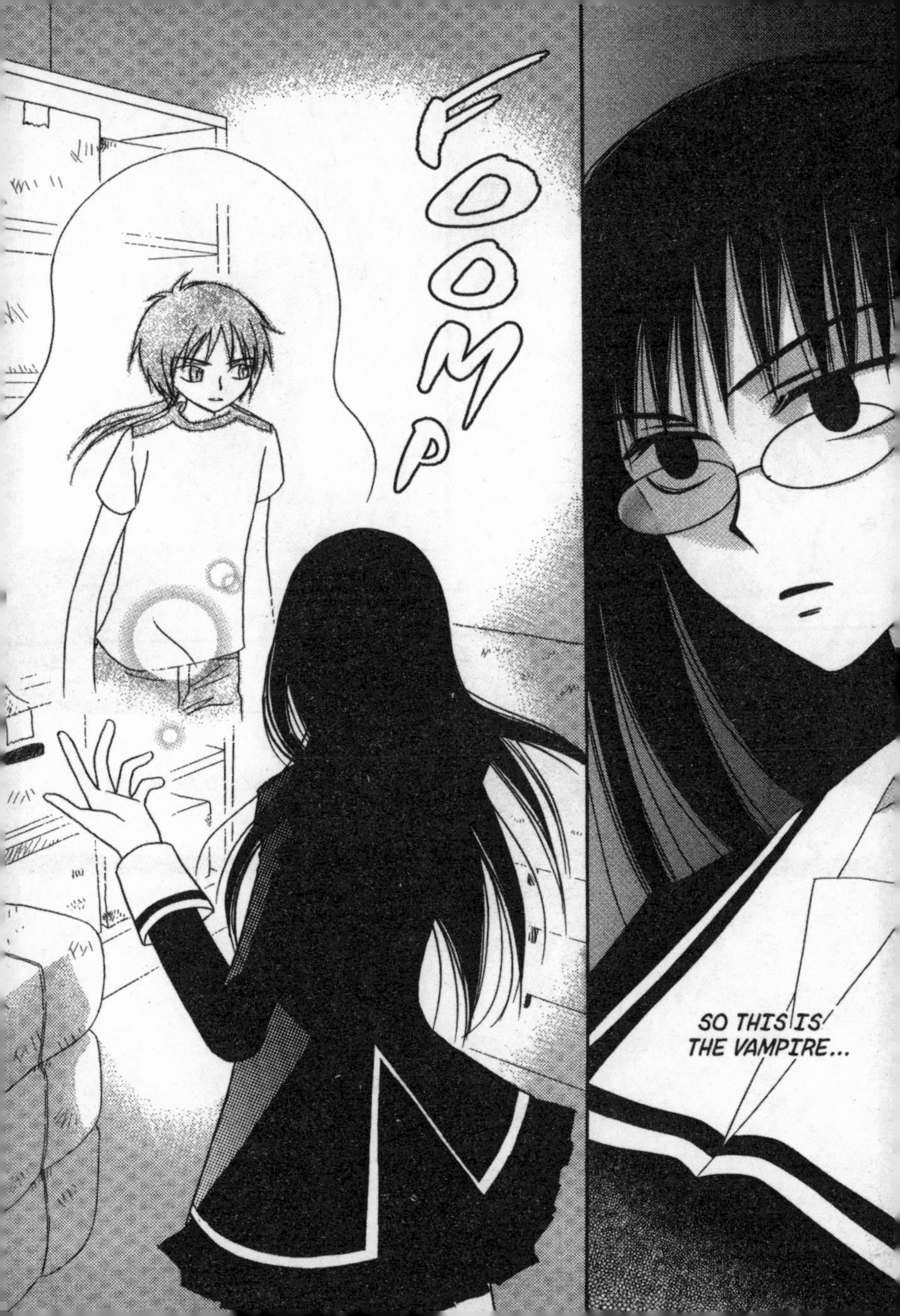
FOOMP
SO THIS IS THE VAMPIRE...

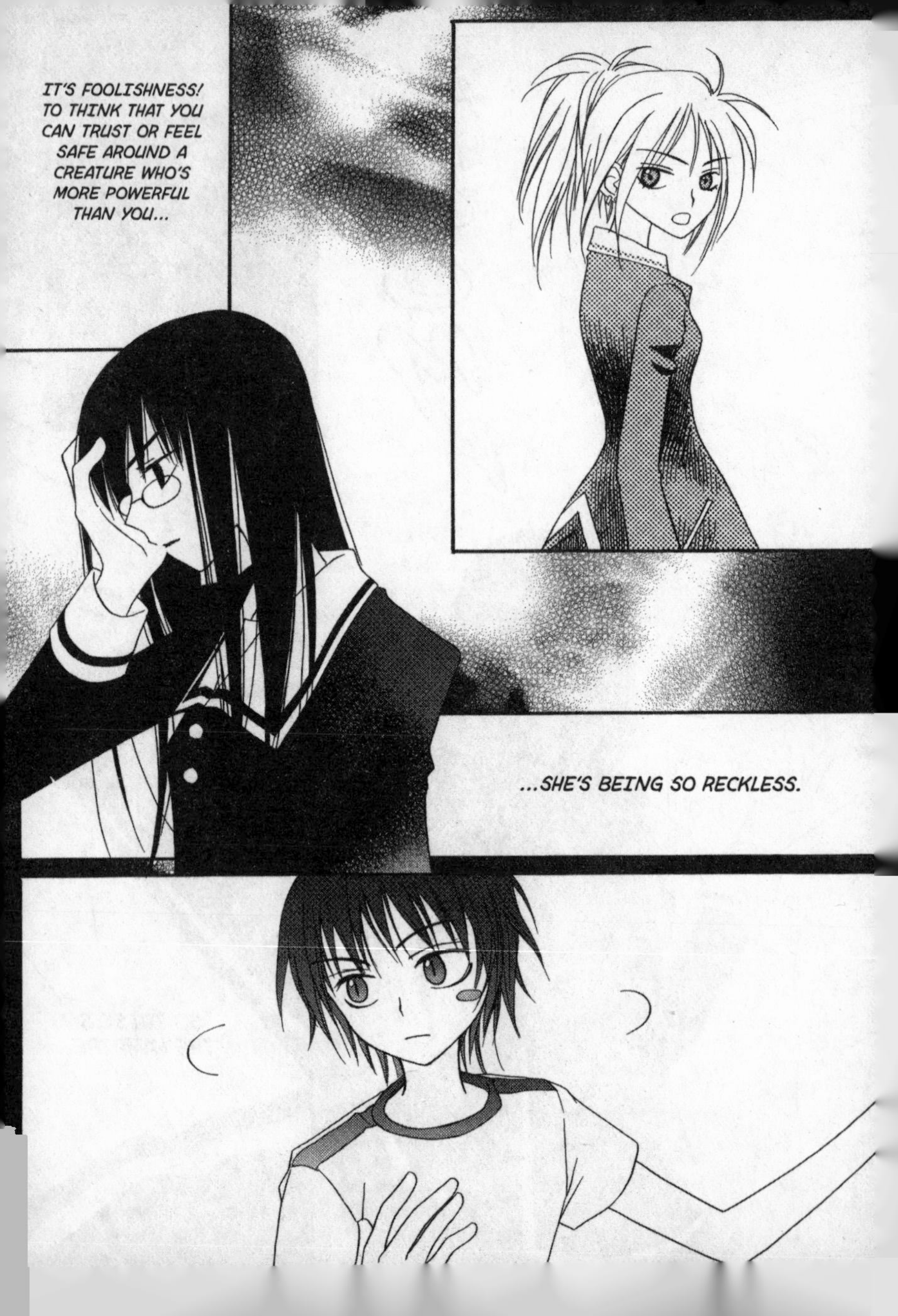
IT'S FOOLISHNESS! TO THINK THAT YOU CAN TRUST OR FEEL SAFE AROUND A CREATURE WHO'S MORE POWERFUL THAN YOU...
...SHE'S BEING SO RECKLESS.

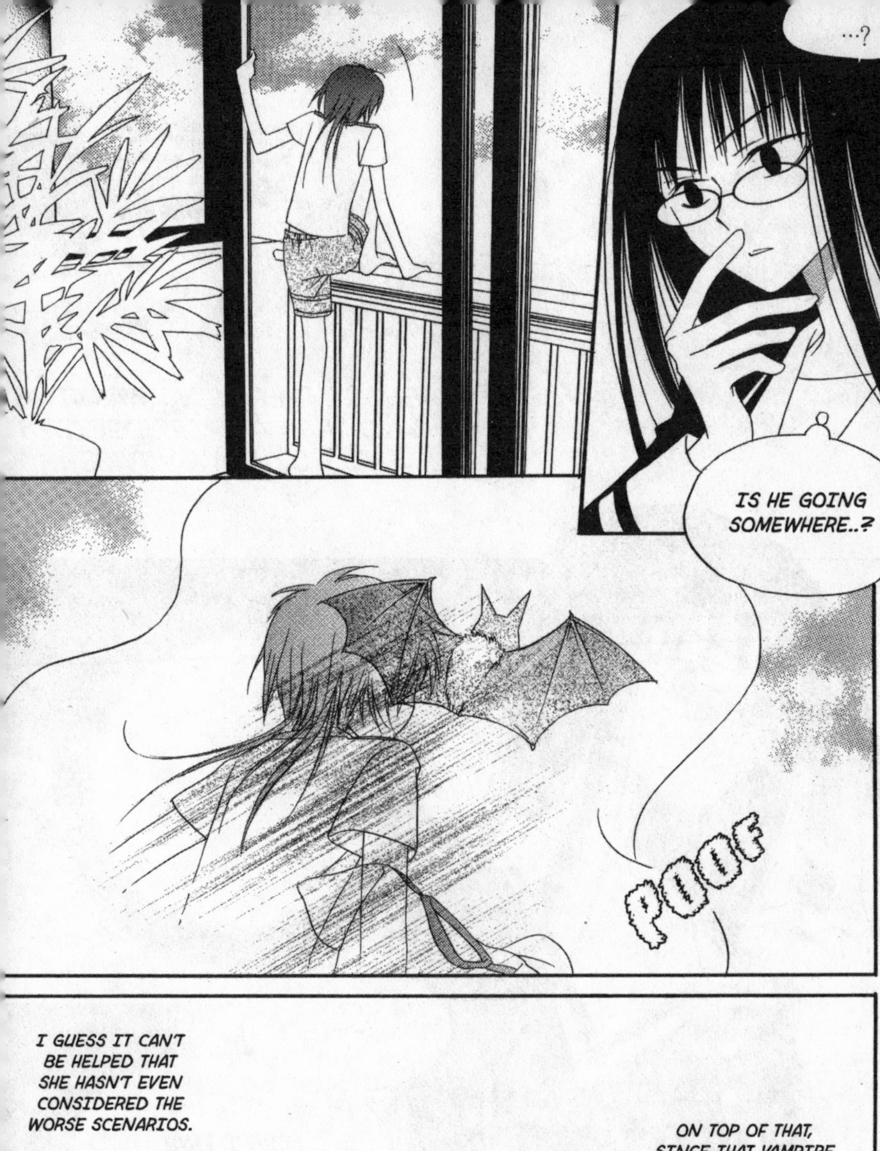
...?
IS HE GOING SOMEWHERE..?
POOF
I GUESS IT CAN'T BE HELPED THAT SHE HASN'T EVEN CONSIDERED THE WORSE SCENARIOS.
ON TOP OF THAT, SINCE THAT VAMPIRE WAS STILL WEAK FROM HIS RECOVERY, SHE'S PROBABLY ONLY SEEN HIS QUIET SIDE.

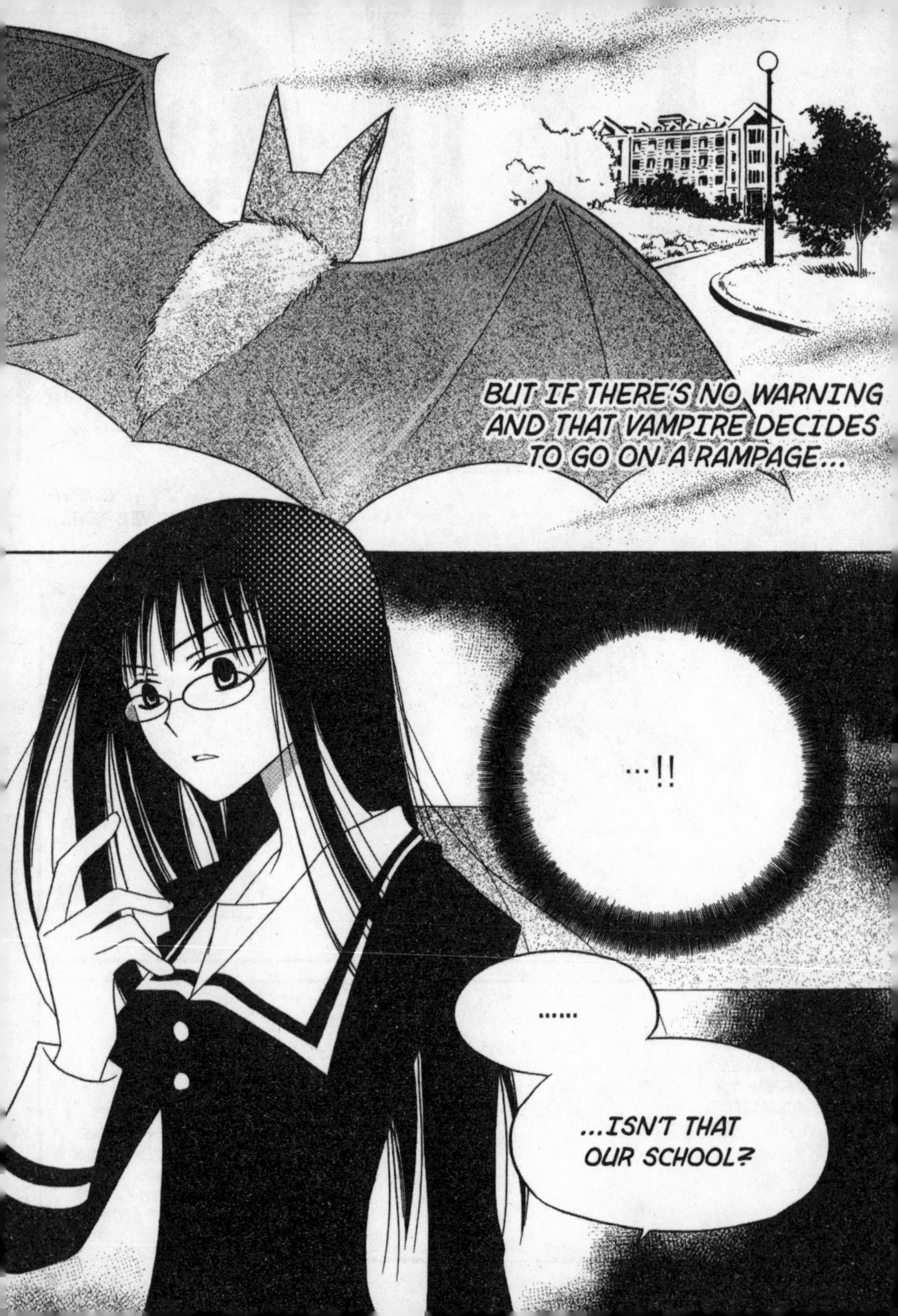
BUT IF THERE'S NO WARNING AND THAT VAMPIRE DECIDES TO GO ON A RAMPAGE...
...!!
......
...ISN'T THAT OUR SCHOOL?

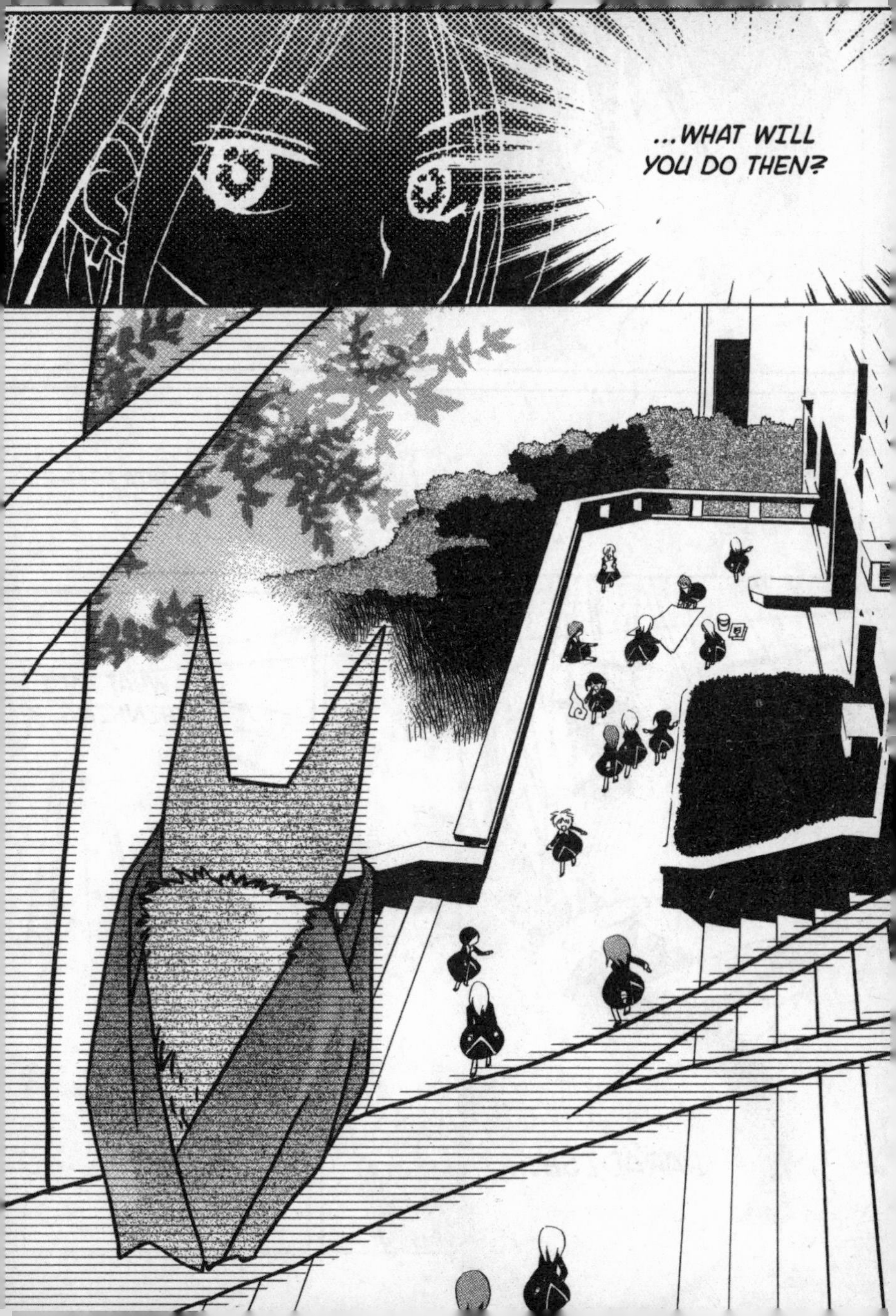
...WHAT WILL YOU DO THEN?

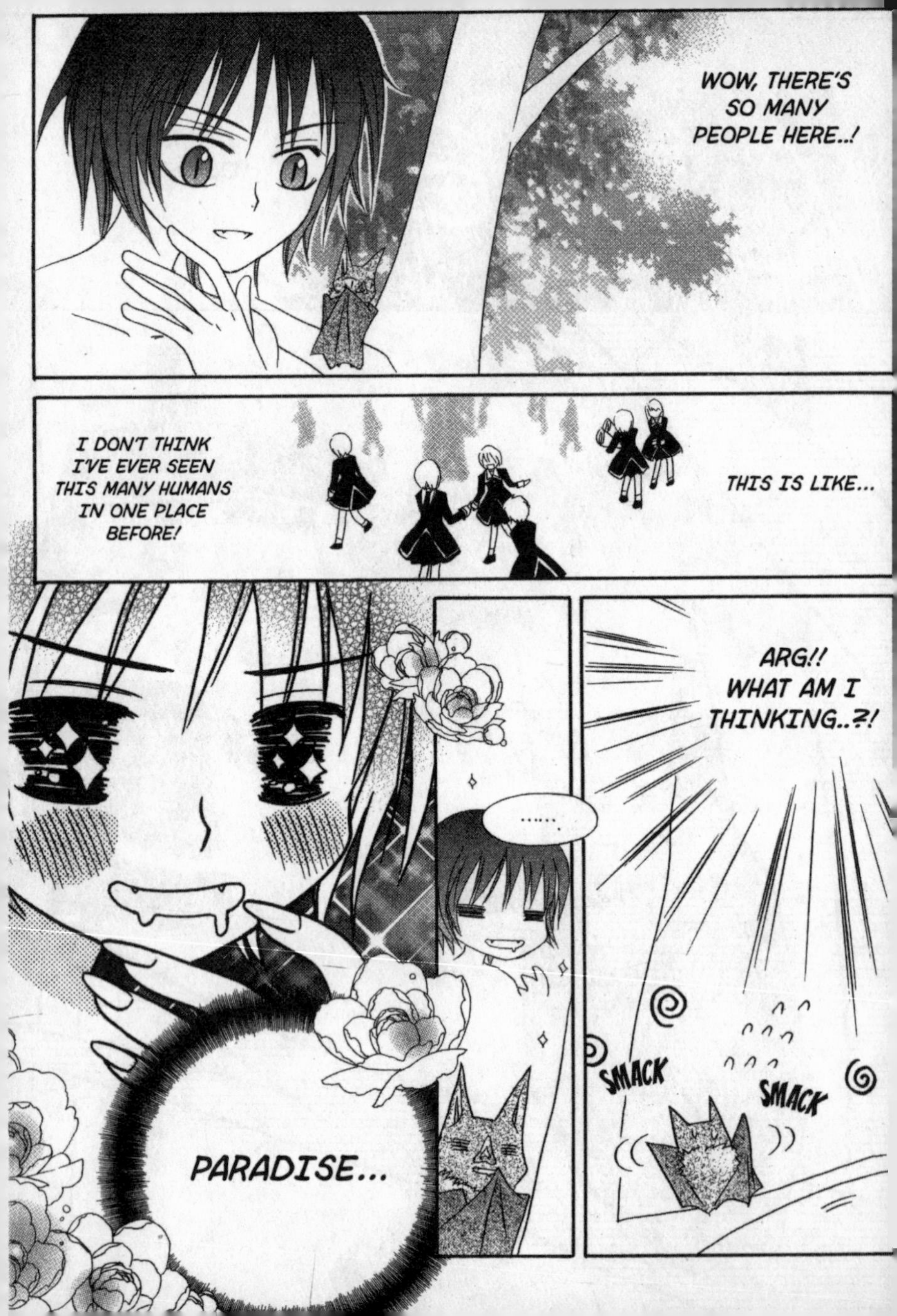

WOW, THERE'S SO MANY PEOPLE HERE..!
I DON'T THINK I'VE EVER SEEN THIS MANY HUMANS IN ONE PLACE BEFORE!
THIS IS LIKE...
PARADISE...
......
ARG!! WHAT AM I THINKING..?!
SMACK
SMACK

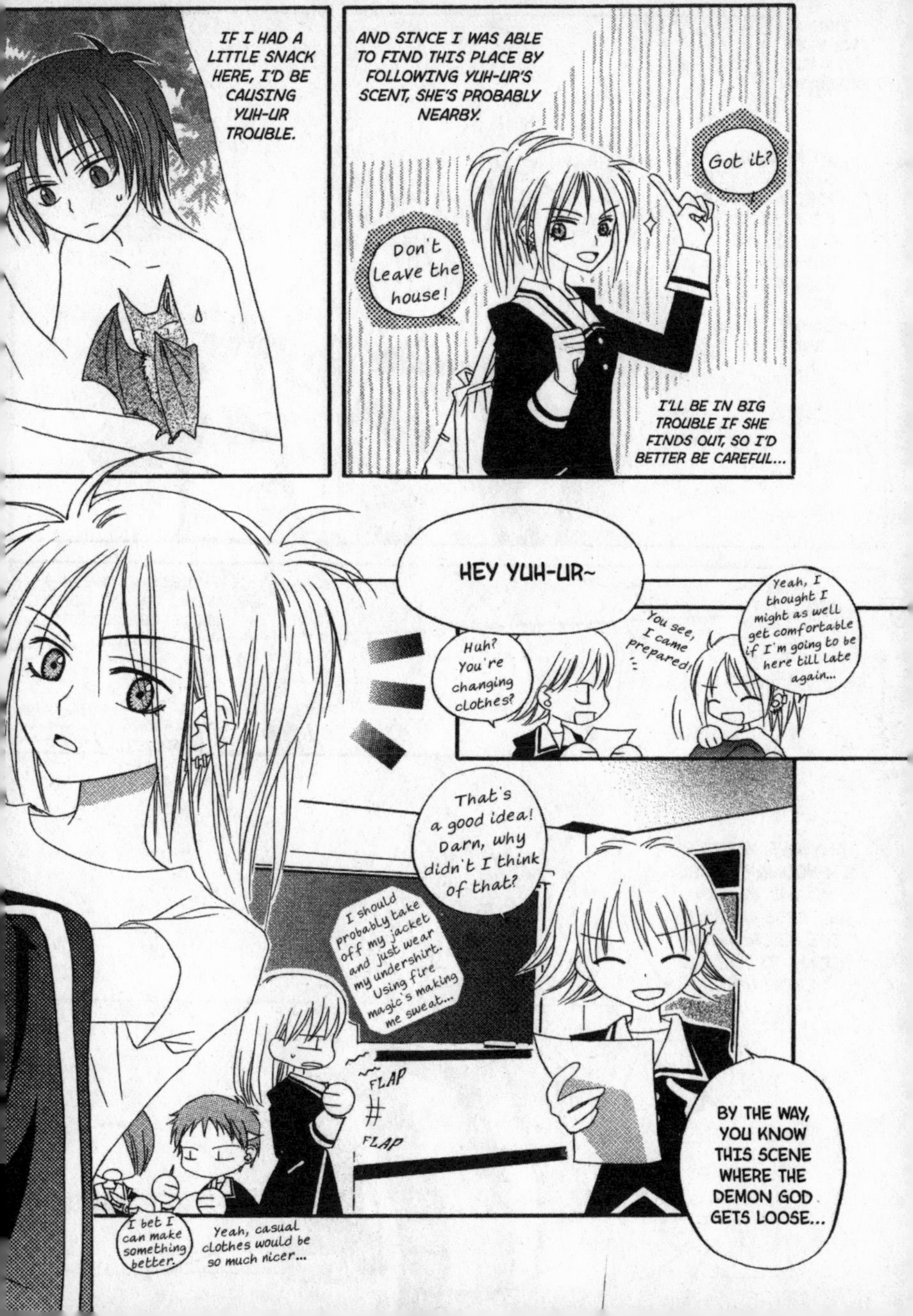
IF I HAD A LITTLE SNACK HERE, I'D BE CAUSING YUH-UR TROUBLE.
AND SINCE I WAS ABLE TO FIND THIS PLACE BY FOLLOWING YUH-UR'S SCENT, SHE'S PROBABLY NEARBY.
Got it?
Don't leave the house!
I'LL BE IN BIG TROUBLE IF SHE FINDS OUT, SO I'D BETTER BE CAREFUL...
HEY YUH-UR~
Huh? You're changing clothes?
You see, I came prepared!
Yeah, I thought I might as well get comfortable if I'm going to be here till late again...
That's a good idea! Darn, why didn't I think of that?
I should probably take off my jacket and just wear my undershirt. Using fire magic's making me sweat...
FLAP
FLAP
I bet I can make something better.
Yeah, casual clothes would be so much nicer...
BY THE WAY, YOU KNOW THIS SCENE WHERE THE DEMON GOD GETS LOOSE...

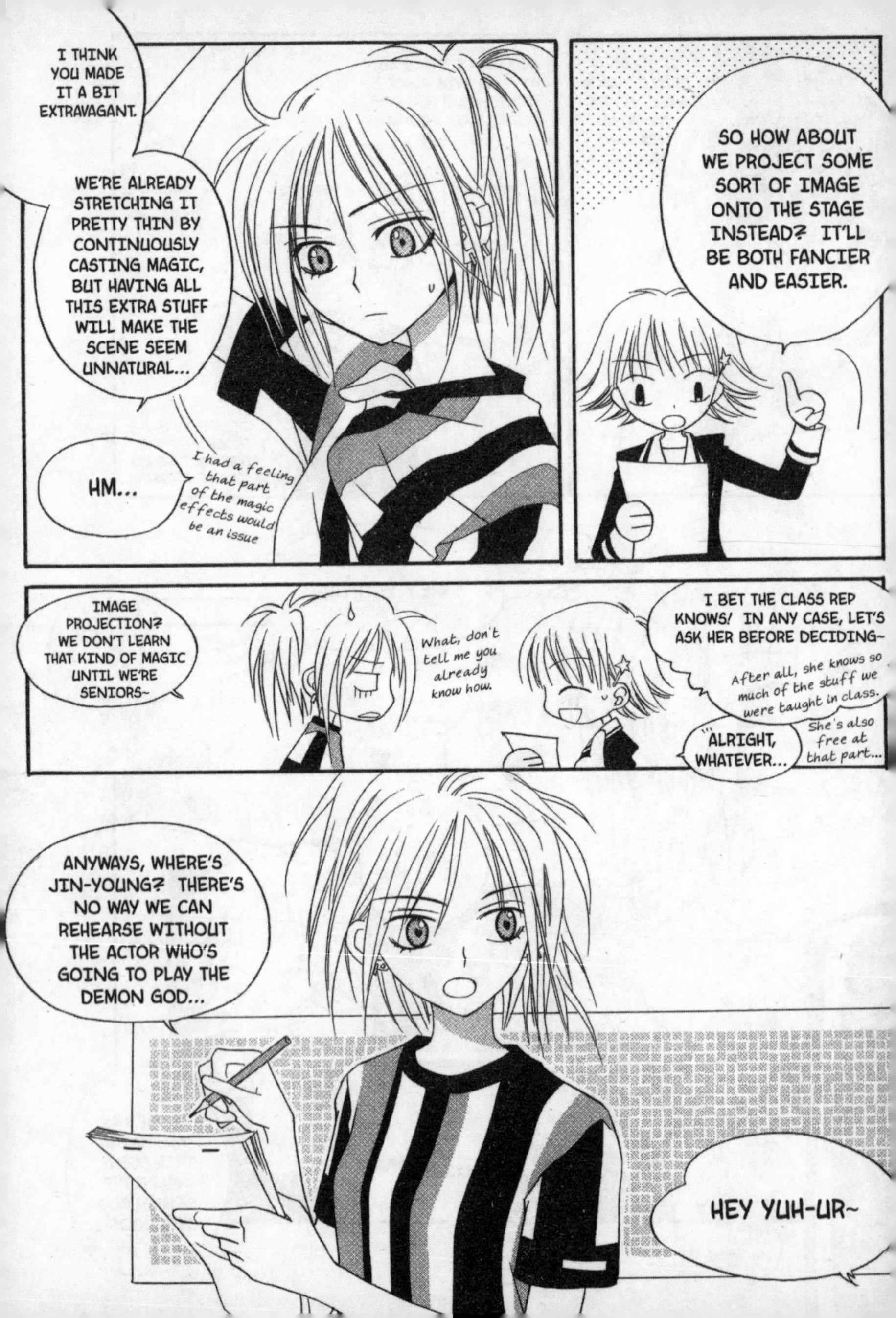
I THINK YOU MADE IT A BIT EXTRAVAGANT.
WE'RE ALREADY STRETCHING IT PRETTY THIN BY CONTINUOUSLY CASTING MAGIC, BUT HAVING ALL THIS EXTRA STUFF WILL MAKE THE SCENE SEEM UNNATURAL...
HM...
I had a feeling that part of the magic effects would be an issue
SO HOW ABOUT WE PROJECT SOME SORT OF IMAGE ONTO THE STAGE INSTEAD? IT'LL BE BOTH FANCIER AND EASIER.
IMAGE PROJECTION? WE DON'T LEARN THAT KIND OF MAGIC UNTIL WE'RE SENIORS~
What, don't tell me you already know how.
I BET THE CLASS REP KNOWS! IN ANY CASE, LET'S ASK HER BEFORE DECIDING~
After all, she knows so much of the stuff we were taught in class.
ALRIGHT, WHATEVER...
She's also free at that part...
ANYWAYS, WHERE'S JIN-YOUNG? THERE'S NO WAY WE CAN REHEARSE WITHOUT THE ACTOR WHO'S GOING TO PLAY THE DEMON GOD...
HEY YUH-UR~

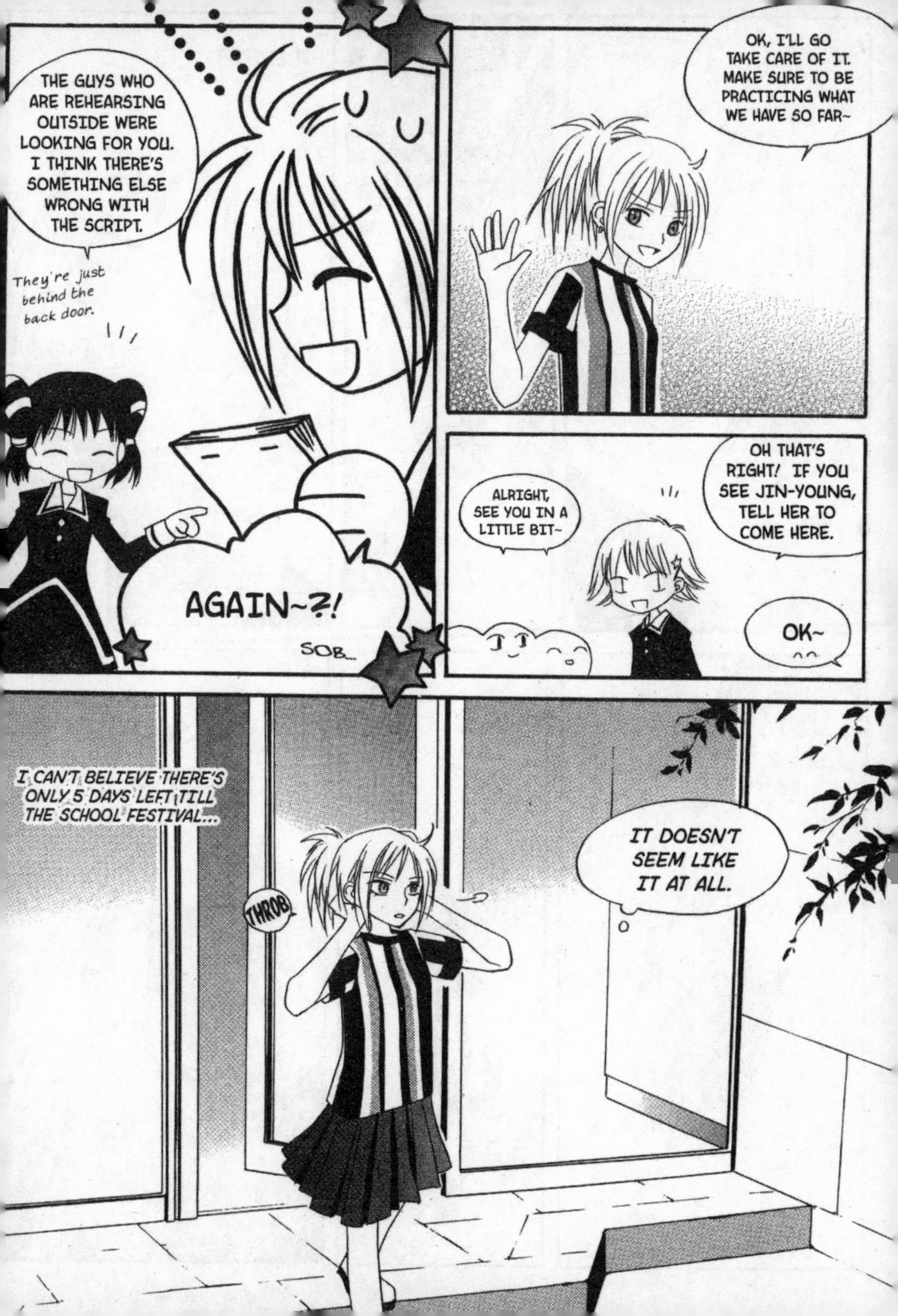
THE GUYS WHO ARE REHEARSING OUTSIDE WERE LOOKING FOR YOU. I THINK THERE'S SOMETHING ELSE WRONG WITH THE SCRIPT.
They're just behind the back door.
AGAIN~?!
SOB...
OK, I'LL GO TAKE CARE OF IT. MAKE SURE TO BE PRACTICING WHAT WE HAVE SO FAR~
ALRIGHT, SEE YOU IN A LITTLE BIT~
OH THAT'S RIGHT! IF YOU SEE JIN-YOUNG, TELL HER TO COME HERE.
OK~
I CAN'T BELIEVE THERE'S ONLY 5 DAYS LEFT TILL THE SCHOOL FESTIVAL...
THROB
IT DOESN'T SEEM LIKE IT AT ALL.

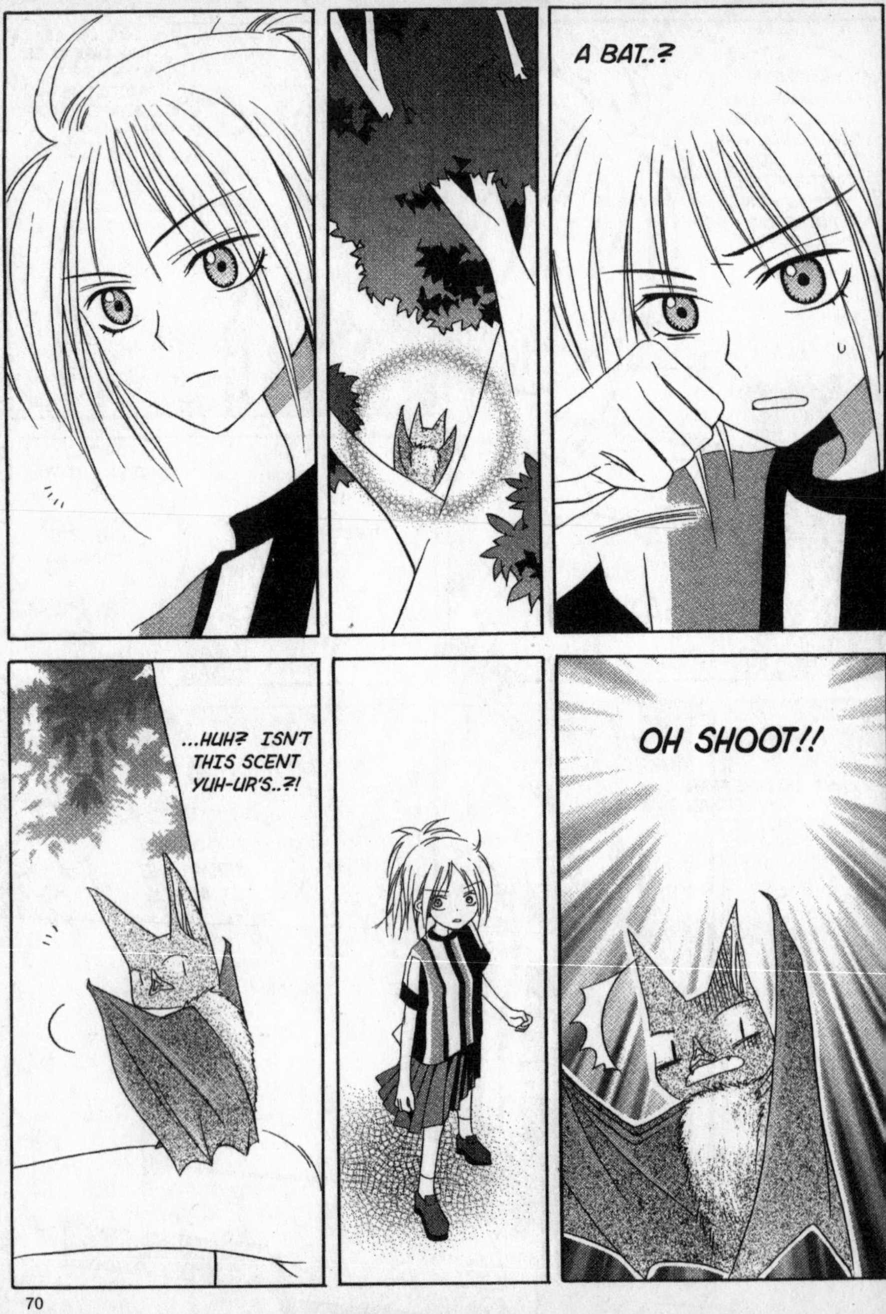
A BAT..?
...HUH? ISN'T THIS SCENT YUH-UR'S..?!
OH SHOOT!!

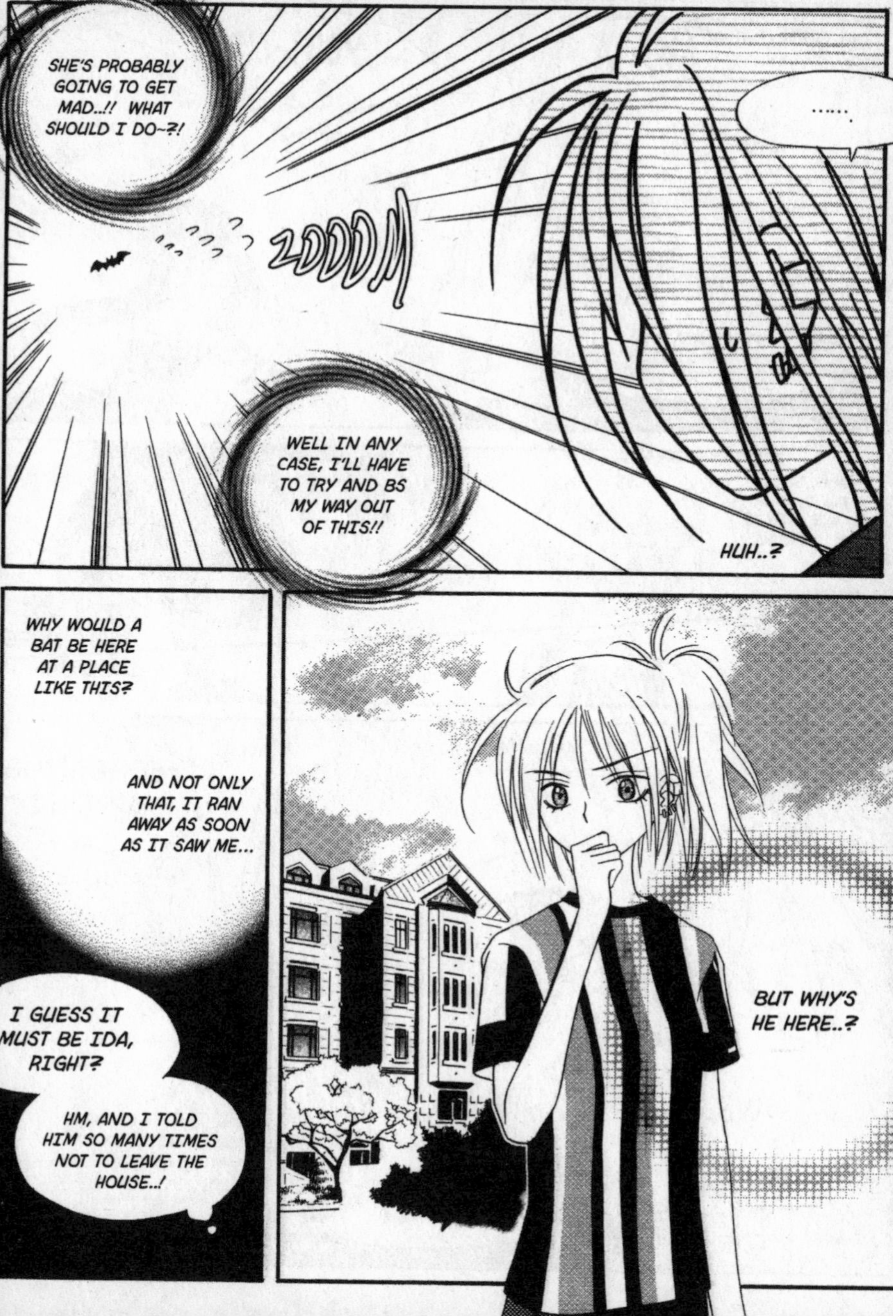
SHE'S PROBABLY GOING TO GET MAD..!! WHAT SHOULD I DO~?!
WELL IN ANY CASE, I'LL HAVE TO TRY AND BS MY WAY OUT OF THIS!!
ZOOOM
......
HUH..?
WHY WOULD A BAT BE HERE AT A PLACE LIKE THIS?
AND NOT ONLY THAT, IT RAN AWAY AS SOON AS IT SAW ME...
I GUESS IT MUST BE IDA, RIGHT?
HM, AND I TOLD HIM SO MANY TIMES NOT TO LEAVE THE HOUSE..!
BUT WHY'S HE HERE..?

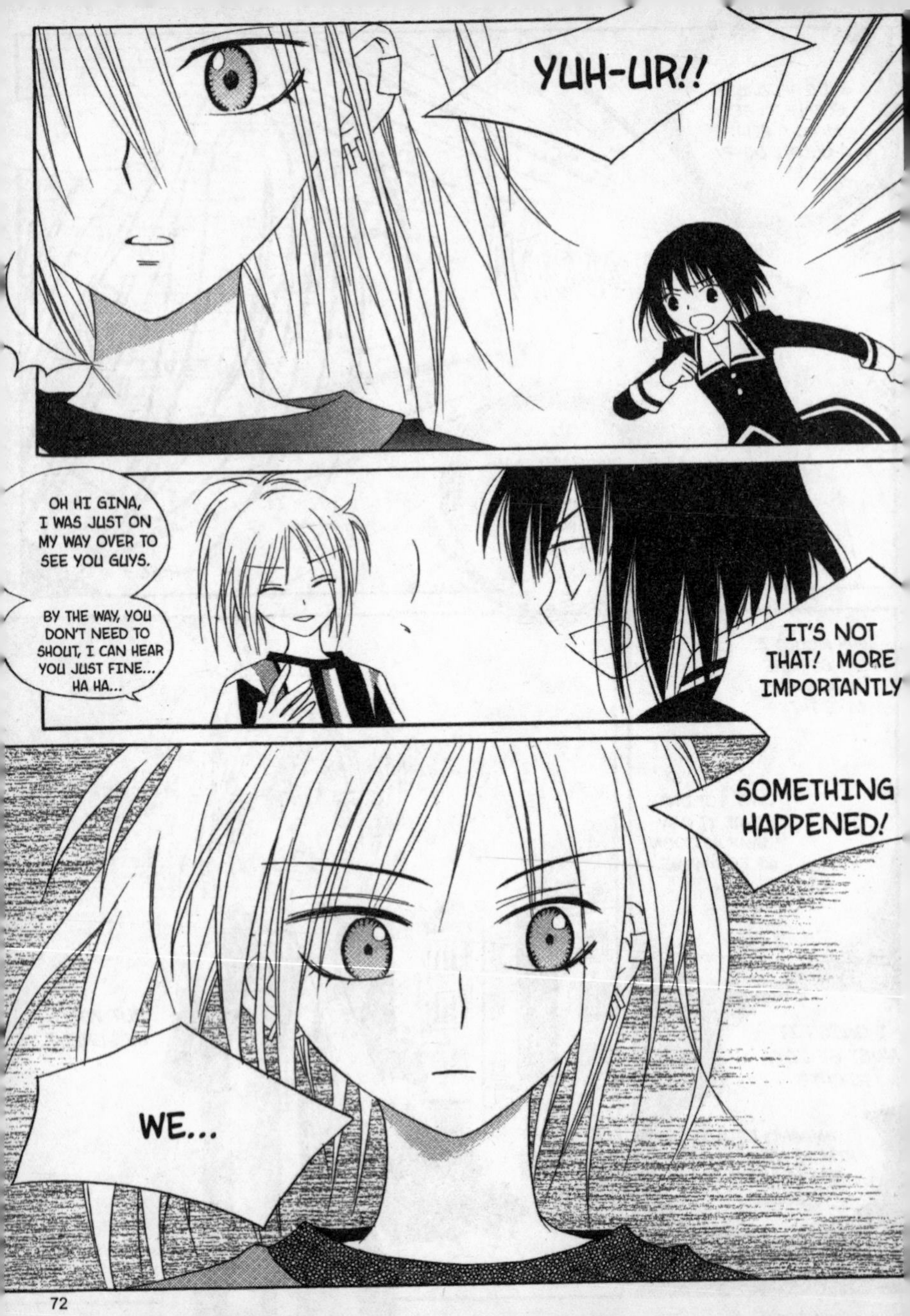
YUH-UR!!
OH HI GINA, I WAS JUST ON MY WAY OVER TO SEE YOU GUYS.
BY THE WAY, YOU DON'T NEED TO SHOUT, I CAN HEAR YOU JUST FINE... HA HA...
IT'S NOT THAT! MORE IMPORTANTLY
SOMETHING HAPPENED!
WE...

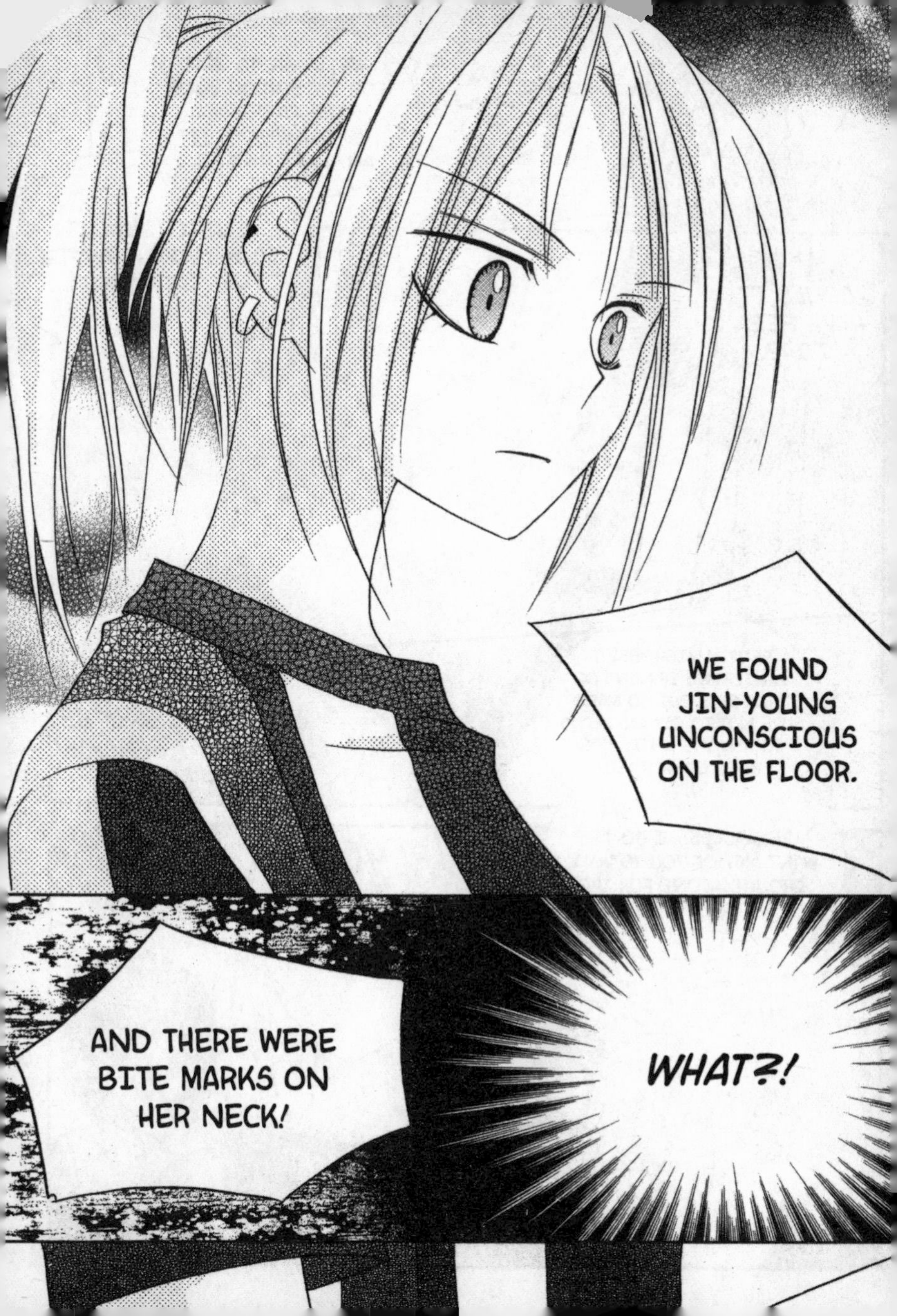
WE FOUND JIN-YOUNG UNCONSCIOUS ON THE FLOOR.
AND THERE WERE BITE MARKS ON HER NECK!
WHAT?!

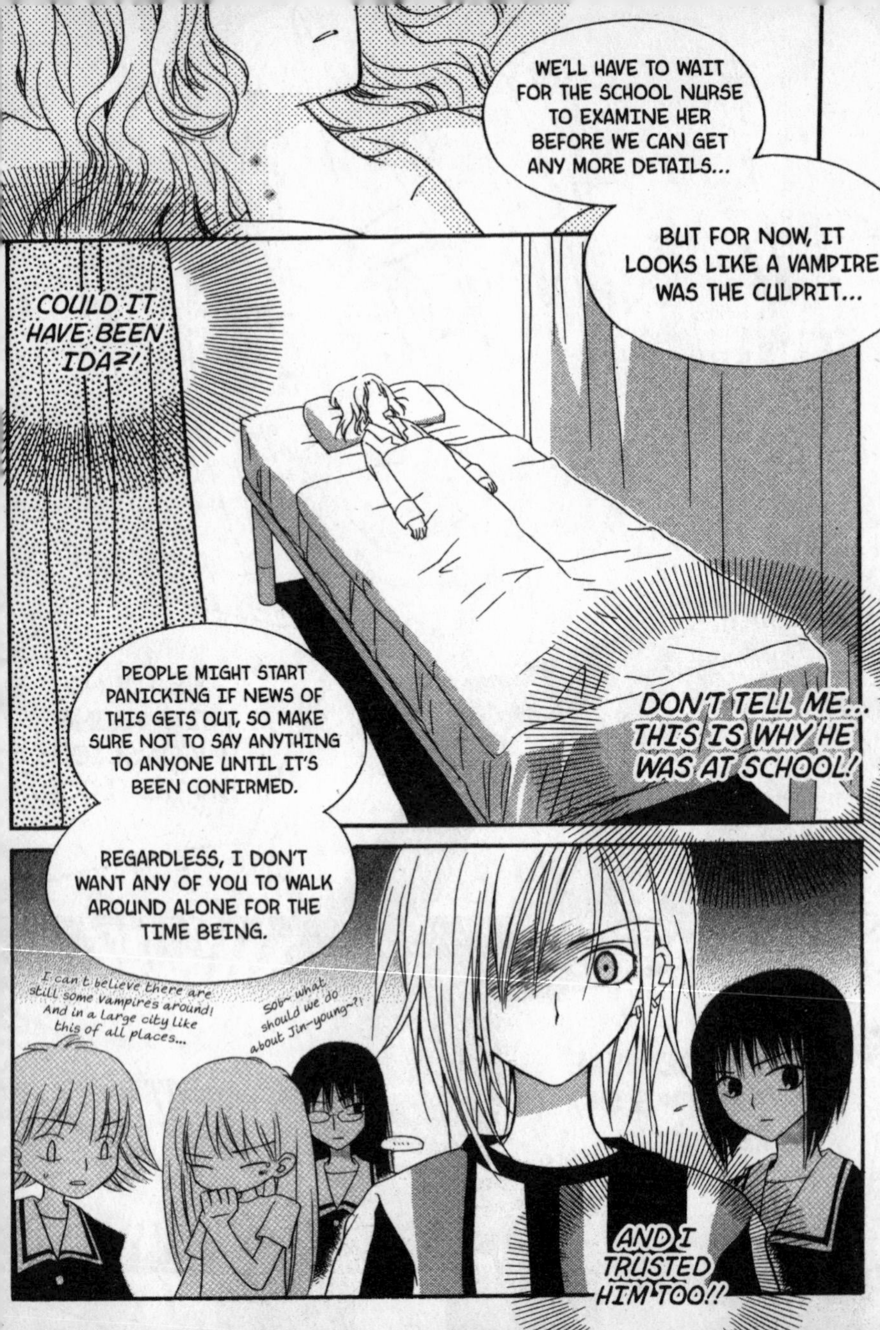
WE'LL HAVE TO WAIT FOR THE SCHOOL NURSE TO EXAMINE HER BEFORE WE CAN GET ANY MORE DETAILS...
BUT FOR NOW, IT LOOKS LIKE A VAMPIRE WAS THE CULPRIT...
COULD IT HAVE BEEN IDA?!
DON'T TELL ME... THIS IS WHY HE WAS AT SCHOOL!
PEOPLE MIGHT START PANICKING IF NEWS OF THIS GETS OUT, SO MAKE SURE NOT TO SAY ANYTHING TO ANYONE UNTIL IT'S BEEN CONFIRMED.
REGARDLESS, I DON'T WANT ANY OF YOU TO WALK AROUND ALONE FOR THE TIME BEING.
I can't believe there are still some vampires around! And in a large city like this of all places...
Sob~ what should we do about Jin-young~?!
AND I TRUSTED HIM TOO!!

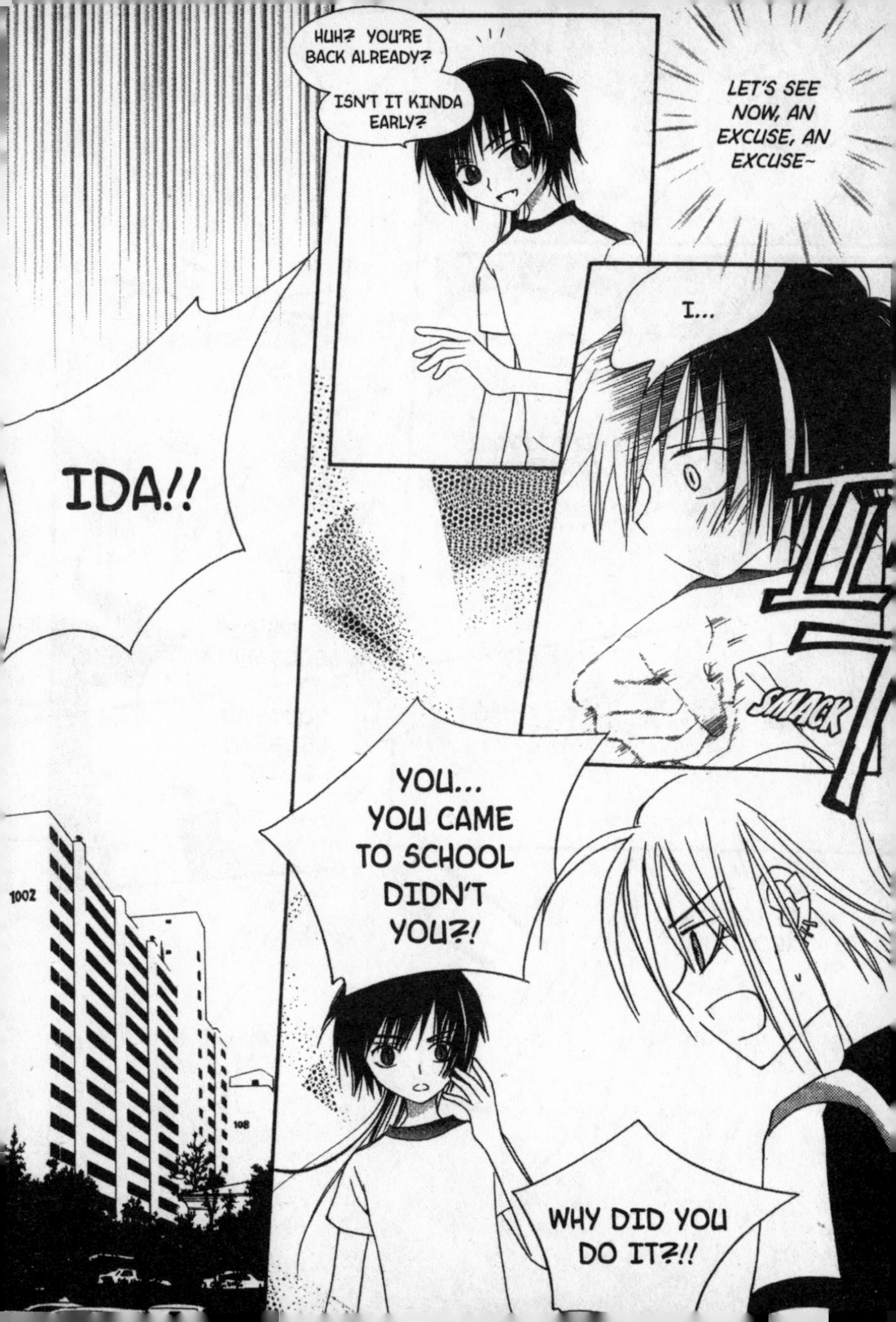
IDA!!
1002
108
HUH? YOU'RE BACK ALREADY?
ISN'T IT KINDA EARLY?
LET'S SEE NOW, AN EXCUSE, AN EXCUSE~
I...
SMACK
YOU... YOU CAME TO SCHOOL DIDN'T YOU?!
WHY DID YOU DO IT?!!

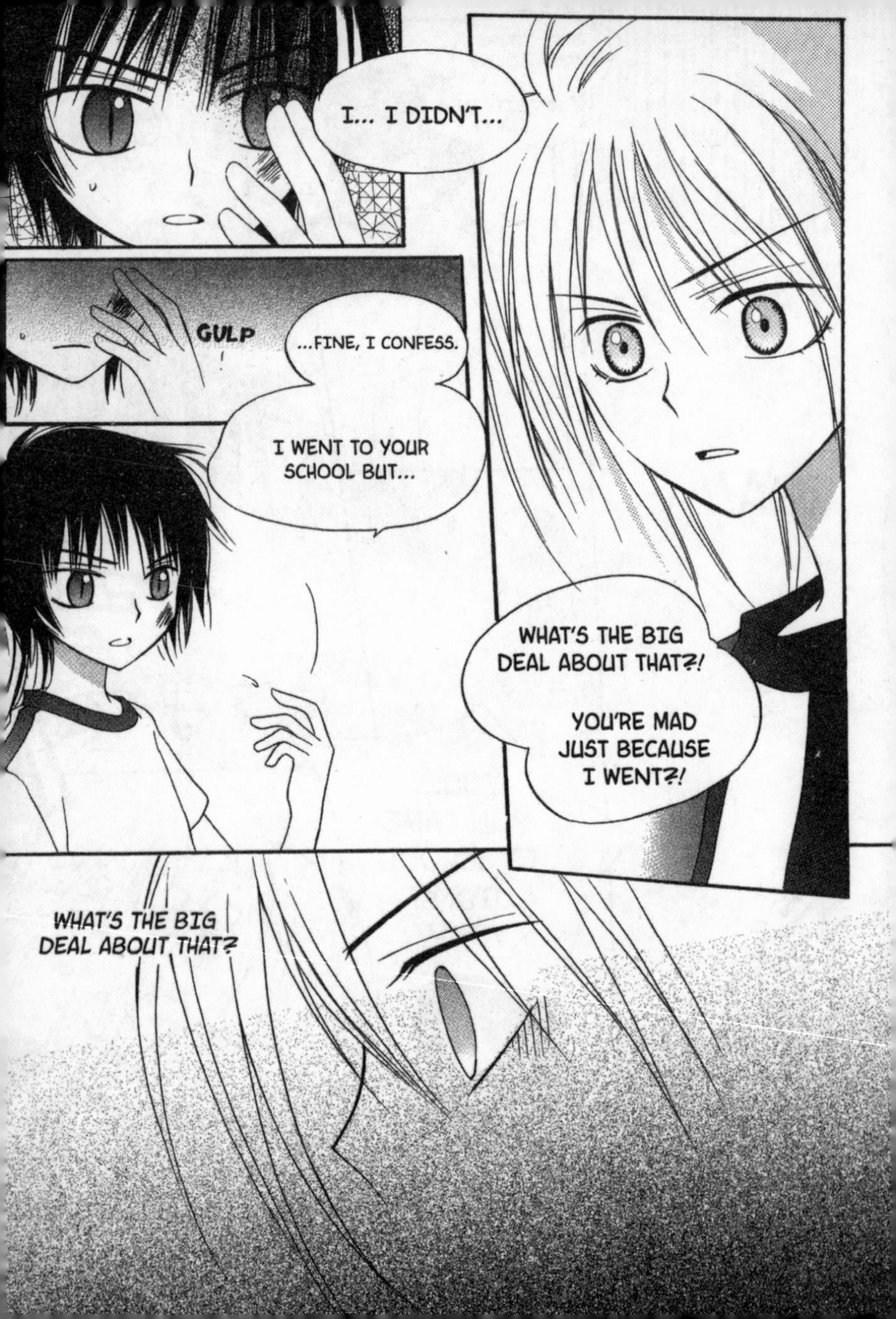
I... I DIDN'T...
GULP
...FINE, I CONFESS.
I WENT TO YOUR SCHOOL BUT...
WHAT'S THE BIG DEAL ABOUT THAT?!
YOU'RE MAD JUST BECAUSE I WENT?!
WHAT'S THE BIG DEAL ABOUT THAT?

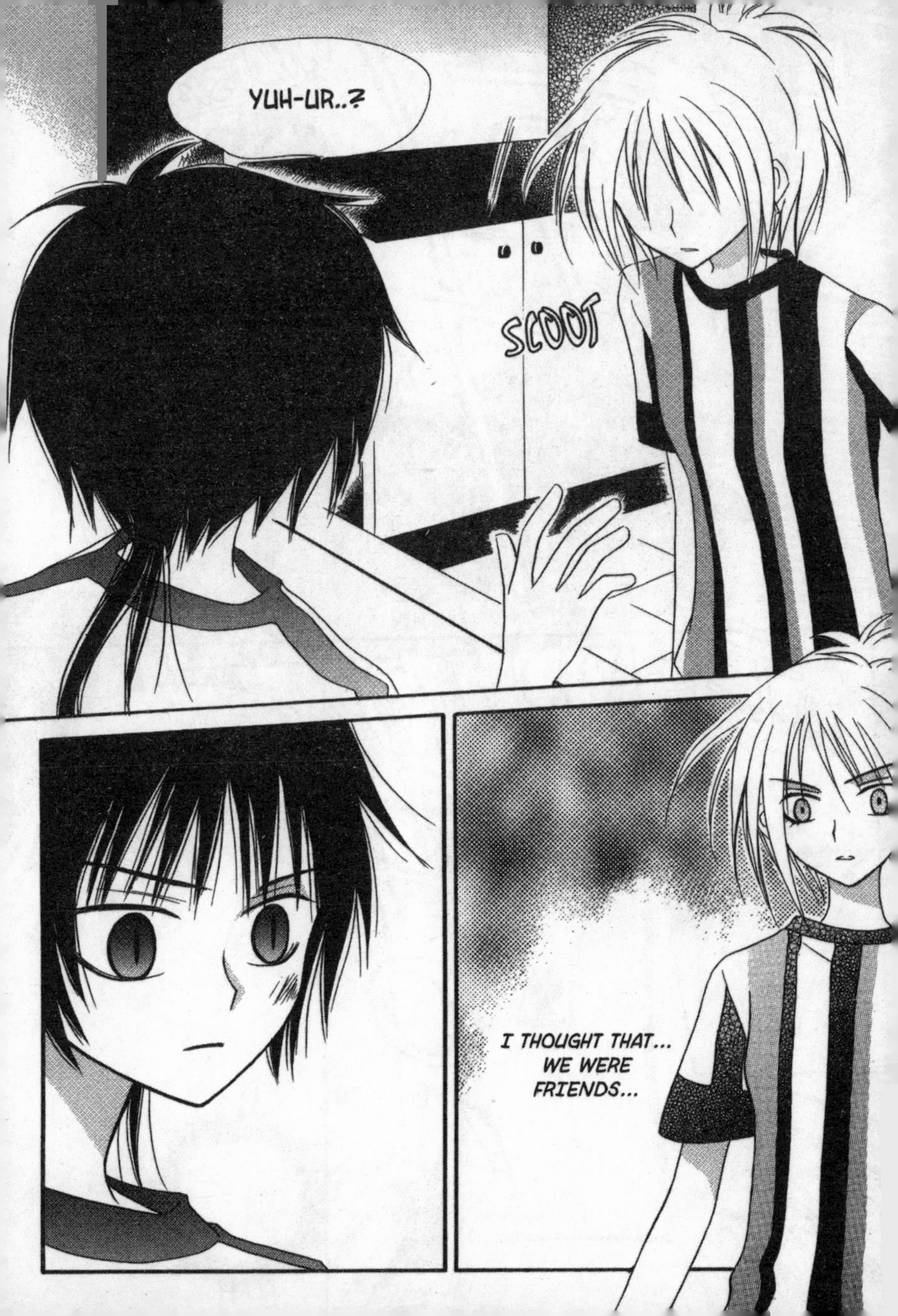
YUH-UR..?
SCOOT
I THOUGHT THAT... WE WERE FRIENDS...

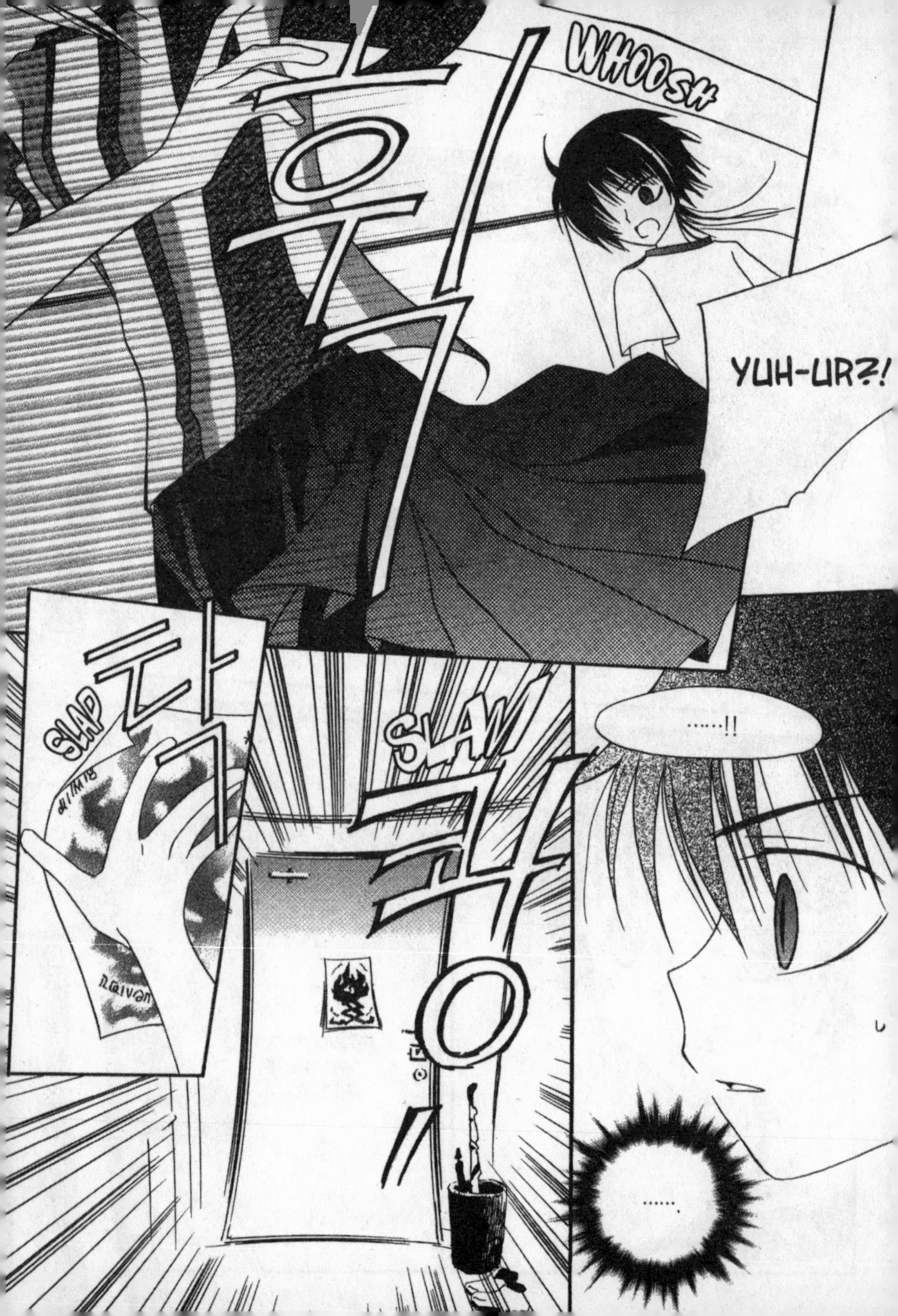
WHOOSH
YUH-UR?!
SLAP
SLAM
......!!
....

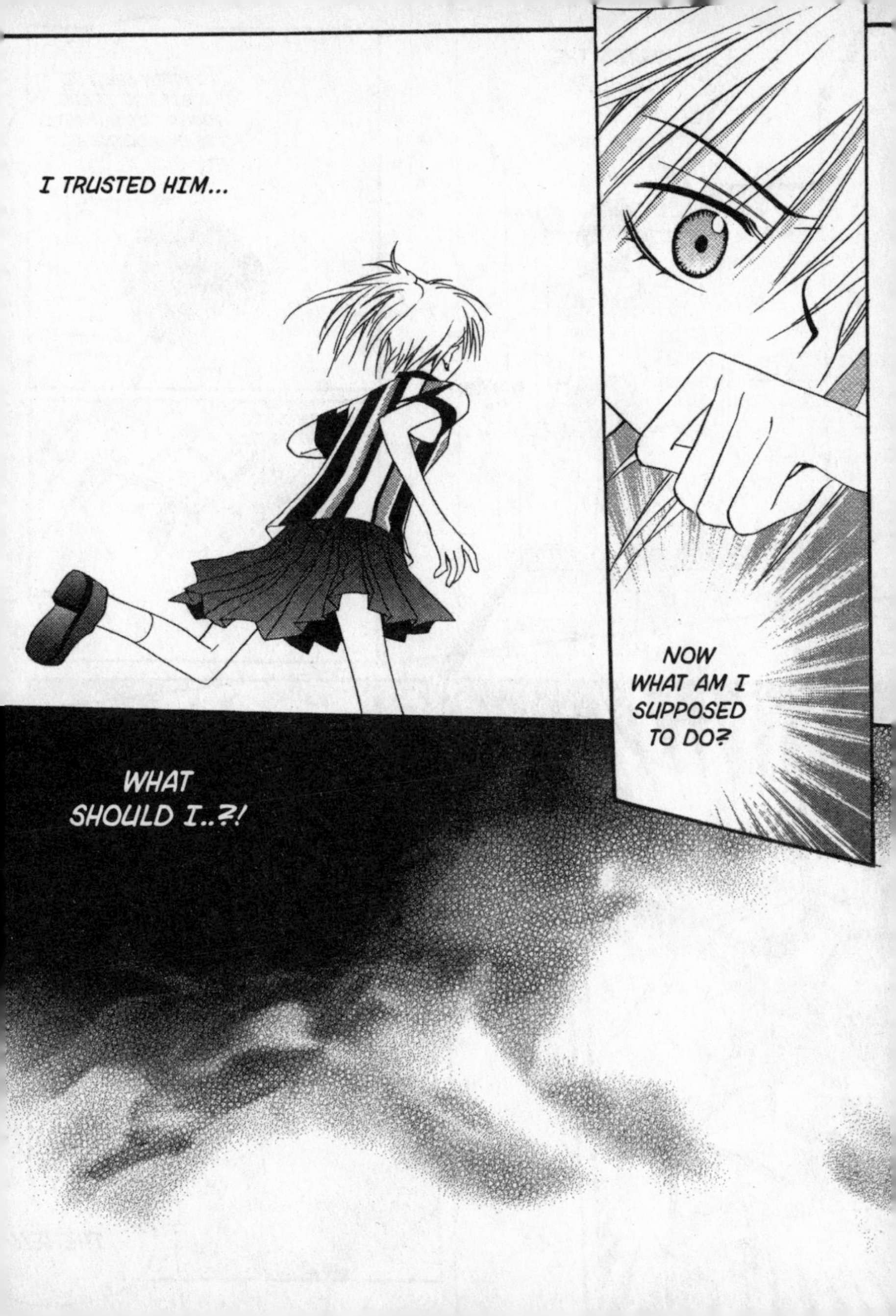
I TRUSTED HIM...
NOW WHAT AM I SUPPOSED TO DO?
WHAT SHOULD I..?!

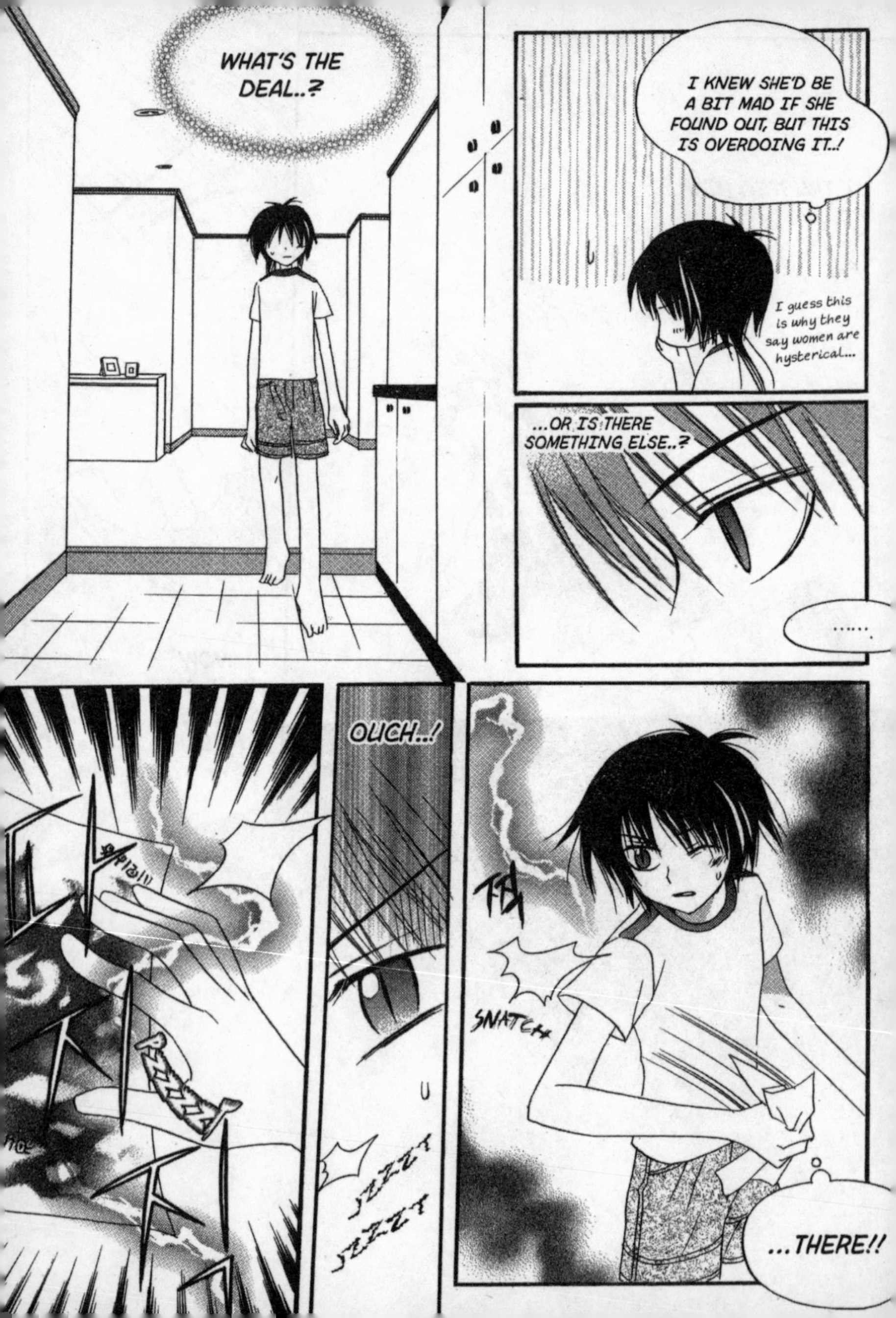
WHAT'S THE DEAL..?
I KNEW SHE'D BE A BIT MAD IF SHE FOUND OUT, BUT THIS IS OVERDOING IT..!
I guess this is why they say women are hysterical...
...OR IS THERE SOMETHING ELSE..?
......
OUCH..!
SNATCH
...THERE!!

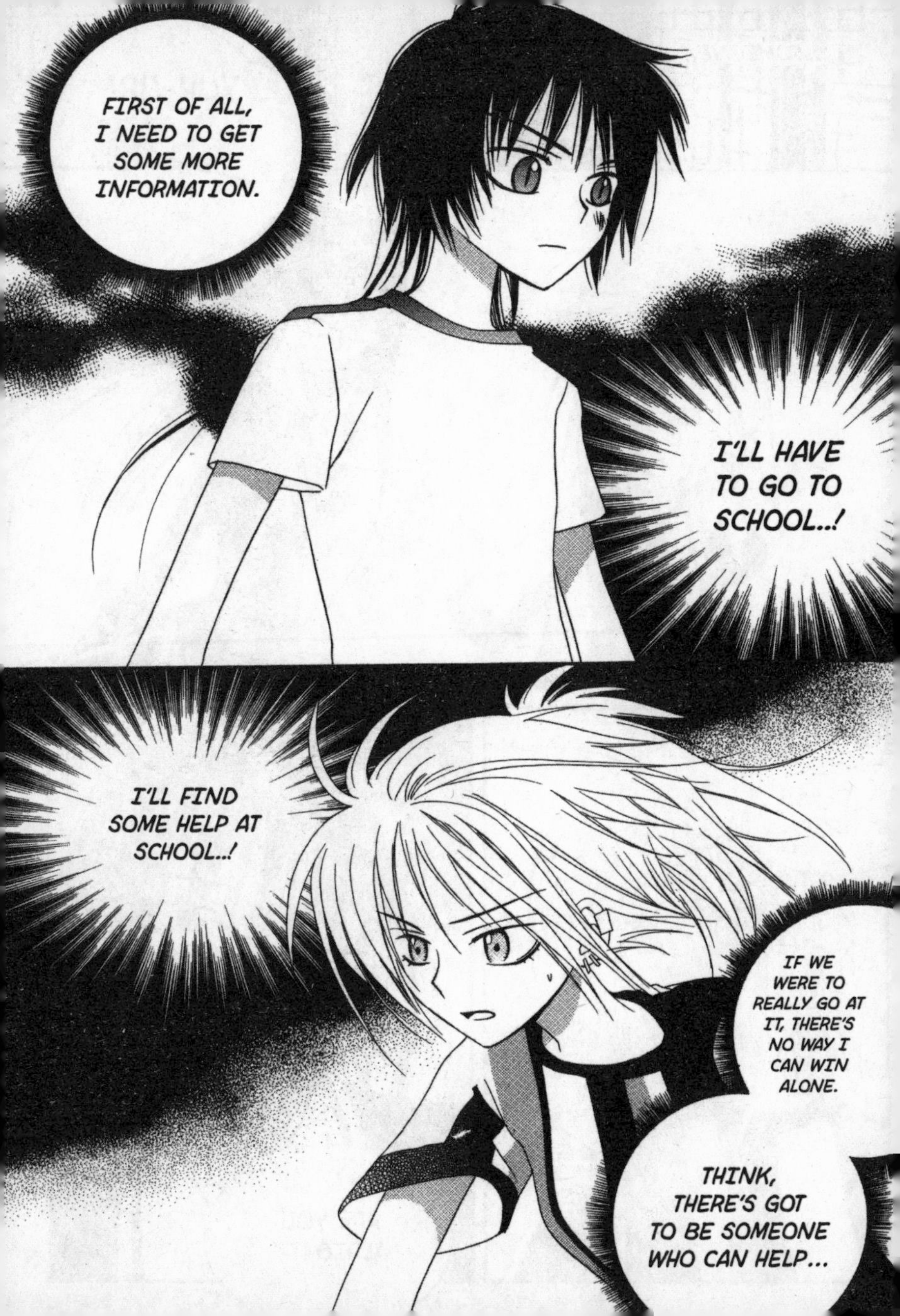
FIRST OF ALL, I NEED TO GET SOME MORE INFORMATION.
I'LL HAVE TO GO TO SCHOOL..!
I'LL FIND SOME HELP AT SCHOOL..!
IF WE WERE TO REALLY GO AT IT, THERE'S NO WAY I CAN WIN ALONE.
THINK, THERE'S GOT TO BE SOMEONE WHO CAN HELP...

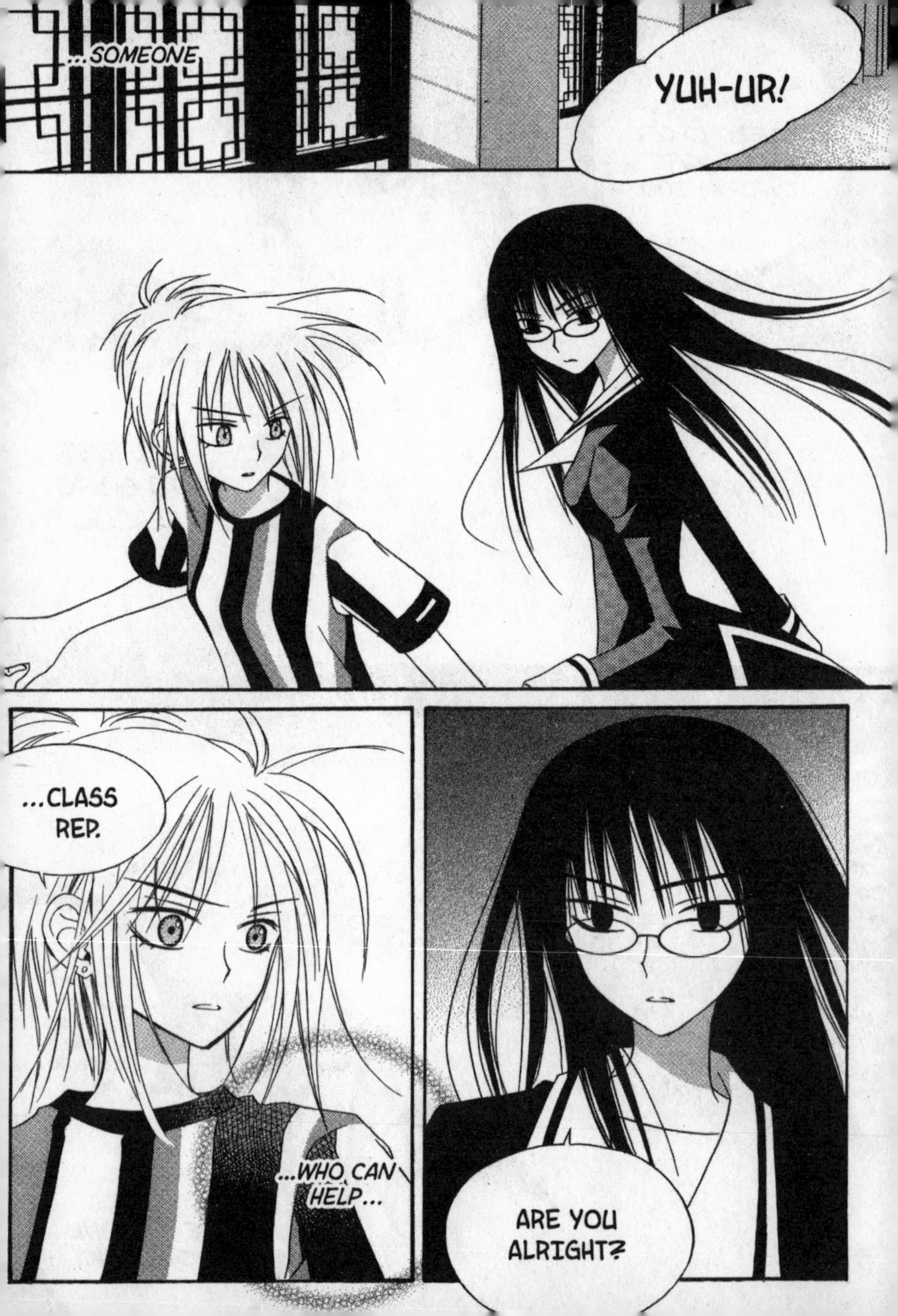
...SOMEONE
YUH-UR!
...CLASS REP.
...WHO CAN HELP...
ARE YOU ALRIGHT?

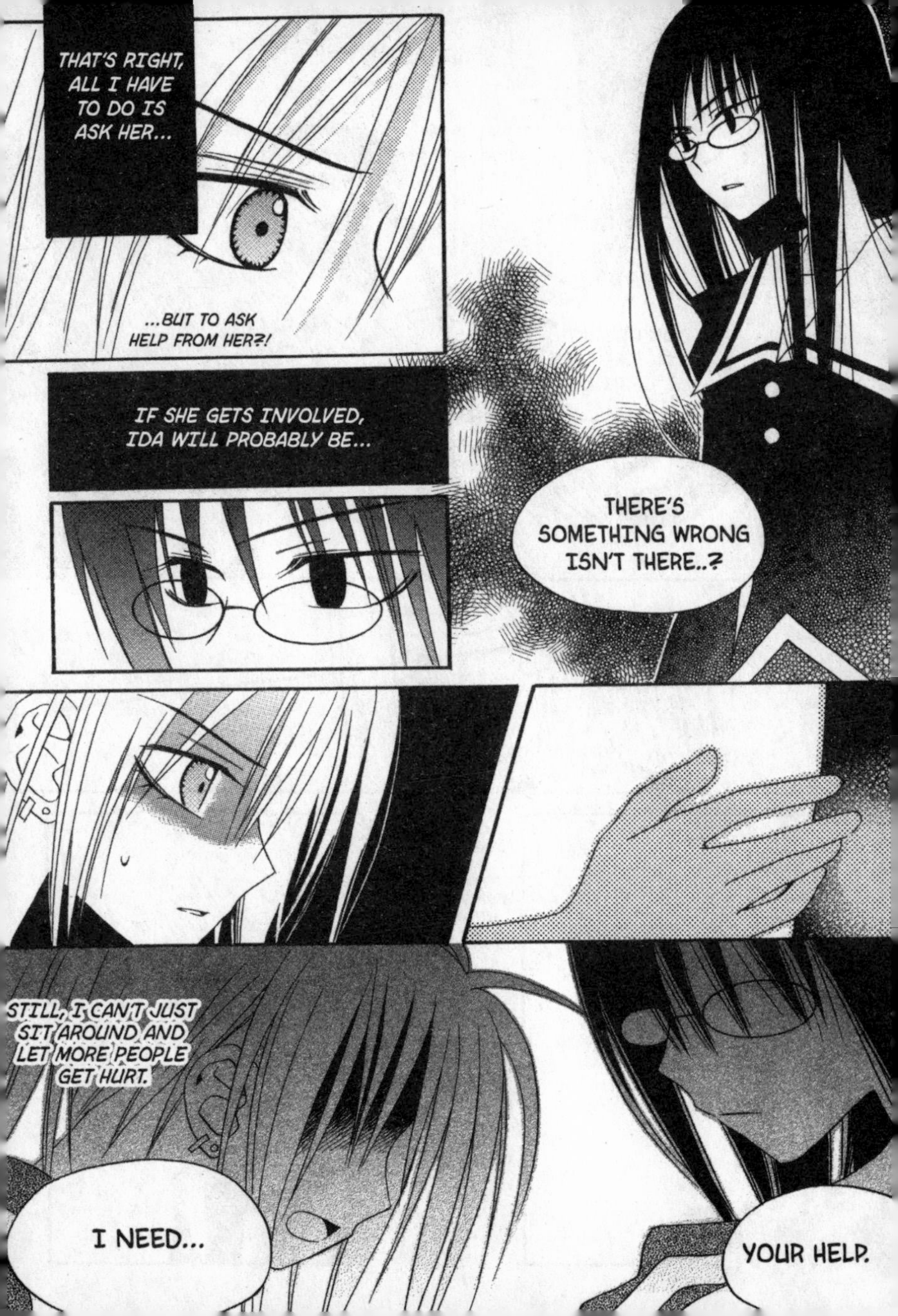
THAT'S RIGHT, ALL I HAVE TO DO IS ASK HER...
...BUT TO ASK HELP FROM HER?!
IF SHE GETS INVOLVED, IDA WILL PROBABLY BE...
THERE'S SOMETHING WRONG ISN'T THERE..?
STILL, I CAN'T JUST SIT AROUND AND LET MORE PEOPLE GET HURT.
I NEED...
YOUR HELP.

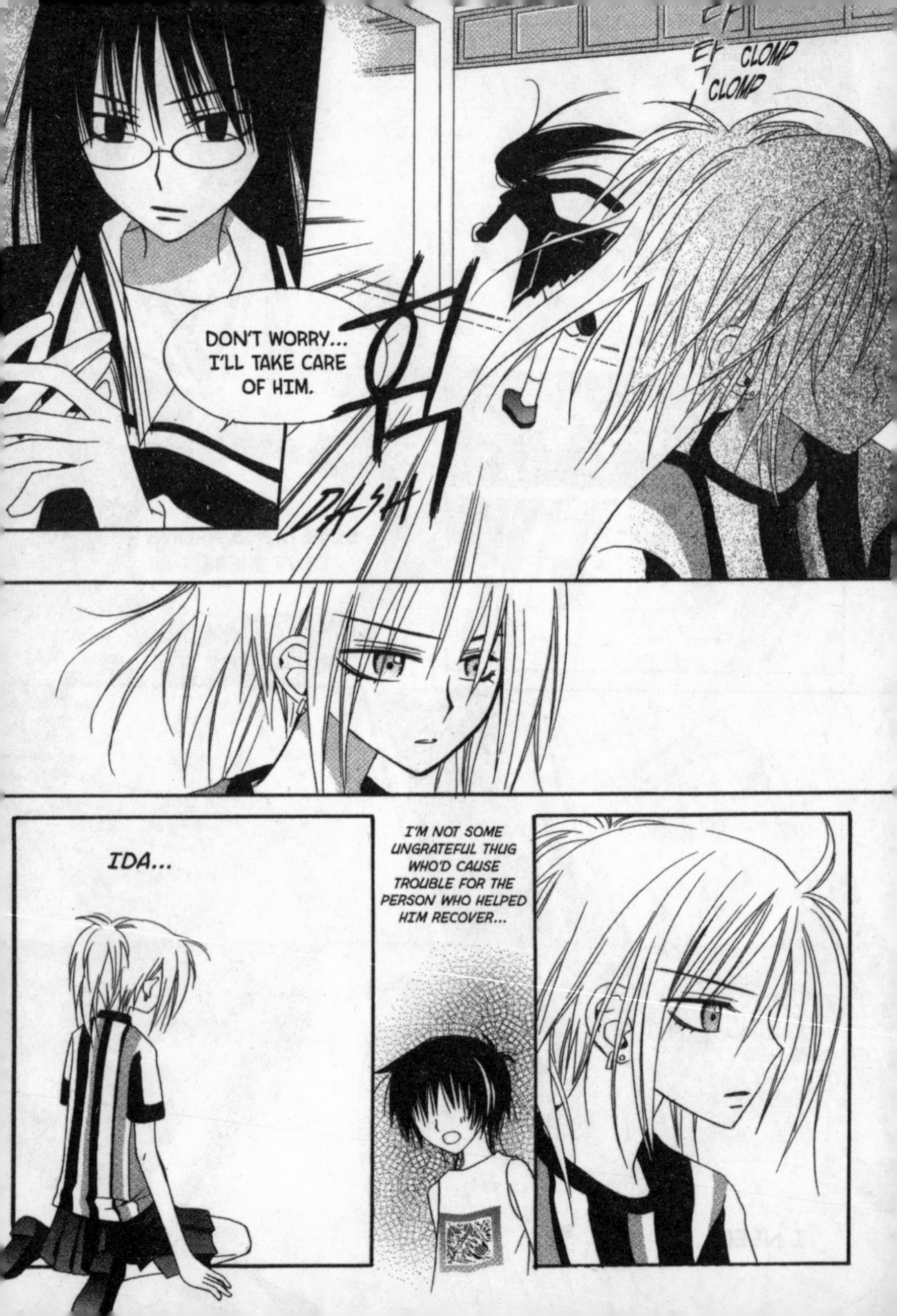
DON'T WORRY... I'LL TAKE CARE OF HIM.
CLOMP
CLOMP
헉
DASH
IDA...
I'M NOT SOME UNGRATEFUL THUG WHO'D CAUSE TROUBLE FOR THE PERSON WHO HELPED HIM RECOVER...

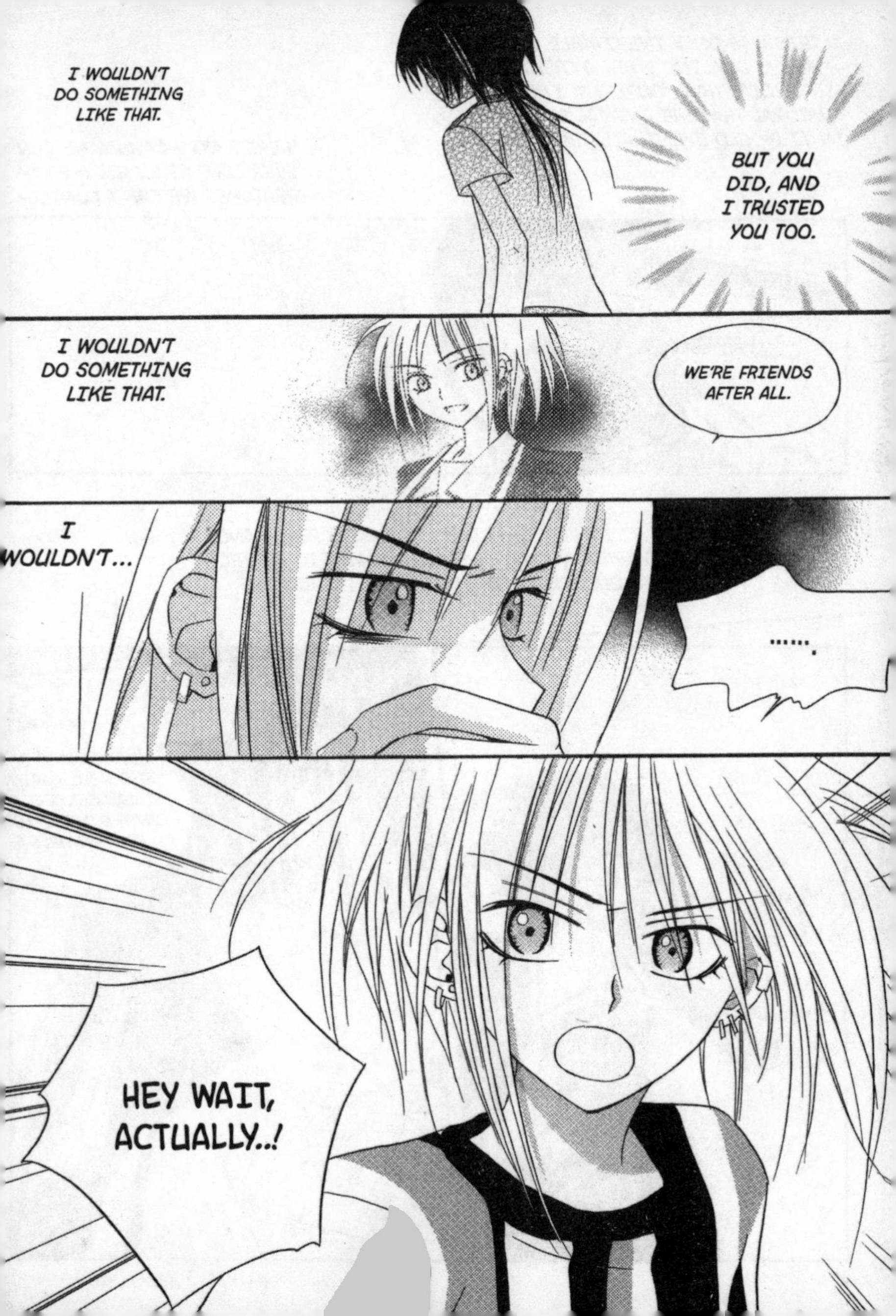
I WOULDN'T DO SOMETHING LIKE THAT.
BUT YOU DID, AND I TRUSTED YOU TOO.
I WOULDN'T DO SOMETHING LIKE THAT.
WE'RE FRIENDS AFTER ALL.
I WOULDN'T...
......
HEY WAIT, ACTUALLY..!

THIS WAS ONLY INEVITABLE WHEN YOU'RE DEALING WITH A CREATURE STRONGER THAN YOURSELF. IT'S ONLY NATURAL THAT THE ANIMAL INSTINCT IN IT WOULD EVENTUALLY TAKE OVER...

THERE'S NO WAY HUMANS CAN EVER LIVE PEACEFULLY WITH CREATURES WE CAN'T CONTROL.

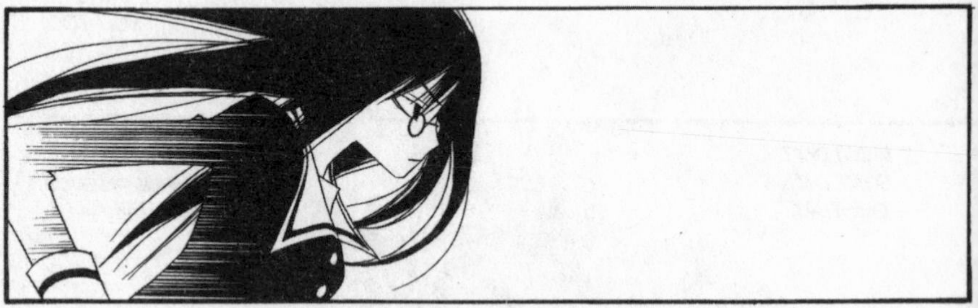

IT ISN'T A QUESTION OF WHAT'S RIGHT AND WHAT'S WRONG. WE SIMPLY HAVE TO PROTECT OURSELVES BY TAKING THE INITIATIVE.

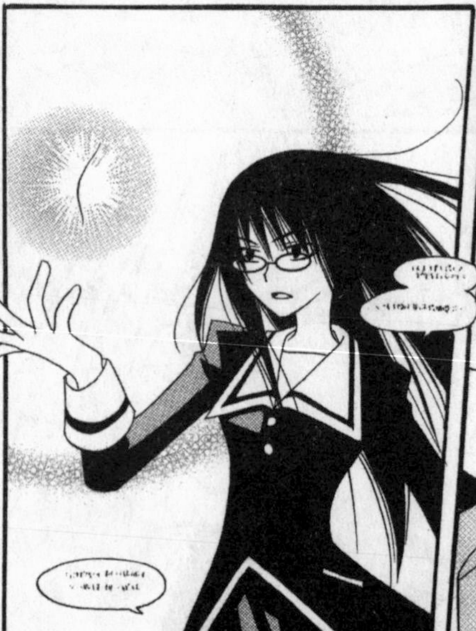

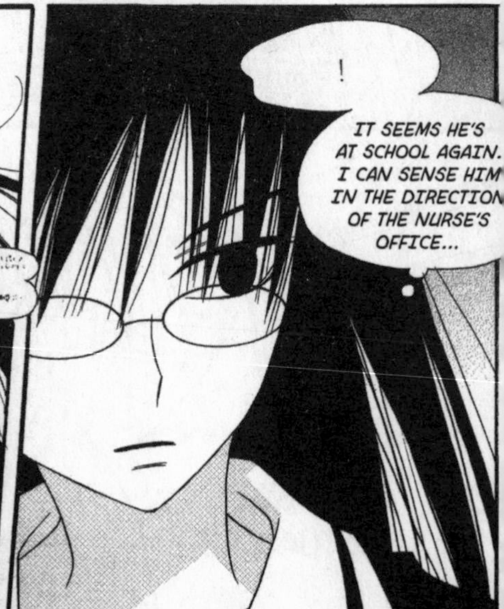
!
IT SEEMS HE'S AT SCHOOL AGAIN. I CAN SENSE HIM IN THE DIRECTION OF THE NURSE'S OFFICE...

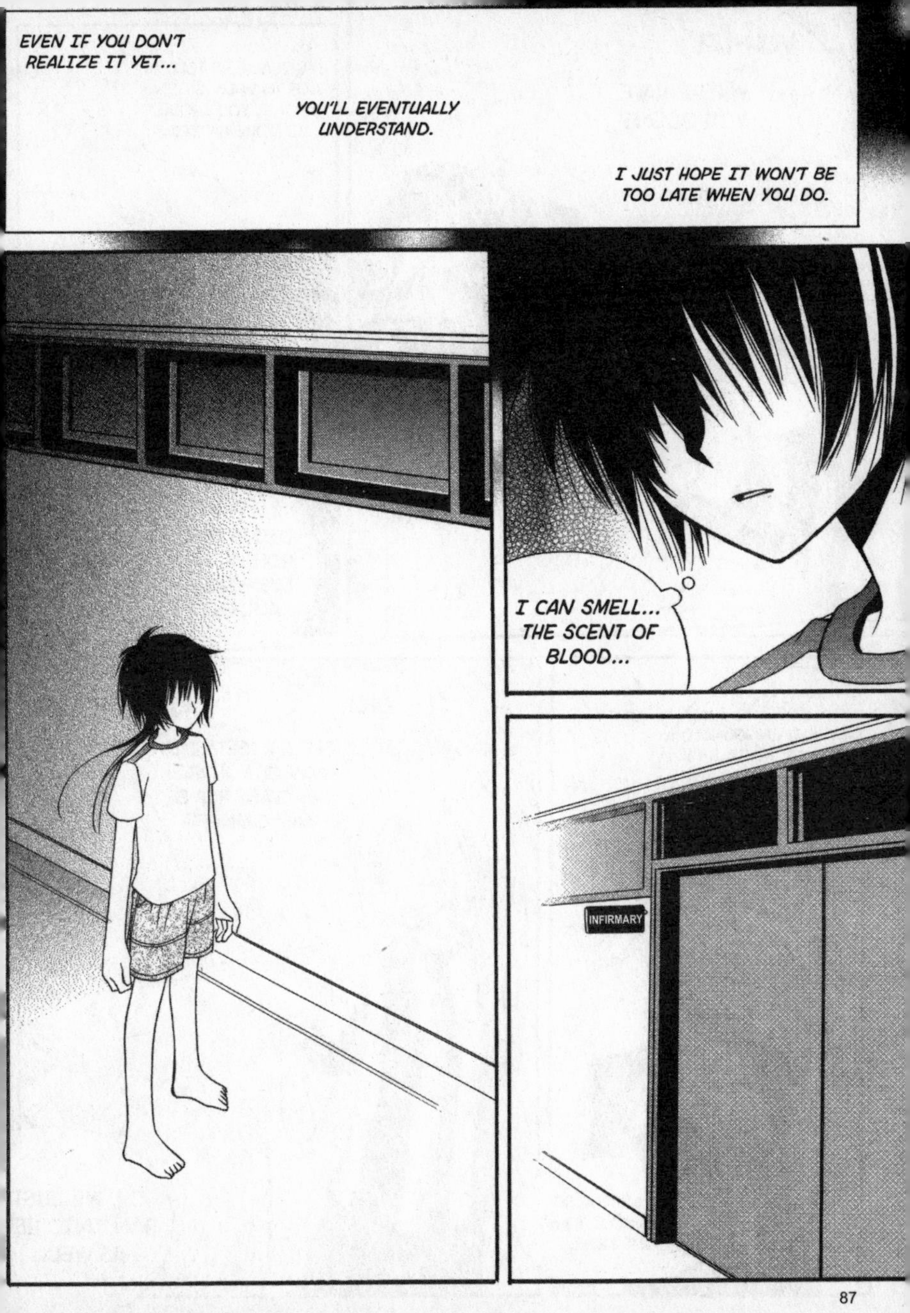
EVEN IF YOU DON'T REALIZE IT YET...
YOU'LL EVENTUALLY UNDERSTAND.
I JUST HOPE IT WON'T BE TOO LATE WHEN YOU DO.
I CAN SMELL... THE SCENT OF BLOOD...
INFIRMARY

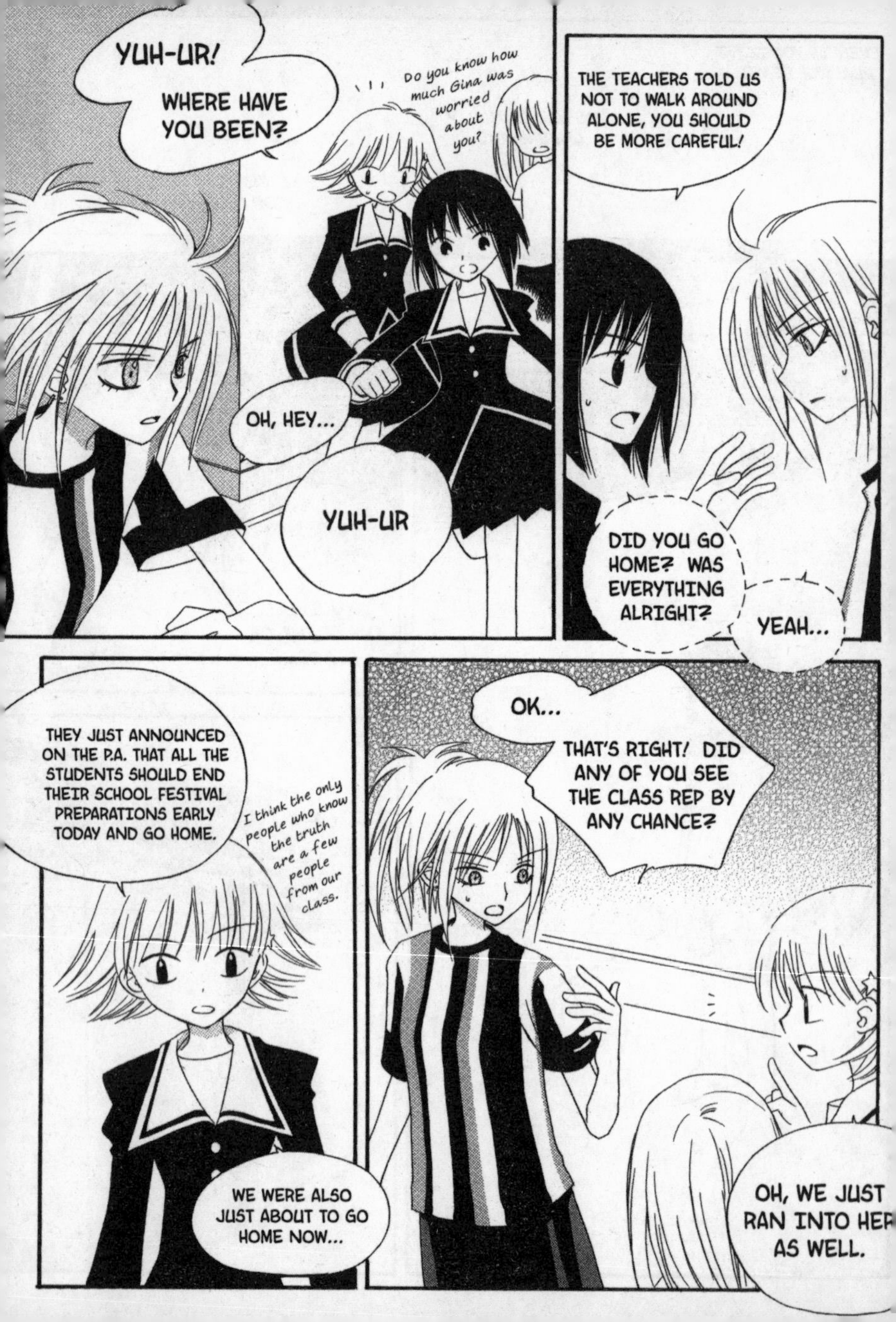

YUH-UR!
WHERE HAVE YOU BEEN?
OH, HEY...
Do you know how much Gina was worried about you?
YUH-UR
THE TEACHERS TOLD US NOT TO WALK AROUND ALONE, YOU SHOULD BE MORE CAREFUL!
DID YOU GO HOME? WAS EVERYTHING ALRIGHT?
YEAH...
THEY JUST ANNOUNCED ON THE P.A. THAT ALL THE STUDENTS SHOULD END THEIR SCHOOL FESTIVAL PREPARATIONS EARLY TODAY AND GO HOME.
I think the only people who know the truth are a few people from our class.
WE WERE ALSO JUST ABOUT TO GO HOME NOW...
OK...
THAT'S RIGHT! DID ANY OF YOU SEE THE CLASS REP BY ANY CHANCE?
OH, WE JUST RAN INTO HER AS WELL.

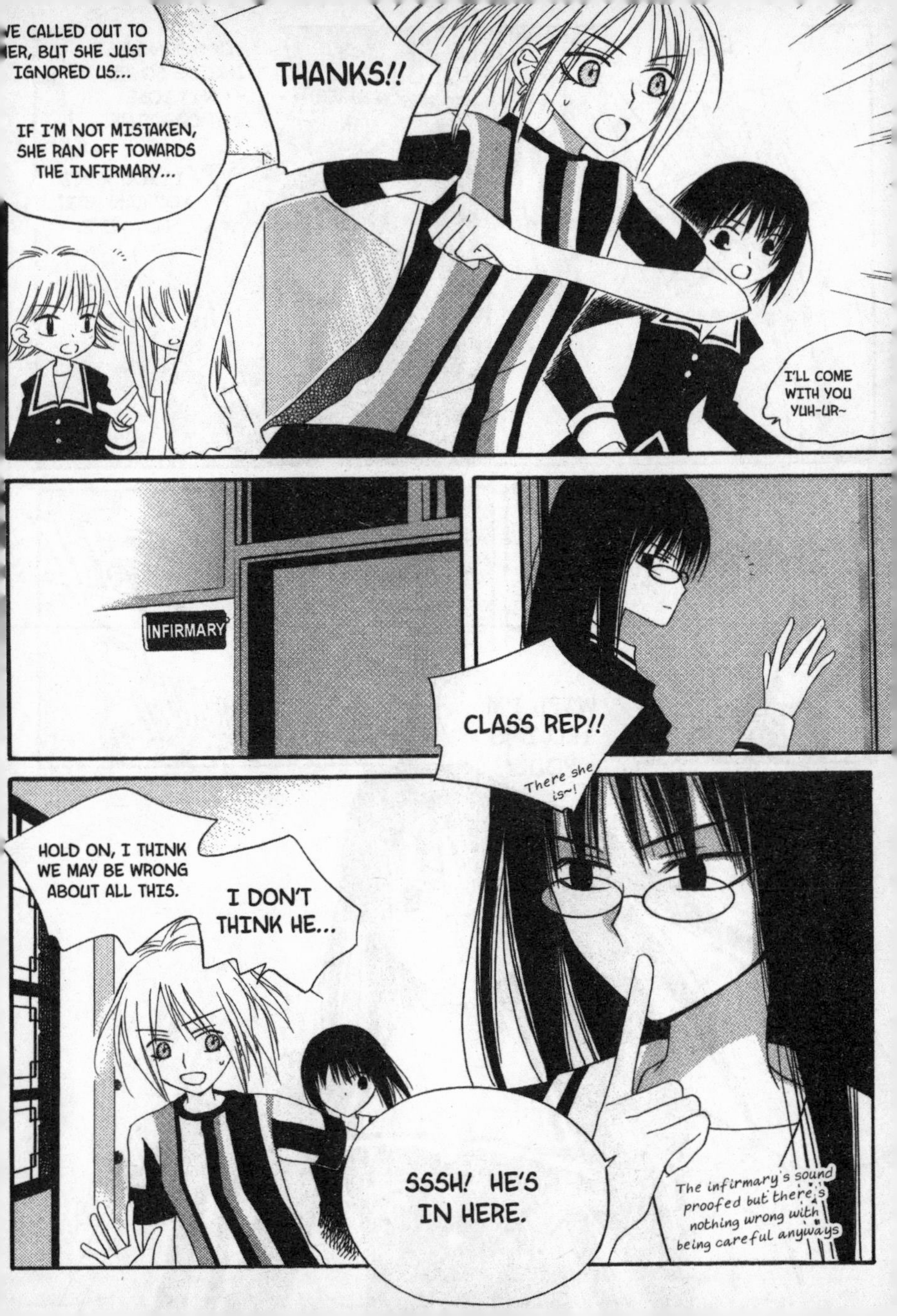

WE CALLED OUT TO HER, BUT SHE JUST IGNORED US...
IF I'M NOT MISTAKEN, SHE RAN OFF TOWARDS THE INFIRMARY...
THANKS!!
I'LL COME WITH YOU YUH-UR~
INFIRMARY
CLASS REP!!
There she is~!
HOLD ON, I THINK WE MAY BE WRONG ABOUT ALL THIS.
I DON'T THINK HE...
SSSH! HE'S IN HERE.
The infirmary's sound proofed but there's nothing wrong with being careful anyways

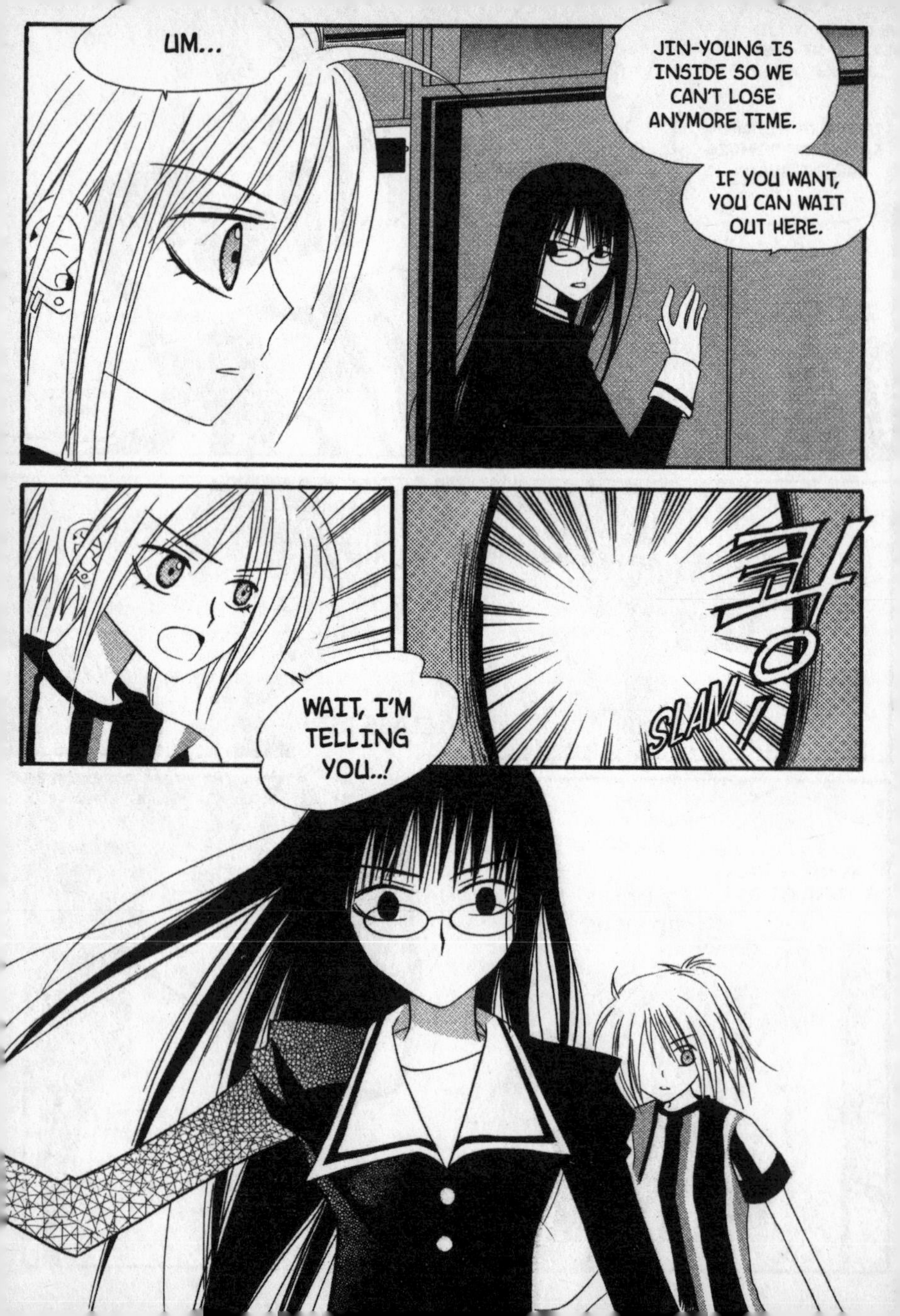
UM...
JIN-YOUNG IS INSIDE SO WE CAN'T LOSE ANYMORE TIME.
IF YOU WANT, YOU CAN WAIT OUT HERE.
WAIT, I'M TELLING YOU..!
쾅
SLAM!

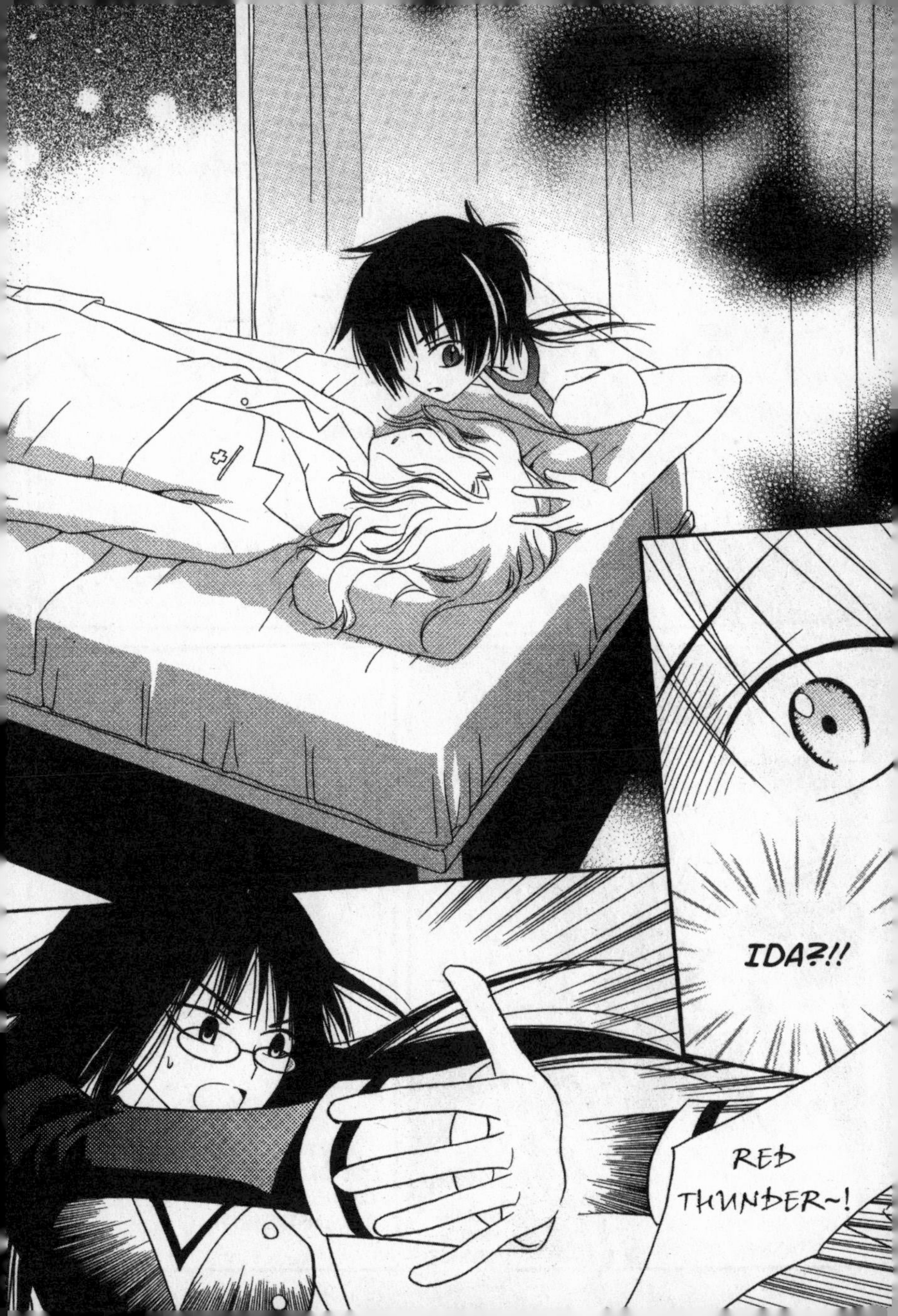
IDA?!!
RED THUNDER~!

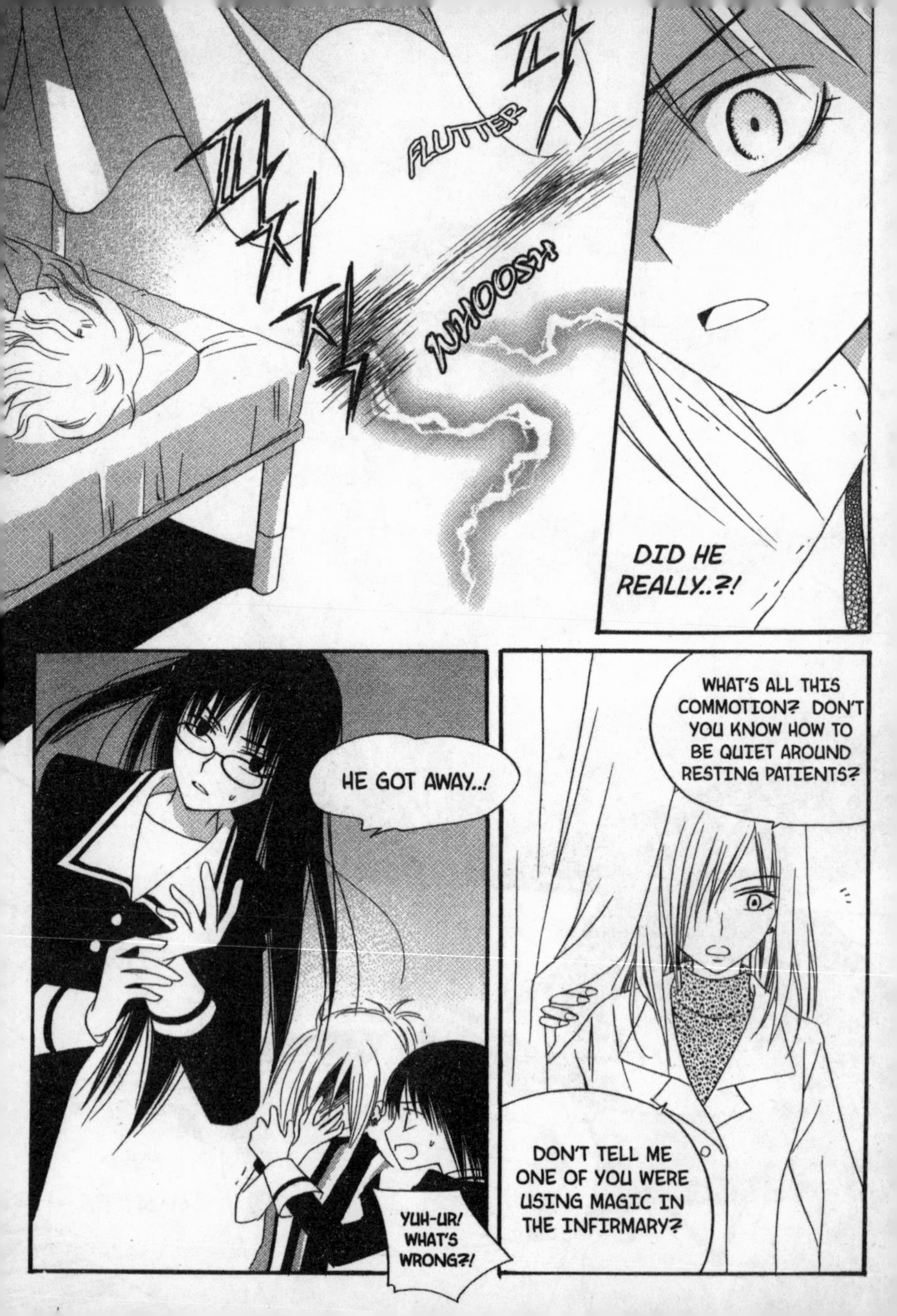
FLUTTER
WHOOSH
DID HE REALLY..?!
HE GOT AWAY..!
YUH-UR! WHAT'S WRONG?!
WHAT'S ALL THIS COMMOTION? DON'T YOU KNOW HOW TO BE QUIET AROUND RESTING PATIENTS?
DON'T TELL ME ONE OF YOU WERE USING MAGIC IN THE INFIRMARY?

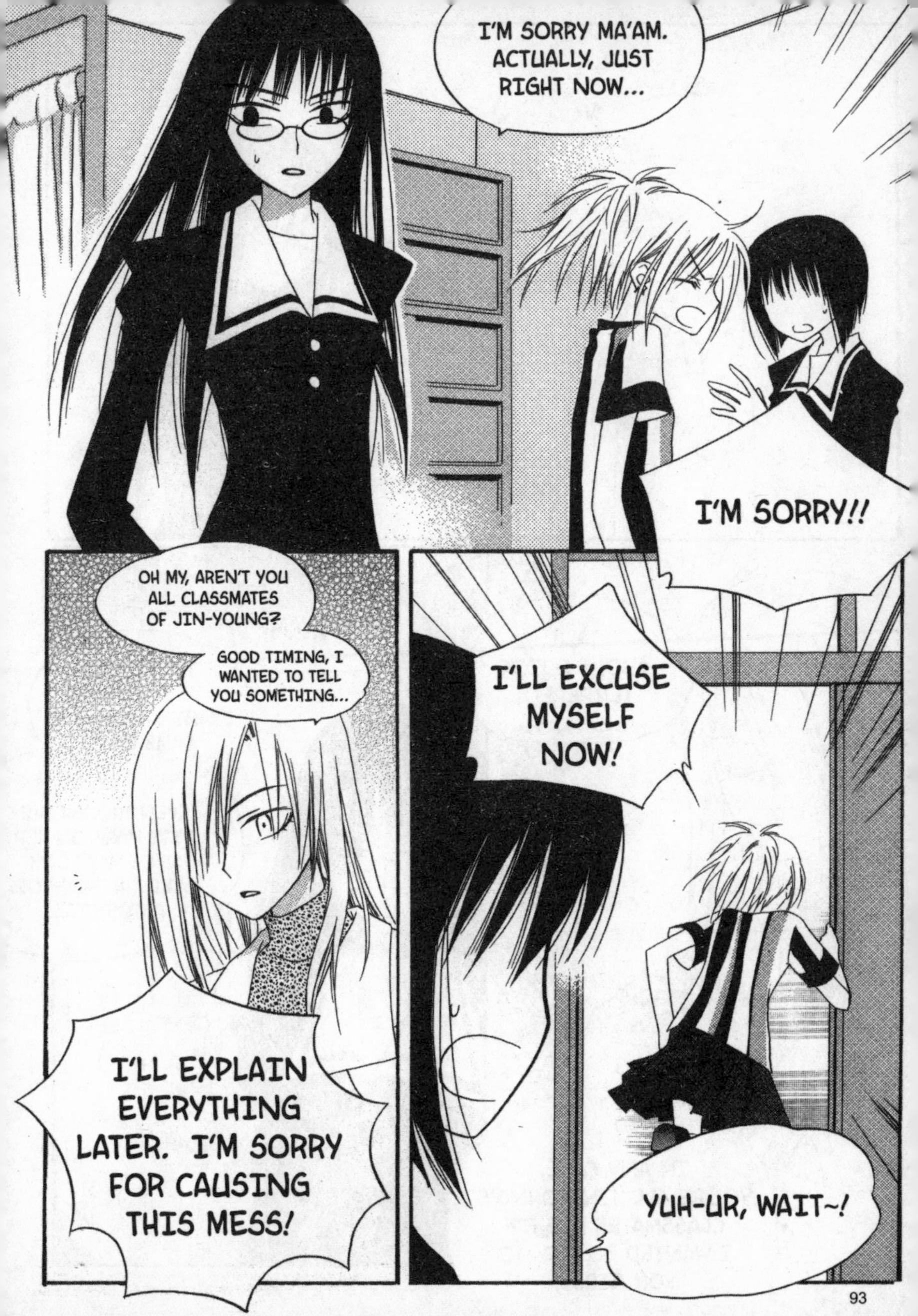

I'M SORRY MA'AM. ACTUALLY, JUST RIGHT NOW...
I'M SORRY!!
OH MY, AREN'T YOU ALL CLASSMATES OF JIN-YOUNG?
GOOD TIMING, I WANTED TO TELL YOU SOMETHING...
I'LL EXPLAIN EVERYTHING LATER. I'M SORRY FOR CAUSING THIS MESS!
I'LL EXCUSE MYSELF NOW!
YUH-UR, WAIT~!

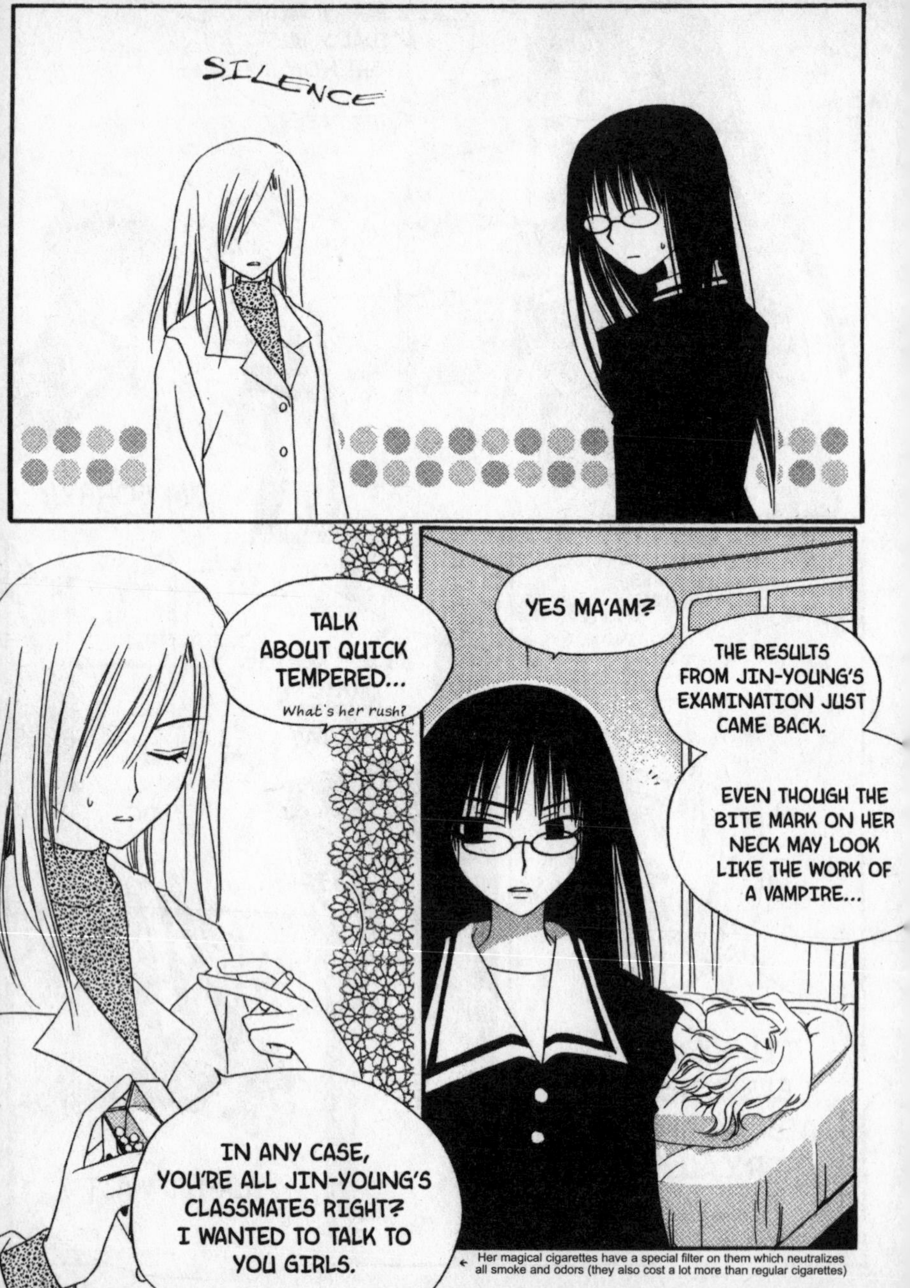
SILENCE
TALK ABOUT QUICK TEMPERED...
What's her rush?
IN ANY CASE, YOU'RE ALL JIN-YOUNG'S CLASSMATES RIGHT? I WANTED TO TALK TO YOU GIRLS.
YES MA'AM?
THE RESULTS FROM JIN-YOUNG'S EXAMINATION JUST CAME BACK.
EVEN THOUGH THE BITE MARK ON HER NECK MAY LOOK LIKE THE WORK OF A VAMPIRE...
← Her magical cigarettes have a special filter on them which neutralizes all smoke and odors (they also cost a lot more than regular cigarettes)

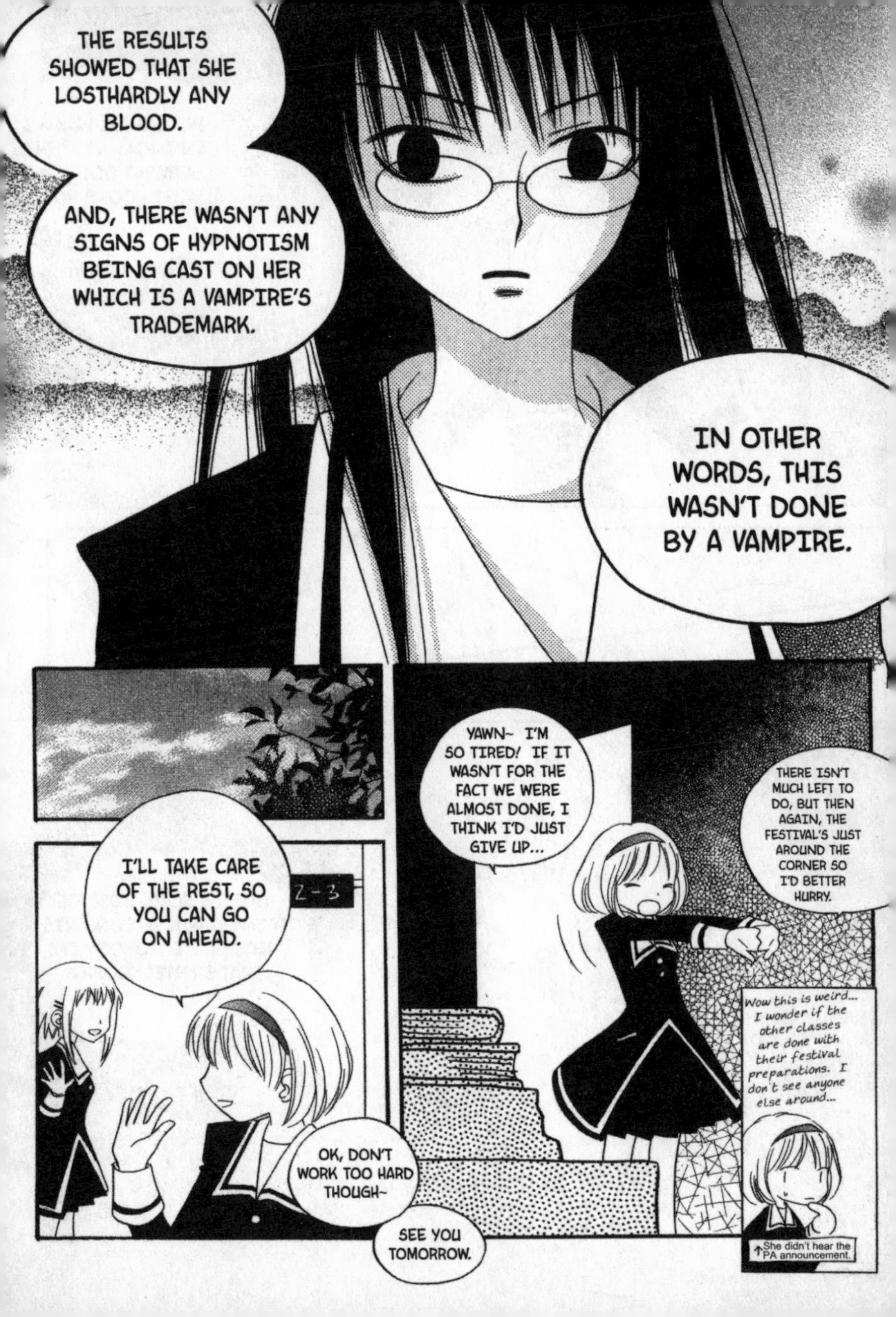
THE RESULTS SHOWED THAT SHE LOSTHARDLY ANY BLOOD.
AND, THERE WASN'T ANY SIGNS OF HYPNOTISM BEING CAST ON HER WHICH IS A VAMPIRE'S TRADEMARK.
IN OTHER WORDS, THIS WASN'T DONE BY A VAMPIRE.
I'LL TAKE CARE OF THE REST, SO YOU CAN GO ON AHEAD.
2-3
OK, DON'T WORK TOO HARD THOUGH~
SEE YOU TOMORROW.
YAWN~ I'M SO TIRED! IF IT WASN'T FOR THE FACT WE WERE ALMOST DONE, I THINK I'D JUST GIVE UP...
THERE ISN'T MUCH LEFT TO DO, BUT THEN AGAIN, THE FESTIVAL'S JUST AROUND THE CORNER SO I'D BETTER HURRY.
Wow this is weird... I wonder if the other classes are done with their festival preparations. I don't see anyone else around...
↑She didn't hear the PA announcement.

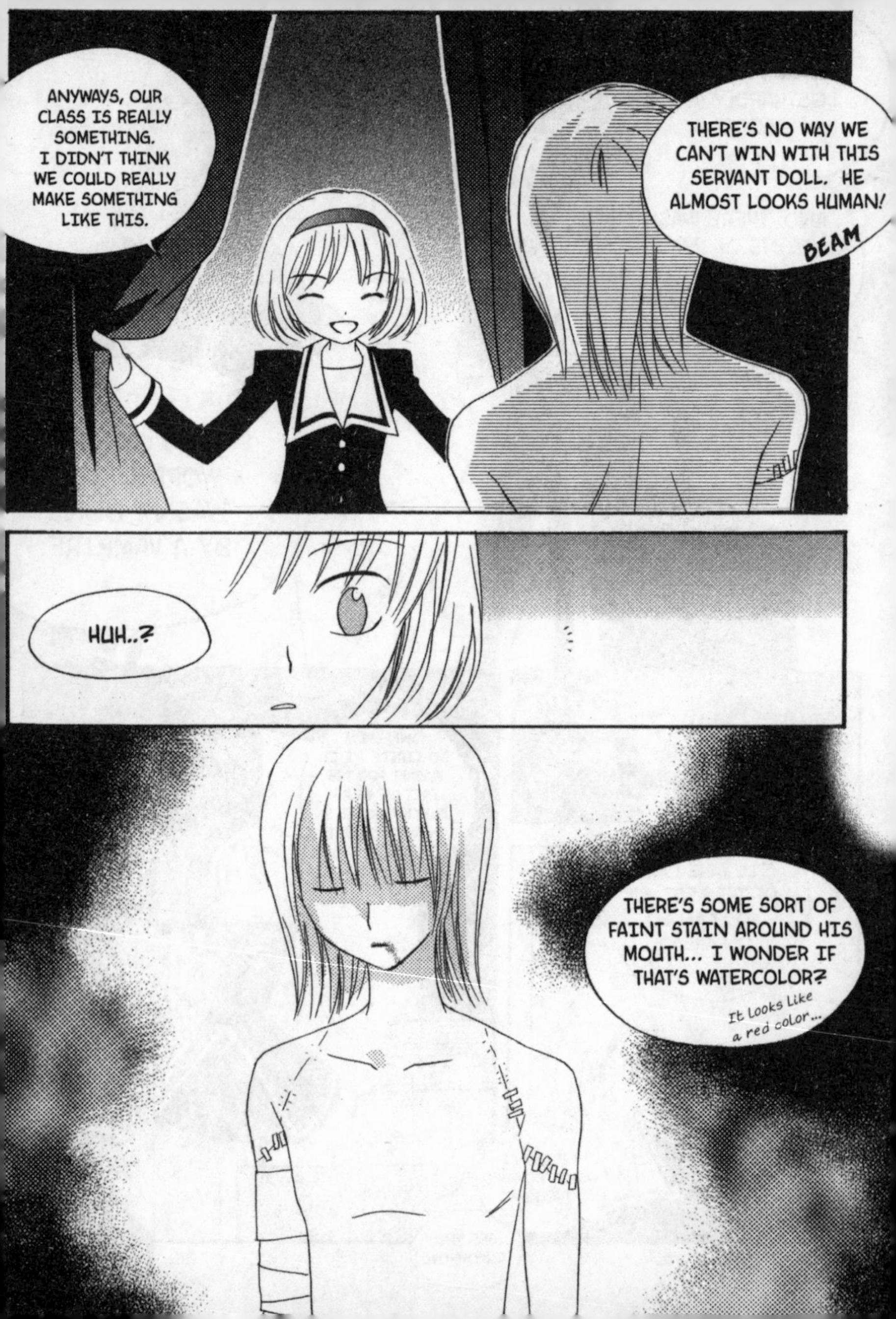
ANYWAYS, OUR CLASS IS REALLY SOMETHING. I DIDN'T THINK WE COULD REALLY MAKE SOMETHING LIKE THIS.
THERE'S NO WAY WE CAN'T WIN WITH THIS SERVANT DOLL. HE ALMOST LOOKS HUMAN!
BEAM
HUH..?
THERE'S SOME SORT OF FAINT STAIN AROUND HIS MOUTH... I WONDER IF THAT'S WATERCOLOR?
It Looks Like a red color...

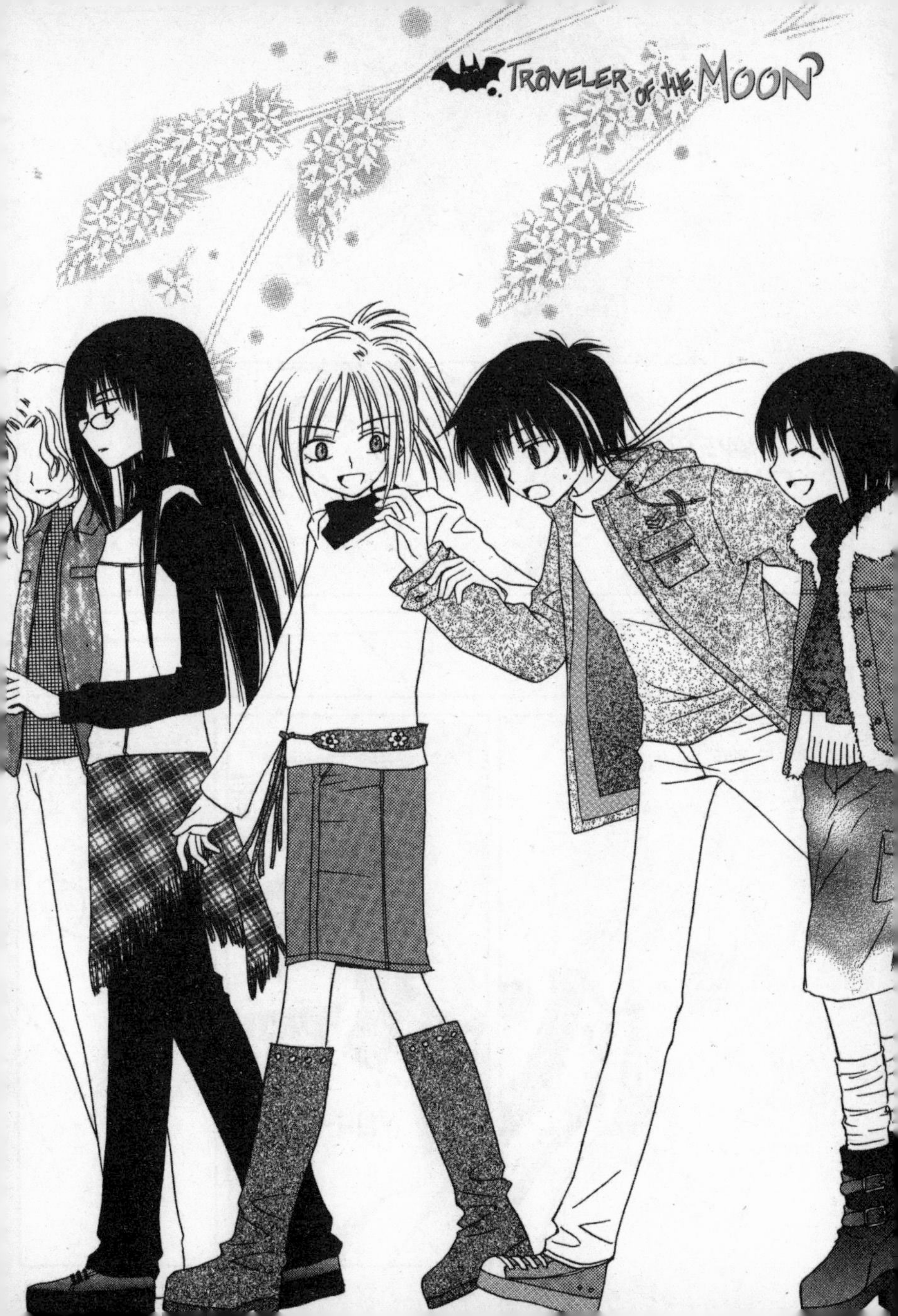
TRAVELER OF THE MOON

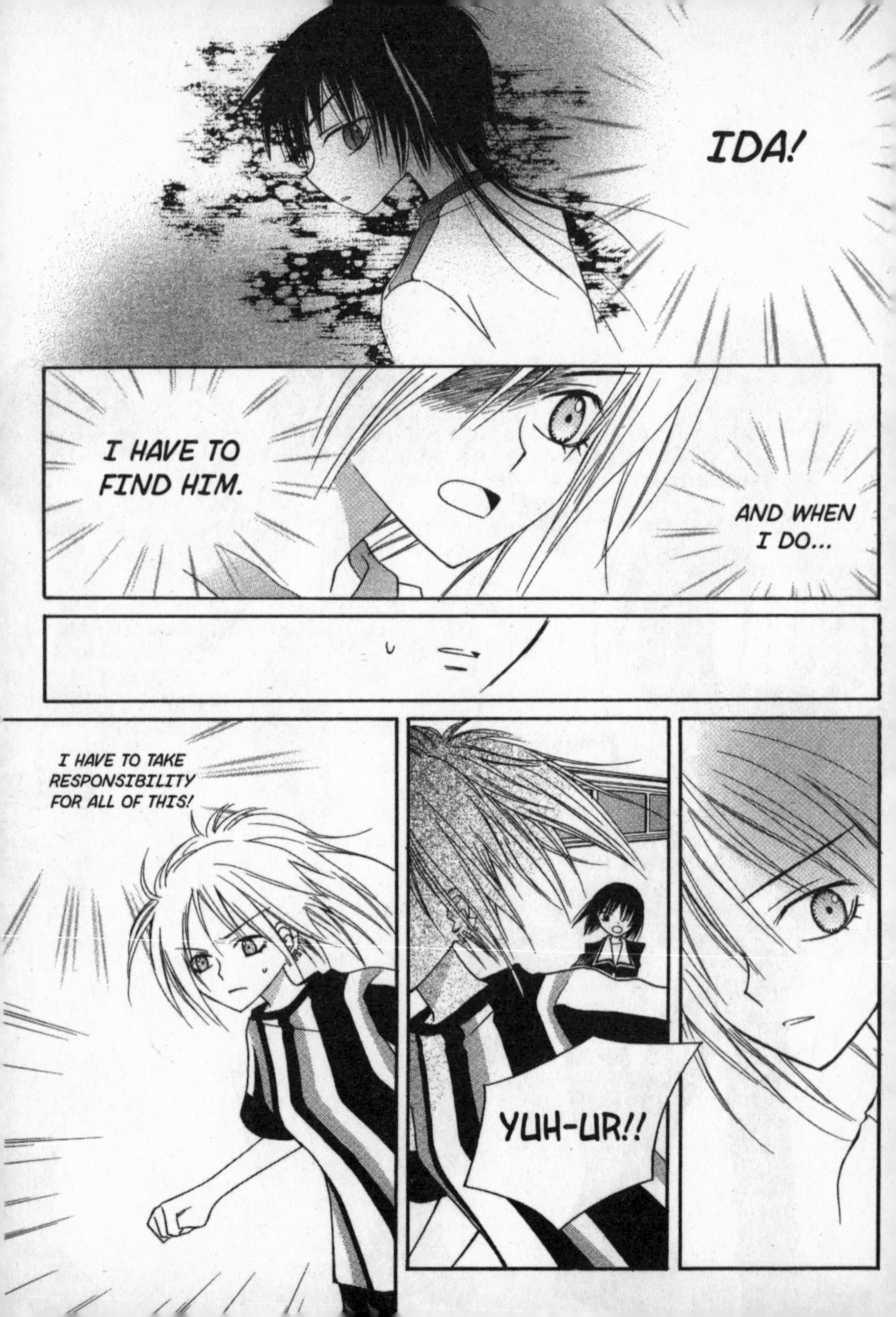
IDA!
I HAVE TO FIND HIM.
AND WHEN I DO...
I HAVE TO TAKE RESPONSIBILITY FOR ALL OF THIS!
YUH-UR!!

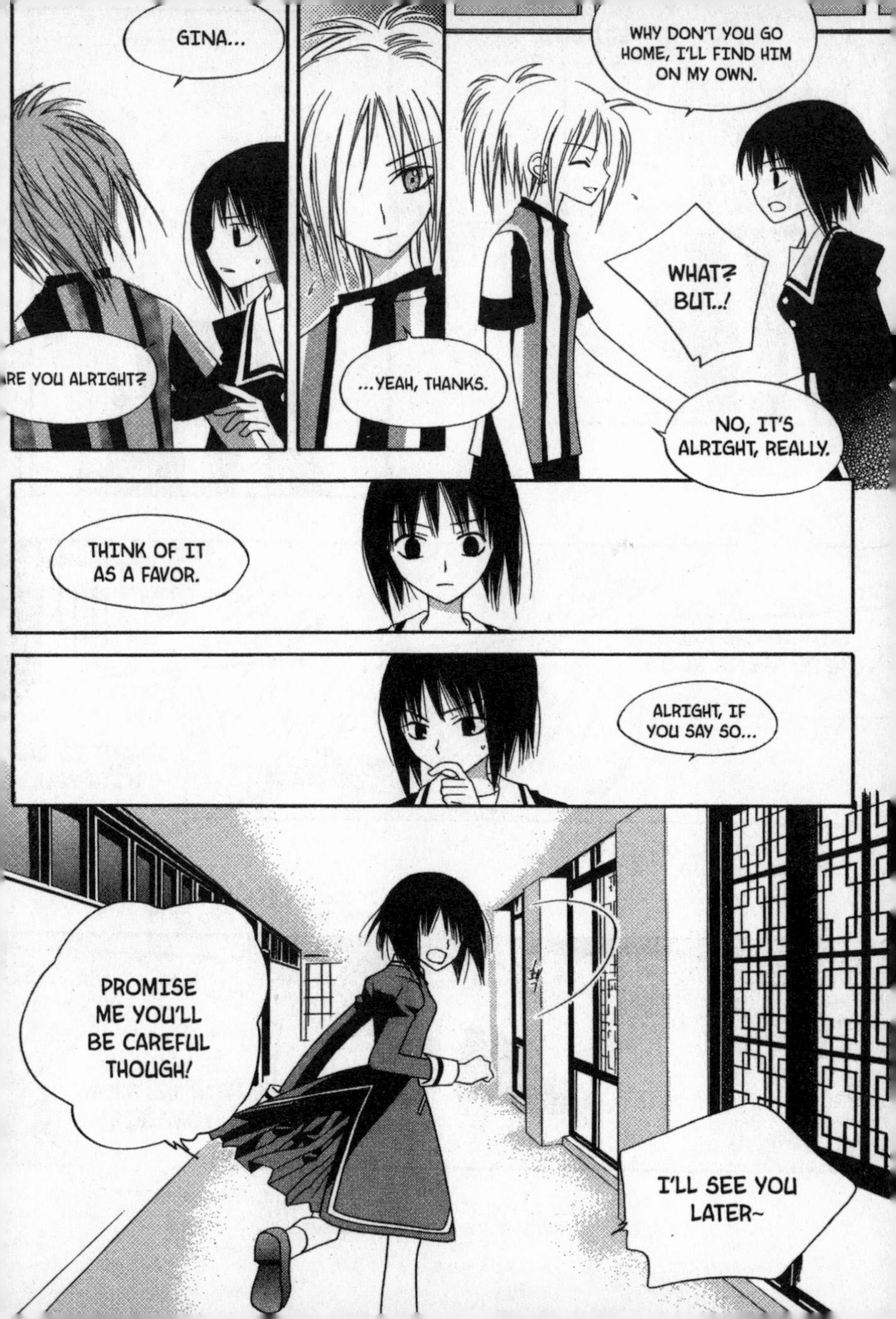
GINA...
RE YOU ALRIGHT?
...YEAH, THANKS.
WHY DON'T YOU GO HOME, I'LL FIND HIM ON MY OWN.
WHAT? BUT..!
NO, IT'S ALRIGHT, REALLY.
THINK OF IT AS A FAVOR.
ALRIGHT, IF YOU SAY SO...
PROMISE ME YOU'LL BE CAREFUL THOUGH!
I'LL SEE YOU LATER~

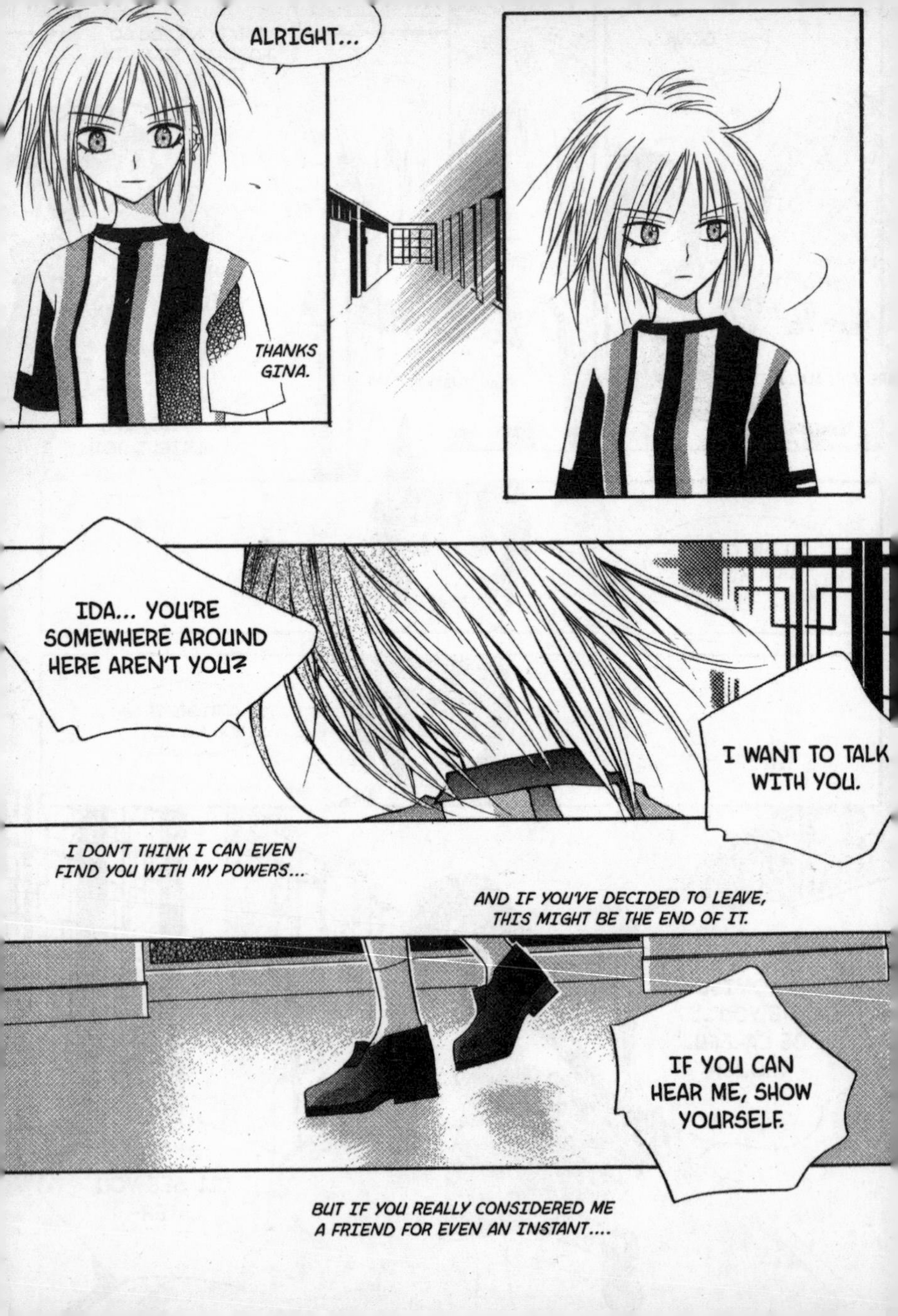
ALRIGHT...
THANKS GINA.
IDA... YOU'RE SOMEWHERE AROUND HERE AREN'T YOU?
I WANT TO TALK WITH YOU.
I DON'T THINK I CAN EVEN FIND YOU WITH MY POWERS...
AND IF YOU'VE DECIDED TO LEAVE, THIS MIGHT BE THE END OF IT.
IF YOU CAN HEAR ME, SHOW YOURSELF.
BUT IF YOU REALLY CONSIDERED ME A FRIEND FOR EVEN AN INSTANT....

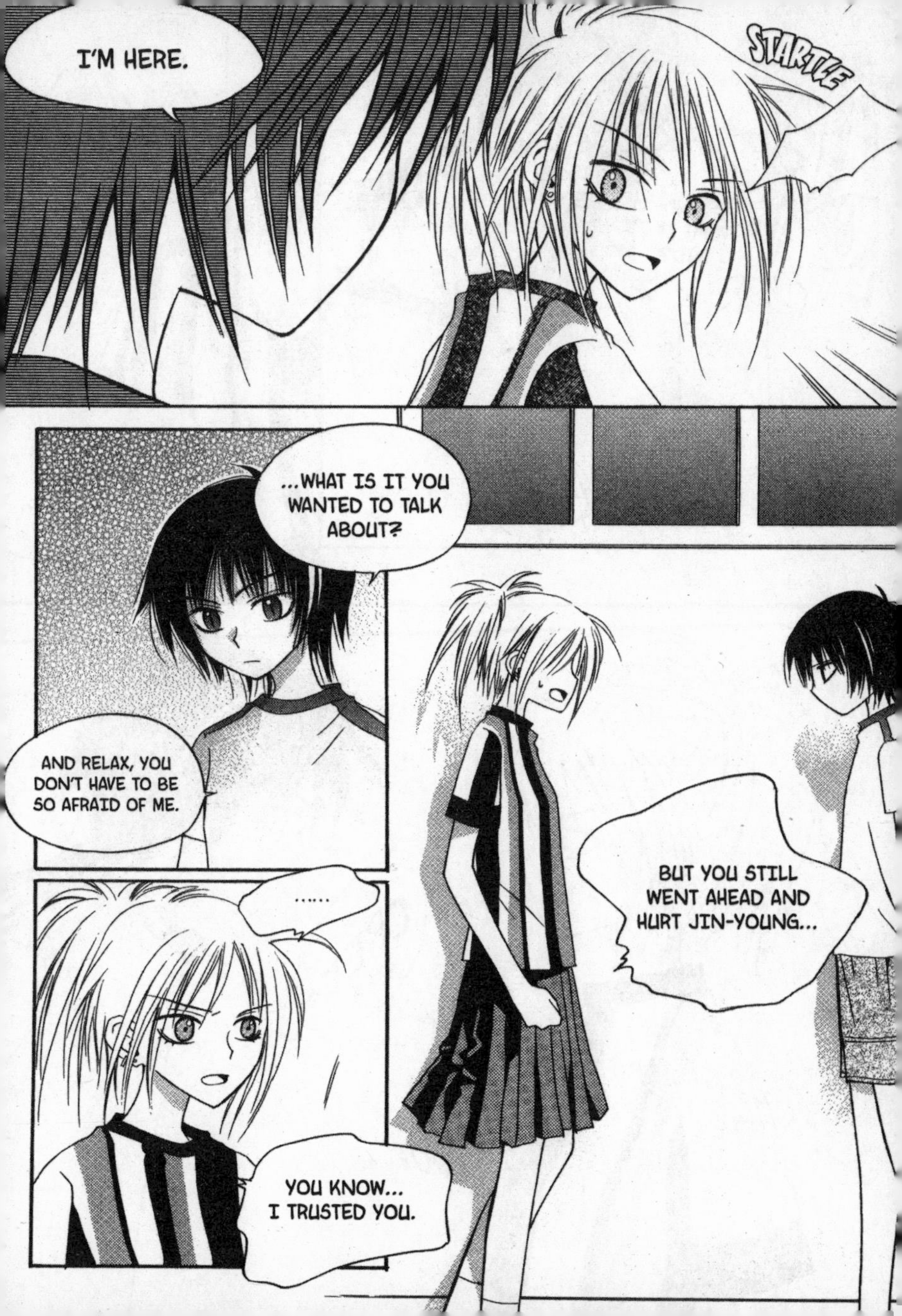
I'M HERE.
STARTLE
...WHAT IS IT YOU WANTED TO TALK ABOUT?
AND RELAX, YOU DON'T HAVE TO BE SO AFRAID OF ME.
BUT YOU STILL WENT AHEAD AND HURT JIN-YOUNG...
......
YOU KNOW... I TRUSTED YOU.

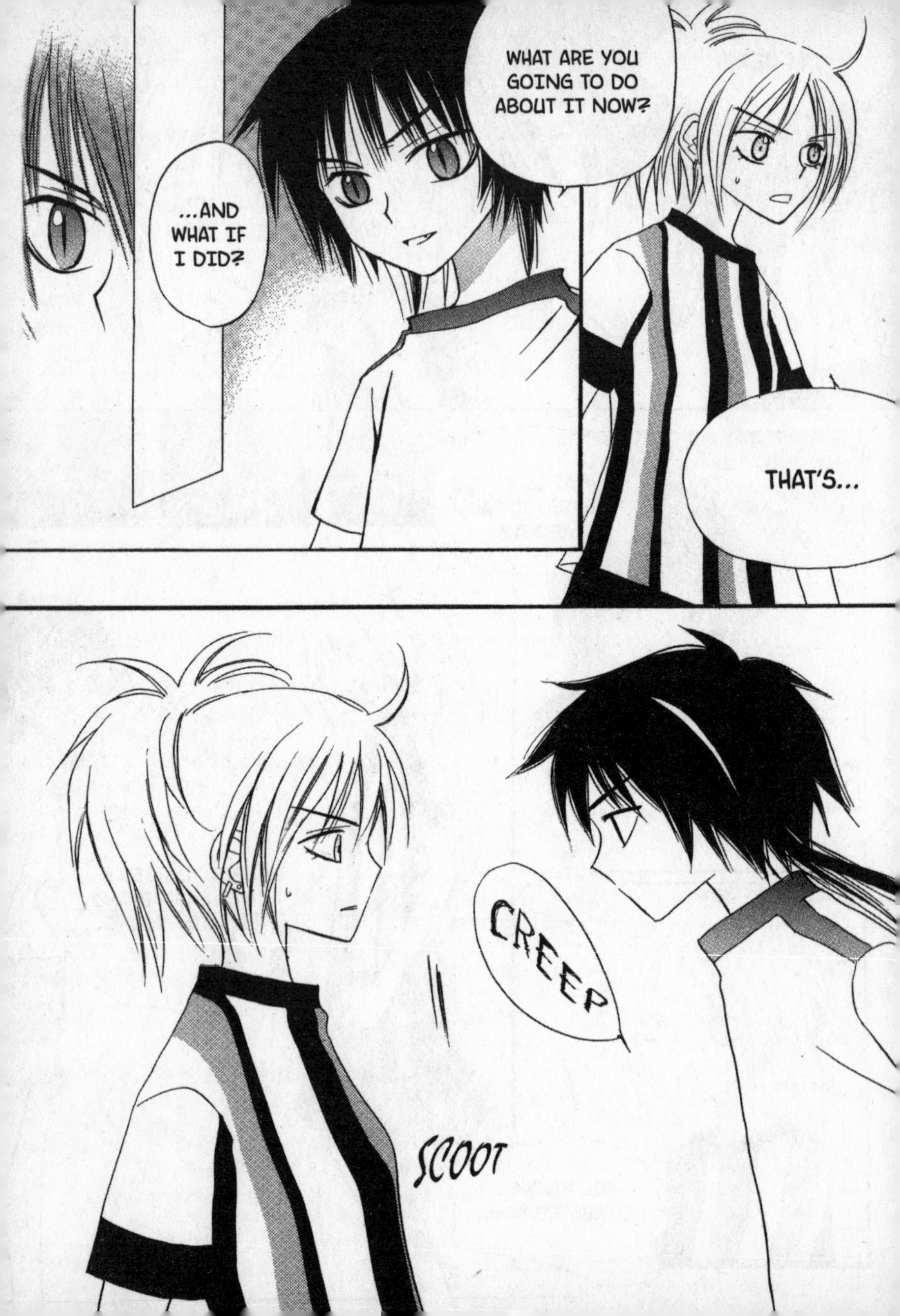
...AND WHAT IF I DID?
WHAT ARE YOU GOING TO DO ABOUT IT NOW?
THAT'S...
CREEP
SCOOT

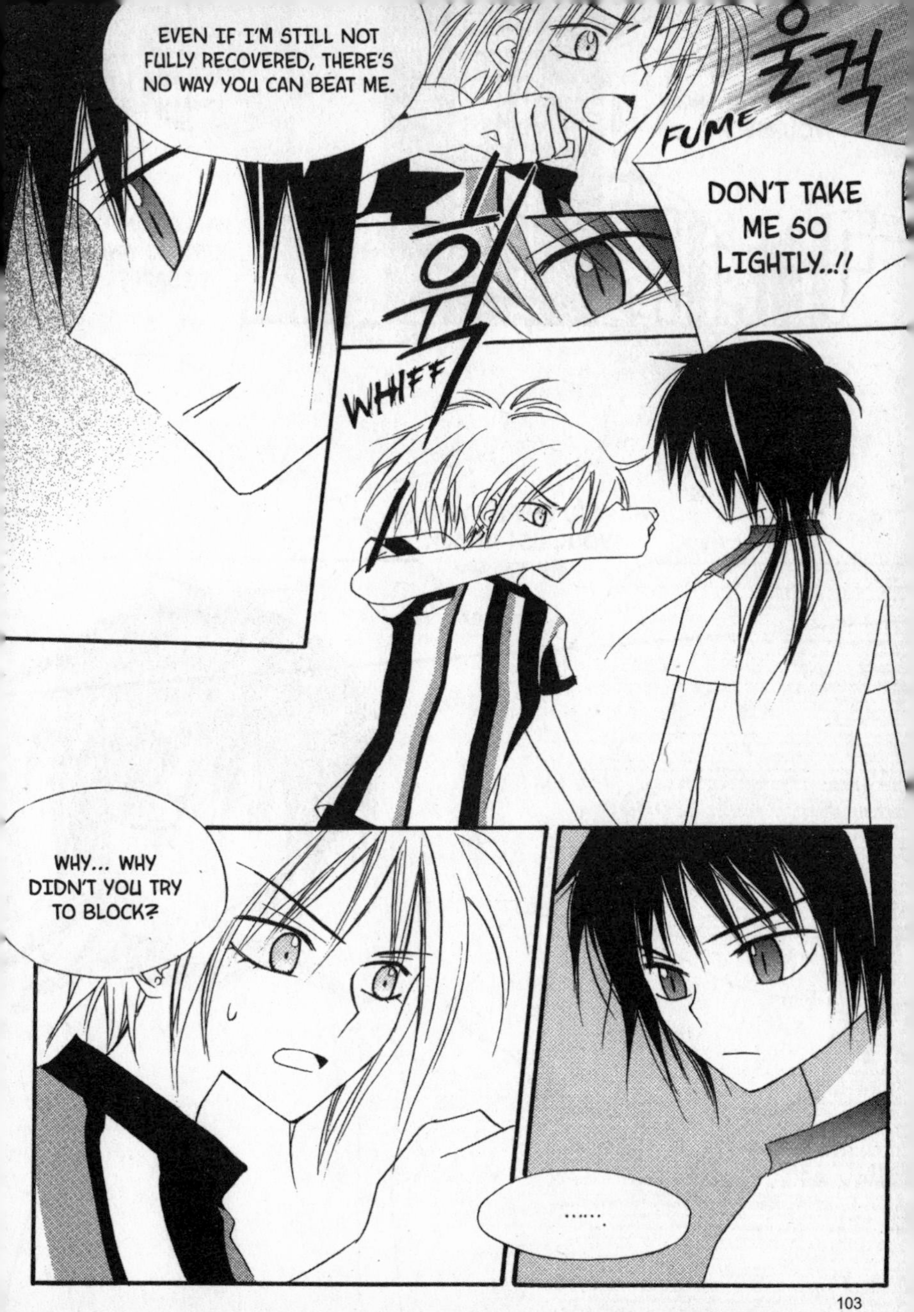
EVEN IF I'M STILL NOT FULLY RECOVERED, THERE'S NO WAY YOU CAN BEAT ME.
울컥
FUME
DON'T TAKE ME SO LIGHTLY..!!
휘익
WHIFF
WHY... WHY DIDN'T YOU TRY TO BLOCK?
......

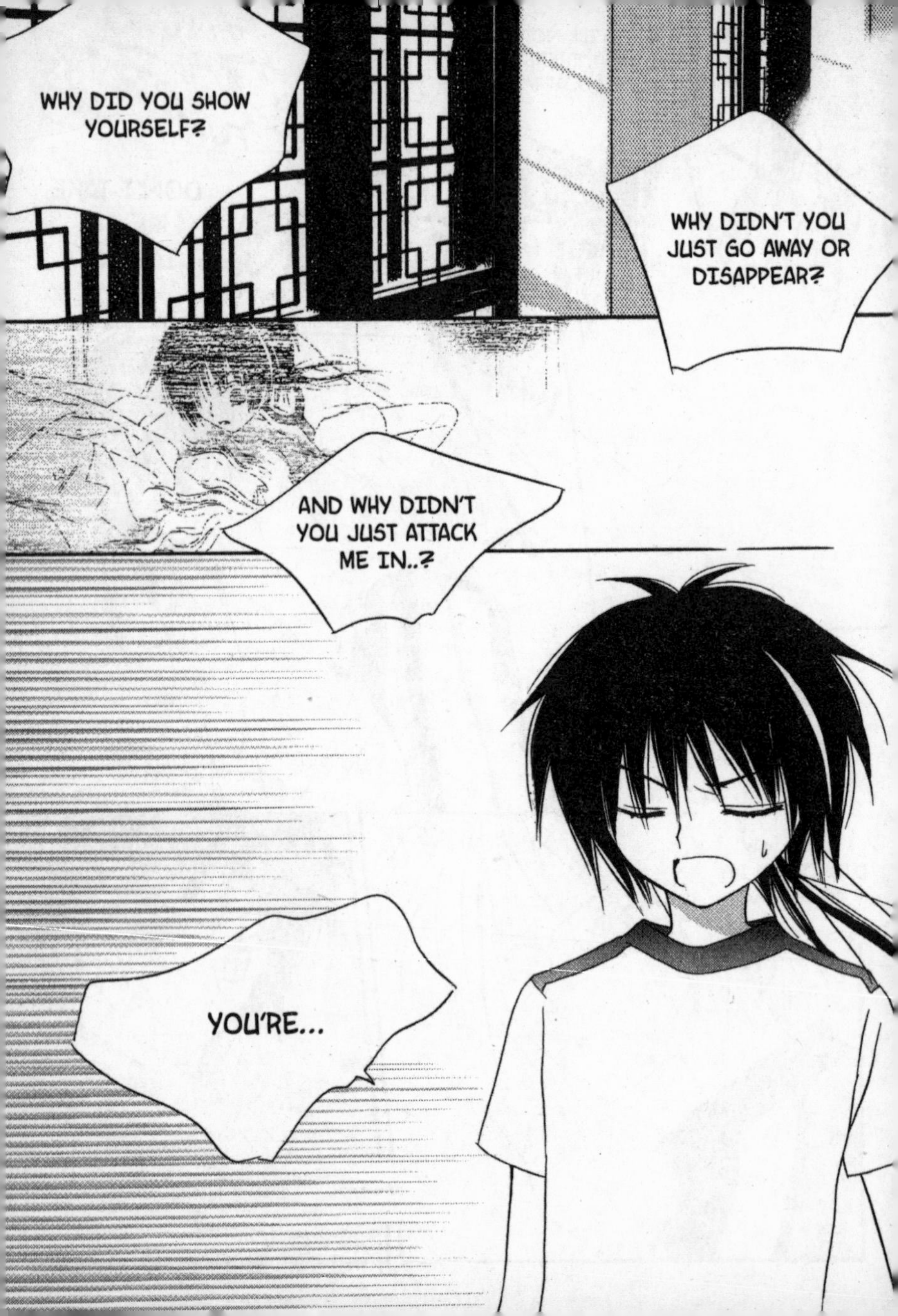
WHY DID YOU SHOW YOURSELF?
WHY DIDN'T YOU JUST GO AWAY OR DISAPPEAR?
AND WHY DIDN'T YOU JUST ATTACK ME IN..?
YOU'RE...

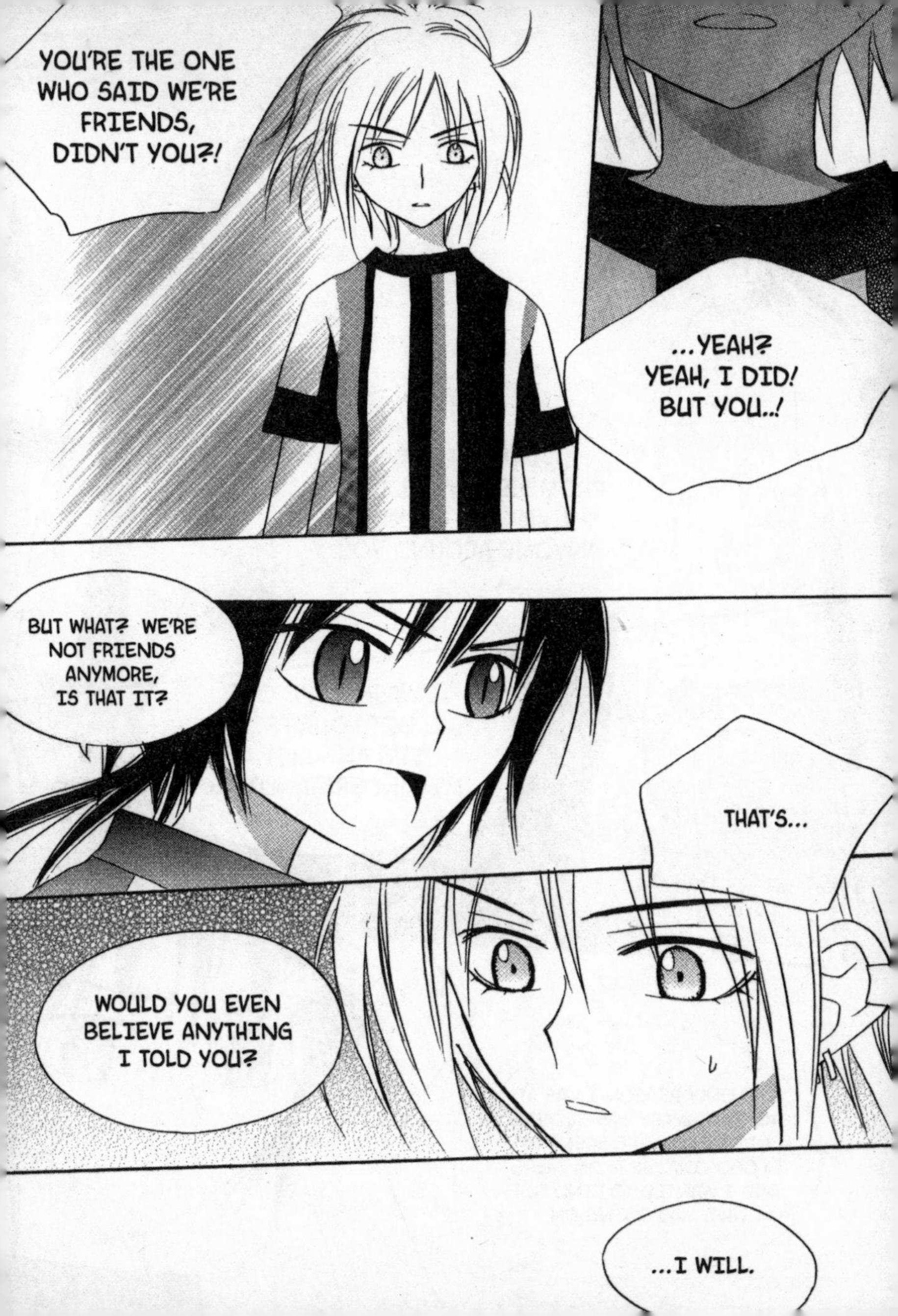
YOU'RE THE ONE WHO SAID WE'RE FRIENDS, DIDN'T YOU?!
...YEAH? YEAH, I DID! BUT YOU..!
BUT WHAT? WE'RE NOT FRIENDS ANYMORE, IS THAT IT?
THAT'S...
WOULD YOU EVEN BELIEVE ANYTHING I TOLD YOU?
...I WILL.

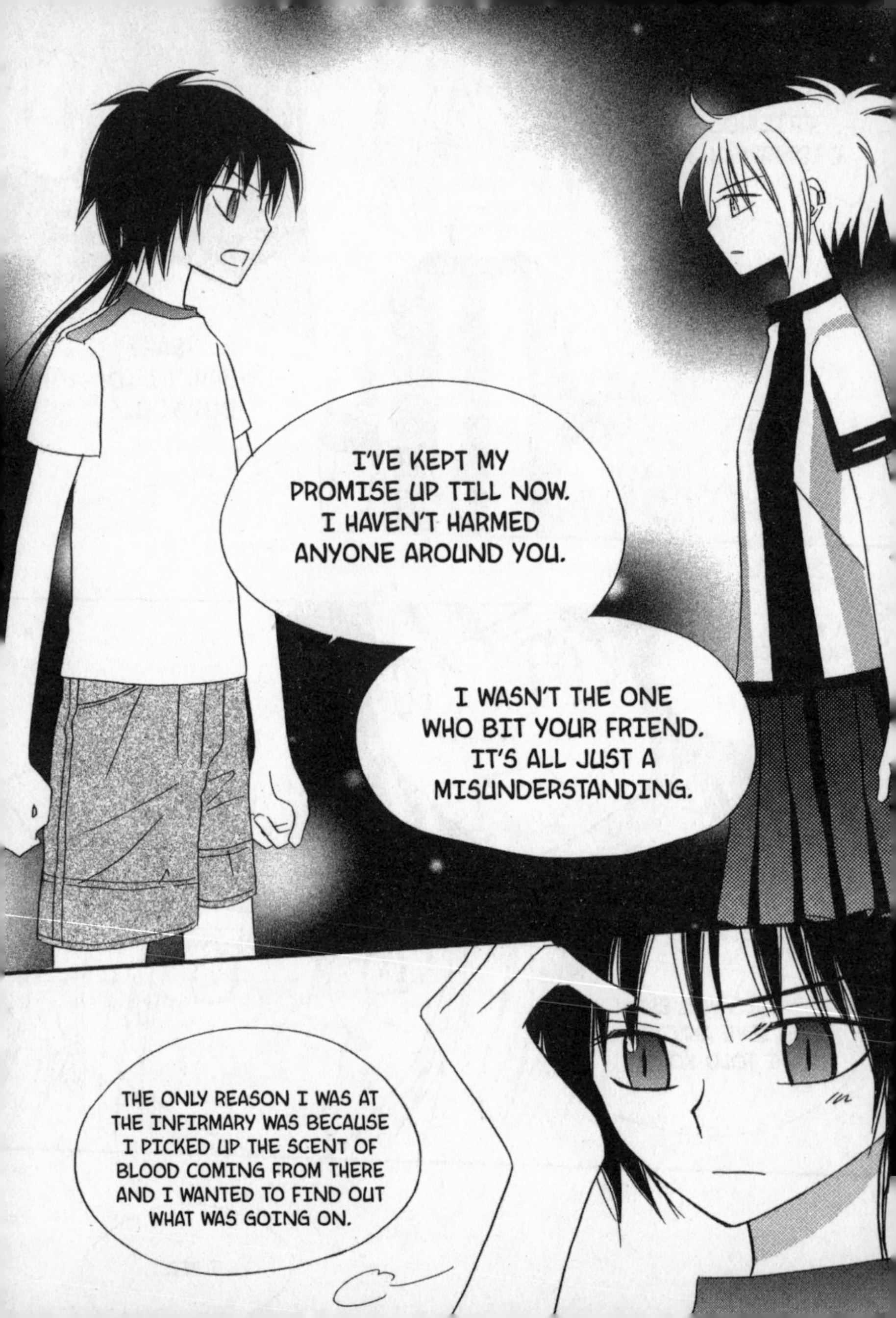
I'VE KEPT MY PROMISE UP TILL NOW. I HAVEN'T HARMED ANYONE AROUND YOU.
I WASN'T THE ONE WHO BIT YOUR FRIEND. IT'S ALL JUST A MISUNDERSTANDING.
THE ONLY REASON I WAS AT THE INFIRMARY WAS BECAUSE I PICKED UP THE SCENT OF BLOOD COMING FROM THERE AND I WANTED TO FIND OUT WHAT WAS GOING ON.

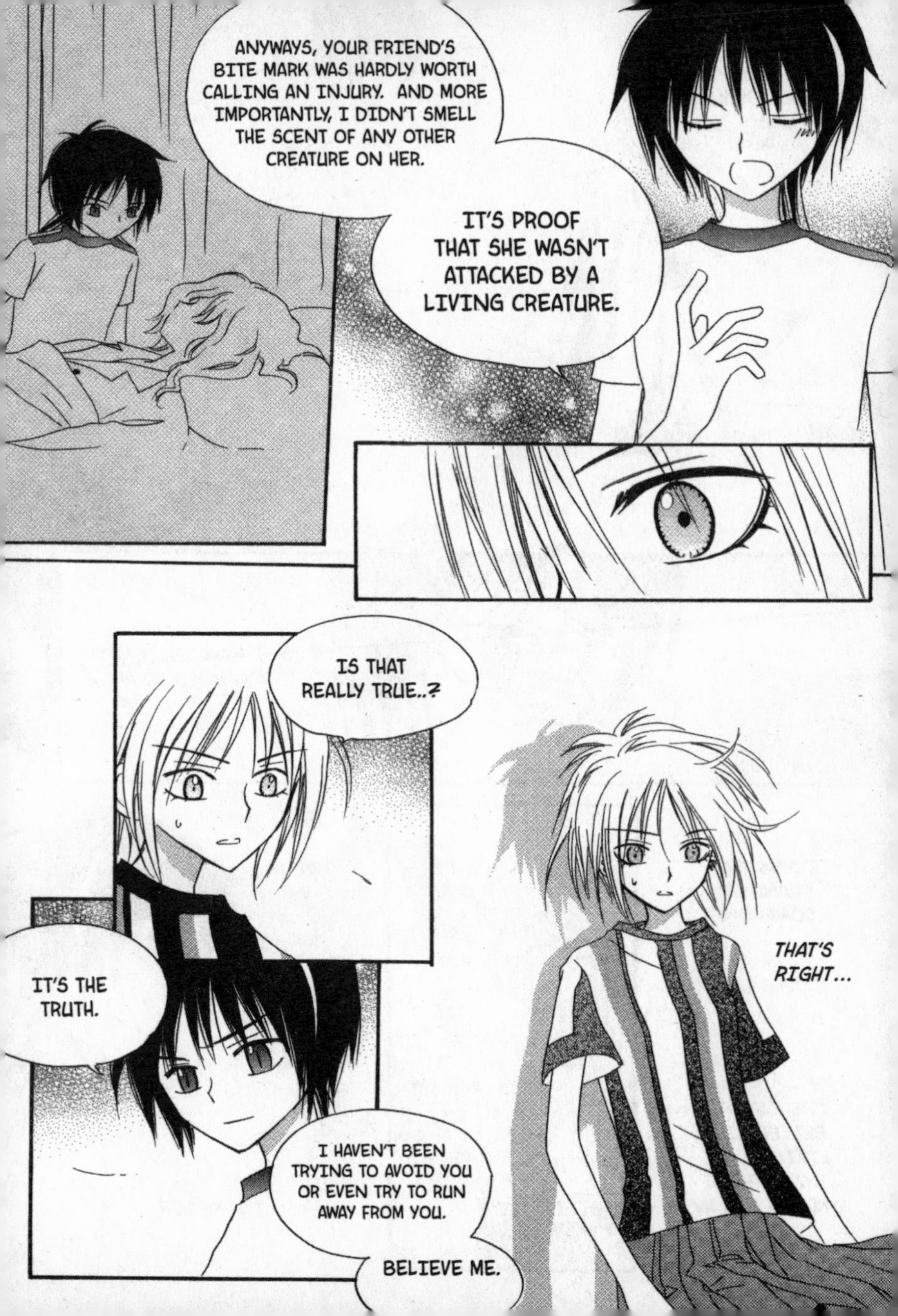
ANYWAYS, YOUR FRIEND'S BITE MARK WAS HARDLY WORTH CALLING AN INJURY. AND MORE IMPORTANTLY, I DIDN'T SMELL THE SCENT OF ANY OTHER CREATURE ON HER.
IT'S PROOF THAT SHE WASN'T ATTACKED BY A LIVING CREATURE.
IS THAT REALLY TRUE..?
IT'S THE TRUTH.
I HAVEN'T BEEN TRYING TO AVOID YOU OR EVEN TRY TO RUN AWAY FROM YOU.
BELIEVE ME.
THAT'S RIGHT...

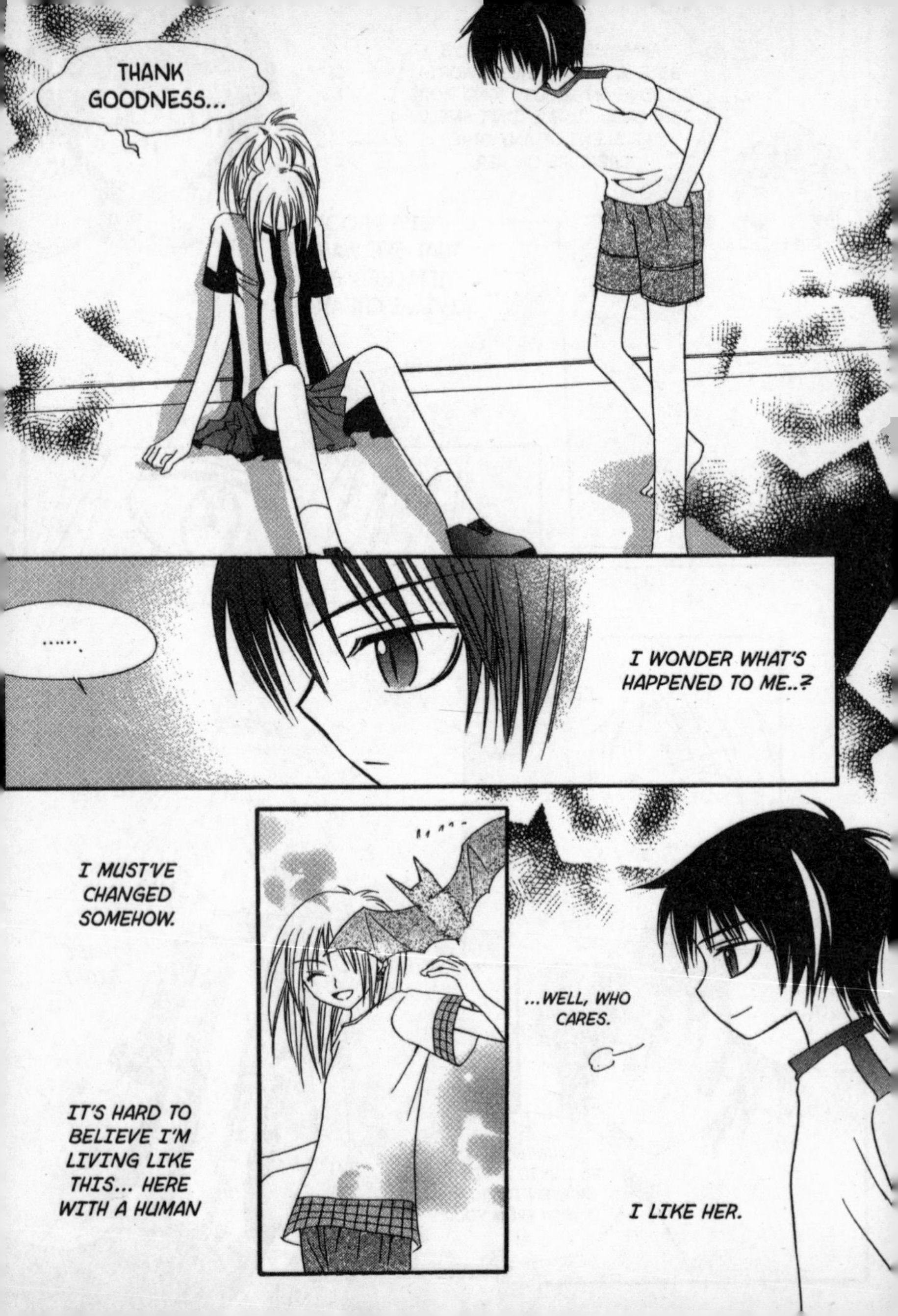
THANK GOODNESS...
......
I WONDER WHAT'S HAPPENED TO ME..?
I MUST'VE CHANGED SOMEHOW.
IT'S HARD TO BELIEVE I'M LIVING LIKE THIS... HERE WITH A HUMAN
...WELL, WHO CARES.
I LIKE HER.

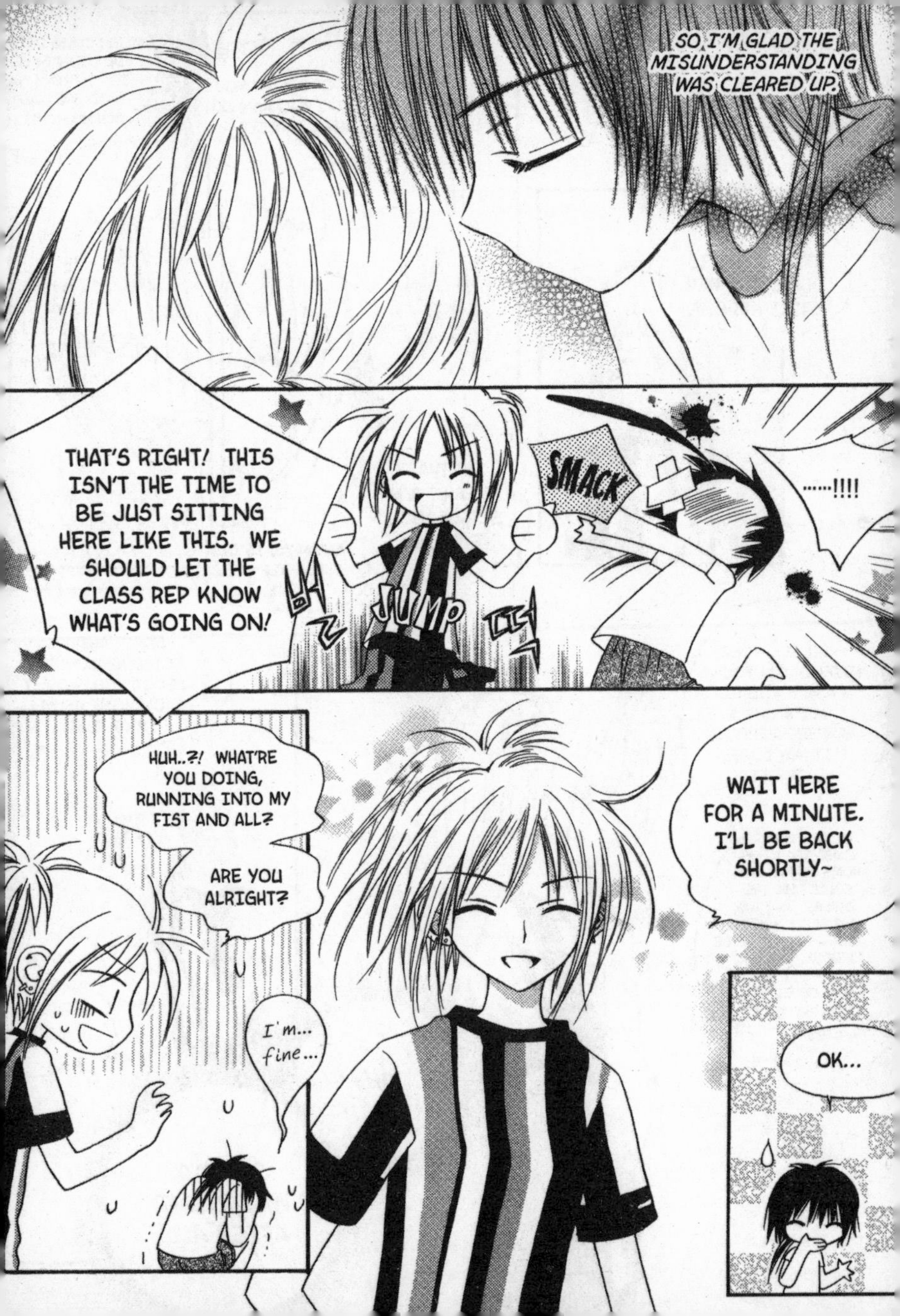
SO I'M GLAD THE MISUNDERSTANDING WAS CLEARED UP.
THAT'S RIGHT! THIS ISN'T THE TIME TO BE JUST SITTING HERE LIKE THIS. WE SHOULD LET THE CLASS REP KNOW WHAT'S GOING ON!
JUMP
SMACK
......!!!!
HUH..?! WHAT'RE YOU DOING, RUNNING INTO MY FIST AND ALL?
ARE YOU ALRIGHT?
I'm... fine...
WAIT HERE FOR A MINUTE. I'LL BE BACK SHORTLY~
OK...

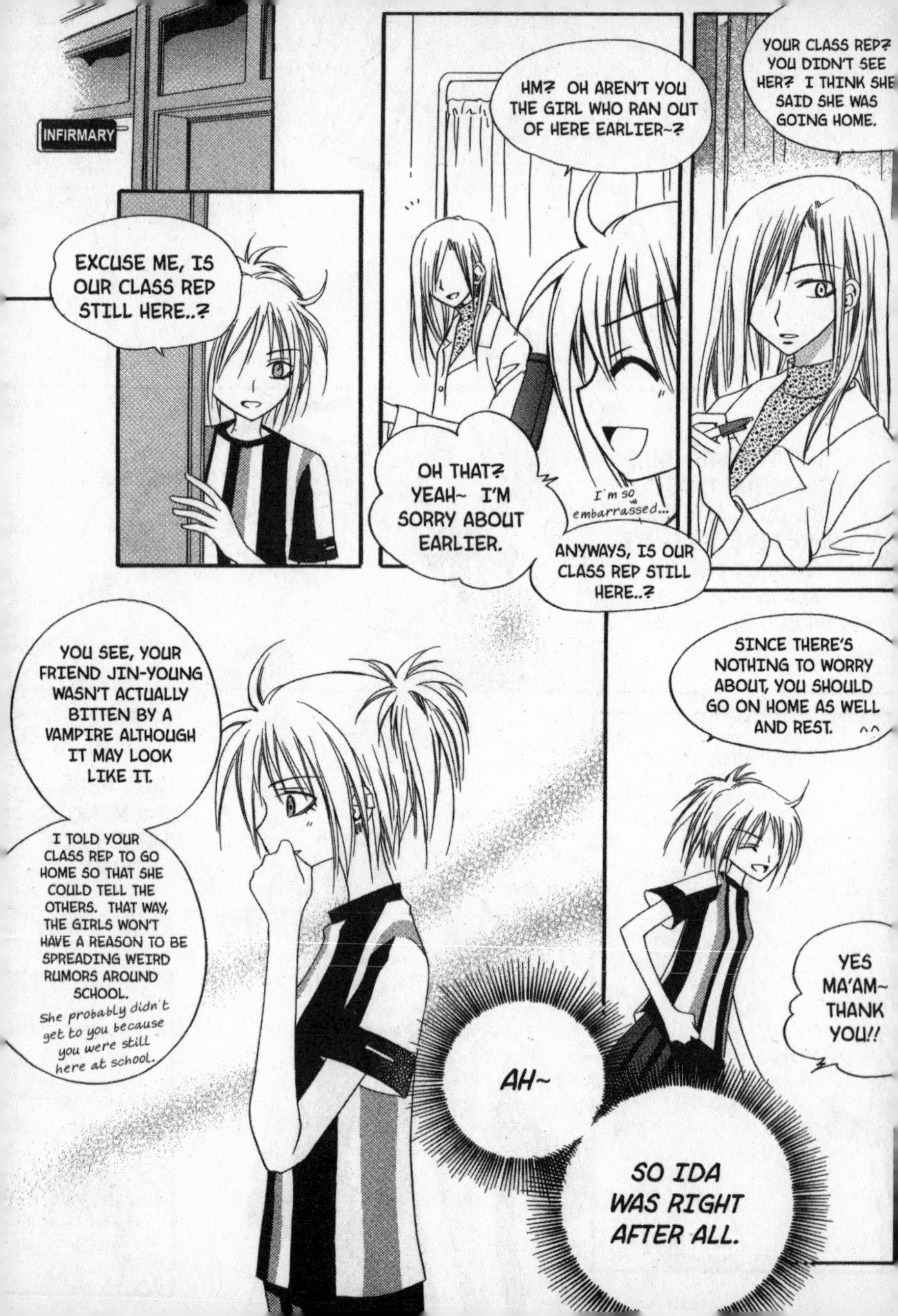
INFIRMARY
EXCUSE ME, IS OUR CLASS REP STILL HERE..?
HM? OH AREN'T YOU THE GIRL WHO RAN OUT OF HERE EARLIER~?
OH THAT? YEAH~ I'M SORRY ABOUT EARLIER.
I'm so embarrassed...
ANYWAYS, IS OUR CLASS REP STILL HERE..?
YOUR CLASS REP? YOU DIDN'T SEE HER? I THINK SHE SAID SHE WAS GOING HOME.
YOU SEE, YOUR FRIEND JIN-YOUNG WASN'T ACTUALLY BITTEN BY A VAMPIRE ALTHOUGH IT MAY LOOK LIKE IT.
I TOLD YOUR CLASS REP TO GO HOME SO THAT SHE COULD TELL THE OTHERS. THAT WAY, THE GIRLS WON'T HAVE A REASON TO BE SPREADING WEIRD RUMORS AROUND SCHOOL.
She probably didn't get to you because you were still here at school.
SINCE THERE'S NOTHING TO WORRY ABOUT, YOU SHOULD GO ON HOME AS WELL AND REST. ^^
YES MA'AM~ THANK YOU!!
AH~
SO IDA WAS RIGHT AFTER ALL.

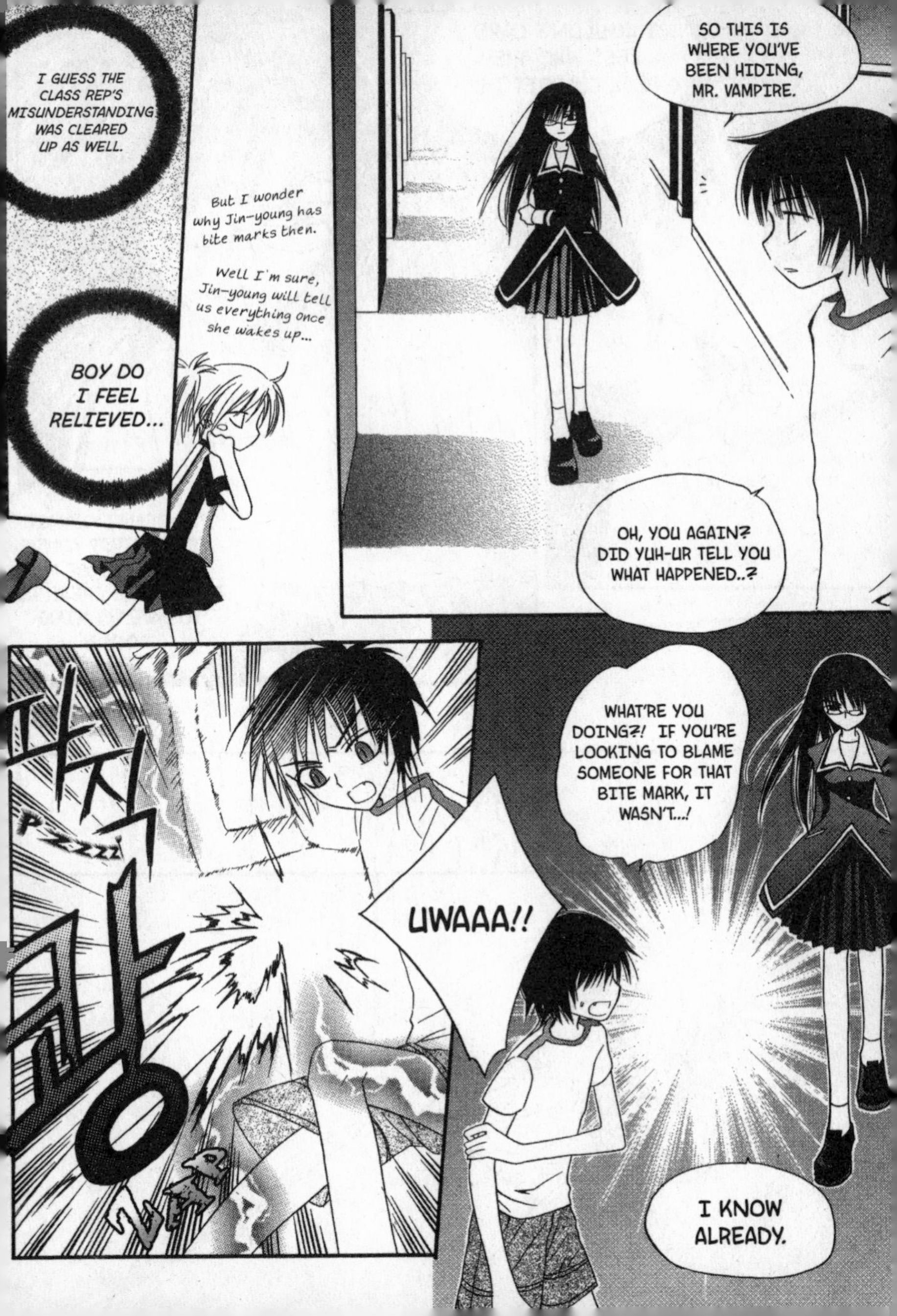
I GUESS THE CLASS REP'S MISUNDERSTANDING WAS CLEARED UP AS WELL.
But I wonder why Jin-young has bite marks then.
Well I'm sure, Jin-young will tell us everything once she wakes up...
BOY DO I FEEL RELIEVED...
SO THIS IS WHERE YOU'VE BEEN HIDING, MR. VAMPIRE.
OH, YOU AGAIN? DID YUH-UR TELL YOU WHAT HAPPENED..?
UWAAA!!
WHAT'RE YOU DOING?! IF YOU'RE LOOKING TO BLAME SOMEONE FOR THAT BITE MARK, IT WASN'T...!
I KNOW ALREADY.

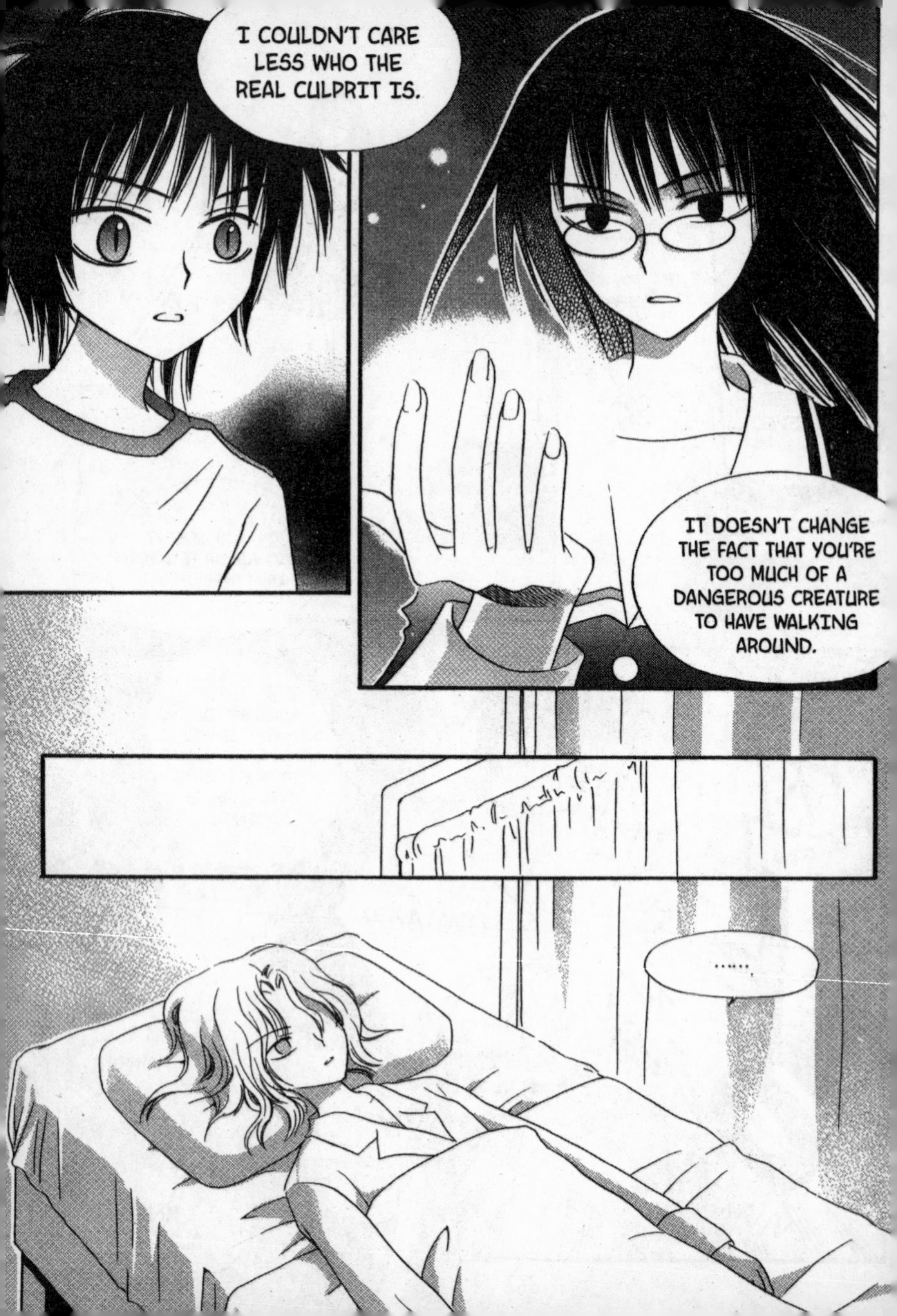
I COULDN'T CARE LESS WHO THE REAL CULPRIT IS.
IT DOESN'T CHANGE THE FACT THAT YOU'RE TOO MUCH OF A DANGEROUS CREATURE TO HAVE WALKING AROUND.
......

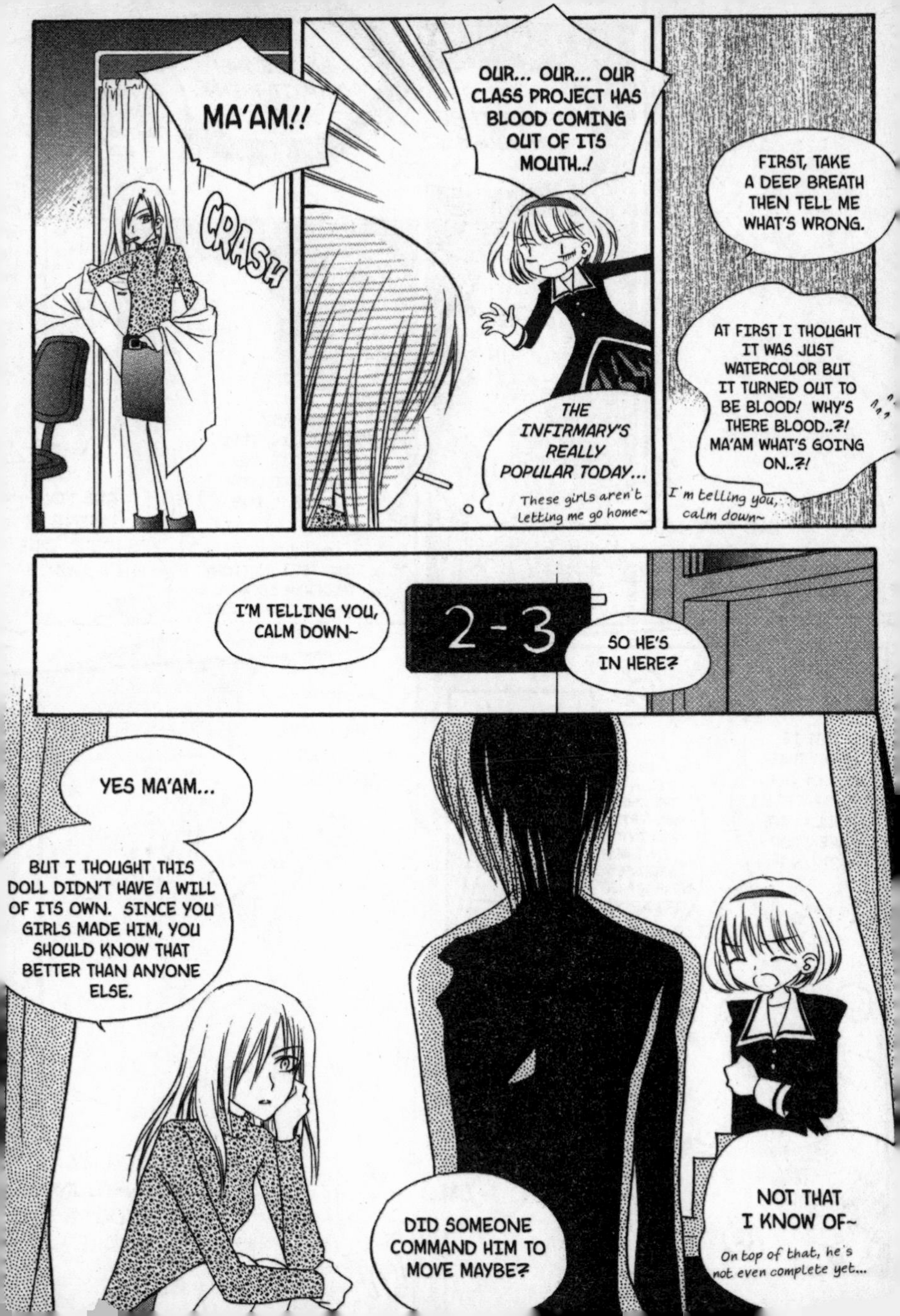
MA'AM!!
CRASH
OUR... OUR... OUR CLASS PROJECT HAS BLOOD COMING OUT OF ITS MOUTH..!
THE INFIRMARY'S REALLY POPULAR TODAY...
These girls aren't letting me go home~
FIRST, TAKE A DEEP BREATH THEN TELL ME WHAT'S WRONG.
AT FIRST I THOUGHT IT WAS JUST WATERCOLOR BUT IT TURNED OUT TO BE BLOOD! WHY'S THERE BLOOD..?! MA'AM WHAT'S GOING ON..?!
I'm telling you, calm down~
I'M TELLING YOU, CALM DOWN~
2-3
SO HE'S IN HERE?
YES MA'AM...
BUT I THOUGHT THIS DOLL DIDN'T HAVE A WILL OF ITS OWN. SINCE YOU GIRLS MADE HIM, YOU SHOULD KNOW THAT BETTER THAN ANYONE ELSE.
DID SOMEONE COMMAND HIM TO MOVE MAYBE?
NOT THAT I KNOW OF~
On top of that, he's not even complete yet...

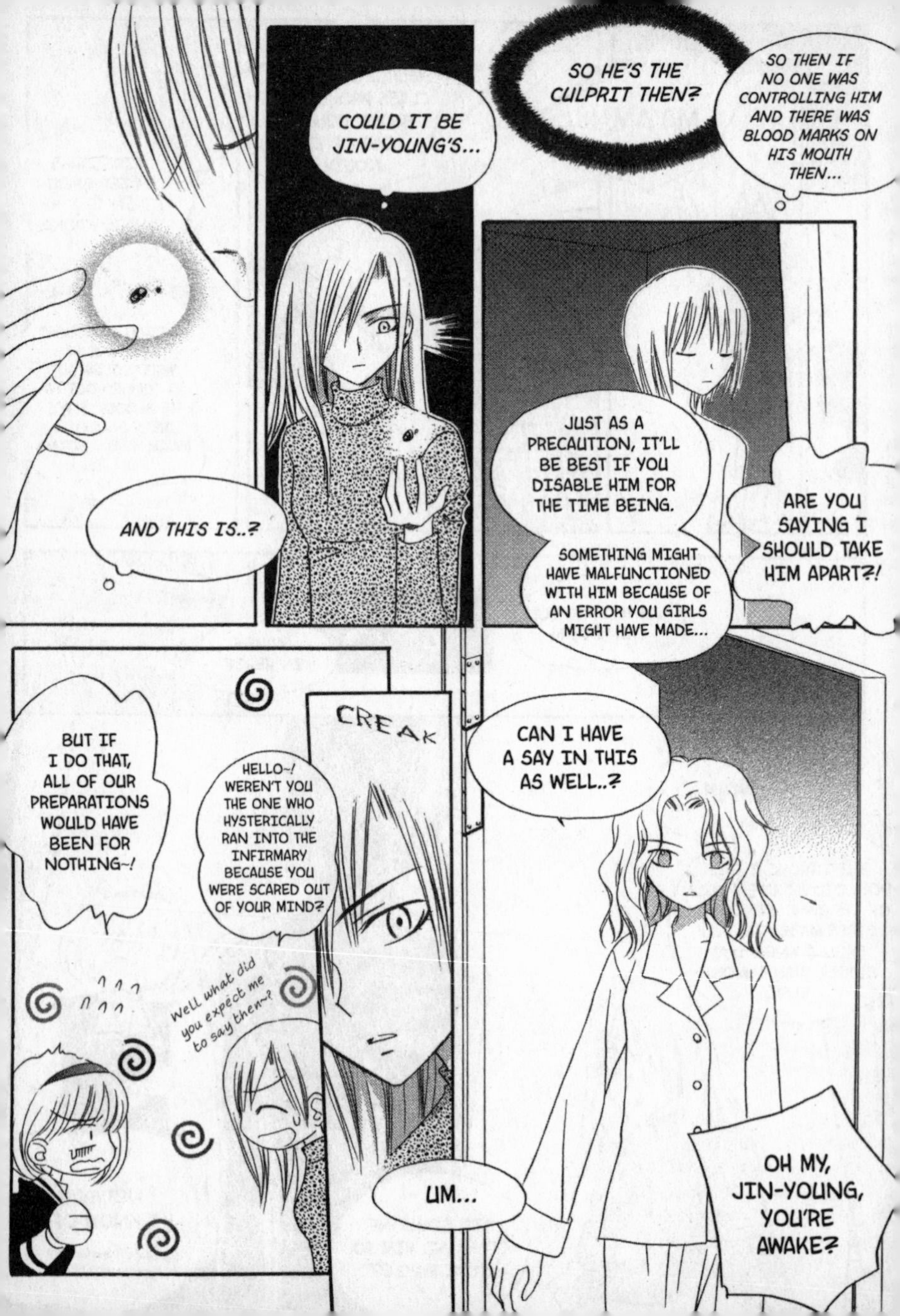
AND THIS IS..?
COULD IT BE JIN-YOUNG'S...
SO HE'S THE CULPRIT THEN?
SO THEN IF NO ONE WAS CONTROLLING HIM AND THERE WAS BLOOD MARKS ON HIS MOUTH THEN...
JUST AS A PRECAUTION, IT'LL BE BEST IF YOU DISABLE HIM FOR THE TIME BEING.
SOMETHING MIGHT HAVE MALFUNCTIONED WITH HIM BECAUSE OF AN ERROR YOU GIRLS MIGHT HAVE MADE...
ARE YOU SAYING I SHOULD TAKE HIM APART?!
BUT IF I DO THAT, ALL OF OUR PREPARATIONS WOULD HAVE BEEN FOR NOTHING~!
HELLO~! WEREN'T YOU THE ONE WHO HYSTERICALLY RAN INTO THE INFIRMARY BECAUSE YOU WERE SCARED OUT OF YOUR MIND?
Well what did you expect me to say then~?
CREAK
UM...
CAN I HAVE A SAY IN THIS AS WELL..?
OH MY, JIN-YOUNG, YOU'RE AWAKE?

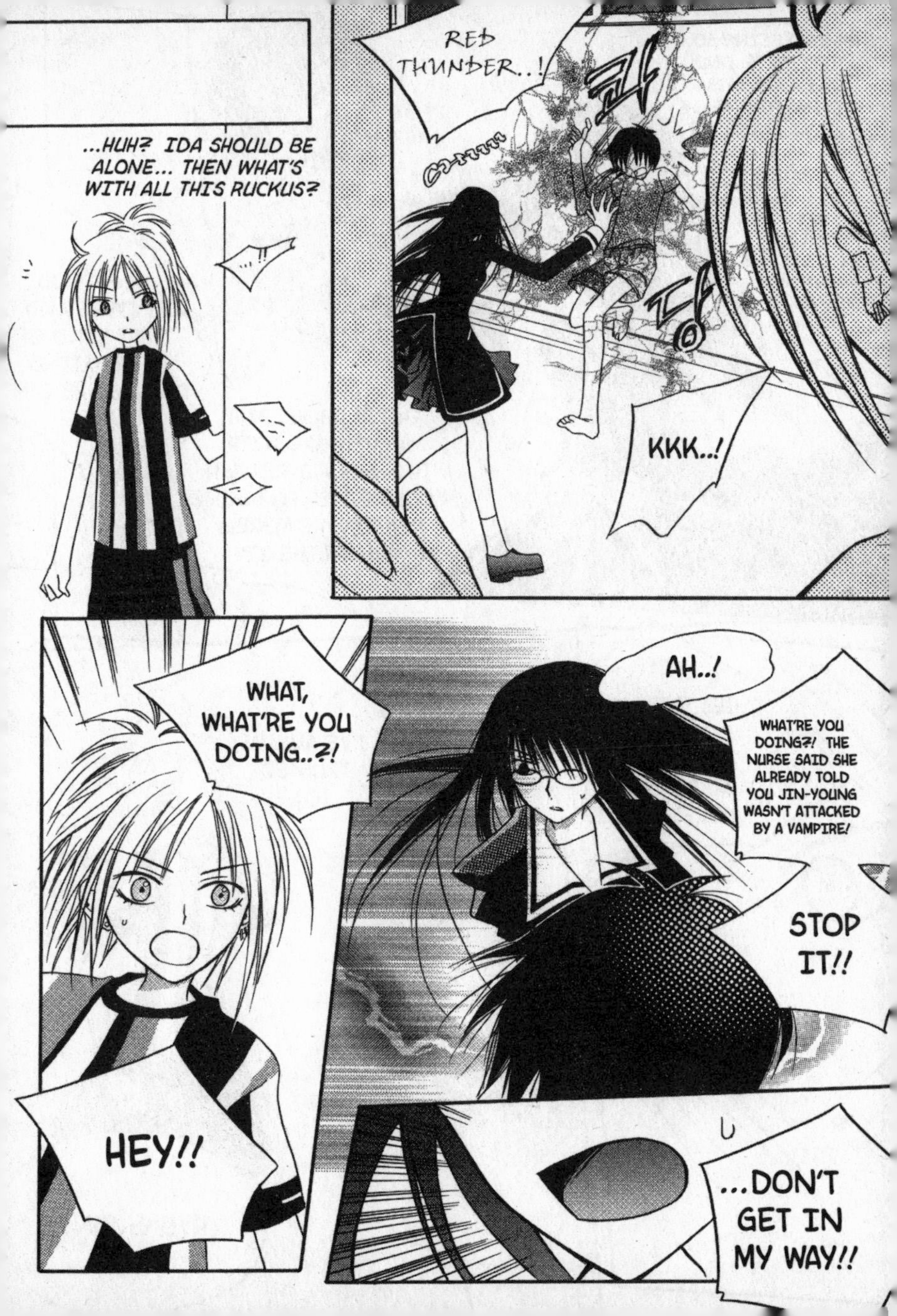
...HUH? IDA SHOULD BE ALONE... THEN WHAT'S WITH ALL THIS RUCKUS?
...!!
RED THUNDER..!
KKK..!
WHAT, WHAT'RE YOU DOING..?!
HEY!!
AH..!
WHAT'RE YOU DOING?! THE NURSE SAID SHE ALREADY TOLD YOU JIN-YOUNG WASN'T ATTACKED BY A VAMPIRE!
STOP IT!!
...DON'T GET IN MY WAY!!

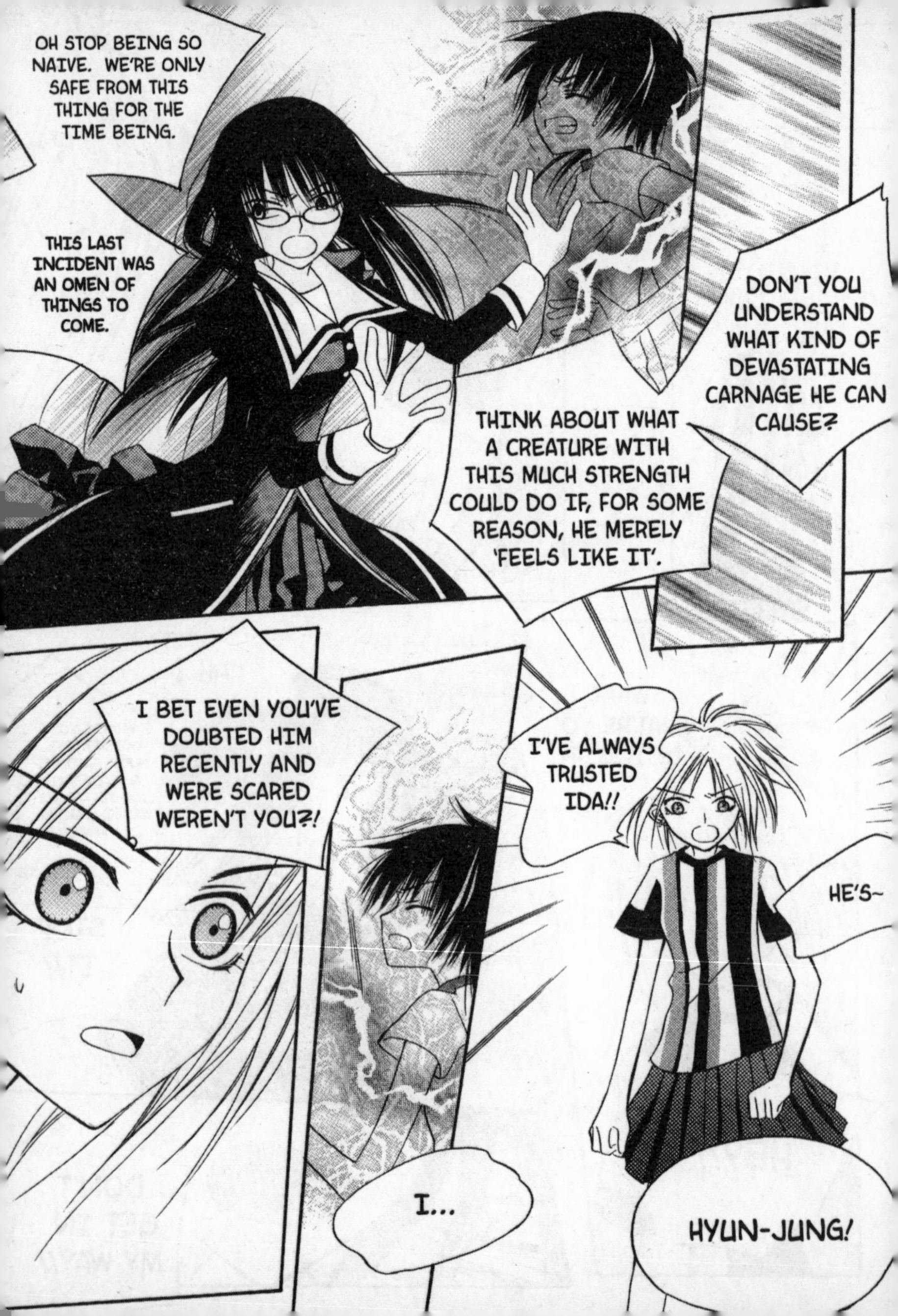
OH STOP BEING SO NAIVE. WE'RE ONLY SAFE FROM THIS THING FOR THE TIME BEING.
THIS LAST INCIDENT WAS AN OMEN OF THINGS TO COME.
DON'T YOU UNDERSTAND WHAT KIND OF DEVASTATING CARNAGE HE CAN CAUSE?
THINK ABOUT WHAT A CREATURE WITH THIS MUCH STRENGTH COULD DO IF, FOR SOME REASON, HE MERELY 'FEELS LIKE IT'.
I BET EVEN YOU'VE DOUBTED HIM RECENTLY AND WERE SCARED WEREN'T YOU?!
I'VE ALWAYS TRUSTED IDA!!
HE'S~
I...
HYUN-JUNG!

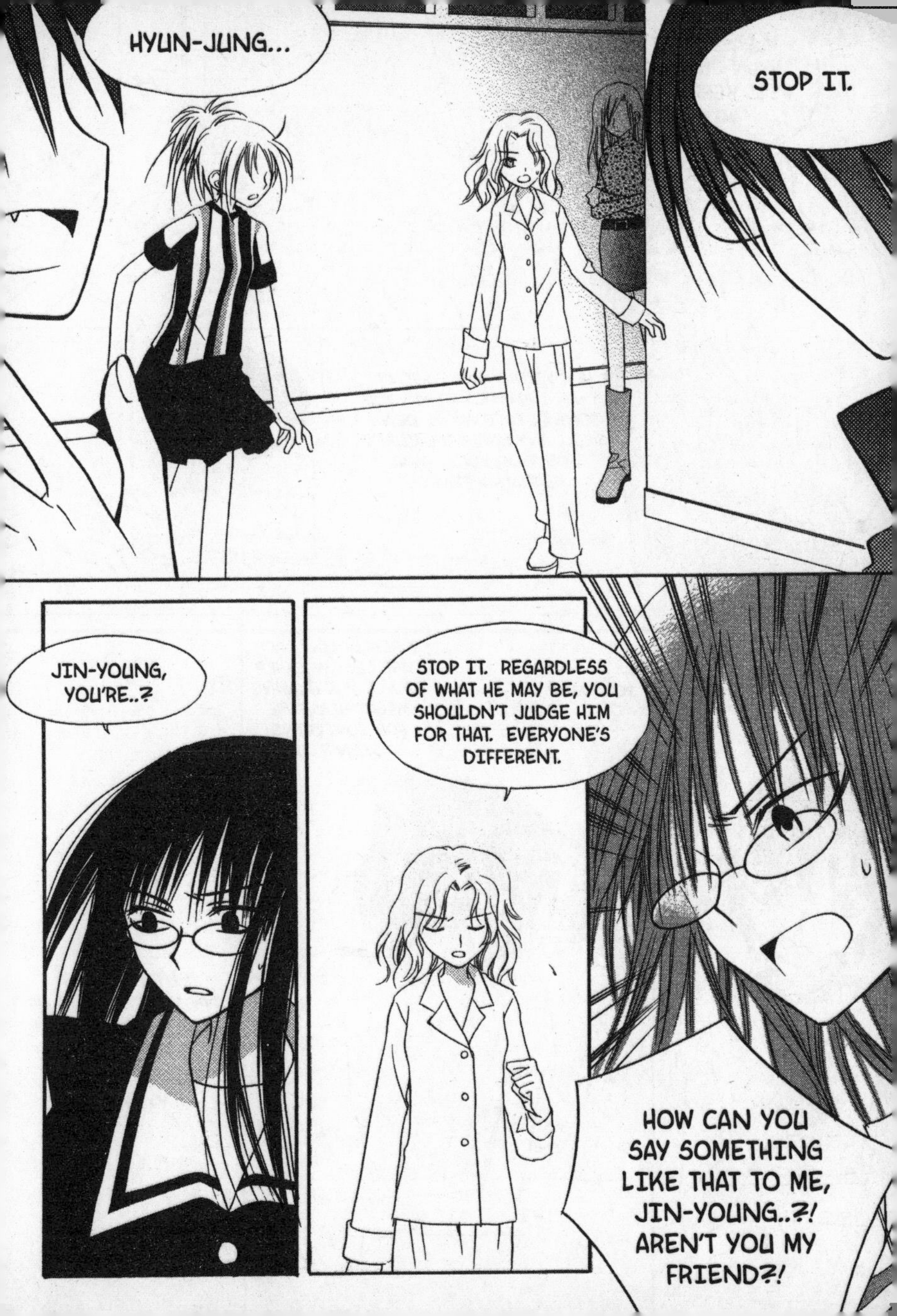
HYUN-JUNG...
STOP IT.
JIN-YOUNG, YOU'RE..?
STOP IT. REGARDLESS OF WHAT HE MAY BE, YOU SHOULDN'T JUDGE HIM FOR THAT. EVERYONE'S DIFFERENT.
HOW CAN YOU SAY SOMETHING LIKE THAT TO ME, JIN-YOUNG..?! AREN'T YOU MY FRIEND?!

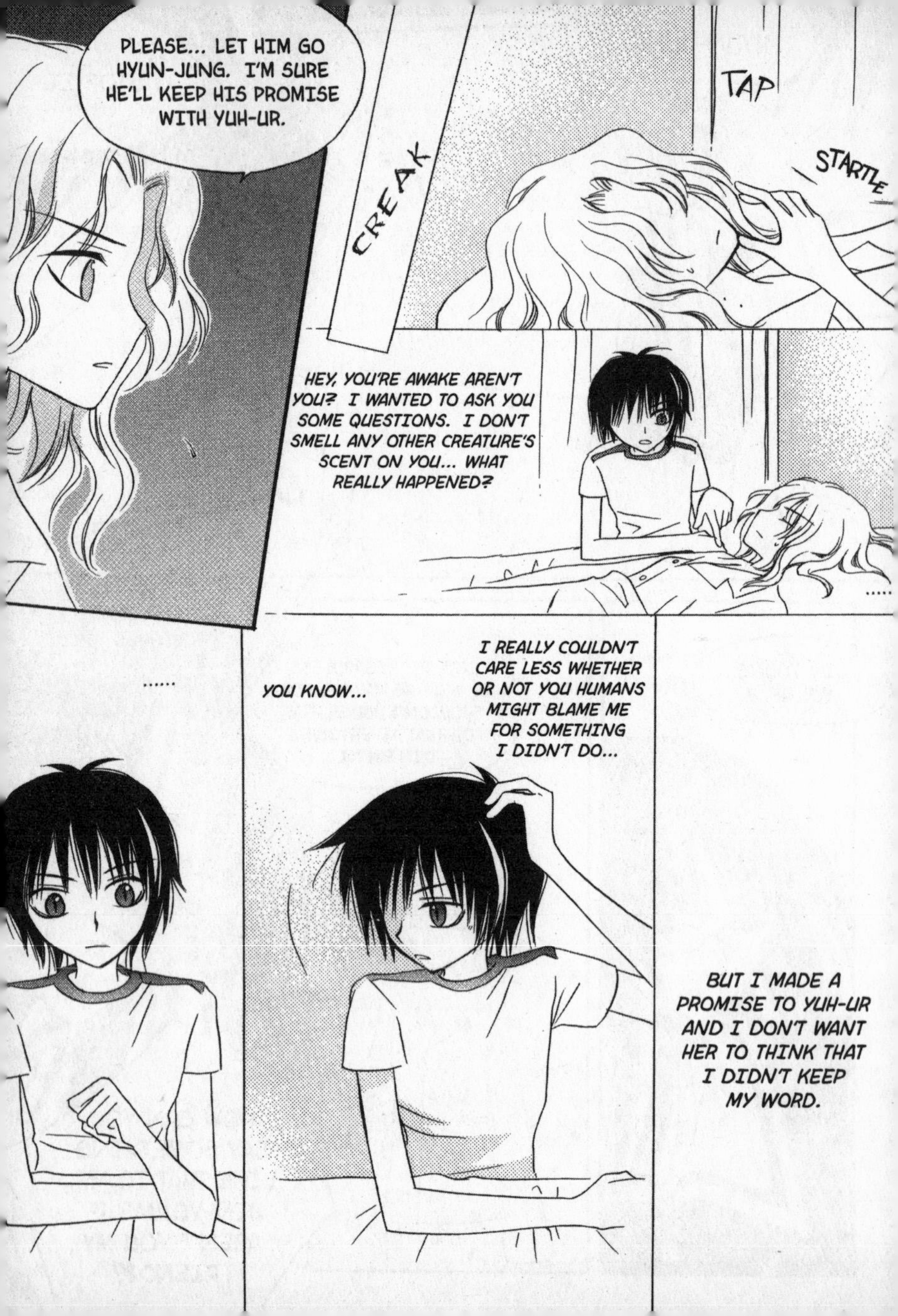
PLEASE... LET HIM GO HYUN-JUNG. I'M SURE HE'LL KEEP HIS PROMISE WITH YUH-UR.
CREAK
TAP
STARTLE
HEY, YOU'RE AWAKE AREN'T YOU? I WANTED TO ASK YOU SOME QUESTIONS. I DON'T SMELL ANY OTHER CREATURE'S SCENT ON YOU... WHAT REALLY HAPPENED?
.....
......
YOU KNOW...
I REALLY COULDN'T CARE LESS WHETHER OR NOT YOU HUMANS MIGHT BLAME ME FOR SOMETHING I DIDN'T DO...
BUT I MADE A PROMISE TO YUH-UR AND I DON'T WANT HER TO THINK THAT I DIDN'T KEEP MY WORD.

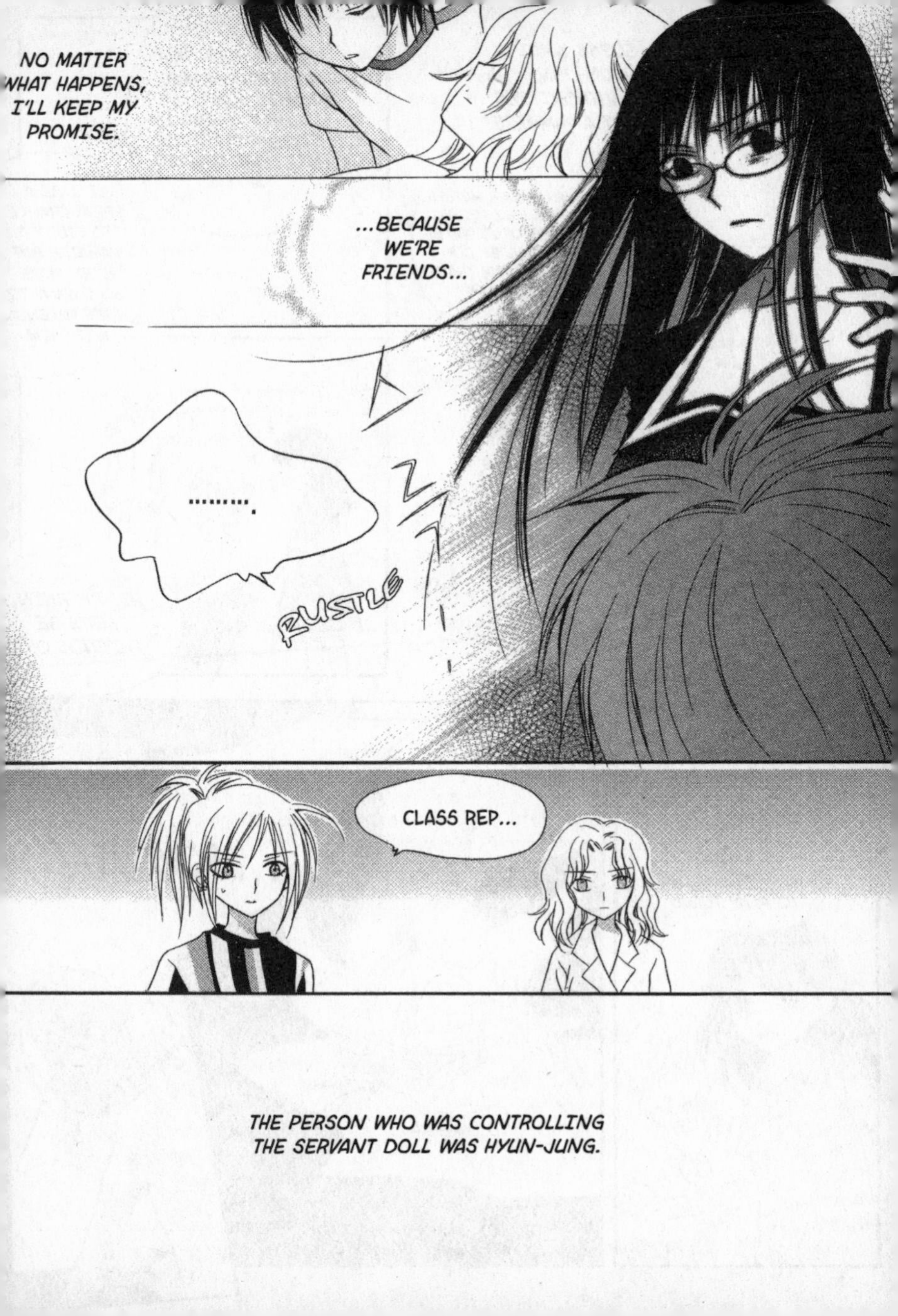
NO MATTER WHAT HAPPENS, I'LL KEEP MY PROMISE.
...BECAUSE WE'RE FRIENDS...
....
RUSTLE
CLASS REP...
THE PERSON WHO WAS CONTROLLING THE SERVANT DOLL WAS HYUN-JUNG.

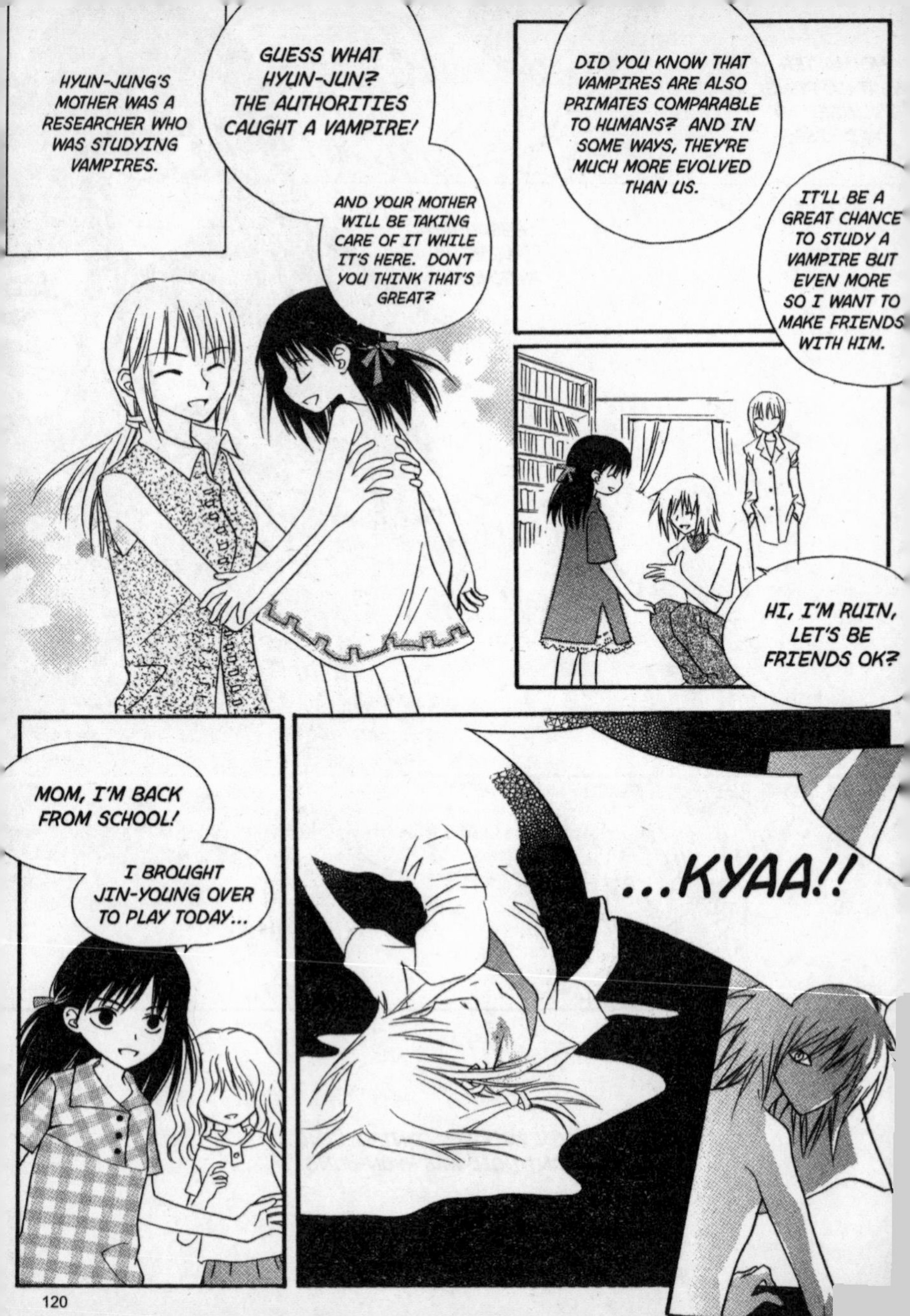
HYUN-JUNG'S MOTHER WAS A RESEARCHER WHO WAS STUDYING VAMPIRES.
GUESS WHAT HYUN-JUN? THE AUTHORITIES CAUGHT A VAMPIRE!
AND YOUR MOTHER WILL BE TAKING CARE OF IT WHILE IT'S HERE. DON'T YOU THINK THAT'S GREAT?
DID YOU KNOW THAT VAMPIRES ARE ALSO PRIMATES COMPARABLE TO HUMANS? AND IN SOME WAYS, THEY'RE MUCH MORE EVOLVED THAN US.
IT'LL BE A GREAT CHANCE TO STUDY A VAMPIRE BUT EVEN MORE SO I WANT TO MAKE FRIENDS WITH HIM.
HI, I'M RUIN, LET'S BE FRIENDS OK?
MOM, I'M BACK FROM SCHOOL!
I BROUGHT JIN-YOUNG OVER TO PLAY TODAY...
...KYAA!!

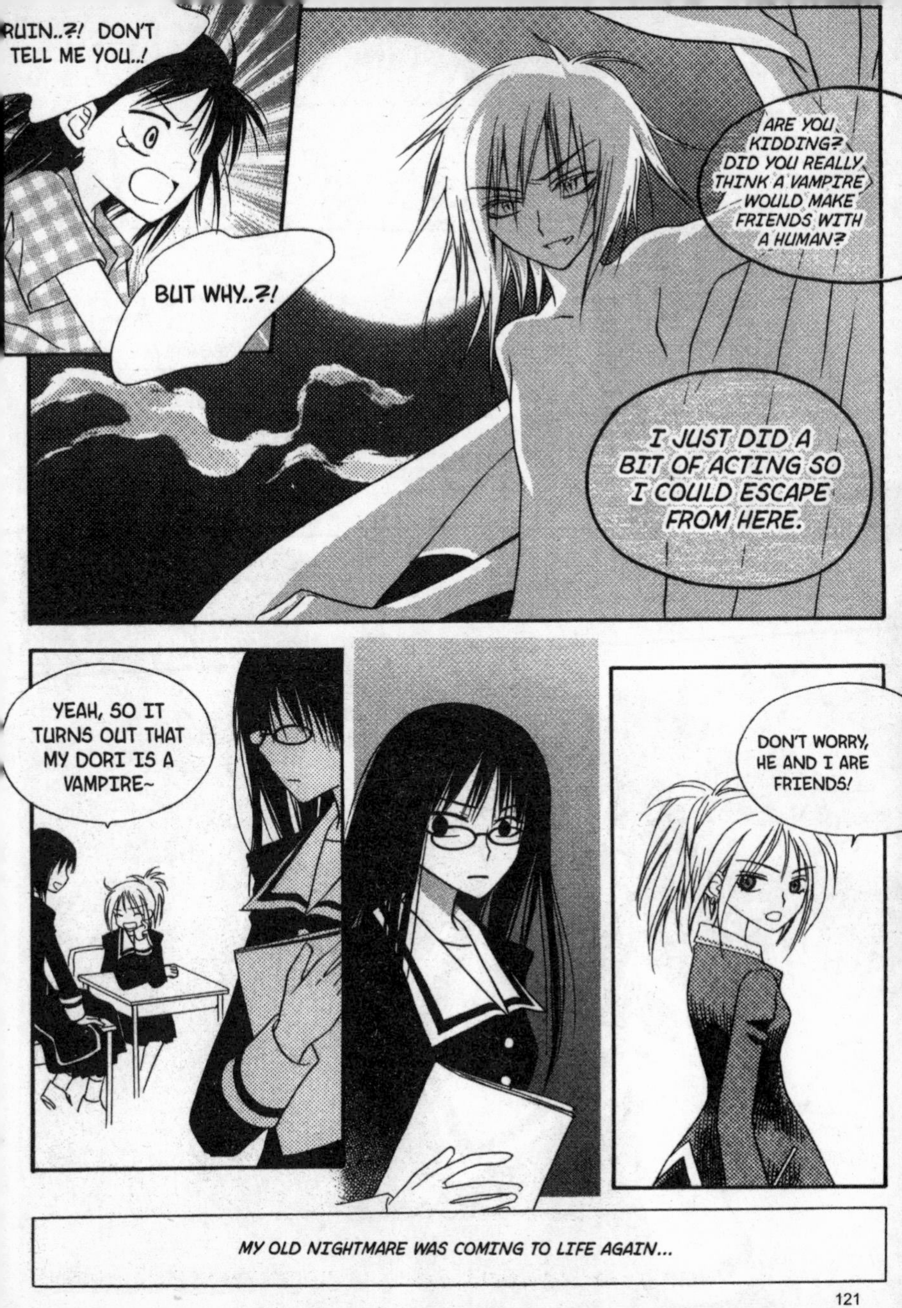

RUIN..?! DON'T TELL ME YOU..!
BUT WHY..?!
ARE YOU KIDDING? DID YOU REALLY THINK A VAMPIRE WOULD MAKE FRIENDS WITH A HUMAN?
I JUST DID A BIT OF ACTING SO I COULD ESCAPE FROM HERE.
YEAH, SO IT TURNS OUT THAT MY DORI IS A VAMPIRE~
DON'T WORRY, HE AND I ARE FRIENDS!
MY OLD NIGHTMARE WAS COMING TO LIFE AGAIN...

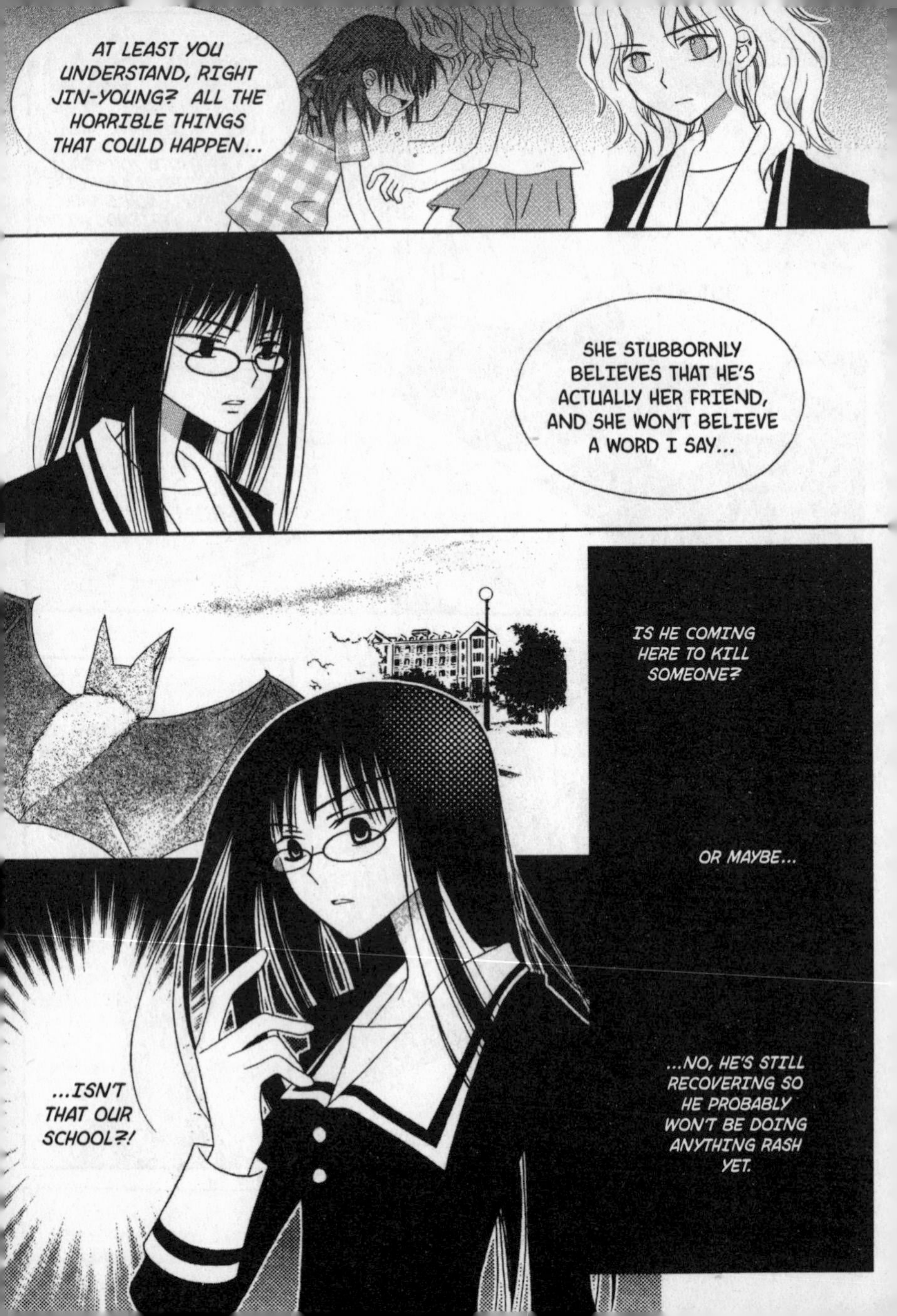
AT LEAST YOU UNDERSTAND, RIGHT JIN-YOUNG? ALL THE HORRIBLE THINGS THAT COULD HAPPEN...
SHE STUBBORNLY BELIEVES THAT HE'S ACTUALLY HER FRIEND, AND SHE WON'T BELIEVE A WORD I SAY...
IS HE COMING HERE TO KILL SOMEONE?
OR MAYBE...
...ISN'T THAT OUR SCHOOL?!
...NO, HE'S STILL RECOVERING SO HE PROBABLY WON'T BE DOING ANYTHING RASH YET.

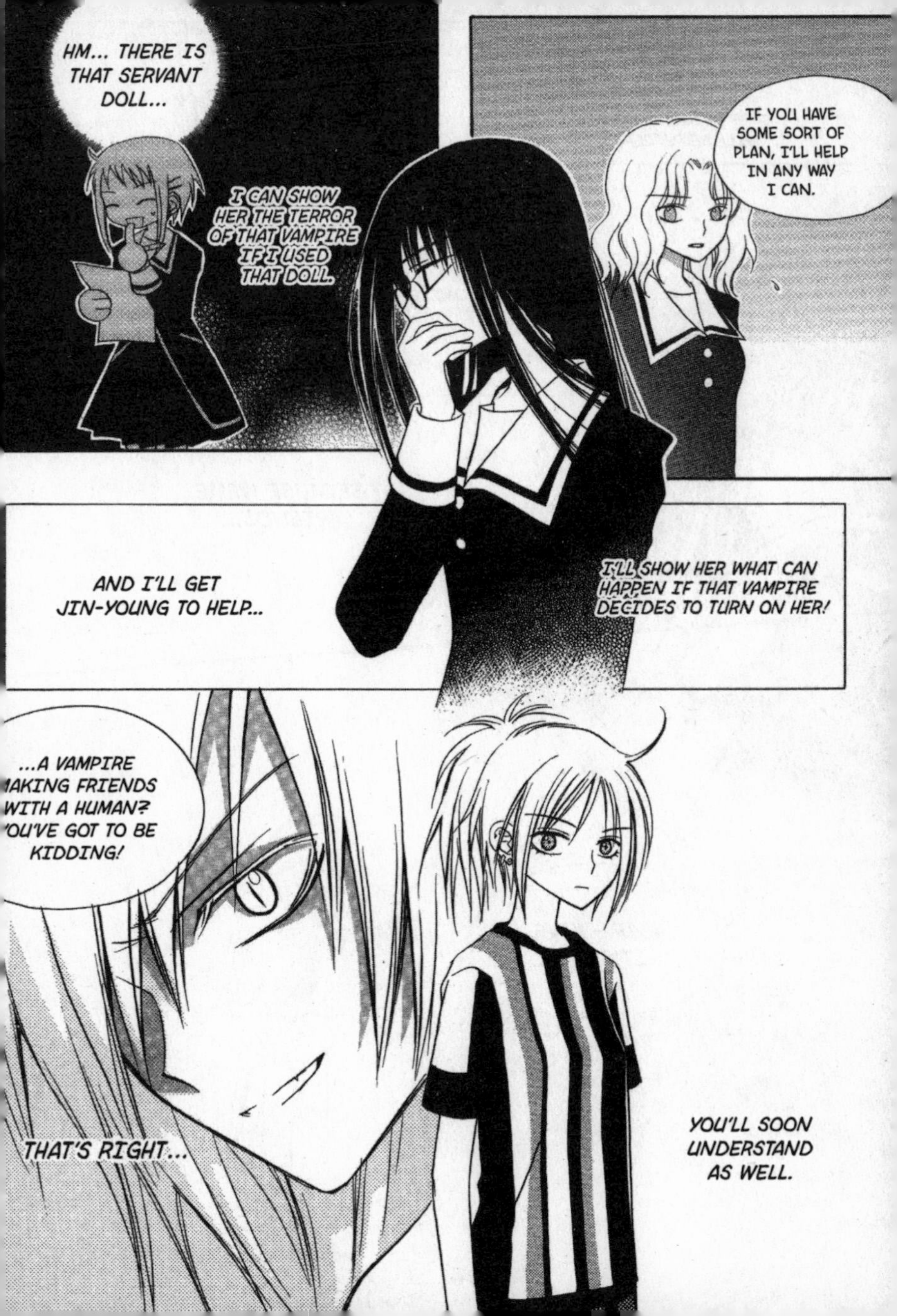
HM... THERE IS THAT SERVANT DOLL...
I CAN SHOW HER THE TERROR OF THAT VAMPIRE IF I USED THAT DOLL.
IF YOU HAVE SOME SORT OF PLAN, I'LL HELP IN ANY WAY I CAN.
AND I'LL GET JIN-YOUNG TO HELP...
I'LL SHOW HER WHAT CAN HAPPEN IF THAT VAMPIRE DECIDES TO TURN ON HER!
...A VAMPIRE AKING FRIENDS WITH A HUMAN? OU'VE GOT TO BE KIDDING!
THAT'S RIGHT...
YOU'LL SOON UNDERSTAND AS WELL.

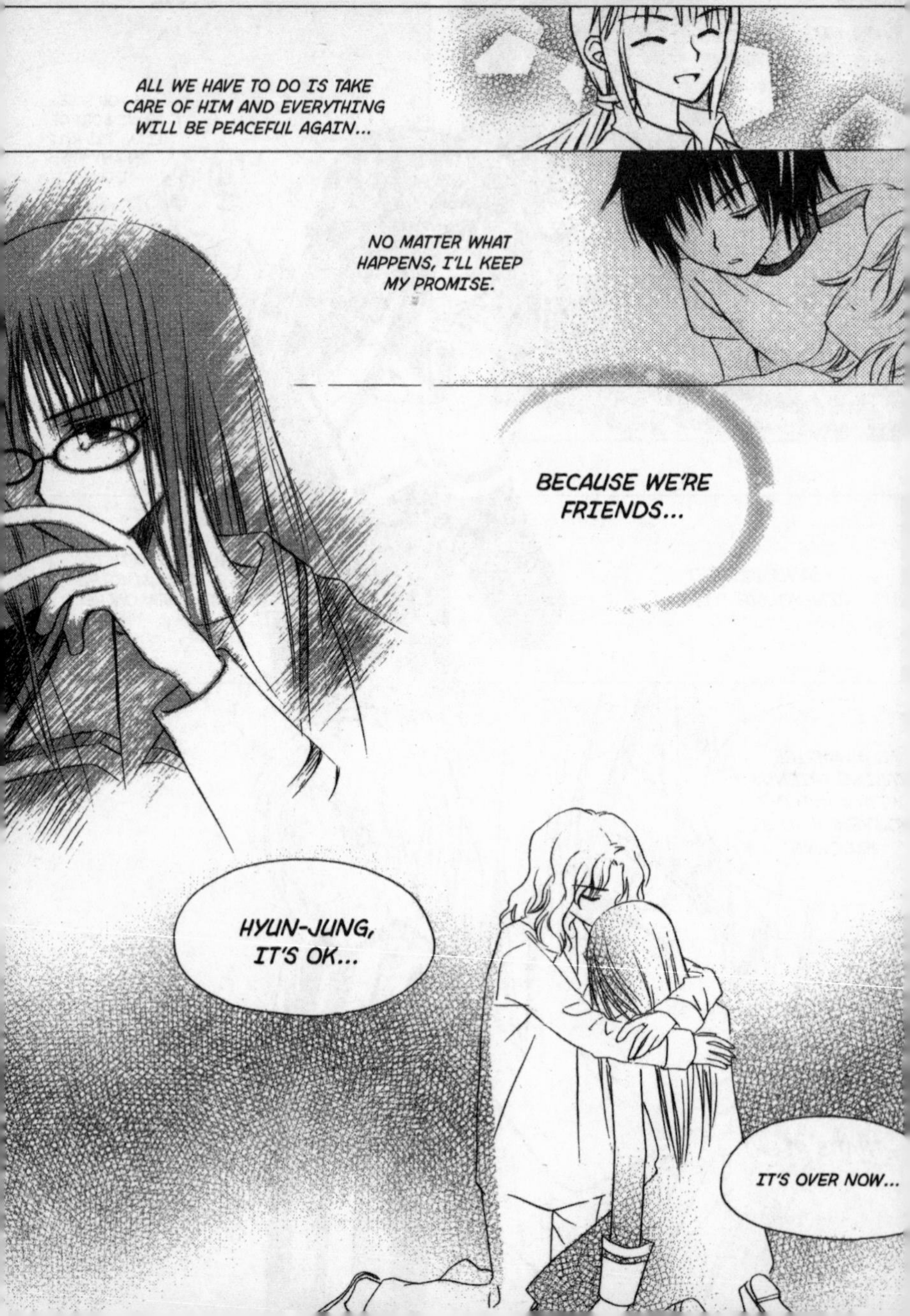
ALL WE HAVE TO DO IS TAKE CARE OF HIM AND EVERYTHING WILL BE PEACEFUL AGAIN...
NO MATTER WHAT HAPPENS, I'LL KEEP MY PROMISE.
BECAUSE WE'RE FRIENDS...
HYUN-JUNG, IT'S OK...
IT'S OVER NOW...

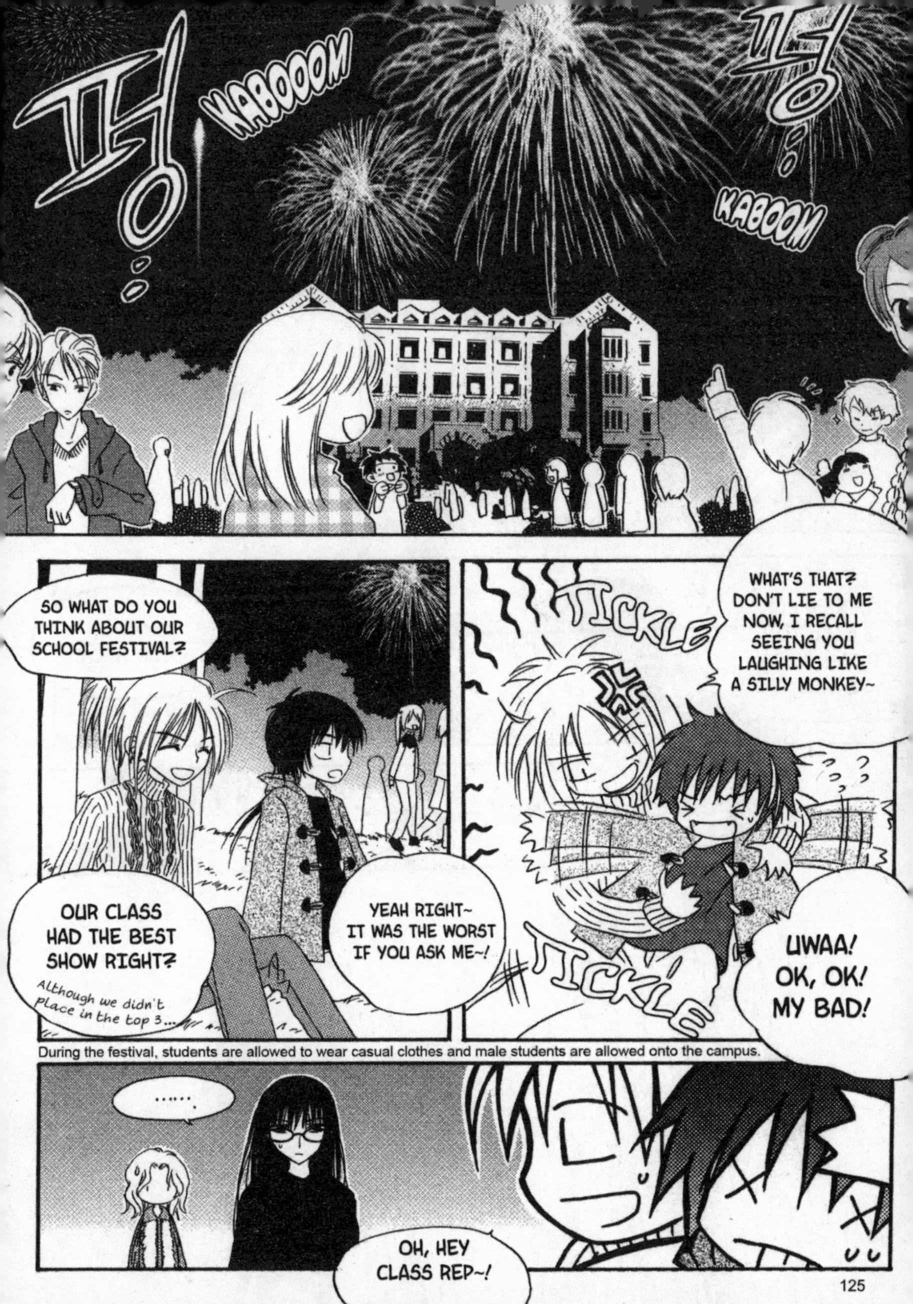
펑
KABOOOM
펑
KABOOM
SO WHAT DO YOU THINK ABOUT OUR SCHOOL FESTIVAL?
OUR CLASS HAD THE BEST SHOW RIGHT?
Although we didn't place in the top 3...
YEAH RIGHT~ IT WAS THE WORST IF YOU ASK ME~!
WHAT'S THAT? DON'T LIE TO ME NOW, I RECALL SEEING YOU LAUGHING LIKE A SILLY MONKEY~
TICKLE
TICKLE
UWAA! OK, OK! MY BAD!
During the festival, students are allowed to wear casual clothes and male students are allowed onto the campus.
......
OH, HEY CLASS REP~!

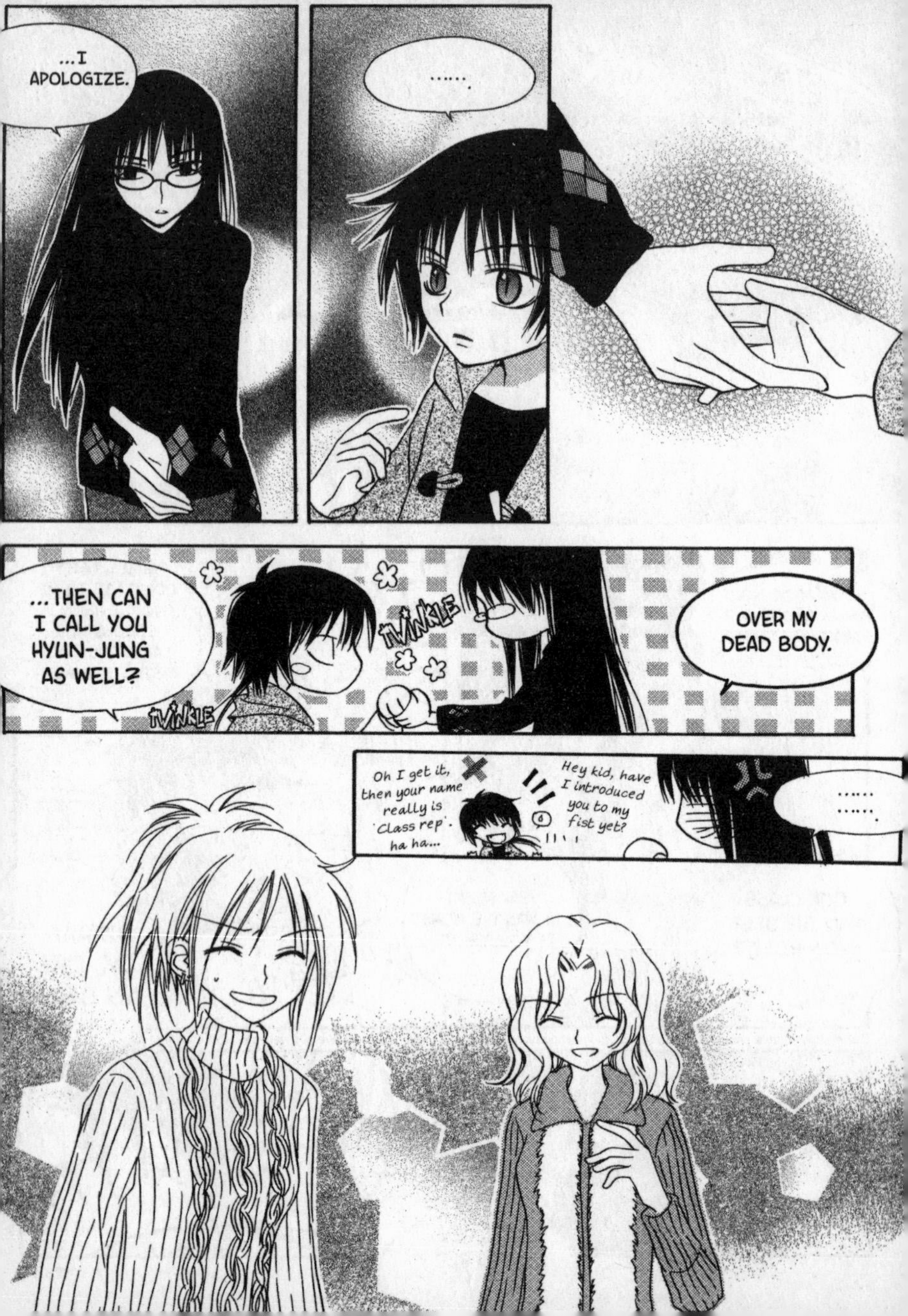
...I APOLOGIZE.
....
...THEN CAN I CALL YOU HYUN-JUNG AS WELL?
TWINKLE
TWINKLE
OVER MY DEAD BODY.
Oh I get it, then your name really is 'Class rep'. ha ha...
Hey kid, have I introduced you to my fist yet?
....

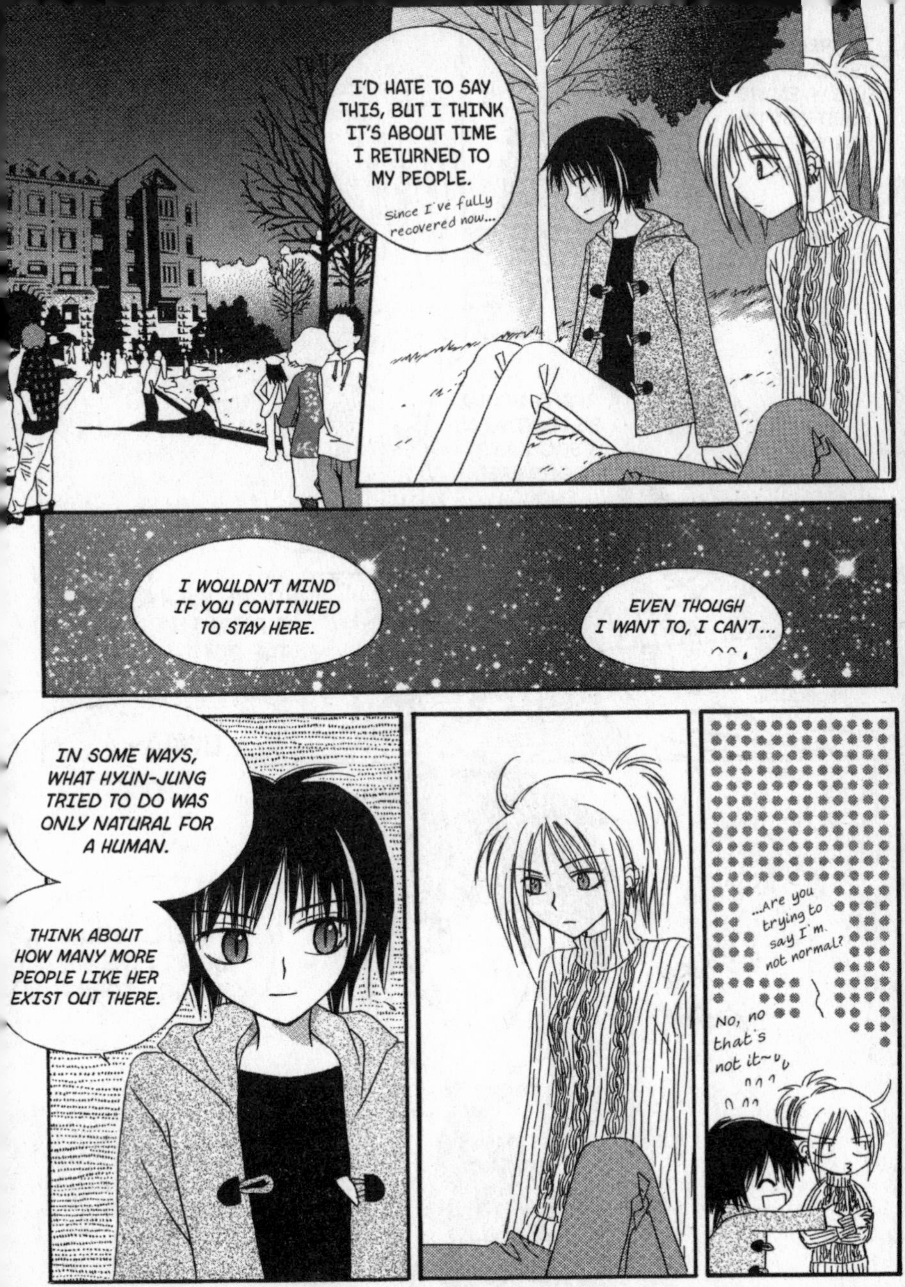
I'D HATE TO SAY THIS, BUT I THINK IT'S ABOUT TIME I RETURNED TO MY PEOPLE.
Since I've fully recovered now...
I WOULDN'T MIND IF YOU CONTINUED TO STAY HERE.
EVEN THOUGH I WANT TO, I CAN'T...
IN SOME WAYS, WHAT HYUN-JUNG TRIED TO DO WAS ONLY NATURAL FOR A HUMAN.
THINK ABOUT HOW MANY MORE PEOPLE LIKE HER EXIST OUT THERE.
...Are you trying to say I'm not normal?
No, no that's not it~

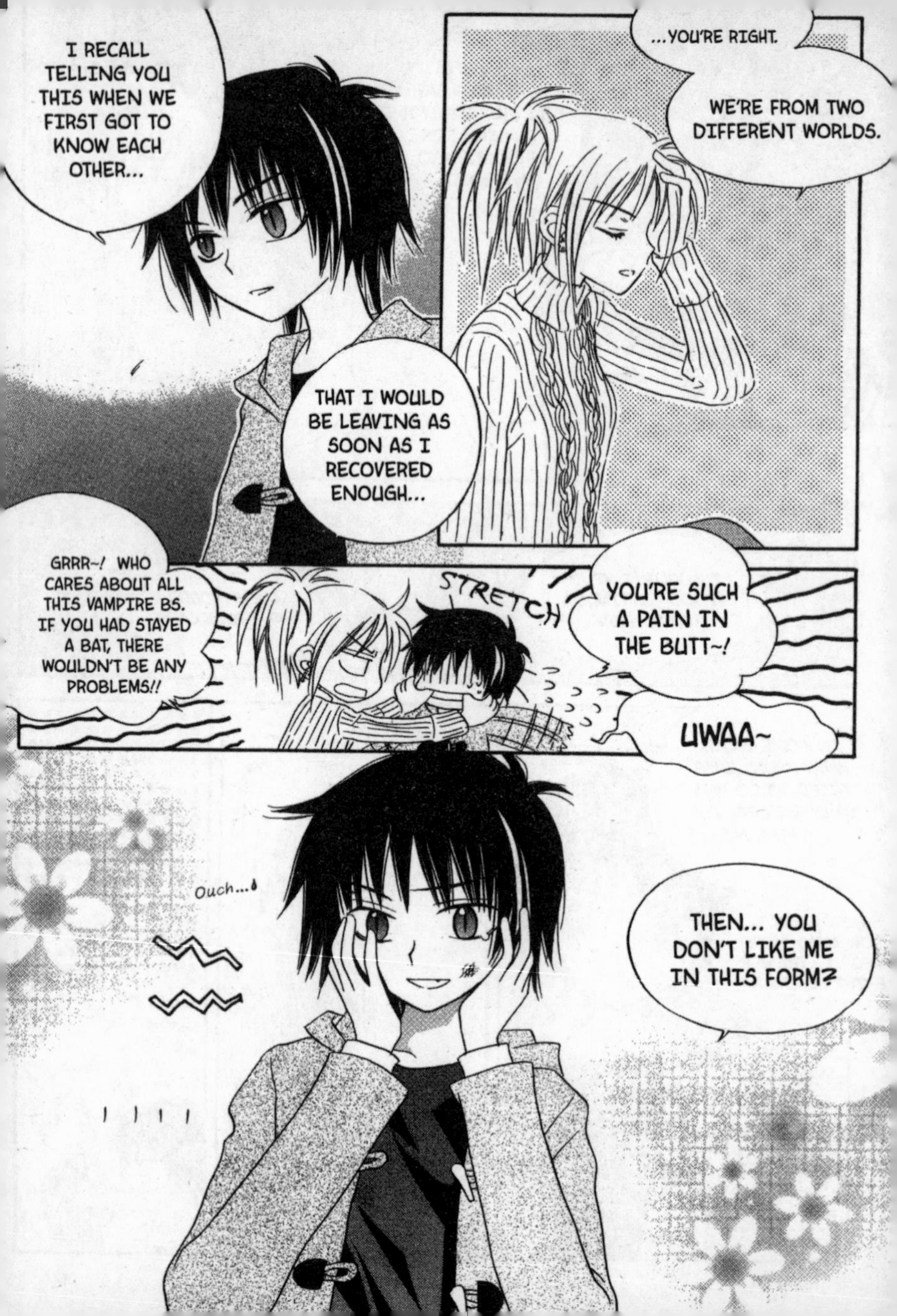
I RECALL TELLING YOU THIS WHEN WE FIRST GOT TO KNOW EACH OTHER...
THAT I WOULD BE LEAVING AS SOON AS I RECOVERED ENOUGH...
...YOU'RE RIGHT.
WE'RE FROM TWO DIFFERENT WORLDS.
GRRR~! WHO CARES ABOUT ALL THIS VAMPIRE BS. IF YOU HAD STAYED A BAT, THERE WOULDN'T BE ANY PROBLEMS!!
STRETCH
YOU'RE SUCH A PAIN IN THE BUTT~!
UWAA~
Ouch...
THEN... YOU DON'T LIKE ME IN THIS FORM?

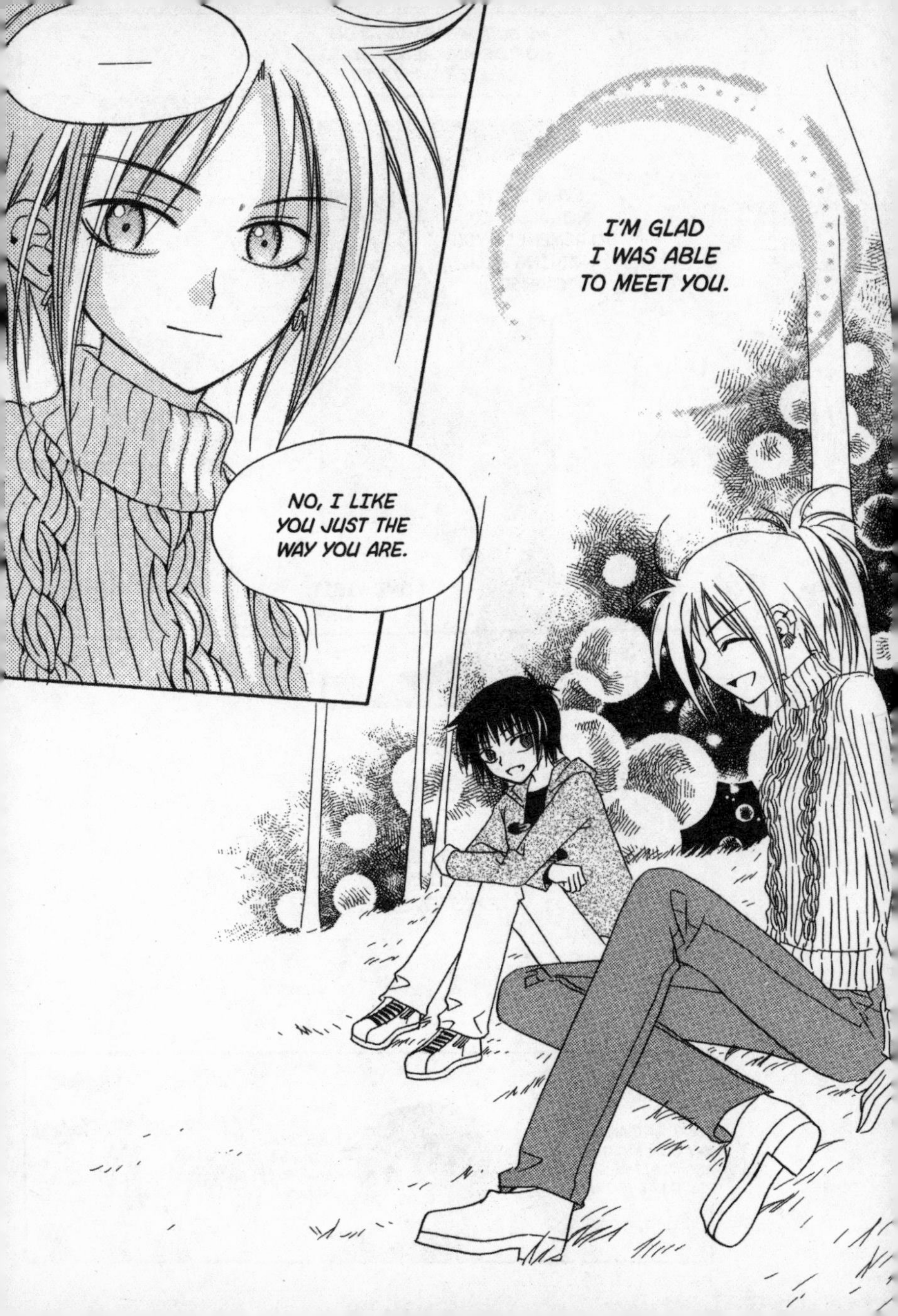
—
NO, I LIKE YOU JUST THE WAY YOU ARE.
I'M GLAD I WAS ABLE TO MEET YOU.

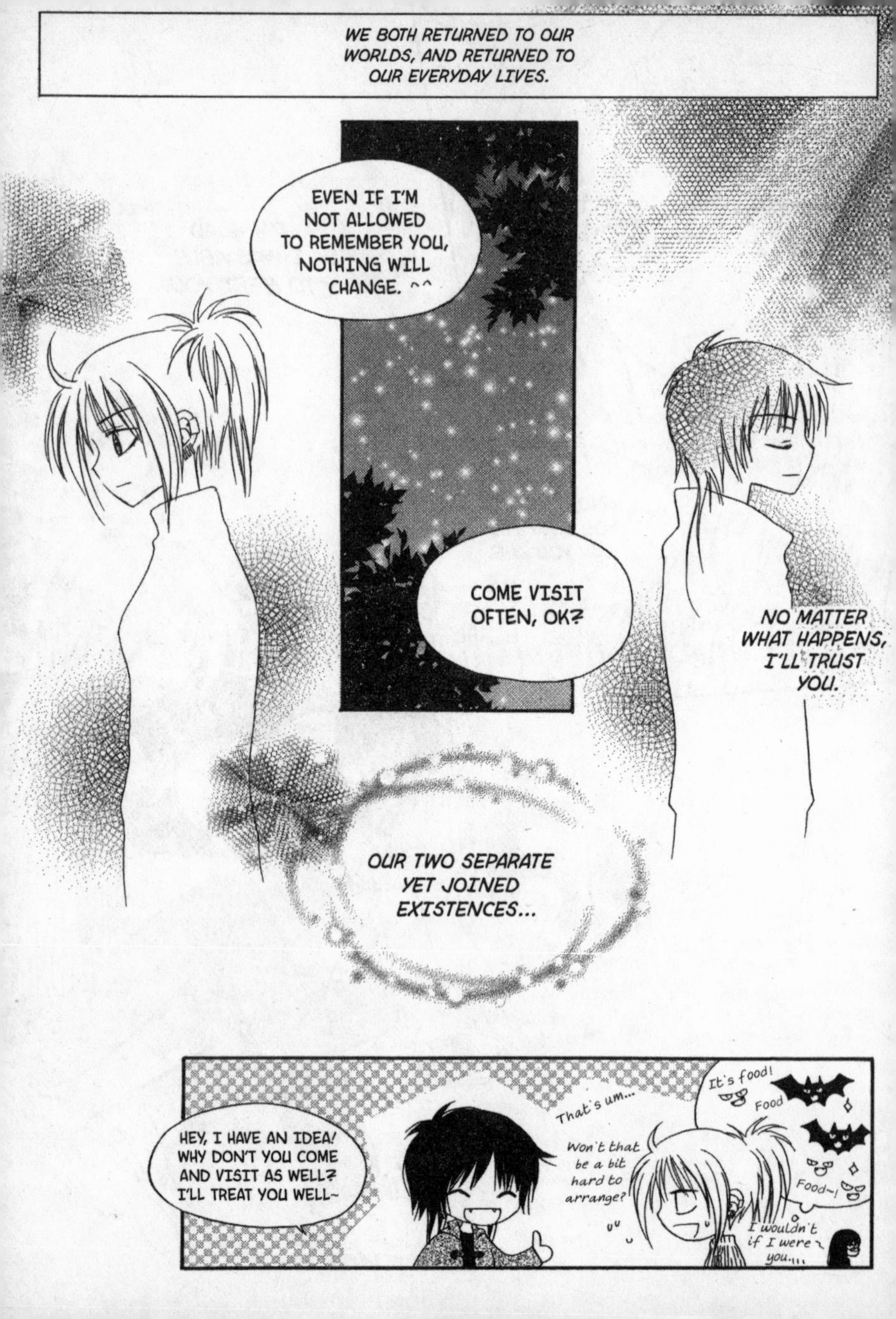
WE BOTH RETURNED TO OUR WORLDS, AND RETURNED TO OUR EVERYDAY LIVES.
EVEN IF I'M NOT ALLOWED TO REMEMBER YOU, NOTHING WILL CHANGE. ^^
COME VISIT OFTEN, OK?
NO MATTER WHAT HAPPENS, I'LL TRUST YOU.
OUR TWO SEPARATE YET JOINED EXISTENCES...
HEY, I HAVE AN IDEA! WHY DON'T YOU COME AND VISIT AS WELL? I'LL TREAT YOU WELL~
That's um...
Won't that be a bit hard to arrange?
It's food!
Food
Food~!
I wouldn't if I were you...

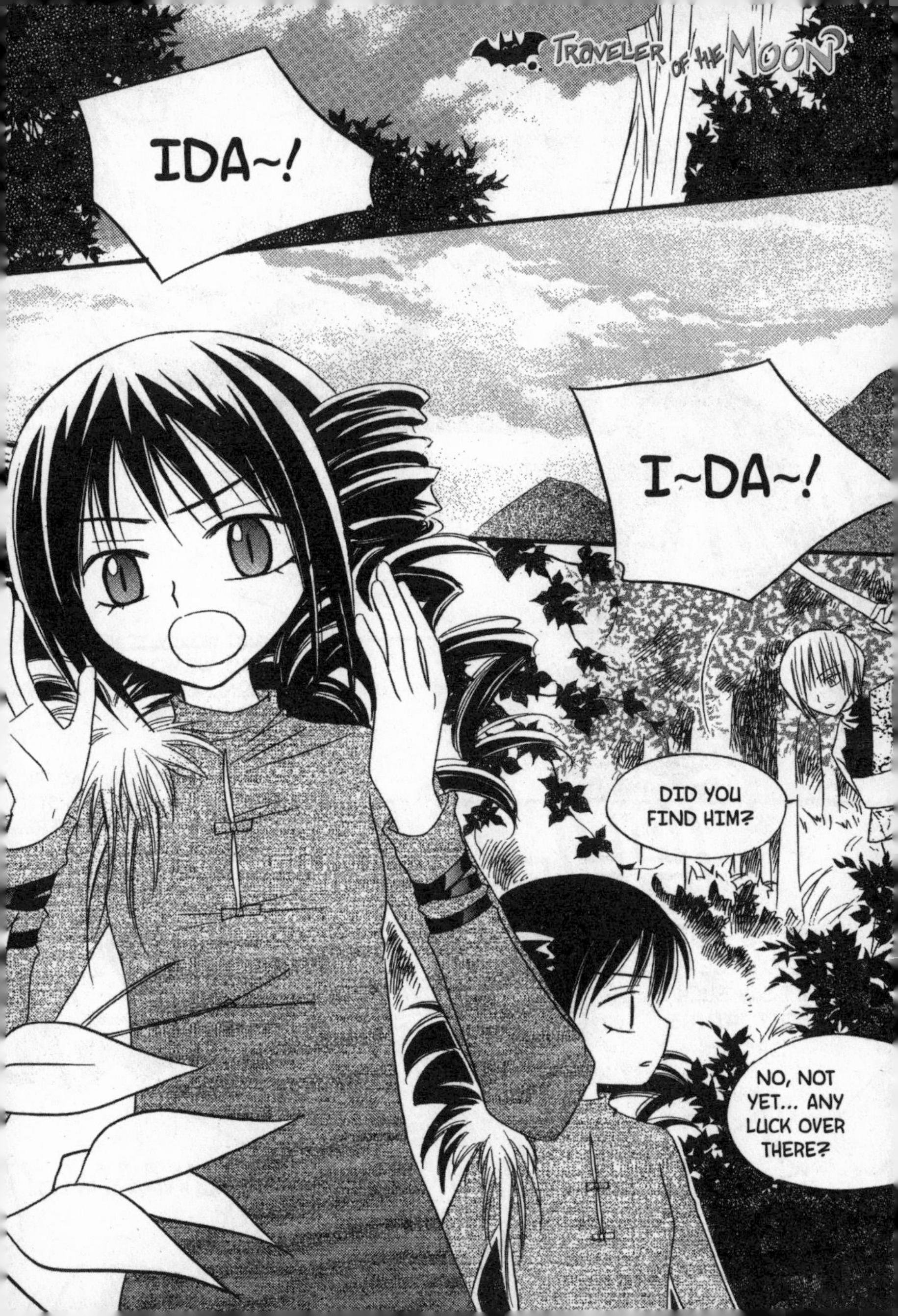
IDA~!
I~DA~!
DID YOU FIND HIM?
NO, NOT YET... ANY LUCK OVER THERE?

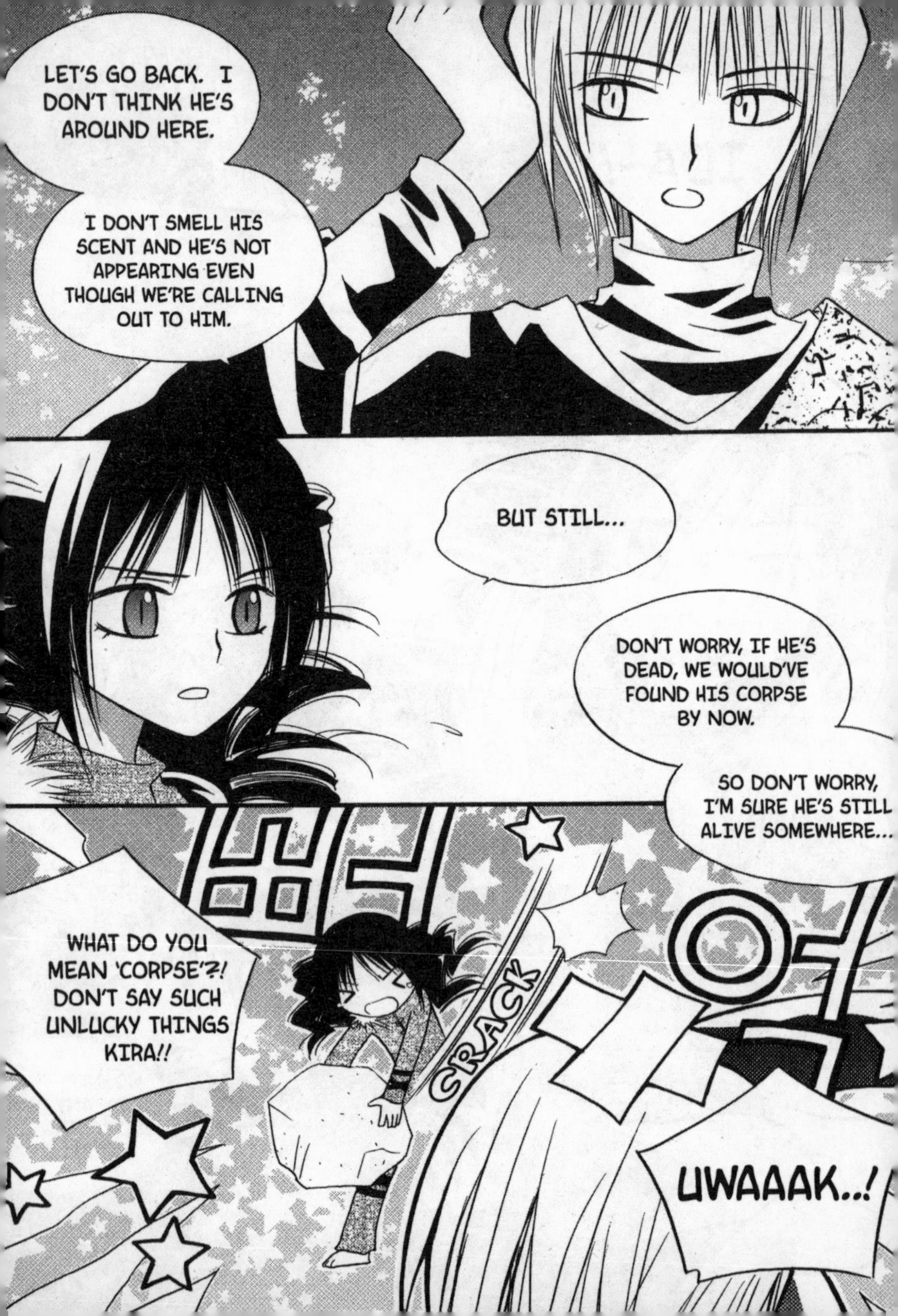
LET'S GO BACK. I DON'T THINK HE'S AROUND HERE.
I DON'T SMELL HIS SCENT AND HE'S NOT APPEARING EVEN THOUGH WE'RE CALLING OUT TO HIM.
BUT STILL...
DON'T WORRY, IF HE'S DEAD, WE WOULD'VE FOUND HIS CORPSE BY NOW.
SO DON'T WORRY, I'M SURE HE'S STILL ALIVE SOMEWHERE...
WHAT DO YOU MEAN 'CORPSE'?! DON'T SAY SUCH UNLUCKY THINGS KIRA!!
CRACK
UWAAAK..!

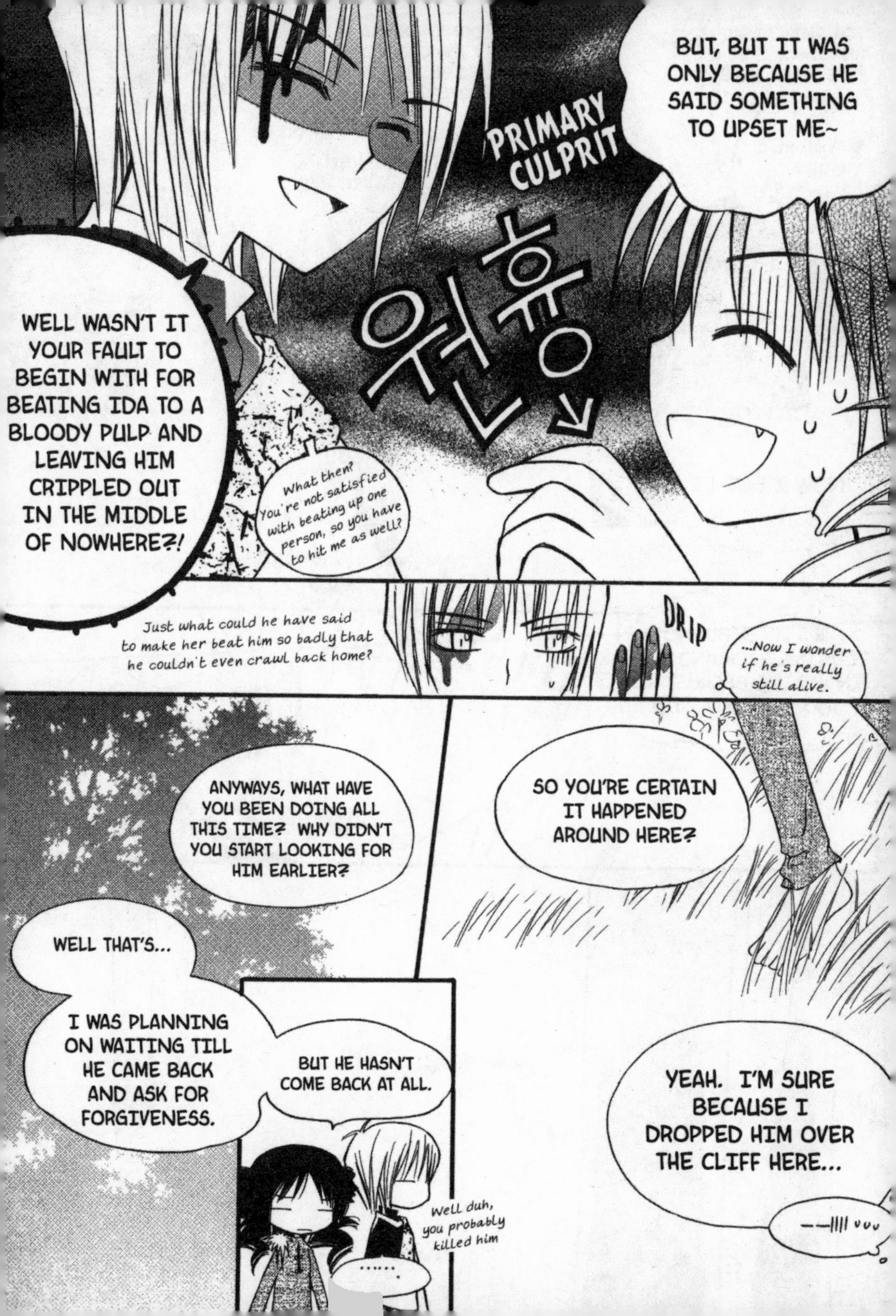
BUT, BUT IT WAS ONLY BECAUSE HE SAID SOMETHING TO UPSET ME~
PRIMARY CULPRIT
원흉
WELL WASN'T IT YOUR FAULT TO BEGIN WITH FOR BEATING IDA TO A BLOODY PULP AND LEAVING HIM CRIPPLED OUT IN THE MIDDLE OF NOWHERE?!
What then? You're not satisfied with beating up one person, so you have to hit me as well?
Just what could he have said to make her beat him so badly that he couldn't even crawl back home?
DRIP
...Now I wonder if he's really still alive.
ANYWAYS, WHAT HAVE YOU BEEN DOING ALL THIS TIME? WHY DIDN'T YOU START LOOKING FOR HIM EARLIER?
WELL THAT'S...
I WAS PLANNING ON WAITING TILL HE CAME BACK AND ASK FOR FORGIVENESS.
BUT HE HASN'T COME BACK AT ALL.
Well duh, you probably killed him
......
SO YOU'RE CERTAIN IT HAPPENED AROUND HERE?
YEAH. I'M SURE BECAUSE I DROPPED HIM OVER THE CLIFF HERE...
--||||

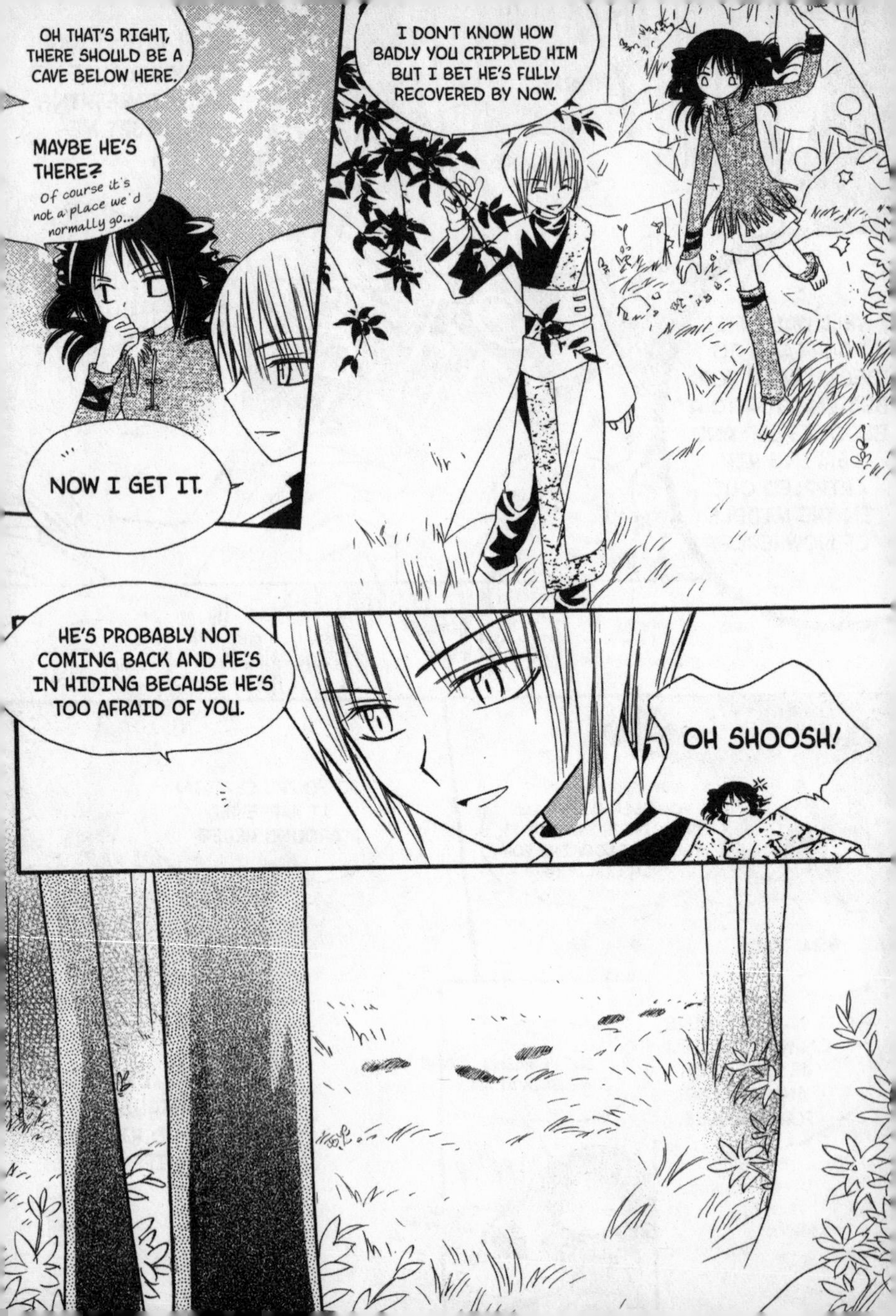
OH THAT'S RIGHT, THERE SHOULD BE A CAVE BELOW HERE.
MAYBE HE'S THERE?
Of course it's not a place we'd normally go...
...
NOW I GET IT.
I DON'T KNOW HOW BADLY YOU CRIPPLED HIM BUT I BET HE'S FULLY RECOVERED BY NOW.
HE'S PROBABLY NOT COMING BACK AND HE'S IN HIDING BECAUSE HE'S TOO AFRAID OF YOU.
OH SHOOSH!

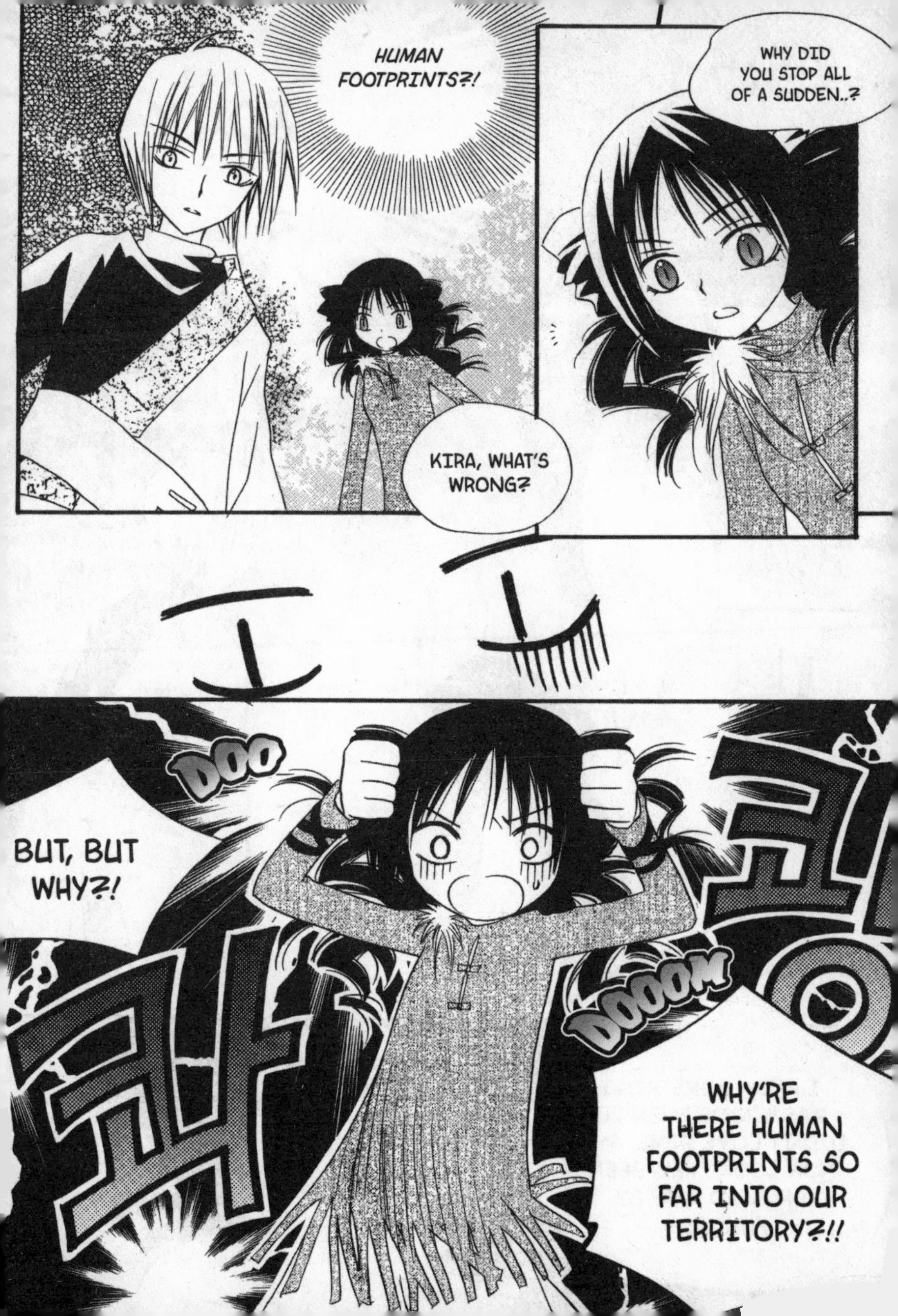
HUMAN FOOTPRINTS?!
KIRA, WHAT'S WRONG?
WHY DID YOU STOP ALL OF A SUDDEN..?
DOO
BUT, BUT WHY?!
DOOOM
WHY'RE THERE HUMAN FOOTPRINTS SO FAR INTO OUR TERRITORY?!!

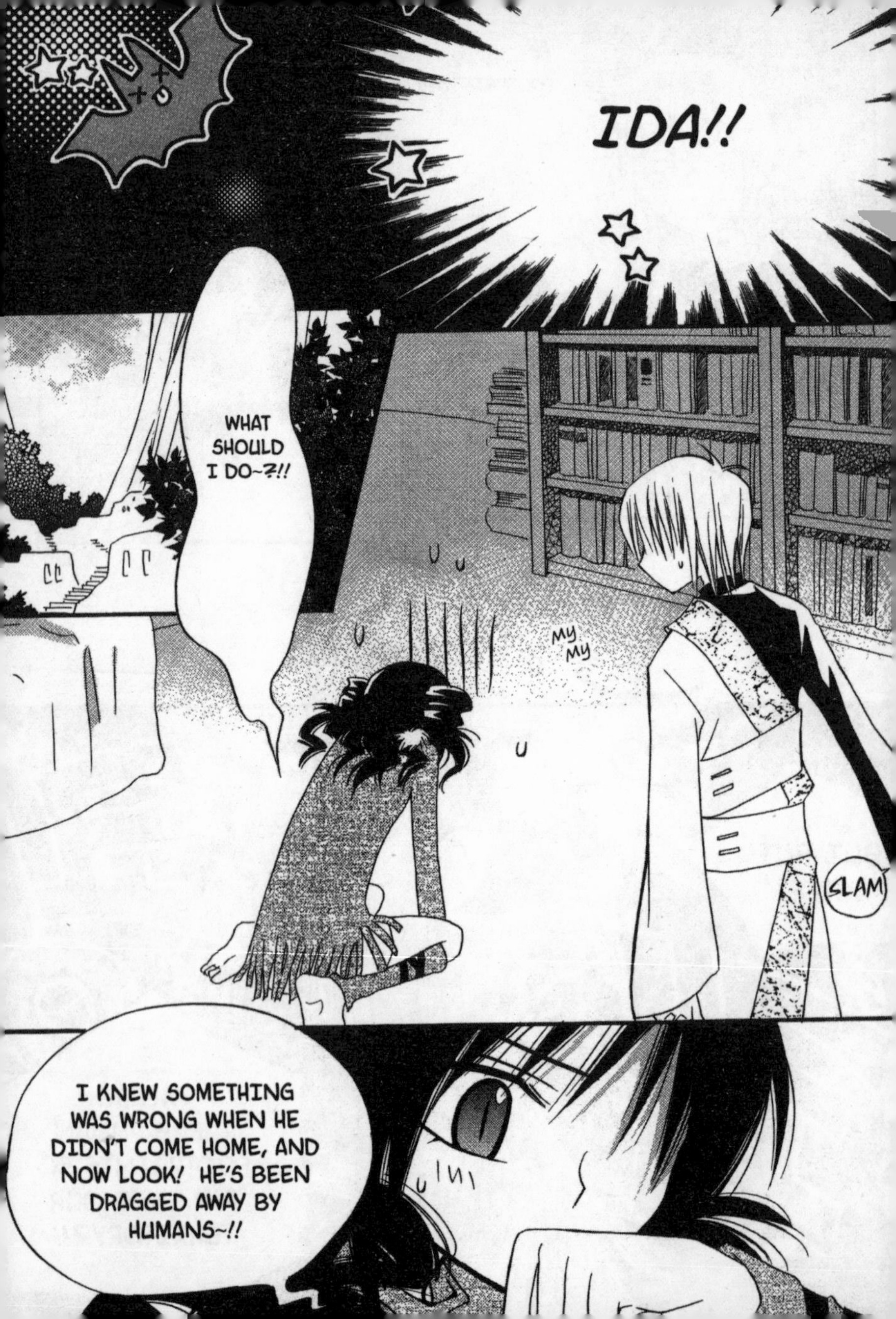
IDA!!
WHAT SHOULD I DO~?!!
MY MY
SLAM
I KNEW SOMETHING WAS WRONG WHEN HE DIDN'T COME HOME, AND NOW LOOK! HE'S BEEN DRAGGED AWAY BY HUMANS~!!

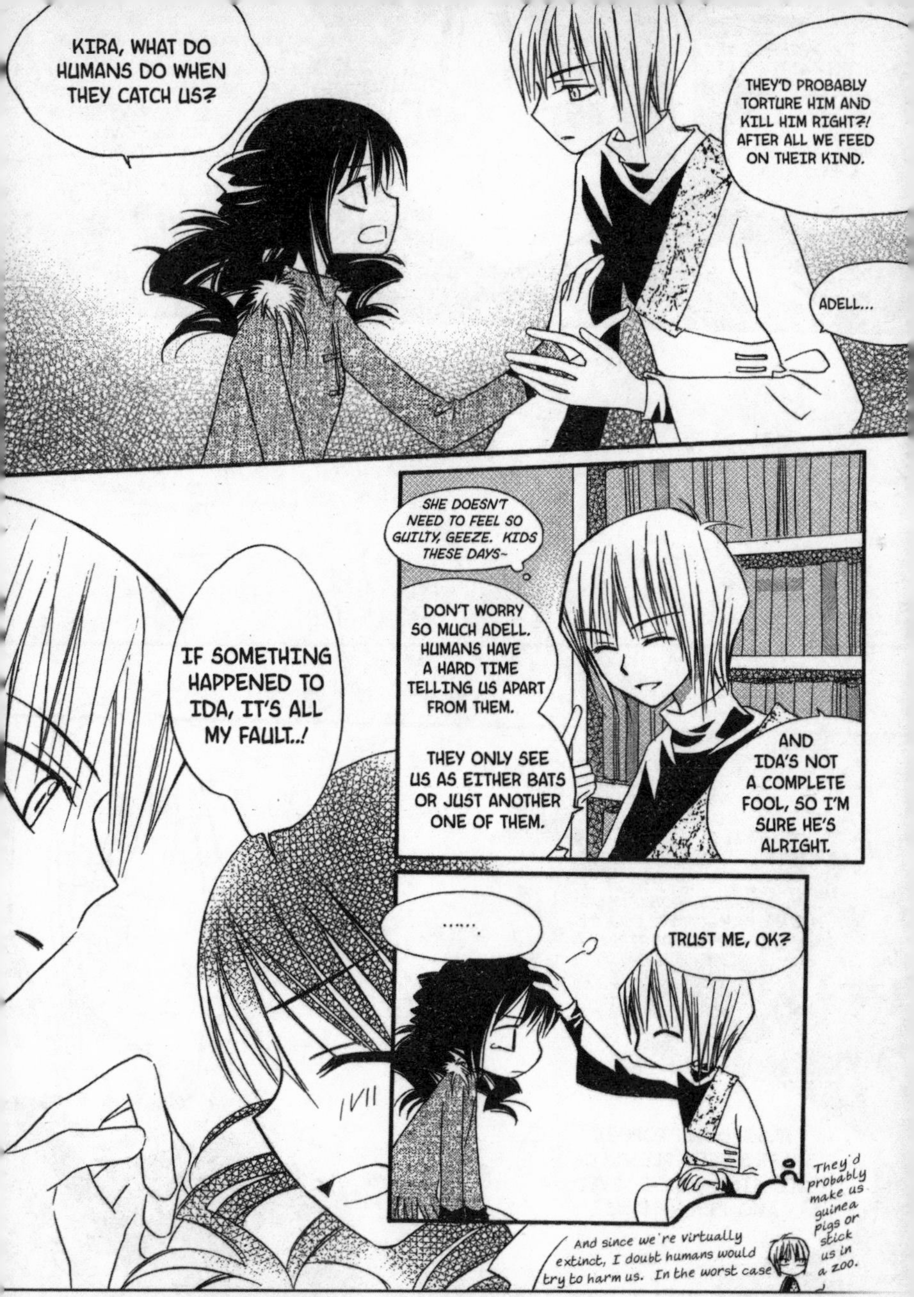
KIRA, WHAT DO HUMANS DO WHEN THEY CATCH US?
THEY'D PROBABLY TORTURE HIM AND KILL HIM RIGHT?! AFTER ALL WE FEED ON THEIR KIND.
ADELL...
IF SOMETHING HAPPENED TO IDA, IT'S ALL MY FAULT..!
SHE DOESN'T NEED TO FEEL SO GUILTY, GEEZE. KIDS THESE DAYS~
DON'T WORRY SO MUCH ADELL. HUMANS HAVE A HARD TIME TELLING US APART FROM THEM.
THEY ONLY SEE US AS EITHER BATS OR JUST ANOTHER ONE OF THEM.
AND IDA'S NOT A COMPLETE FOOL, SO I'M SURE HE'S ALRIGHT.
......
TRUST ME, OK?
And since we're virtually extinct, I doubt humans would try to harm us. In the worst case
They'd probably make us guinea pigs or stick us in a zoo.

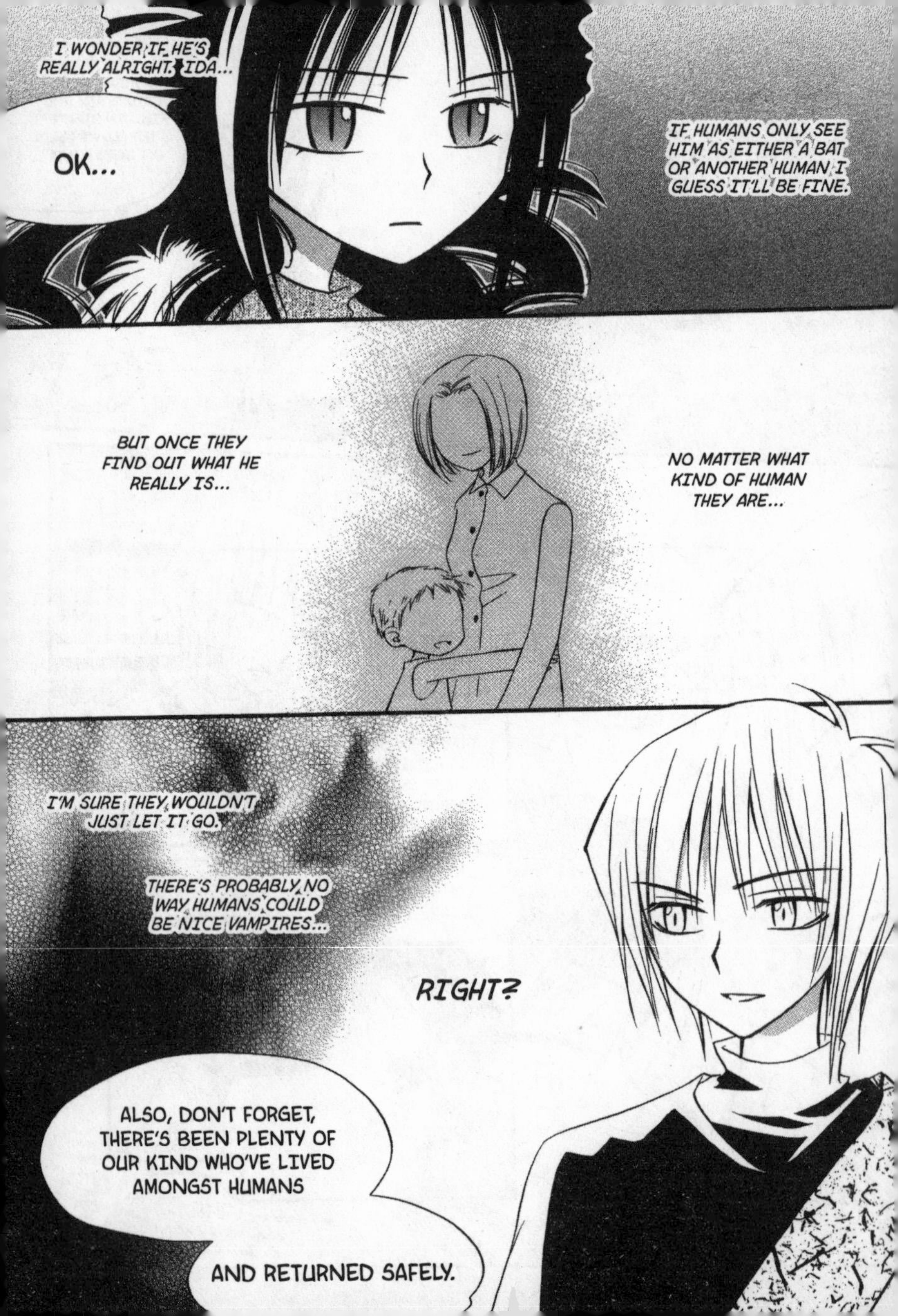
I WONDER IF HE'S REALLY ALRIGHT. IDA...
OK...
IF HUMANS ONLY SEE HIM AS EITHER A BAT OR ANOTHER HUMAN I GUESS IT'LL BE FINE.
BUT ONCE THEY FIND OUT WHAT HE REALLY IS...
NO MATTER WHAT KIND OF HUMAN THEY ARE...
I'M SURE THEY WOULDN'T JUST LET IT GO.
THERE'S PROBABLY NO WAY HUMANS COULD BE NICE VAMPIRES...
RIGHT?
ALSO, DON'T FORGET, THERE'S BEEN PLENTY OF OUR KIND WHO'VE LIVED AMONGST HUMANS
AND RETURNED SAFELY.

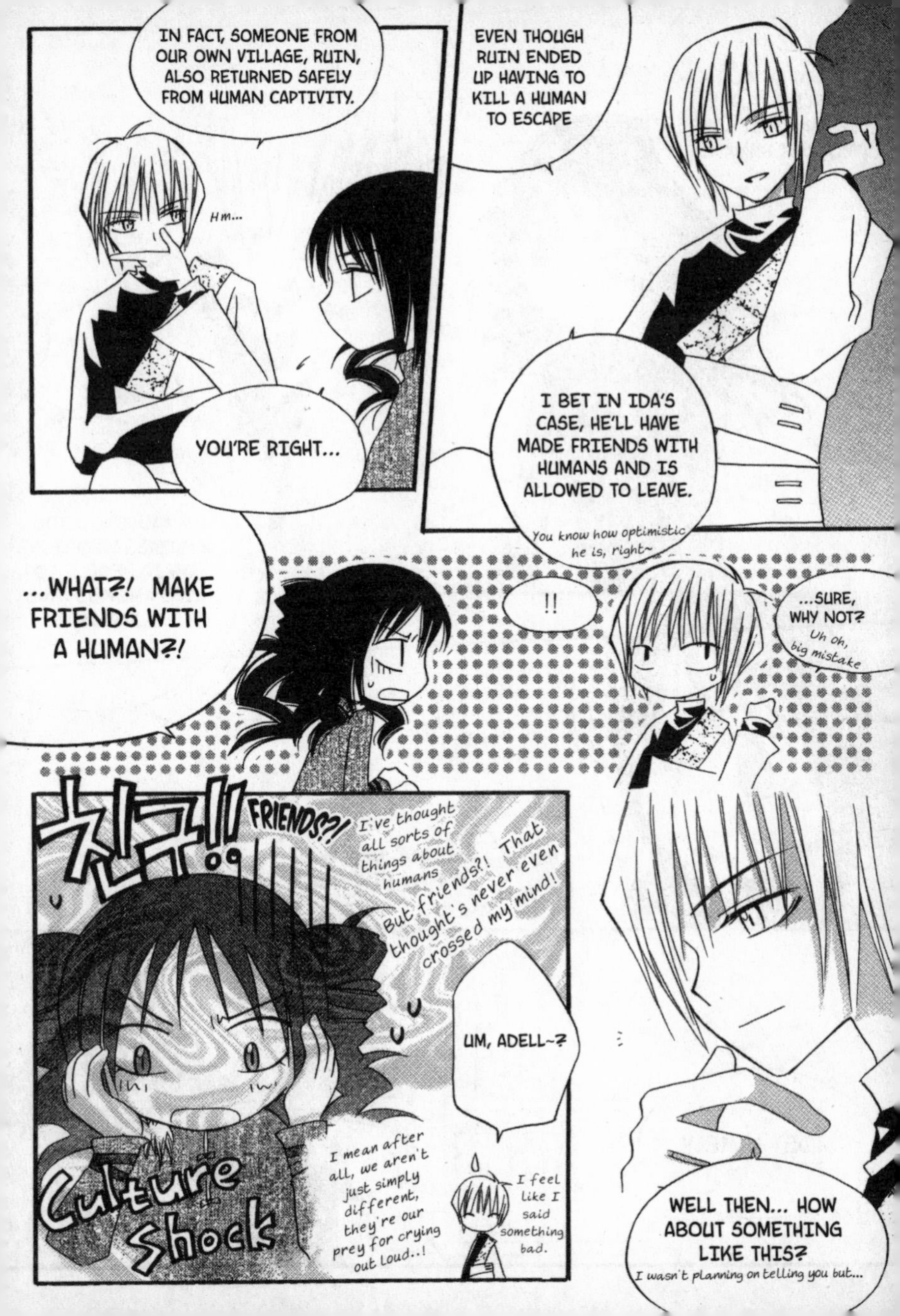
IN FACT, SOMEONE FROM OUR OWN VILLAGE, RUIN, ALSO RETURNED SAFELY FROM HUMAN CAPTIVITY.
Hm...
YOU'RE RIGHT...
EVEN THOUGH RUIN ENDED UP HAVING TO KILL A HUMAN TO ESCAPE
I BET IN IDA'S CASE, HE'LL HAVE MADE FRIENDS WITH HUMANS AND IS ALLOWED TO LEAVE.
You know how optimistic he is, right~
...WHAT?! MAKE FRIENDS WITH A HUMAN?!
!!
...SURE, WHY NOT?
Uh oh, big mistake
FRIENDS?!
I've thought all sorts of things about humans
But friends?! That thought's never even crossed my mind!
Culture Shock
UM, ADELL~?
I mean after all, we aren't just simply different, they're our prey for crying out loud..!
I feel like I said something bad.
WELL THEN... HOW ABOUT SOMETHING LIKE THIS?
I wasn't planning on telling you but...

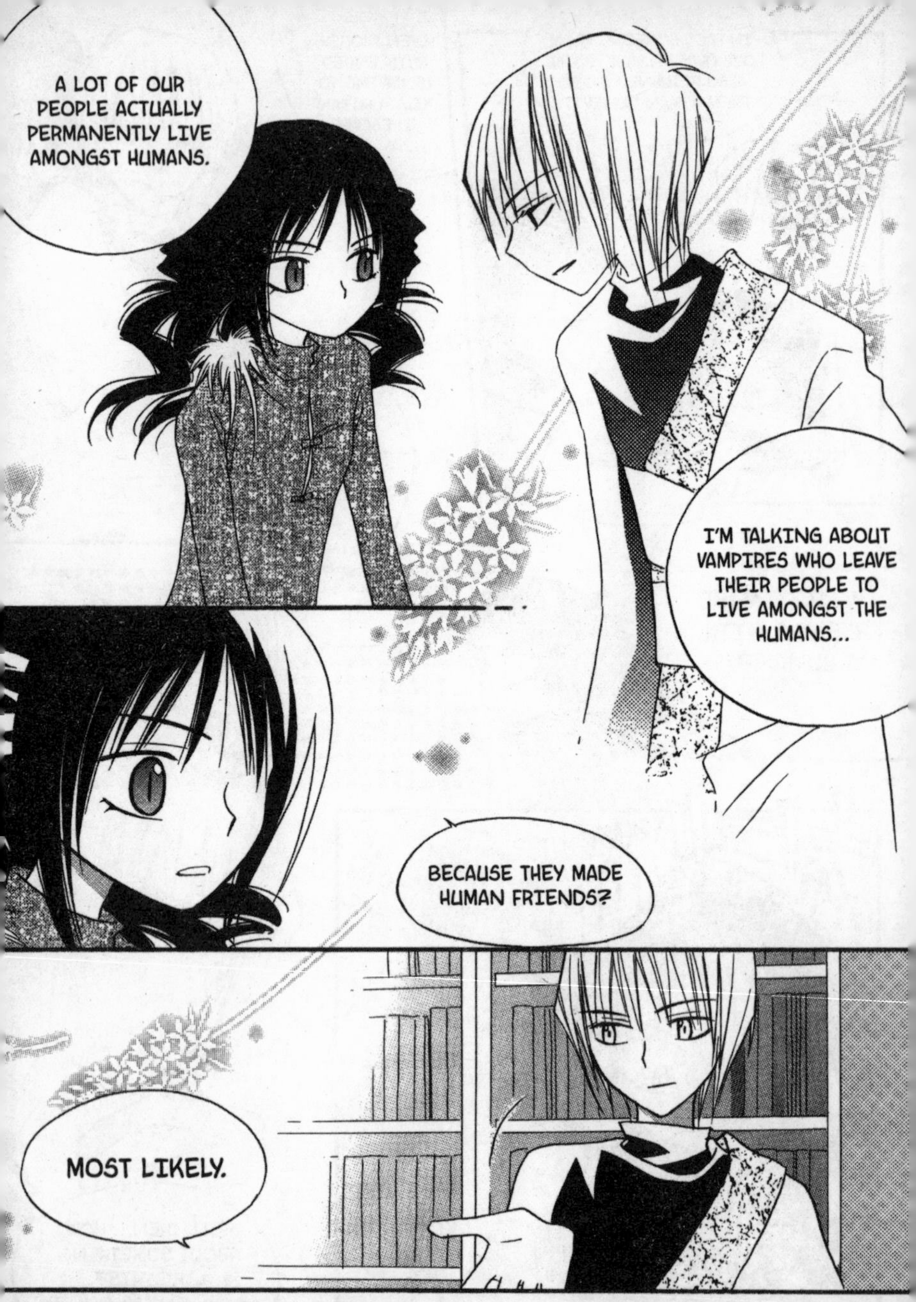
A LOT OF OUR PEOPLE ACTUALLY PERMANENTLY LIVE AMONGST HUMANS.
I'M TALKING ABOUT VAMPIRES WHO LEAVE THEIR PEOPLE TO LIVE AMONGST THE HUMANS...
BECAUSE THEY MADE HUMAN FRIENDS?
MOST LIKELY.

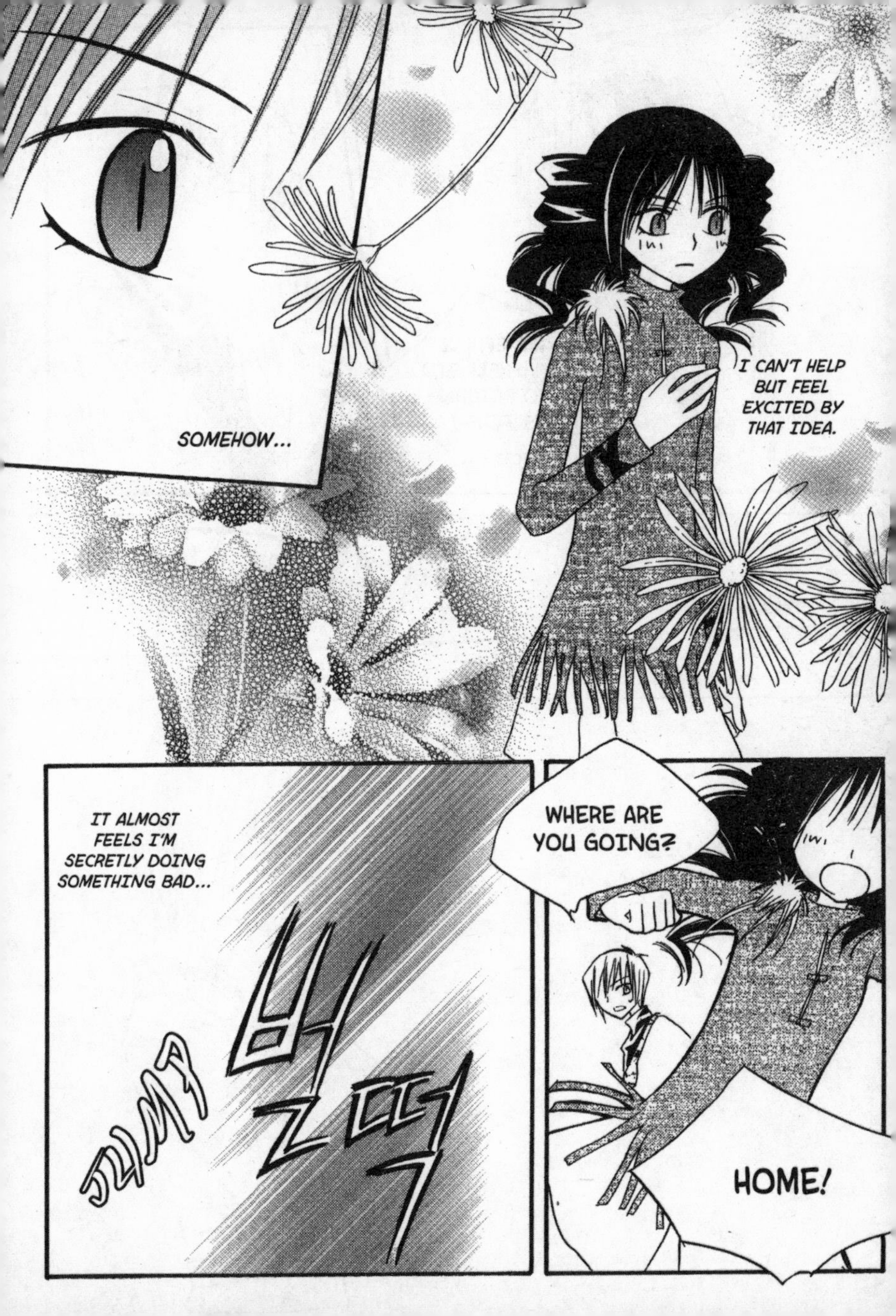
SOMEHOW...
I CAN'T HELP BUT FEEL EXCITED BY THAT IDEA.
IT ALMOST FEELS I'M SECRETLY DOING SOMETHING BAD...
WHERE ARE YOU GOING?
HOME!

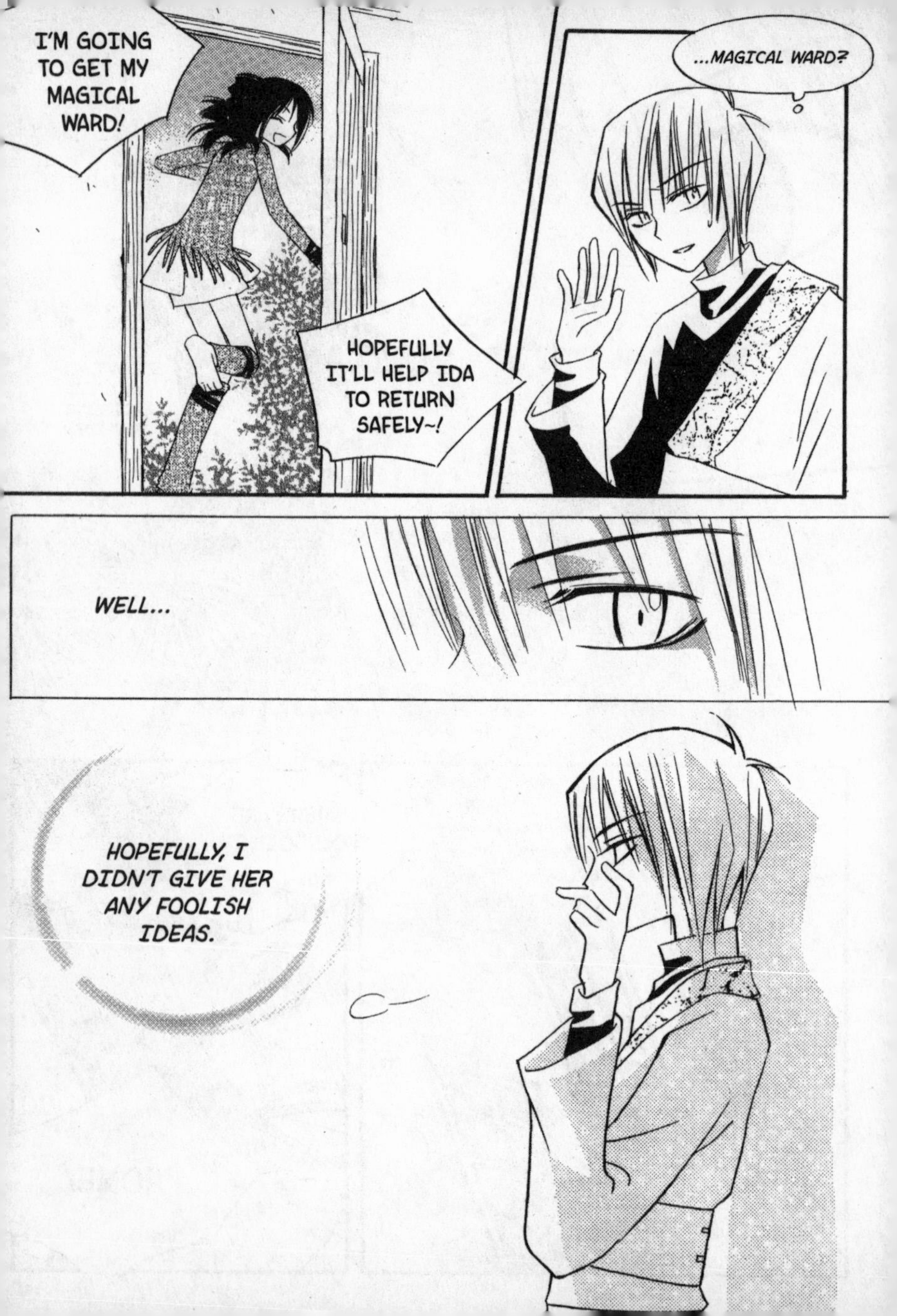
I'M GOING TO GET MY MAGICAL WARD!
HOPEFULLY IT'LL HELP IDA TO RETURN SAFELY~!
...MAGICAL WARD?
WELL...
HOPEFULLY, I DIDN'T GIVE HER ANY FOOLISH IDEAS.

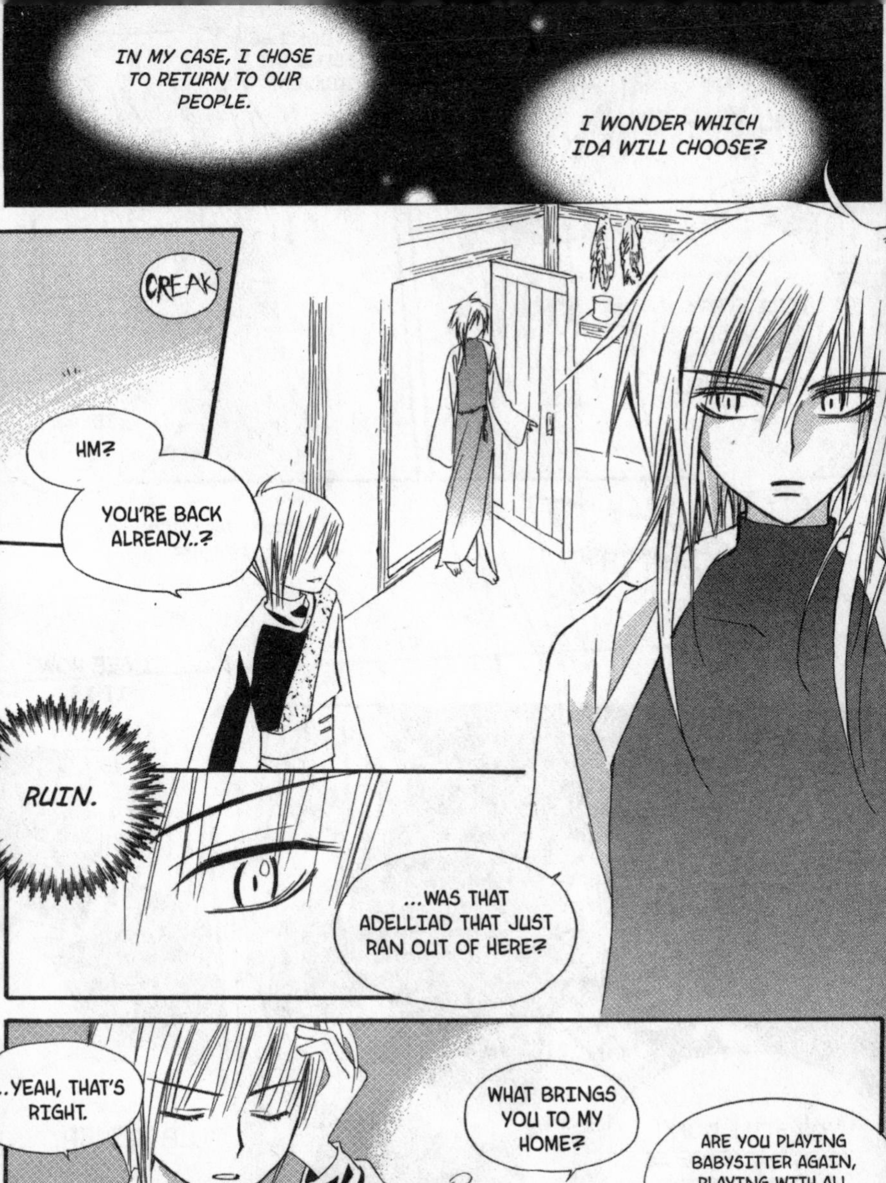
IN MY CASE, I CHOSE TO RETURN TO OUR PEOPLE.
I WONDER WHICH IDA WILL CHOOSE?
CREAK
HM?
YOU'RE BACK ALREADY..?
RUIN.
...WAS THAT ADELLIAD THAT JUST RAN OUT OF HERE?
...YEAH, THAT'S RIGHT.
WHAT BRINGS YOU TO MY HOME?
ARE YOU PLAYING BABYSITTER AGAIN, PLAYING WITH ALL THE NEIGHBORHOOD KIDS AND ALL?

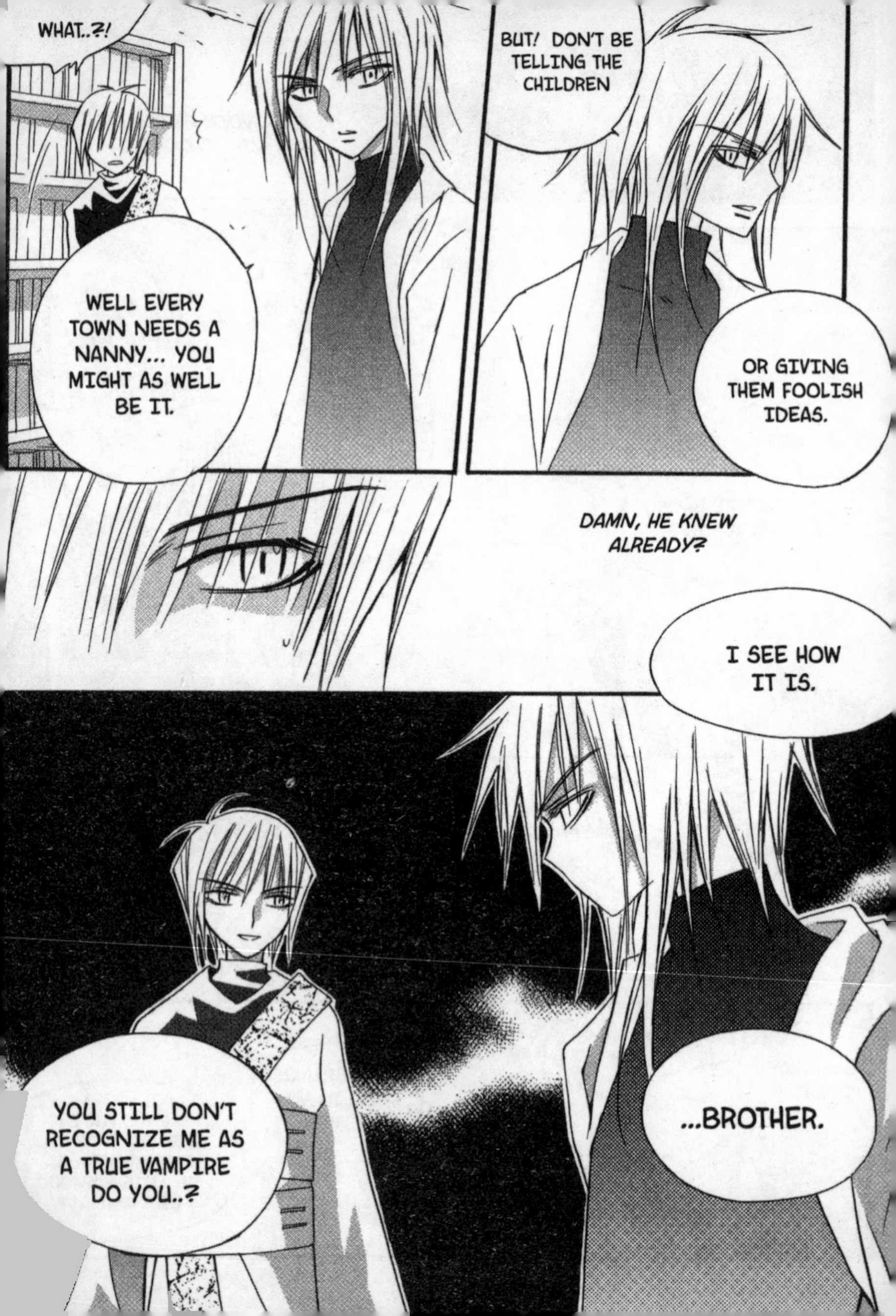
WHAT..?!
WELL EVERY TOWN NEEDS A NANNY... YOU MIGHT AS WELL BE IT.
BUT! DON'T BE TELLING THE CHILDREN
OR GIVING THEM FOOLISH IDEAS.
DAMN, HE KNEW ALREADY?
I SEE HOW IT IS.
YOU STILL DON'T RECOGNIZE ME AS A TRUE VAMPIRE DO YOU..?
...BROTHER.

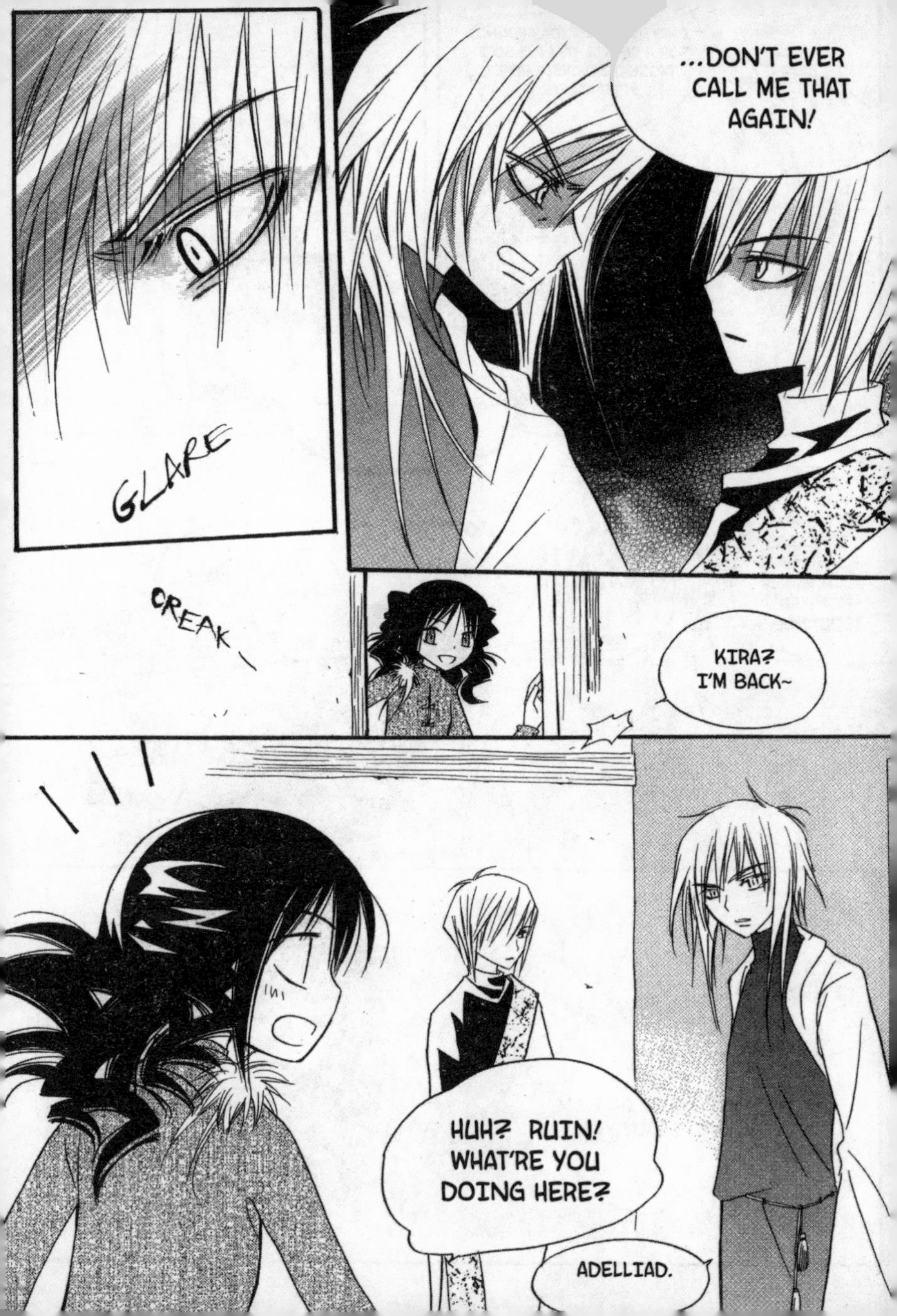
GLARE
...DON'T EVER CALL ME THAT AGAIN!
CREAK
KIRA? I'M BACK~
HUH? RUIN! WHAT'RE YOU DOING HERE?
ADELLIAD.

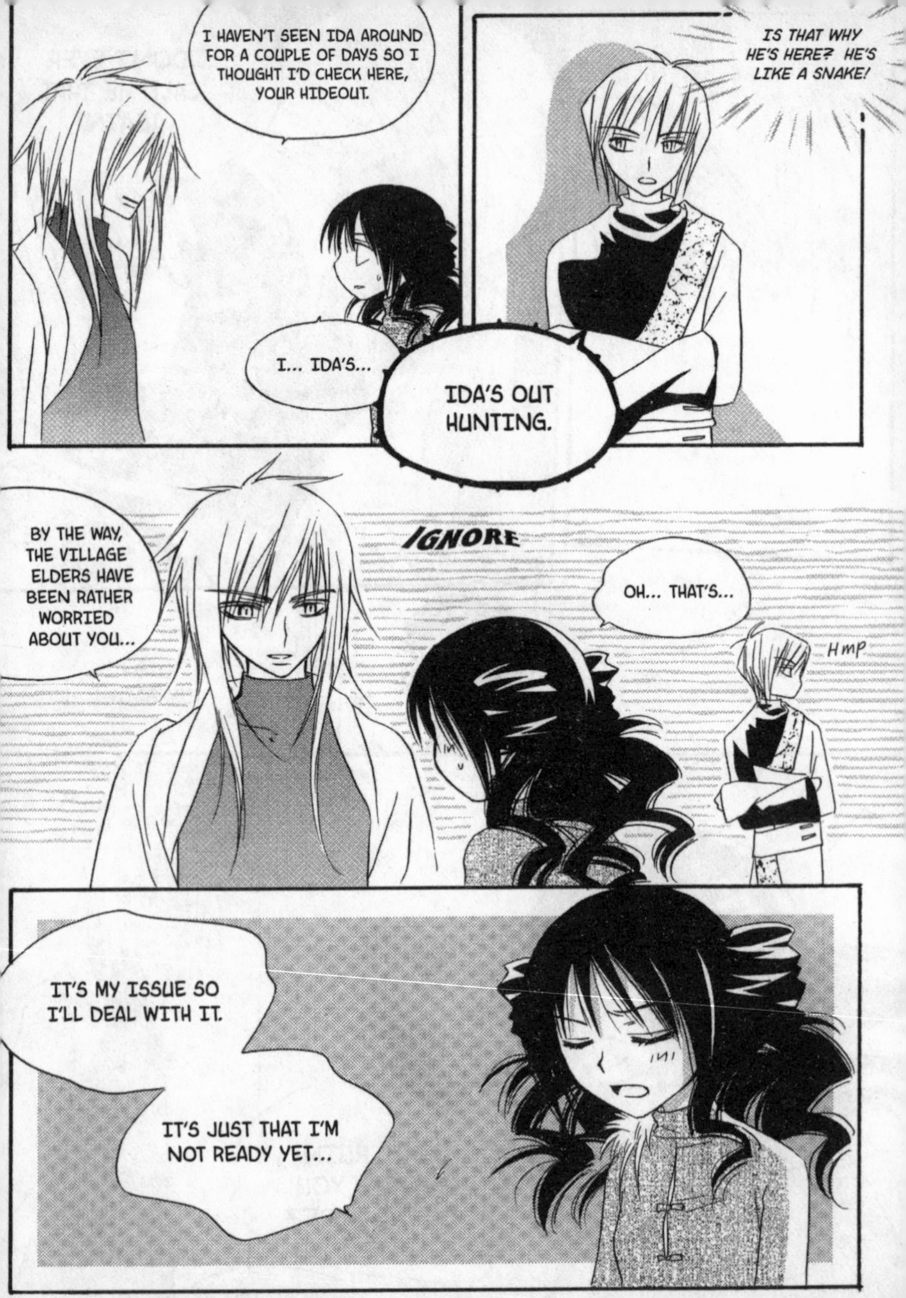
I HAVEN'T SEEN IDA AROUND FOR A COUPLE OF DAYS SO I THOUGHT I'D CHECK HERE, YOUR HIDEOUT.
I... IDA'S...
IS THAT WHY HE'S HERE? HE'S LIKE A SNAKE!
IDA'S OUT HUNTING.
BY THE WAY, THE VILLAGE ELDERS HAVE BEEN RATHER WORRIED ABOUT YOU...
IGNORE
OH... THAT'S...
Hmp
IT'S MY ISSUE SO I'LL DEAL WITH IT.
IT'S JUST THAT I'M NOT READY YET...

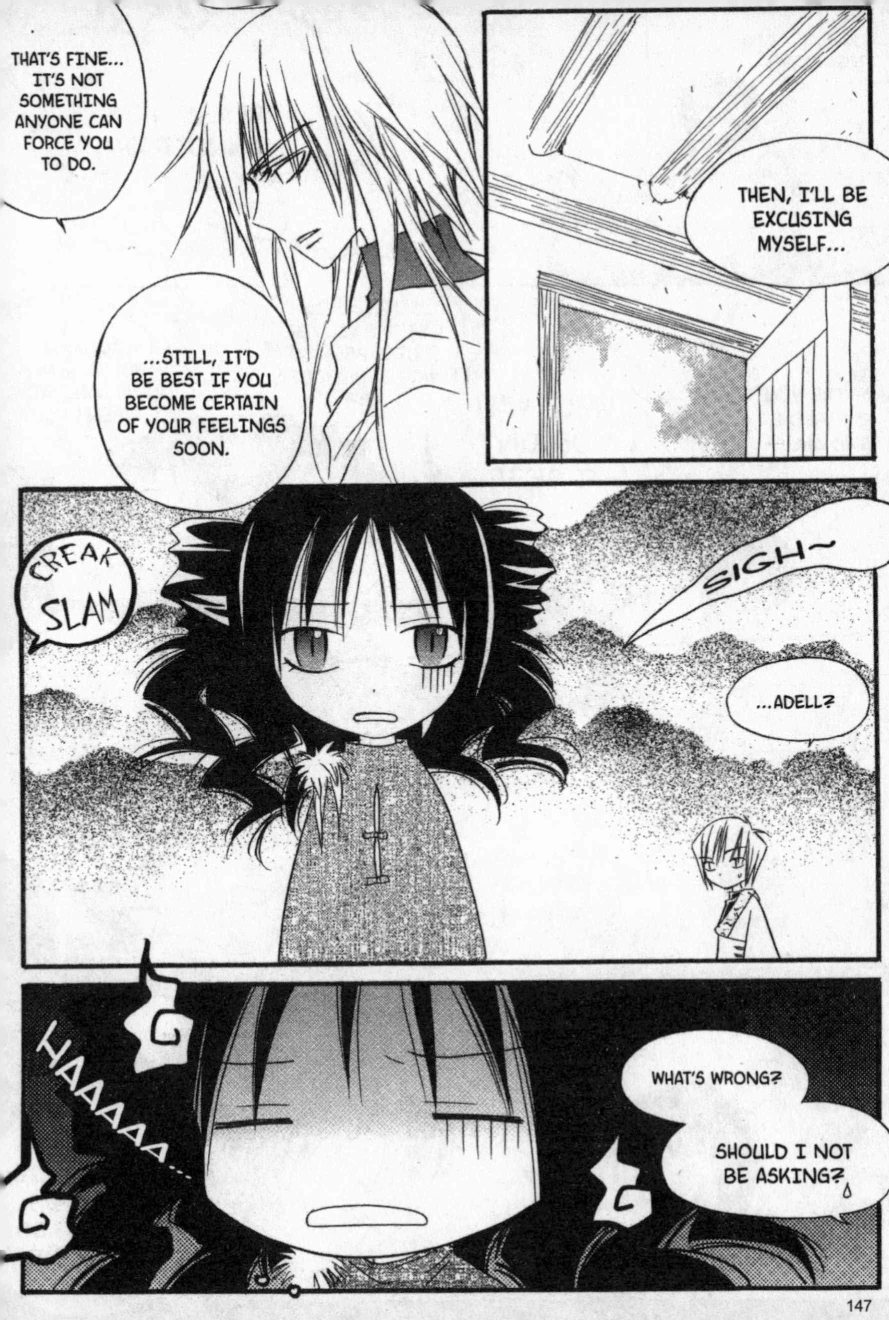
THAT'S FINE... IT'S NOT SOMETHING ANYONE CAN FORCE YOU TO DO.
...STILL, IT'D BE BEST IF YOU BECOME CERTAIN OF YOUR FEELINGS SOON.
THEN, I'LL BE EXCUSING MYSELF...
CREAK
SLAM
SIGH~
...ADELL?
HAAAAAA...
WHAT'S WRONG?
SHOULD I NOT BE ASKING?

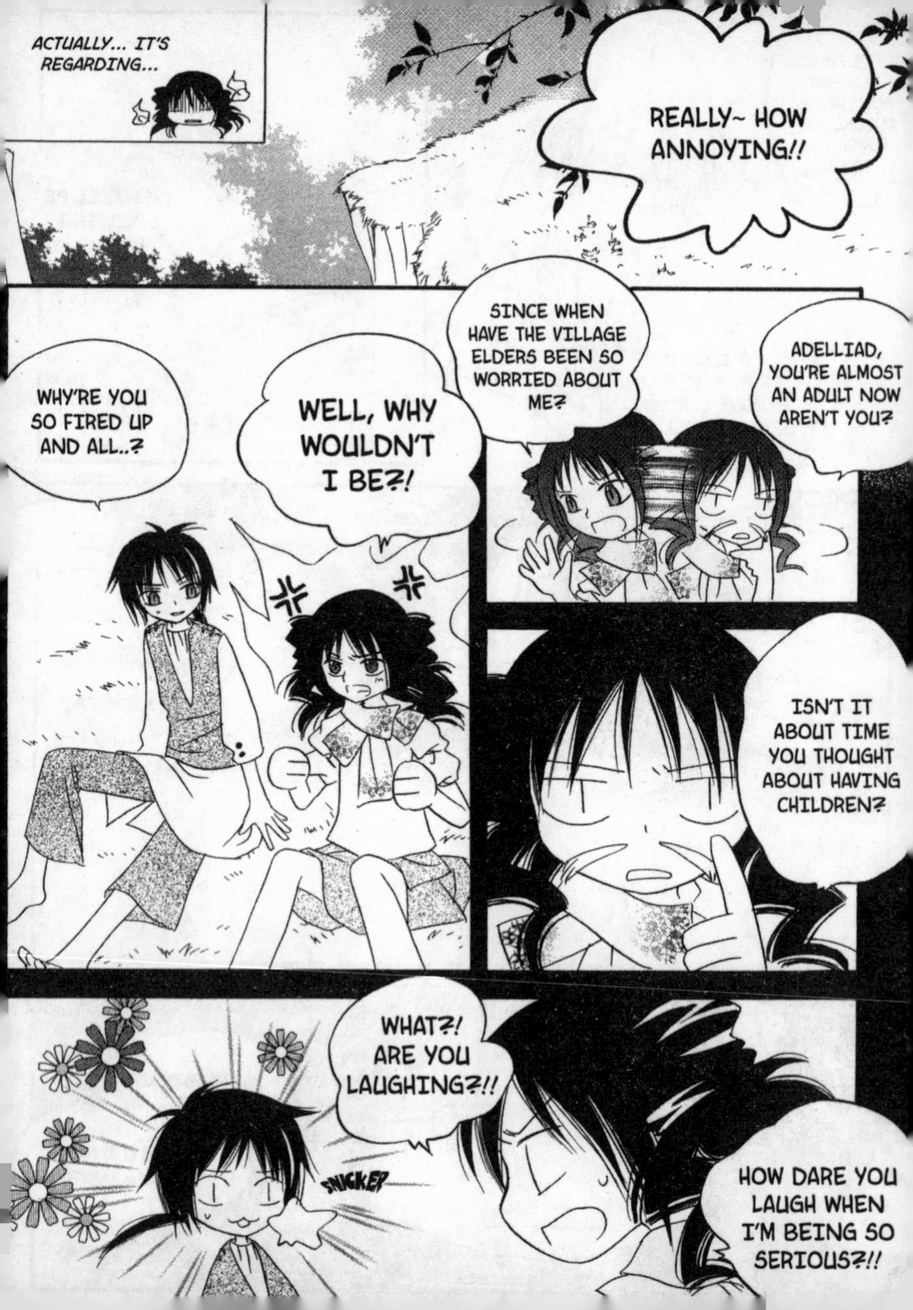
ACTUALLY... IT'S REGARDING...
REALLY~ HOW ANNOYING!!
WHY'RE YOU SO FIRED UP AND ALL..?
WELL, WHY WOULDN'T I BE?!
SINCE WHEN HAVE THE VILLAGE ELDERS BEEN SO WORRIED ABOUT ME?
ADELLIAD, YOU'RE ALMOST AN ADULT NOW AREN'T YOU?
ISN'T IT ABOUT TIME YOU THOUGHT ABOUT HAVING CHILDREN?
WHAT?! ARE YOU LAUGHING?!!
SNICKER
HOW DARE YOU LAUGH WHEN I'M BEING SO SERIOUS?!!

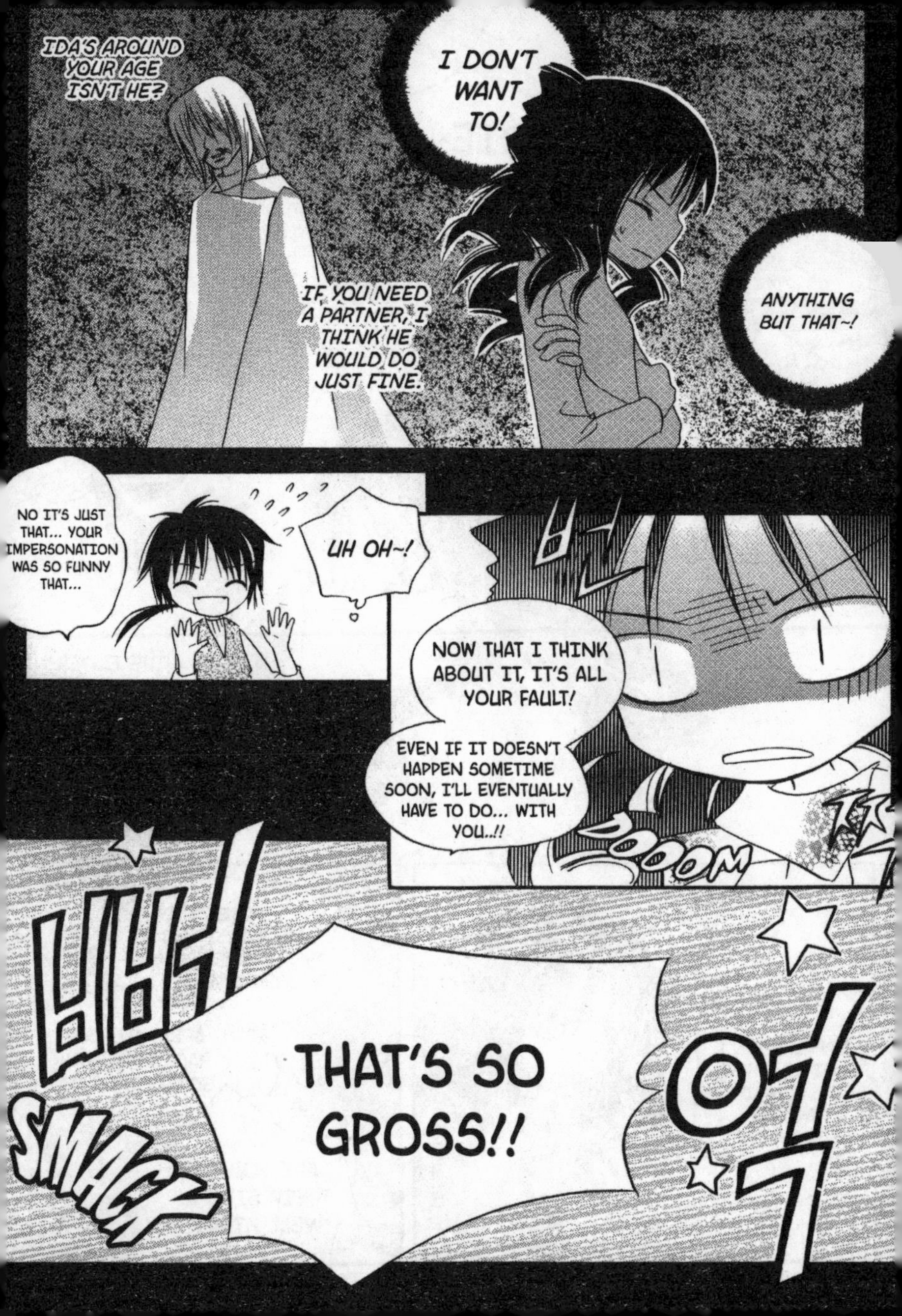
IDA'S AROUND YOUR AGE ISN'T HE?
I DON'T WANT TO!
IF YOU NEED A PARTNER, I THINK HE WOULD DO JUST FINE.
ANYTHING BUT THAT~!
NO IT'S JUST THAT... YOUR IMPERSONATION WAS SO FUNNY THAT...
UH OH~!
NOW THAT I THINK ABOUT IT, IT'S ALL YOUR FAULT!
EVEN IF IT DOESN'T HAPPEN SOMETIME SOON, I'LL EVENTUALLY HAVE TO DO... WITH YOU..!!
DOOOM
SMACK
THAT'S SO GROSS!!

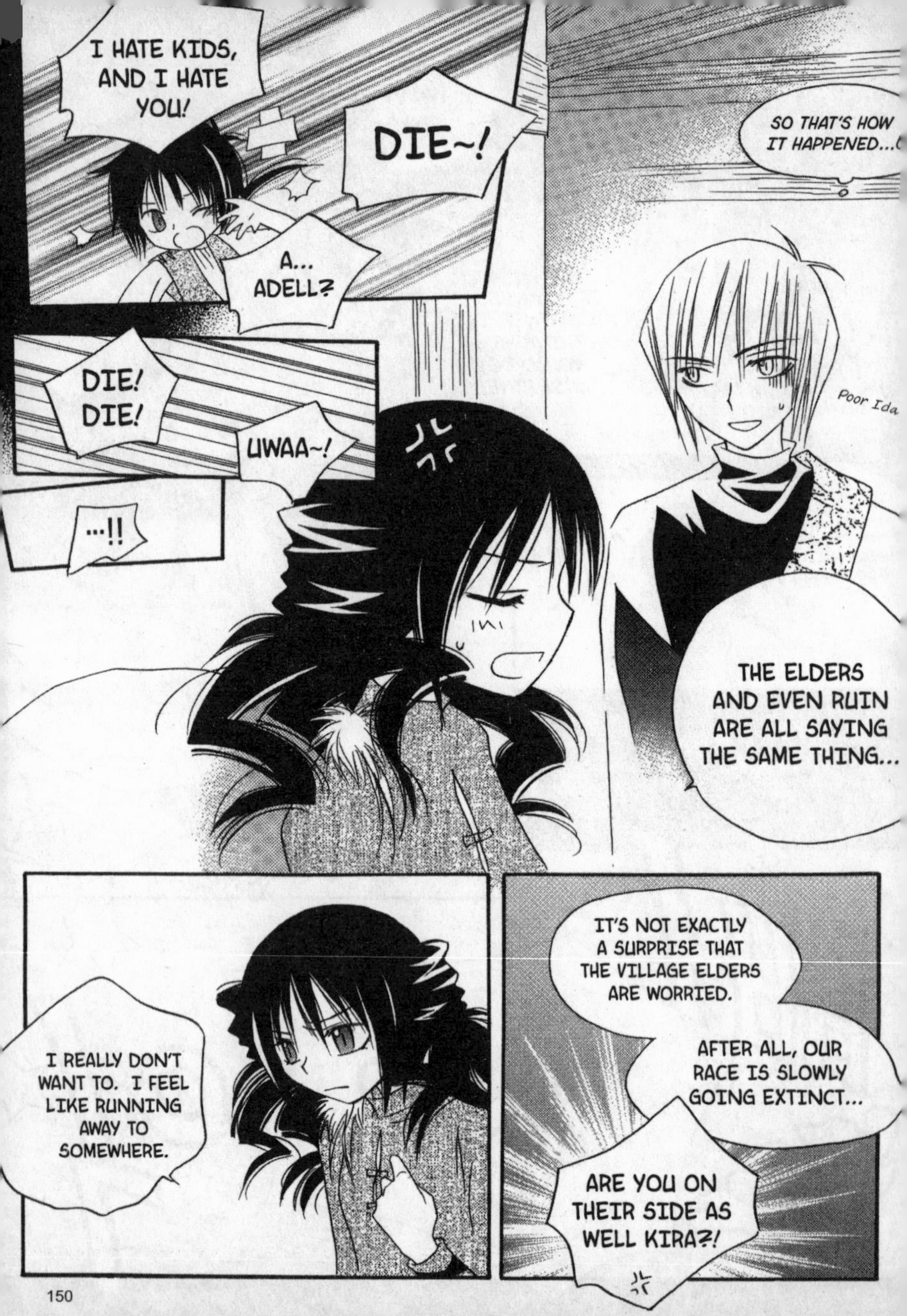
I HATE KIDS, AND I HATE YOU!
DIE~!
A... ADELL?
DIE! DIE!
UWAA~!
...!!
SO THAT'S HOW IT HAPPENED...
Poor Ida
THE ELDERS AND EVEN RUIN ARE ALL SAYING THE SAME THING...
I REALLY DON'T WANT TO. I FEEL LIKE RUNNING AWAY TO SOMEWHERE.
IT'S NOT EXACTLY A SURPRISE THAT THE VILLAGE ELDERS ARE WORRIED.
AFTER ALL, OUR RACE IS SLOWLY GOING EXTINCT...
ARE YOU ON THEIR SIDE AS WELL KIRA?!

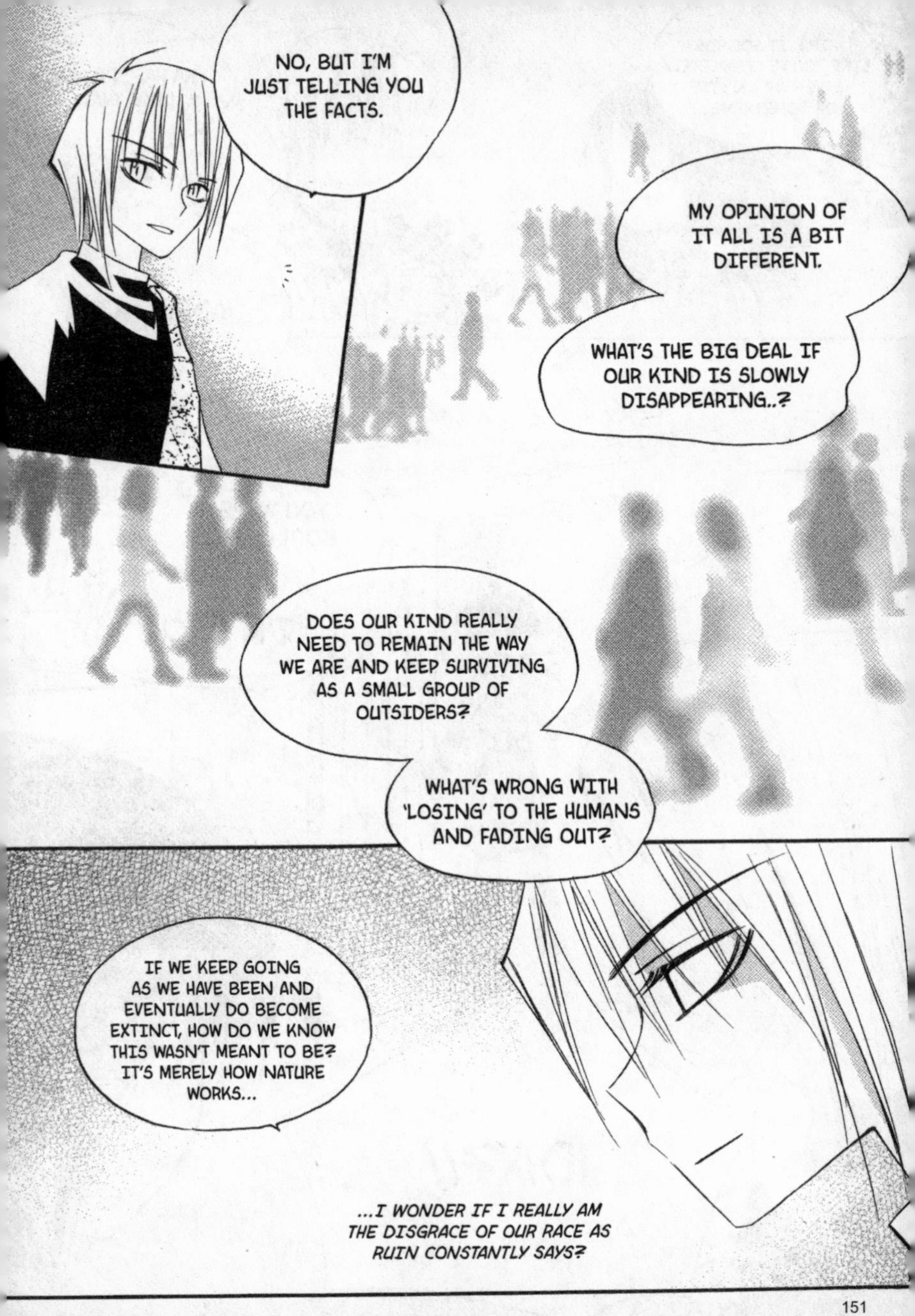
NO, BUT I'M JUST TELLING YOU THE FACTS.
MY OPINION OF IT ALL IS A BIT DIFFERENT.
WHAT'S THE BIG DEAL IF OUR KIND IS SLOWLY DISAPPEARING..?
DOES OUR KIND REALLY NEED TO REMAIN THE WAY WE ARE AND KEEP SURVIVING AS A SMALL GROUP OF OUTSIDERS?
WHAT'S WRONG WITH 'LOSING' TO THE HUMANS AND FADING OUT?
IF WE KEEP GOING AS WE HAVE BEEN AND EVENTUALLY DO BECOME EXTINCT, HOW DO WE KNOW THIS WASN'T MEANT TO BE? IT'S MERELY HOW NATURE WORKS...
...I WONDER IF I REALLY AM THE DISGRACE OF OUR RACE AS RUIN CONSTANTLY SAYS?

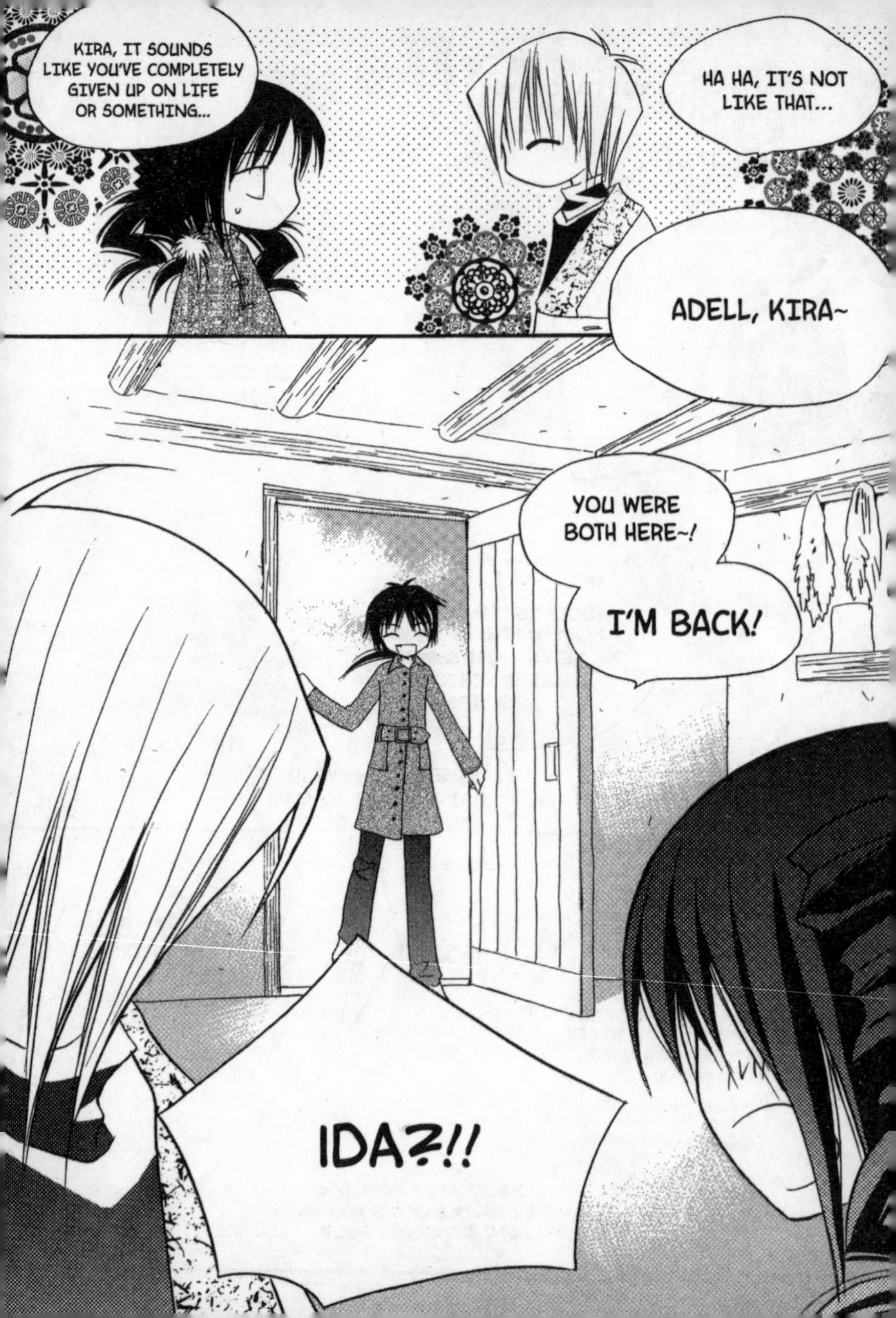
KIRA, IT SOUNDS LIKE YOU'VE COMPLETELY GIVEN UP ON LIFE OR SOMETHING...
HA HA, IT'S NOT LIKE THAT...
ADELL, KIRA~
YOU WERE BOTH HERE~!
I'M BACK!
IDA?!!

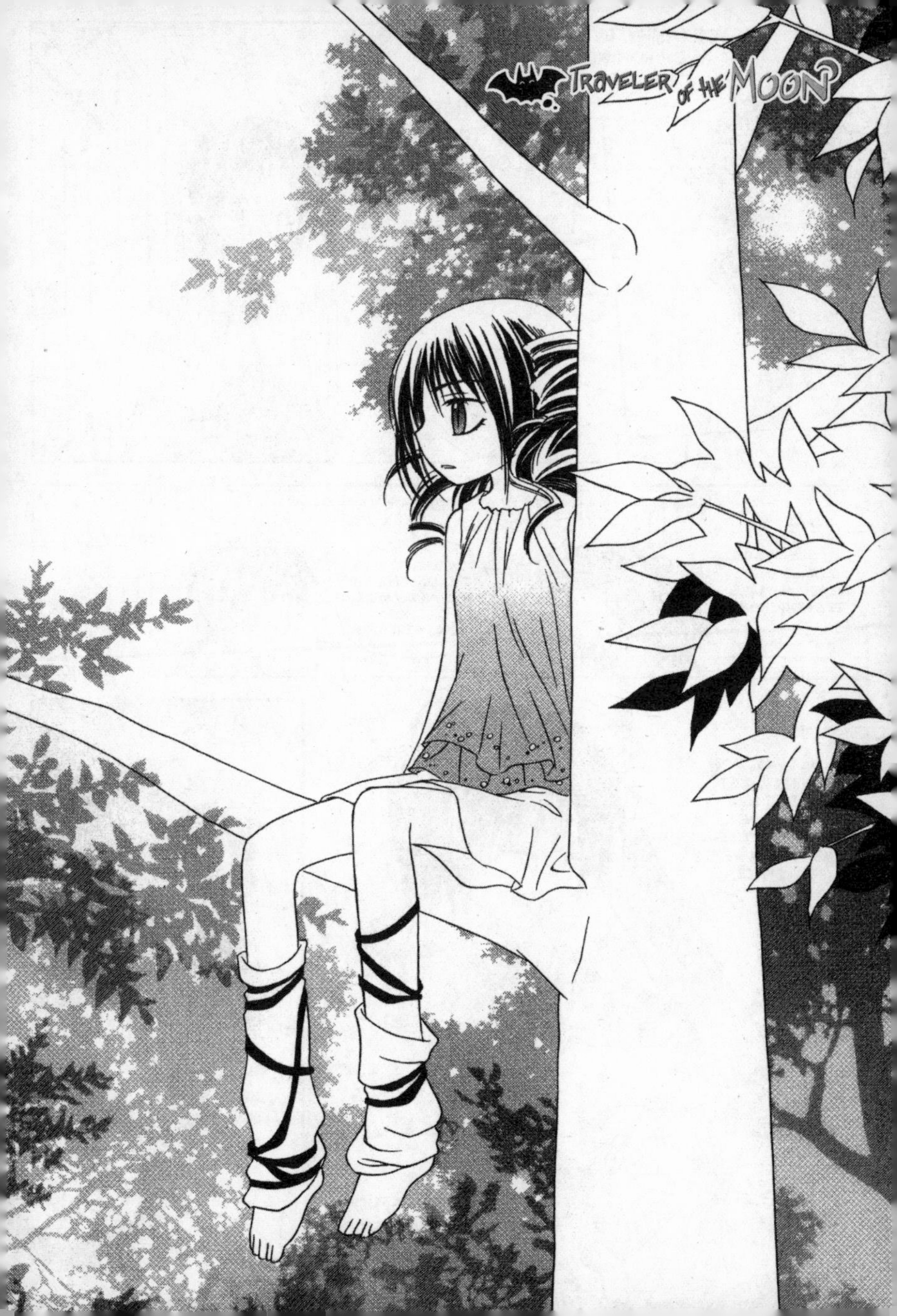
Traveler of the Moon

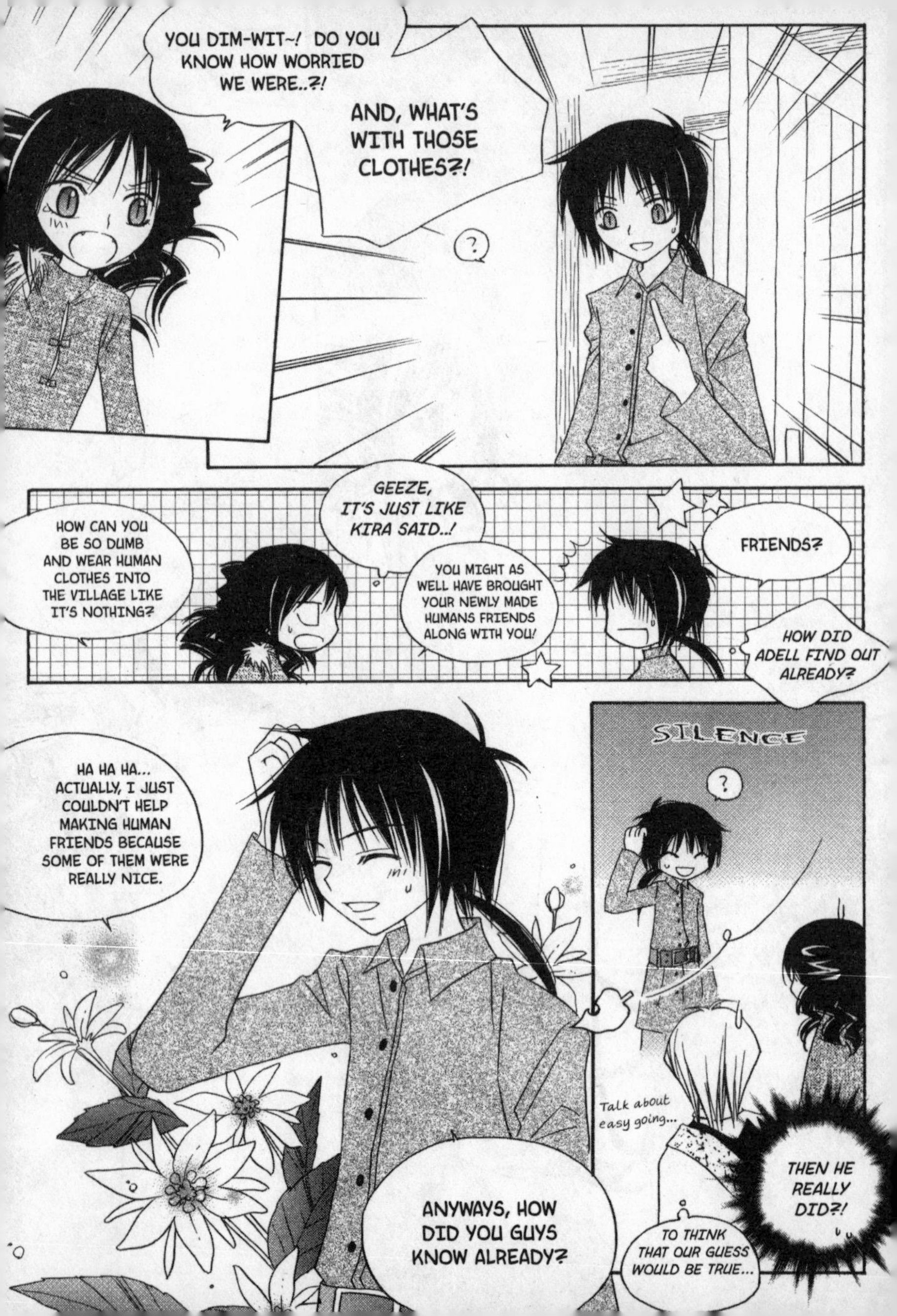
YOU DIM-WIT~! DO YOU KNOW HOW WORRIED WE WERE..?!
AND, WHAT'S WITH THOSE CLOTHES?!
?
HOW CAN YOU BE SO DUMB AND WEAR HUMAN CLOTHES INTO THE VILLAGE LIKE IT'S NOTHING?
GEEZE, IT'S JUST LIKE KIRA SAID..!
YOU MIGHT AS WELL HAVE BROUGHT YOUR NEWLY MADE HUMANS FRIENDS ALONG WITH YOU!
FRIENDS?
HOW DID ADELL FIND OUT ALREADY?
HA HA HA... ACTUALLY, I JUST COULDN'T HELP MAKING HUMAN FRIENDS BECAUSE SOME OF THEM WERE REALLY NICE.
ANYWAYS, HOW DID YOU GUYS KNOW ALREADY?
SILENCE
?
Talk about easy going...
THEN HE REALLY DID?!
TO THINK THAT OUR GUESS WOULD BE TRUE...

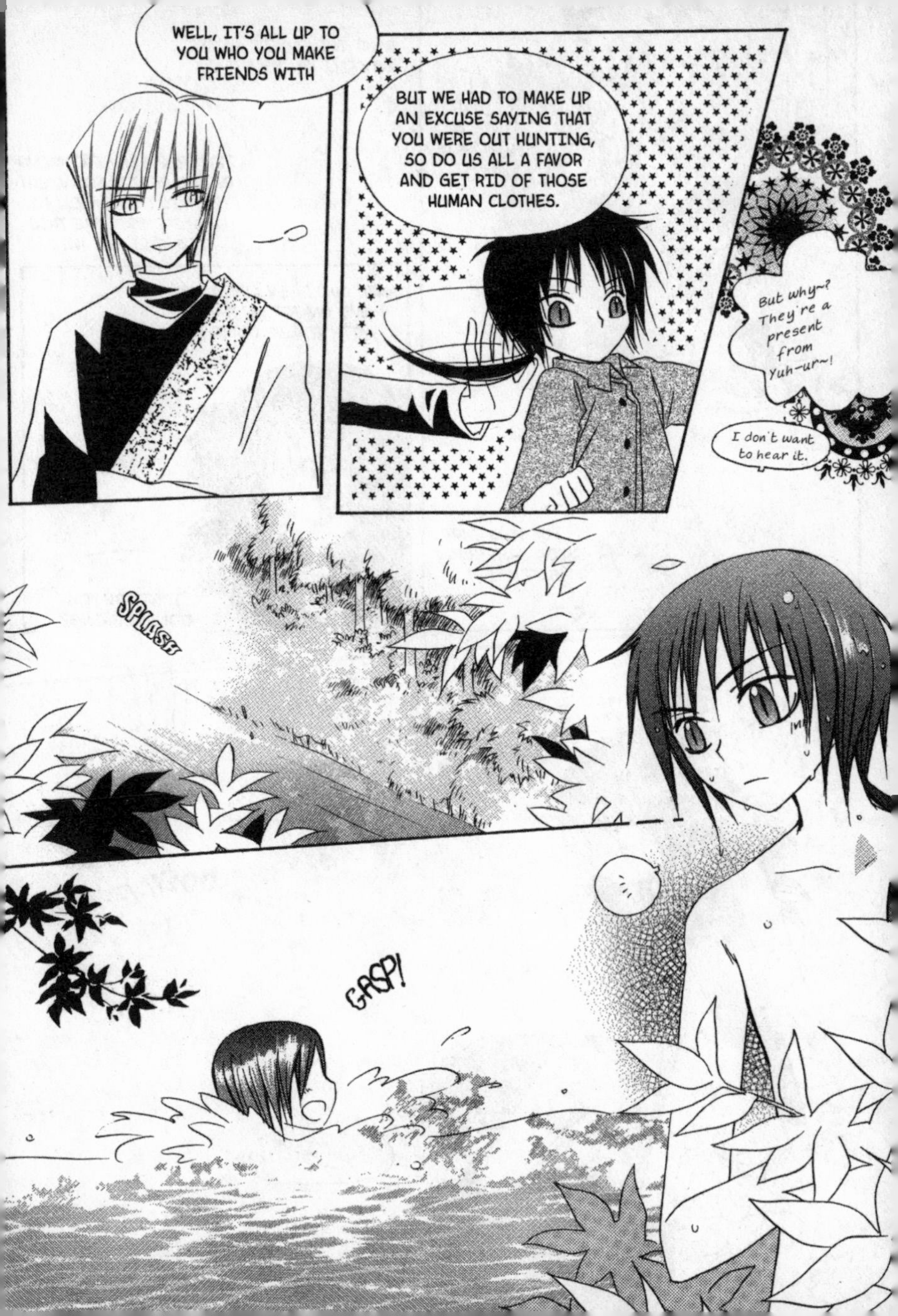
WELL, IT'S ALL UP TO YOU WHO YOU MAKE FRIENDS WITH
BUT WE HAD TO MAKE UP AN EXCUSE SAYING THAT YOU WERE OUT HUNTING, SO DO US ALL A FAVOR AND GET RID OF THOSE HUMAN CLOTHES.
But why~? They're a present from Yuh-ur~!
I don't want to hear it.
SPLASH
GASP!

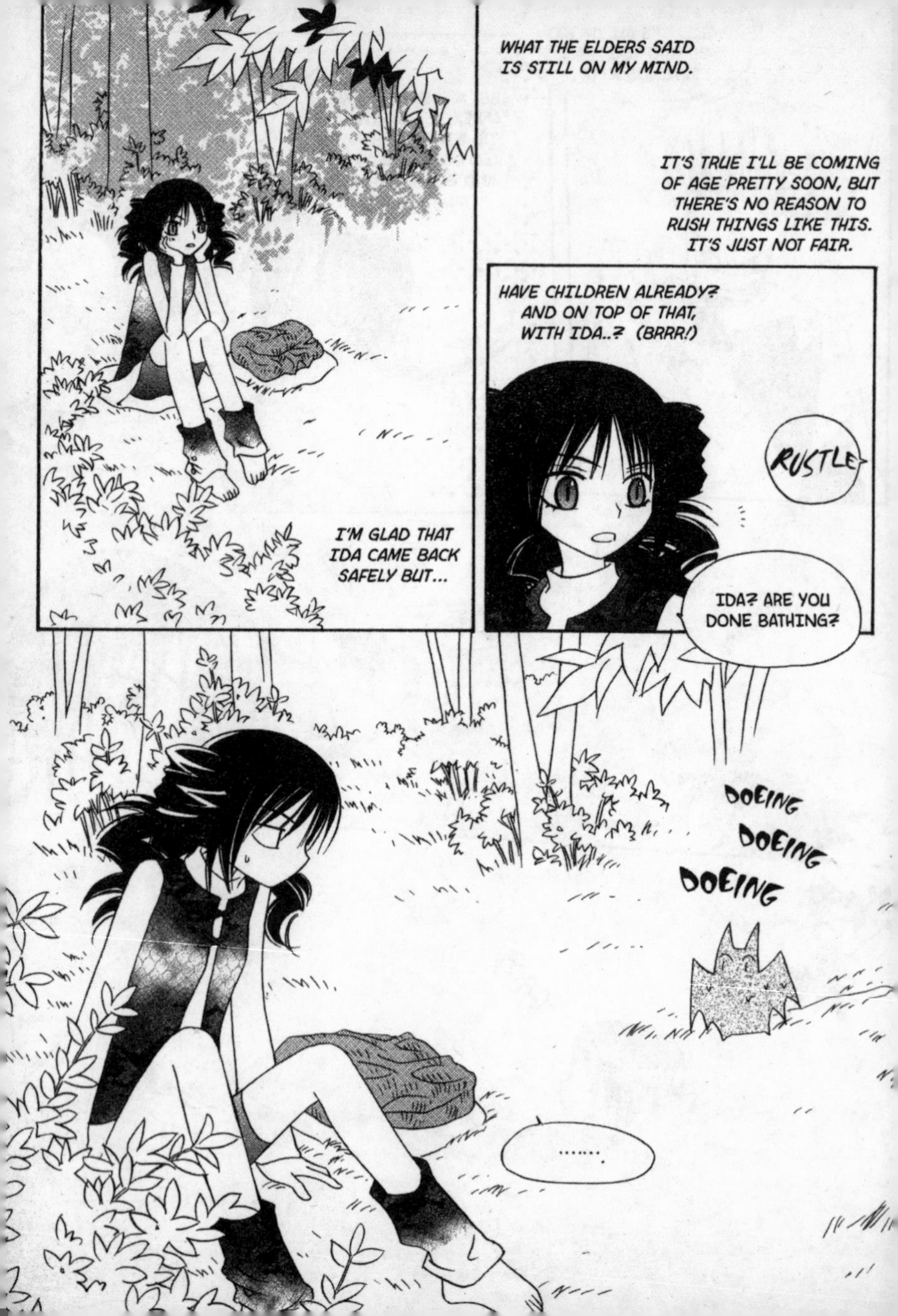
WHAT THE ELDERS SAID IS STILL ON MY MIND.
I'M GLAD THAT IDA CAME BACK SAFELY BUT...
IT'S TRUE I'LL BE COMING OF AGE PRETTY SOON, BUT THERE'S NO REASON TO RUSH THINGS LIKE THIS. IT'S JUST NOT FAIR.
HAVE CHILDREN ALREADY? AND ON TOP OF THAT, WITH IDA..? (BRRR!)
RUSTLE
IDA? ARE YOU DONE BATHING?
DOEING
DOEING
DOEING
....

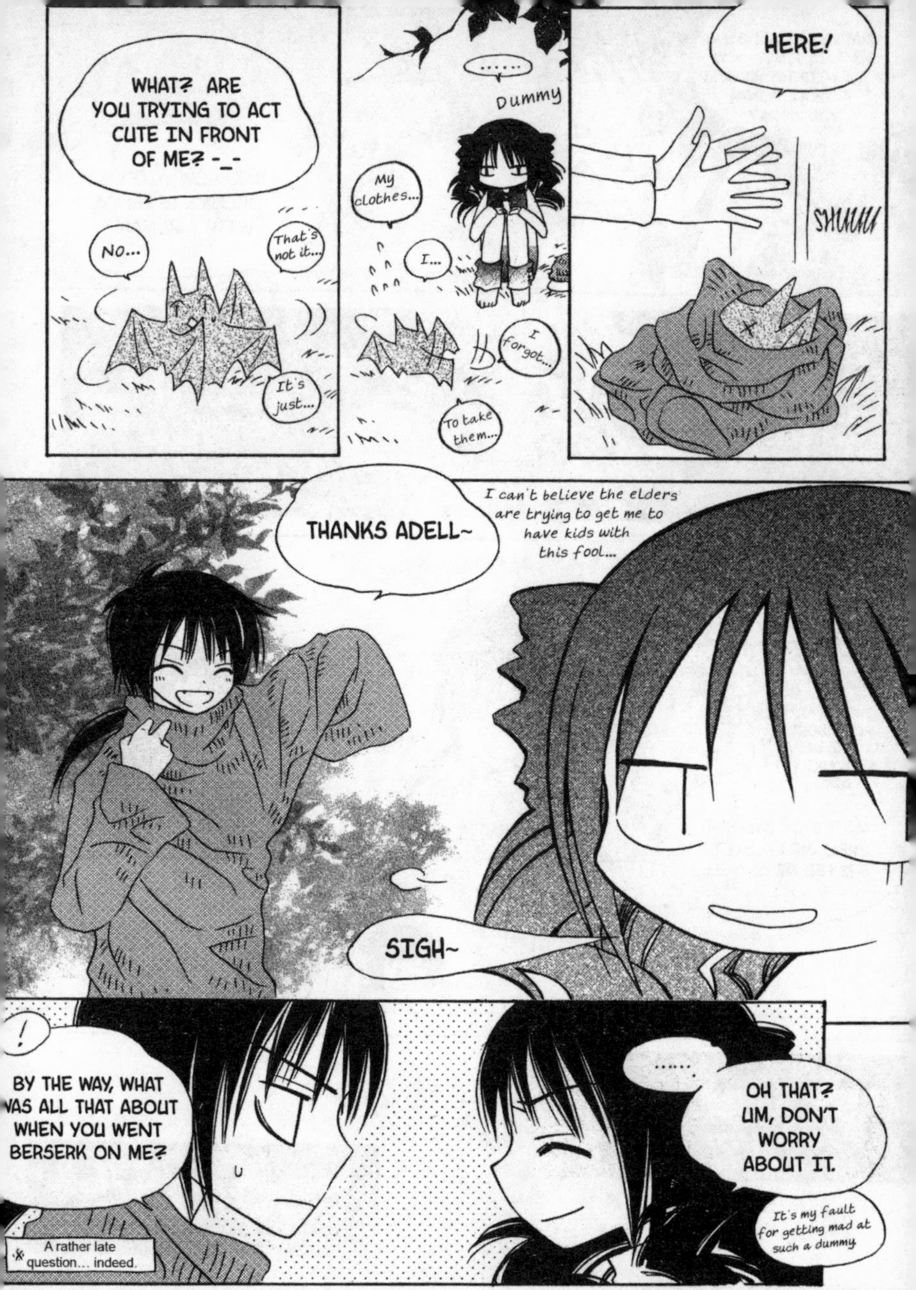
WHAT? ARE YOU TRYING TO ACT CUTE IN FRONT OF ME? -_-
No...
That's not it...
It's just...
......
Dummy
My clothes...
I...
I forgot...
To take them...
HERE!
SHUUUU
THANKS ADELL~
I can't believe the elders are trying to get me to have kids with this fool...
SIGH~
!
BY THE WAY, WHAT WAS ALL THAT ABOUT WHEN YOU WENT BERSERK ON ME?
A rather late question... indeed.
......
OH THAT? UM, DON'T WORRY ABOUT IT.
It's my fault for getting mad at such a dummy

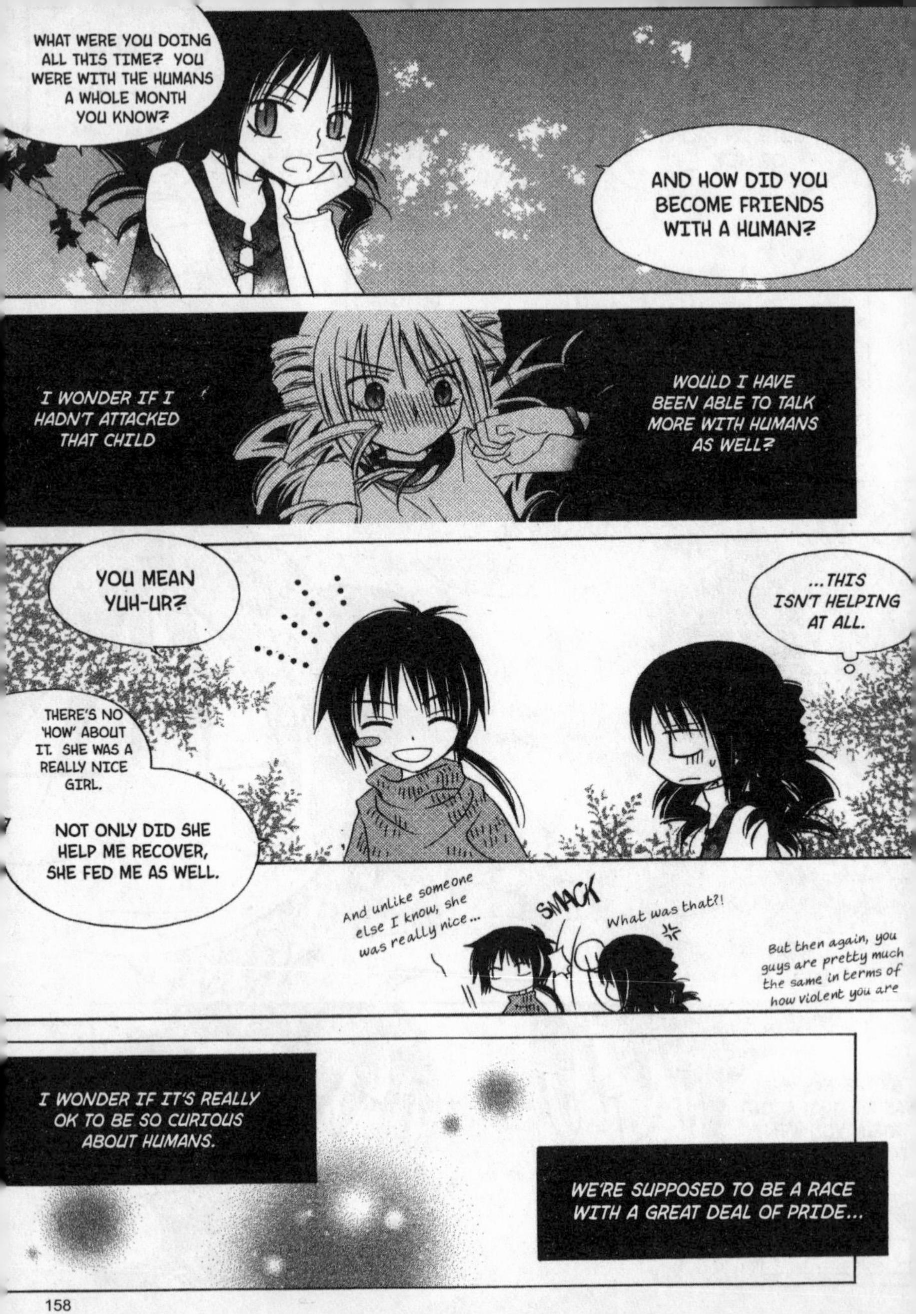

WHAT WERE YOU DOING ALL THIS TIME? YOU WERE WITH THE HUMANS A WHOLE MONTH YOU KNOW?
AND HOW DID YOU BECOME FRIENDS WITH A HUMAN?
I WONDER IF I HADN'T ATTACKED THAT CHILD
WOULD I HAVE BEEN ABLE TO TALK MORE WITH HUMANS AS WELL?
YOU MEAN YUH-UR?
THERE'S NO 'HOW' ABOUT IT. SHE WAS A REALLY NICE GIRL.
NOT ONLY DID SHE HELP ME RECOVER, SHE FED ME AS WELL.
...THIS ISN'T HELPING AT ALL.
And unlike someone else I know, she was really nice...
SMACK
What was that?!
But then again, you guys are pretty much the same in terms of how violent you are
I WONDER IF IT'S REALLY OK TO BE SO CURIOUS ABOUT HUMANS.
WE'RE SUPPOSED TO BE A RACE WITH A GREAT DEAL OF PRIDE...

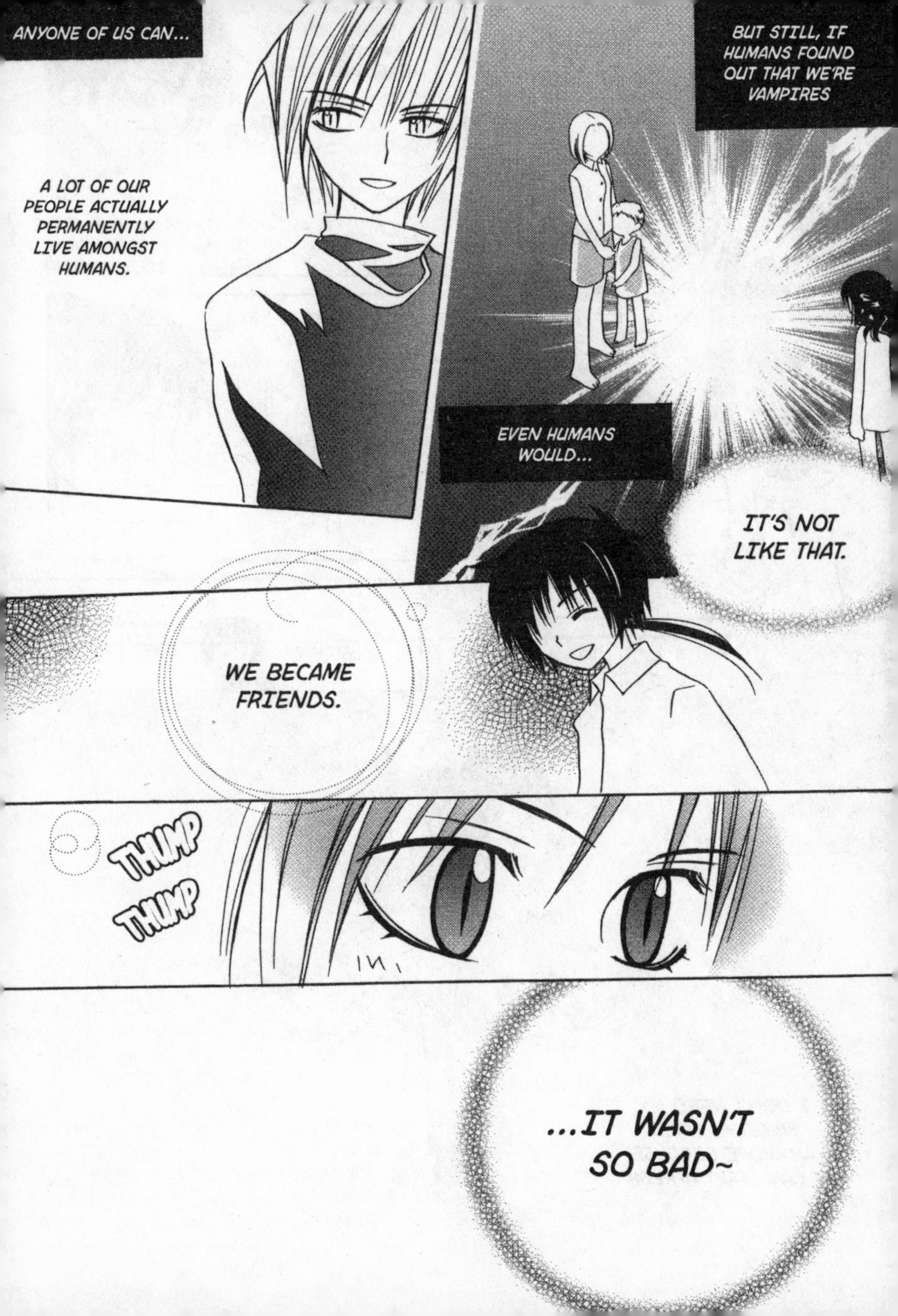
ANYONE OF US CAN...
A LOT OF OUR PEOPLE ACTUALLY PERMANENTLY LIVE AMONGST HUMANS.
BUT STILL, IF HUMANS FOUND OUT THAT WE'RE VAMPIRES
EVEN HUMANS WOULD...
IT'S NOT LIKE THAT.
WE BECAME FRIENDS.
THUMP THUMP
...IT WASN'T SO BAD~

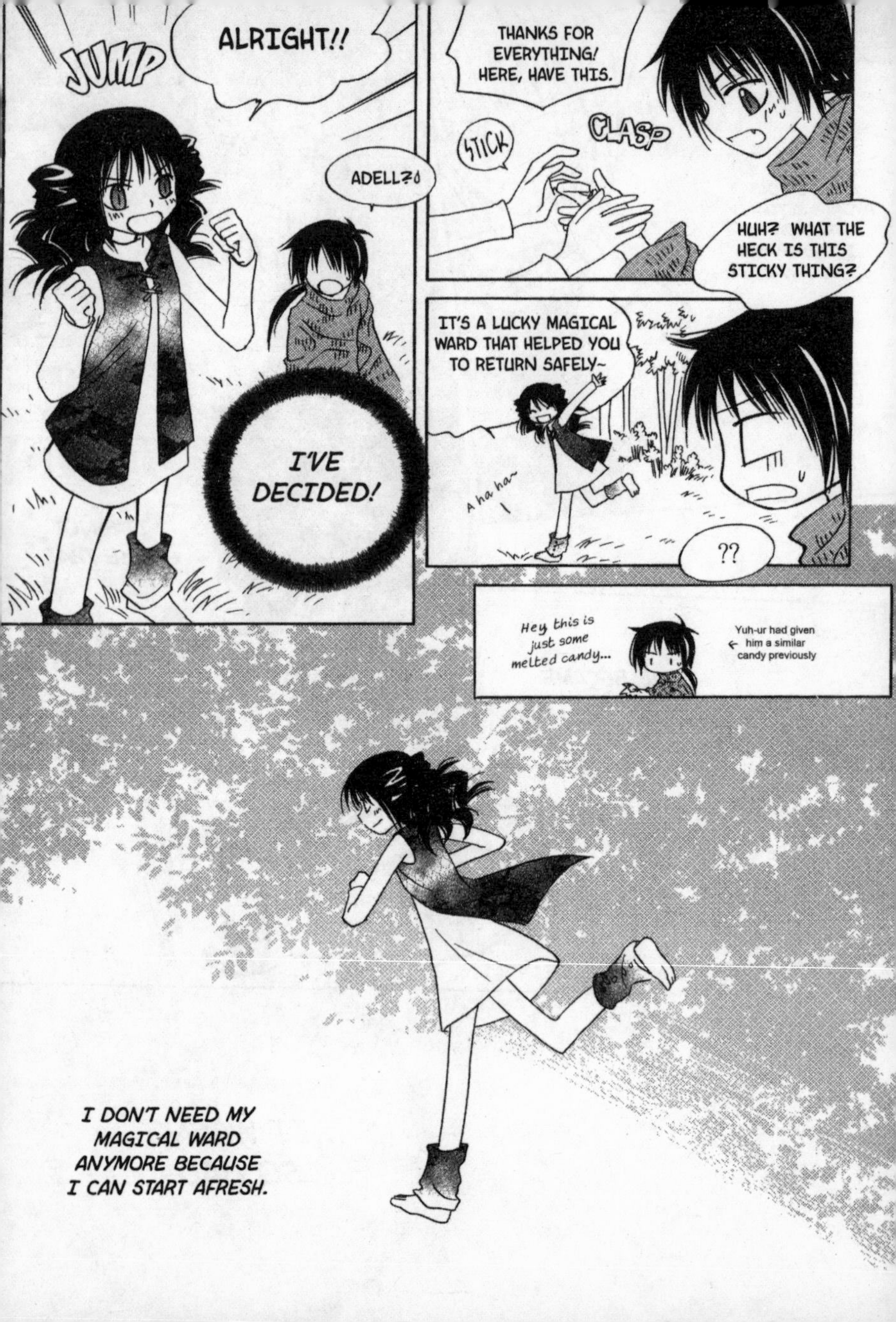
JUMP
ALRIGHT!!
ADELL?!
I'VE DECIDED!
THANKS FOR EVERYTHING! HERE, HAVE THIS.
STICK
CLASP
HUH? WHAT THE HECK IS THIS STICKY THING?
IT'S A LUCKY MAGICAL WARD THAT HELPED YOU TO RETURN SAFELY~
A ha ha~
??
Hey this is just some melted candy...
Yuh-ur had given him a similar candy previously
I DON'T NEED MY MAGICAL WARD ANYMORE BECAUSE I CAN START AFRESH.

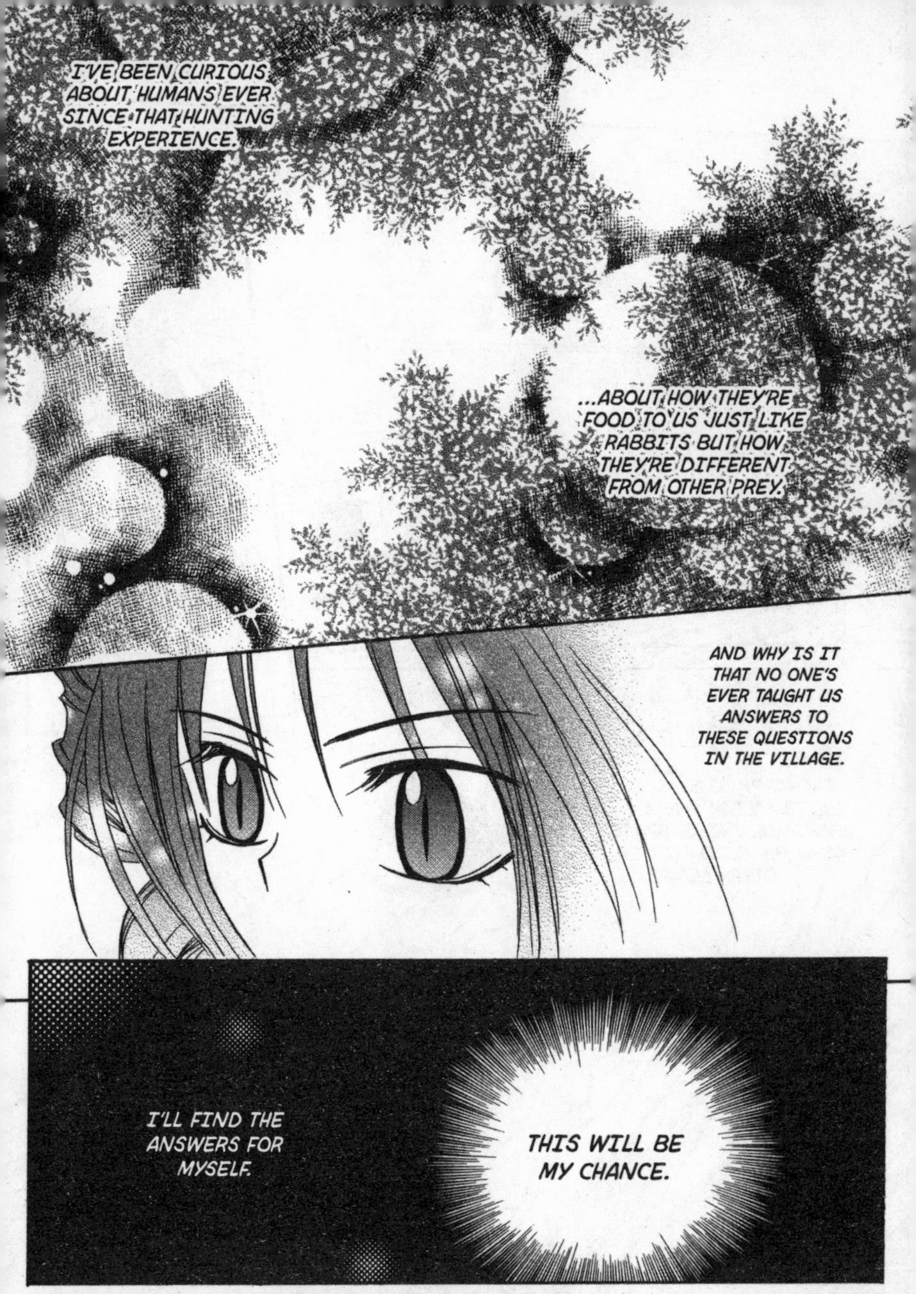
I'VE BEEN CURIOUS ABOUT HUMANS EVER SINCE THAT HUNTING EXPERIENCE.
...ABOUT HOW THEY'RE FOOD TO US JUST LIKE RABBITS BUT HOW THEY'RE DIFFERENT FROM OTHER PREY.
AND WHY IS IT THAT NO ONE'S EVER TAUGHT US ANSWERS TO THESE QUESTIONS IN THE VILLAGE.
I'LL FIND THE ANSWERS FOR MYSELF.
THIS WILL BE MY CHANCE.

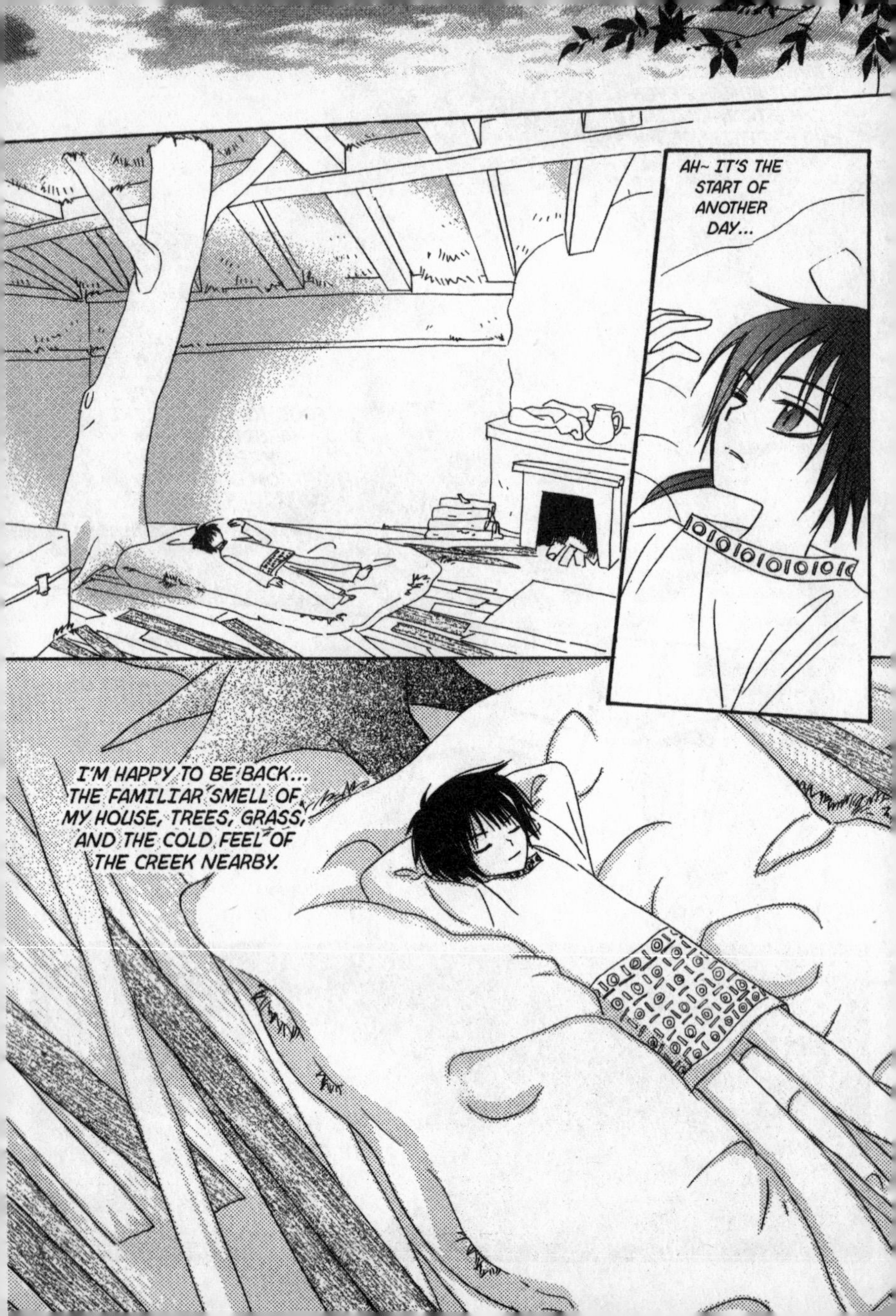
AH~ IT'S THE START OF ANOTHER DAY...
I'M HAPPY TO BE BACK... THE FAMILIAR SMELL OF MY HOUSE, TREES, GRASS, AND THE COLD FEEL OF THE CREEK NEARBY.

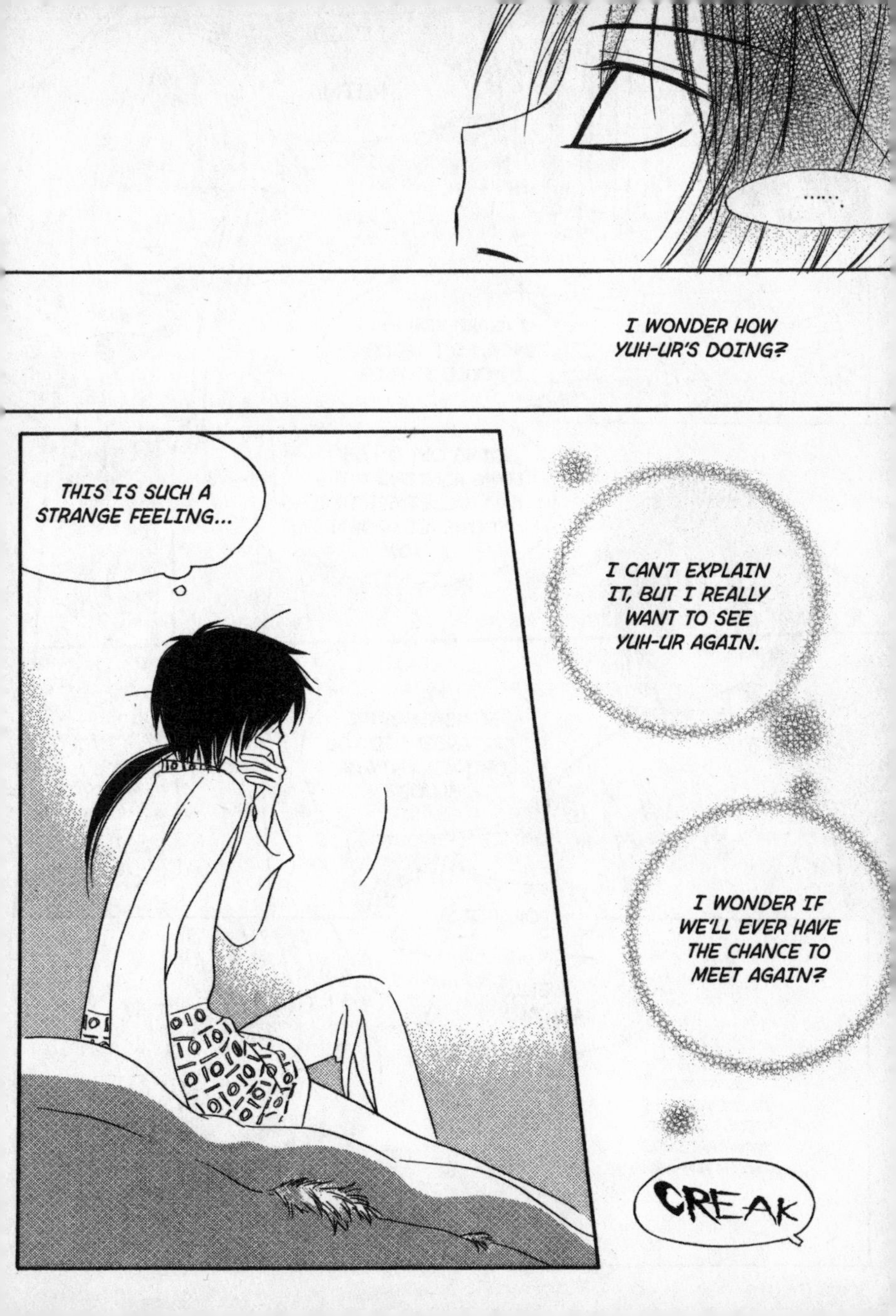
......
I WONDER HOW YUH-UR'S DOING?
THIS IS SUCH A STRANGE FEELING...
I CAN'T EXPLAIN IT, BUT I REALLY WANT TO SEE YUH-UR AGAIN.
I WONDER IF WE'LL EVER HAVE THE CHANCE TO MEET AGAIN?
CREAK

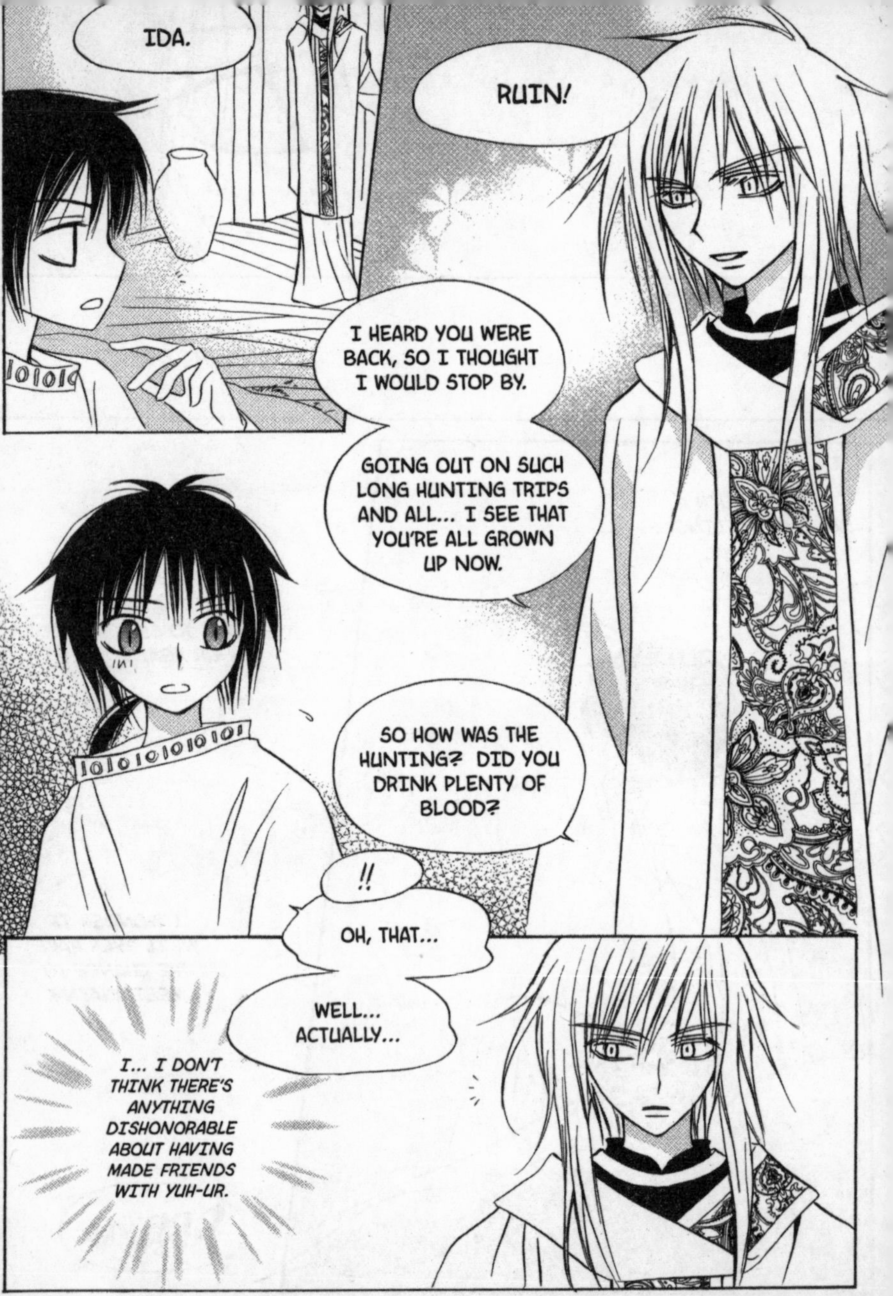
IDA.
RUIN!
I HEARD YOU WERE BACK, SO I THOUGHT I WOULD STOP BY.
GOING OUT ON SUCH LONG HUNTING TRIPS AND ALL... I SEE THAT YOU'RE ALL GROWN UP NOW.
SO HOW WAS THE HUNTING? DID YOU DRINK PLENTY OF BLOOD?
!!
OH, THAT...
WELL... ACTUALLY...
I... I DON'T THINK THERE'S ANYTHING DISHONORABLE ABOUT HAVING MADE FRIENDS WITH YUH-UR.

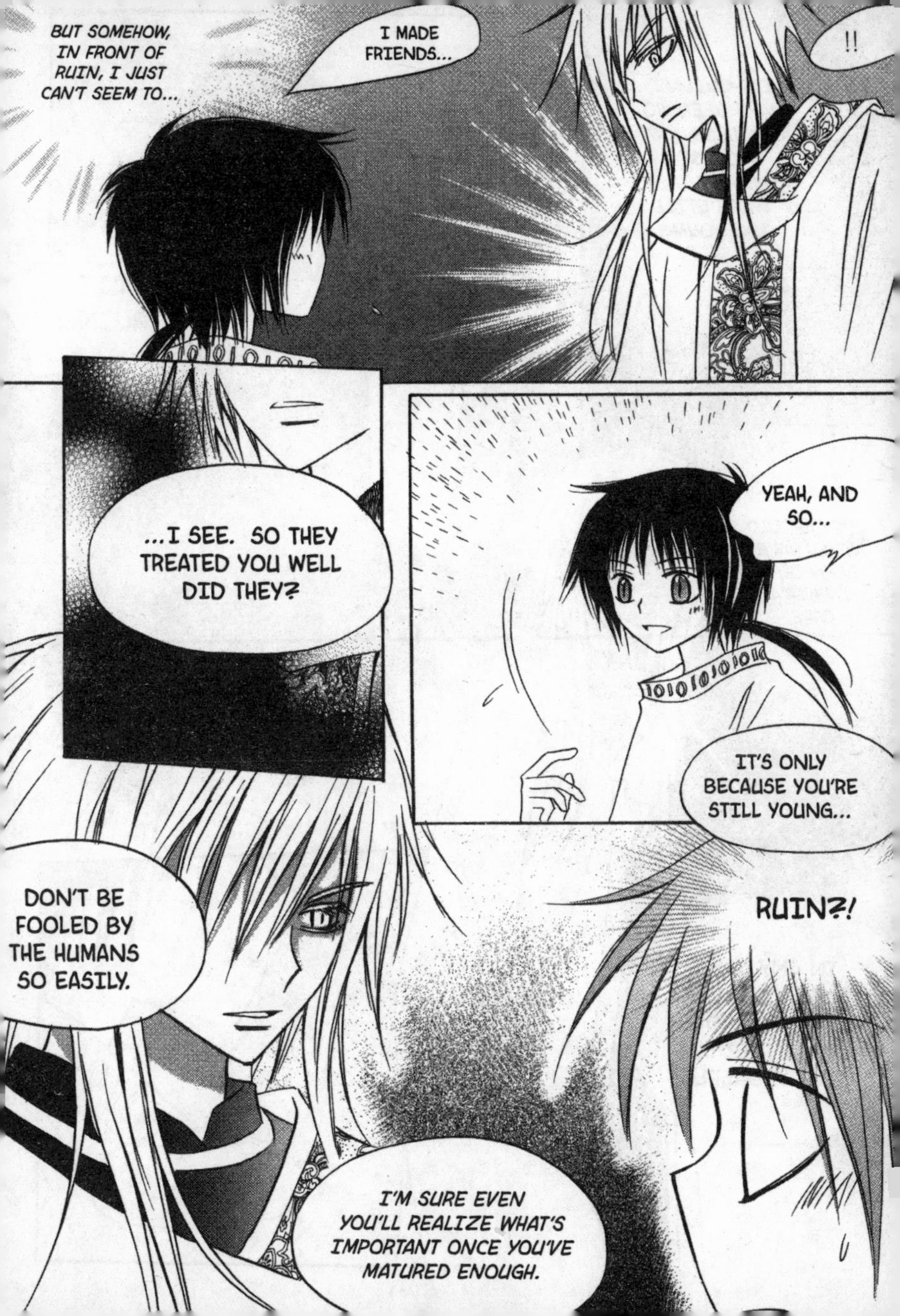
BUT SOMEHOW, IN FRONT OF RUIN, I JUST CAN'T SEEM TO...
I MADE FRIENDS...
!!
...I SEE. SO THEY TREATED YOU WELL DID THEY?
YEAH, AND SO...
IT'S ONLY BECAUSE YOU'RE STILL YOUNG...
DON'T BE FOOLED BY THE HUMANS SO EASILY.
RUIN?!
I'M SURE EVEN YOU'LL REALIZE WHAT'S IMPORTANT ONCE YOU'VE MATURED ENOUGH.

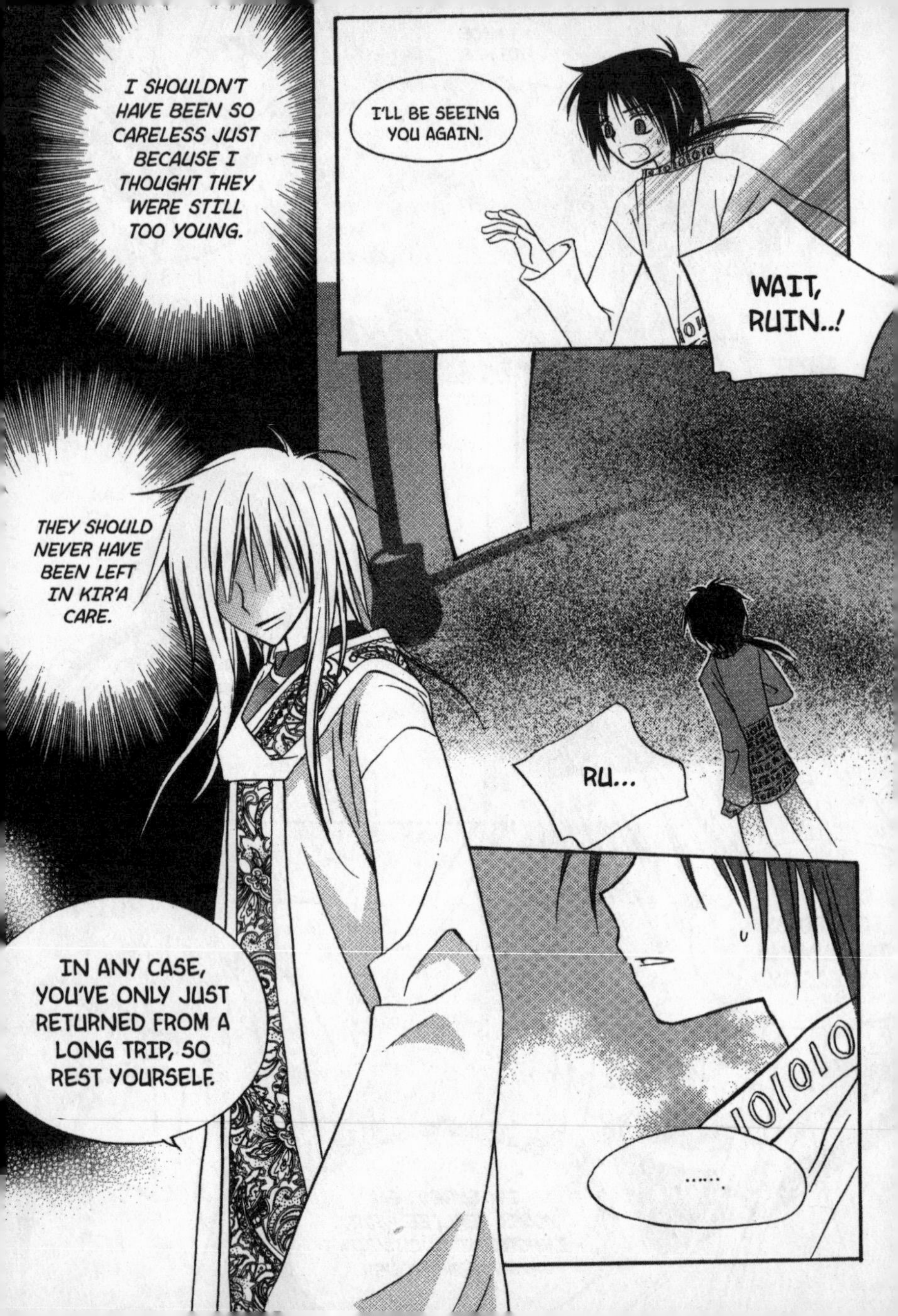
I SHOULDN'T HAVE BEEN SO CARELESS JUST BECAUSE I THOUGHT THEY WERE STILL TOO YOUNG.
THEY SHOULD NEVER HAVE BEEN LEFT IN KIR'A CARE.
IN ANY CASE, YOU'VE ONLY JUST RETURNED FROM A LONG TRIP, SO REST YOURSELF.
I'LL BE SEEING YOU AGAIN.
WAIT, RUIN..!
RU...
......

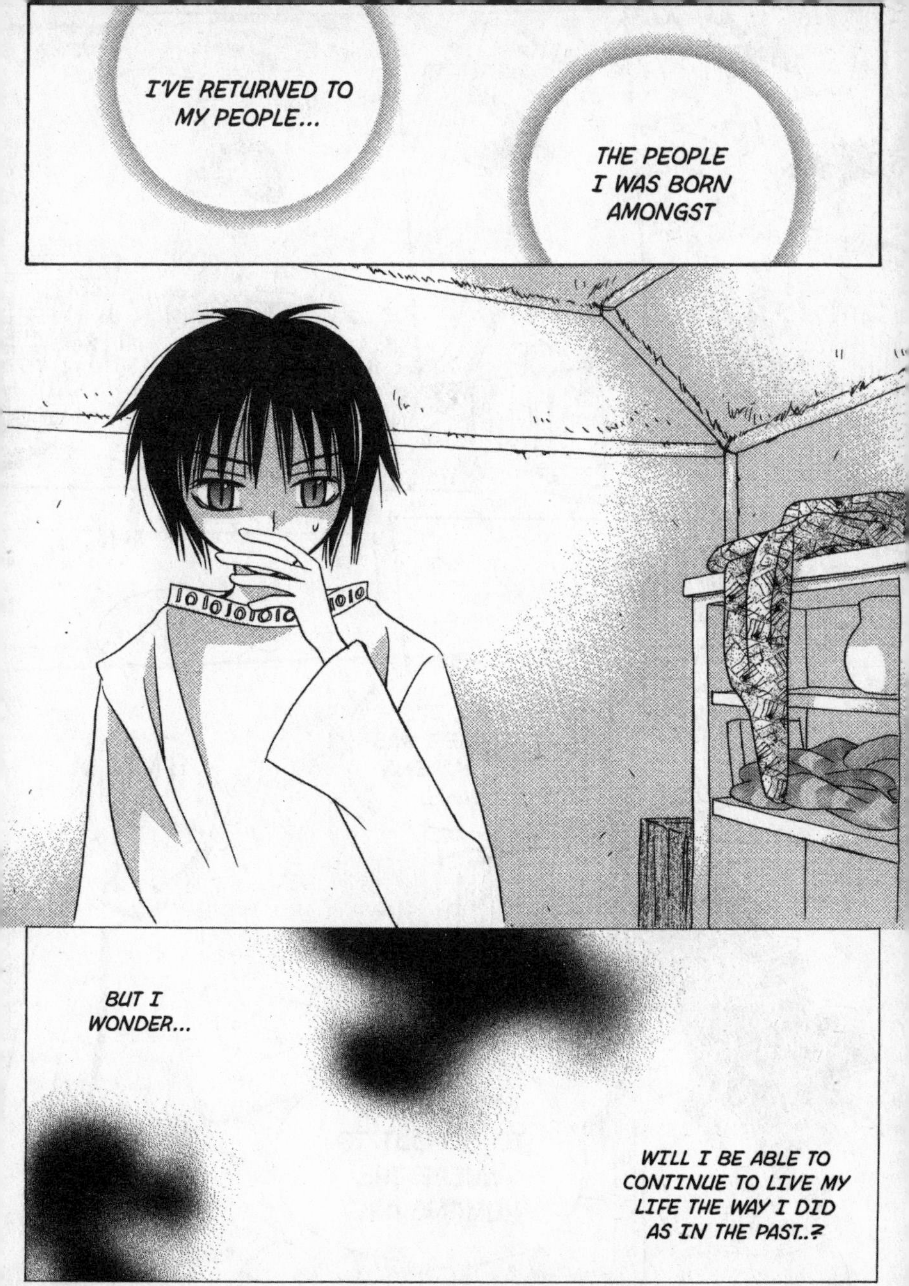
I'VE RETURNED TO MY PEOPLE...
THE PEOPLE I WAS BORN AMONGST
BUT I WONDER...
WILL I BE ABLE TO CONTINUE TO LIVE MY LIFE THE WAY I DID AS IN THE PAST..?

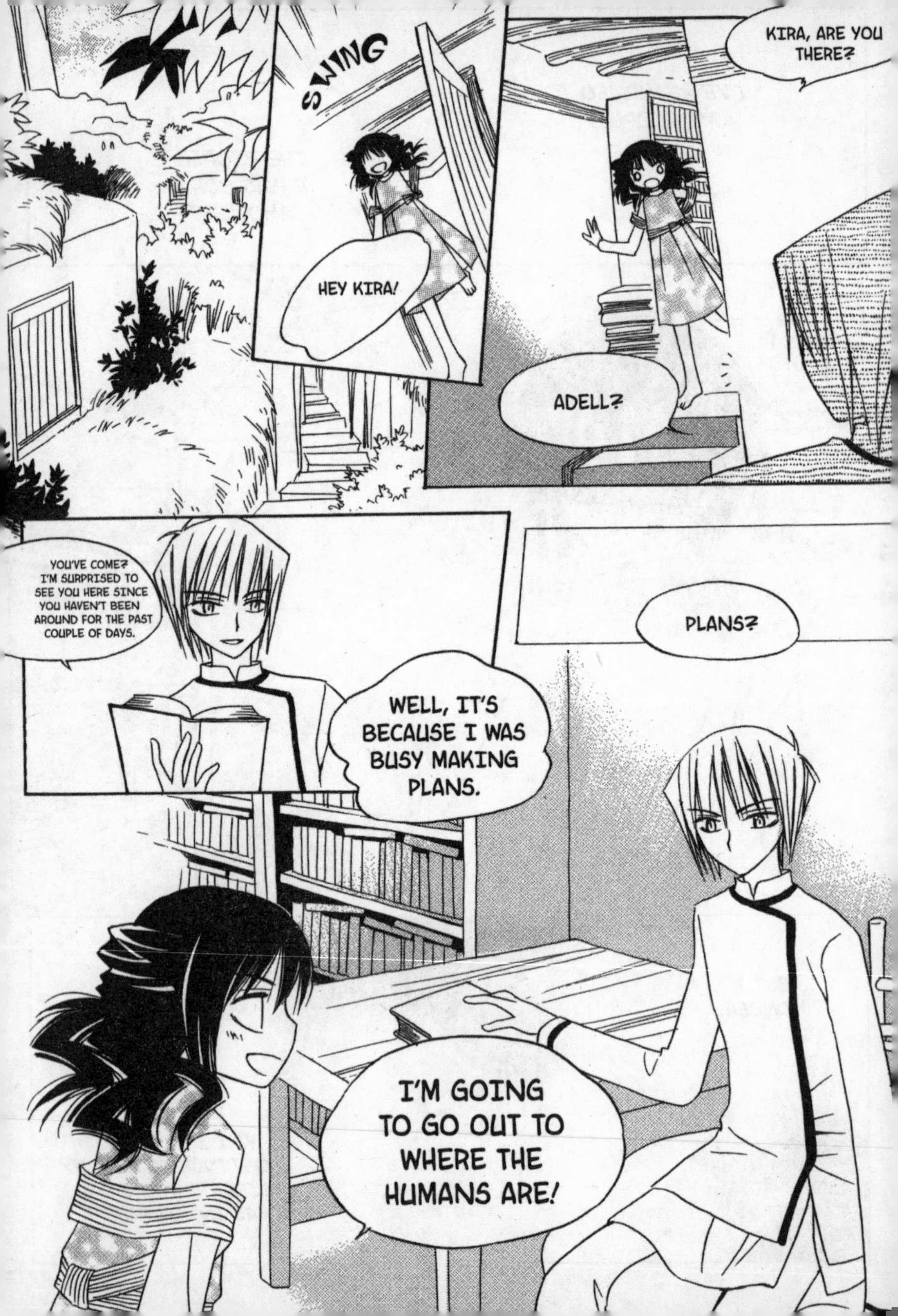
SWING
HEY KIRA!
KIRA, ARE YOU THERE?
ADELL?
YOU'VE COME? I'M SURPRISED TO SEE YOU HERE SINCE YOU HAVEN'T BEEN AROUND FOR THE PAST COUPLE OF DAYS.
PLANS?
WELL, IT'S BECAUSE I WAS BUSY MAKING PLANS.
I'M GOING TO GO OUT TO WHERE THE HUMANS ARE!

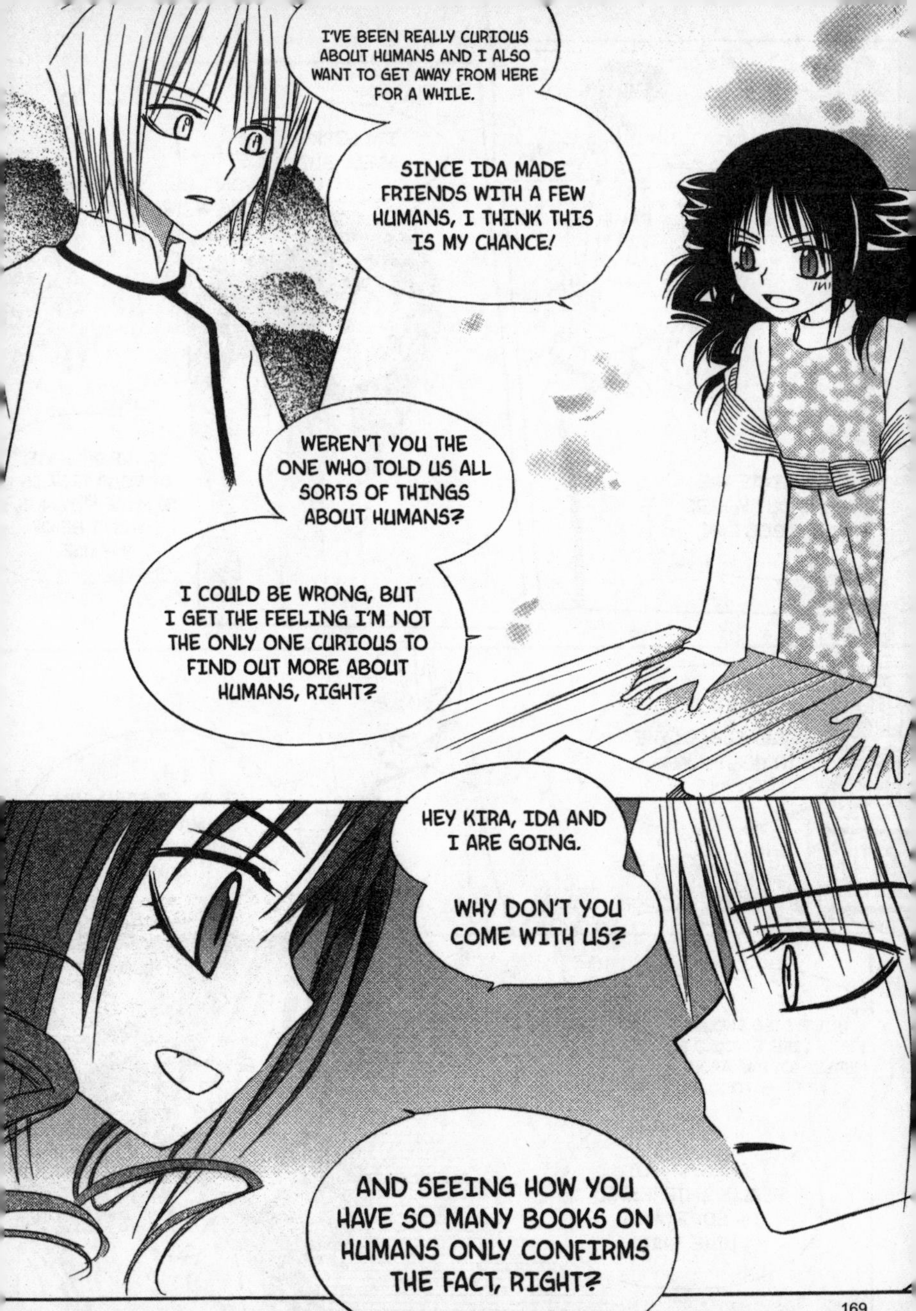
I'VE BEEN REALLY CURIOUS ABOUT HUMANS AND I ALSO WANT TO GET AWAY FROM HERE FOR A WHILE.
SINCE IDA MADE FRIENDS WITH A FEW HUMANS, I THINK THIS IS MY CHANCE!
WEREN'T YOU THE ONE WHO TOLD US ALL SORTS OF THINGS ABOUT HUMANS?
I COULD BE WRONG, BUT I GET THE FEELING I'M NOT THE ONLY ONE CURIOUS TO FIND OUT MORE ABOUT HUMANS, RIGHT?
HEY KIRA, IDA AND I ARE GOING.
WHY DON'T YOU COME WITH US?
AND SEEING HOW YOU HAVE SO MANY BOOKS ON HUMANS ONLY CONFIRMS THE FACT, RIGHT?

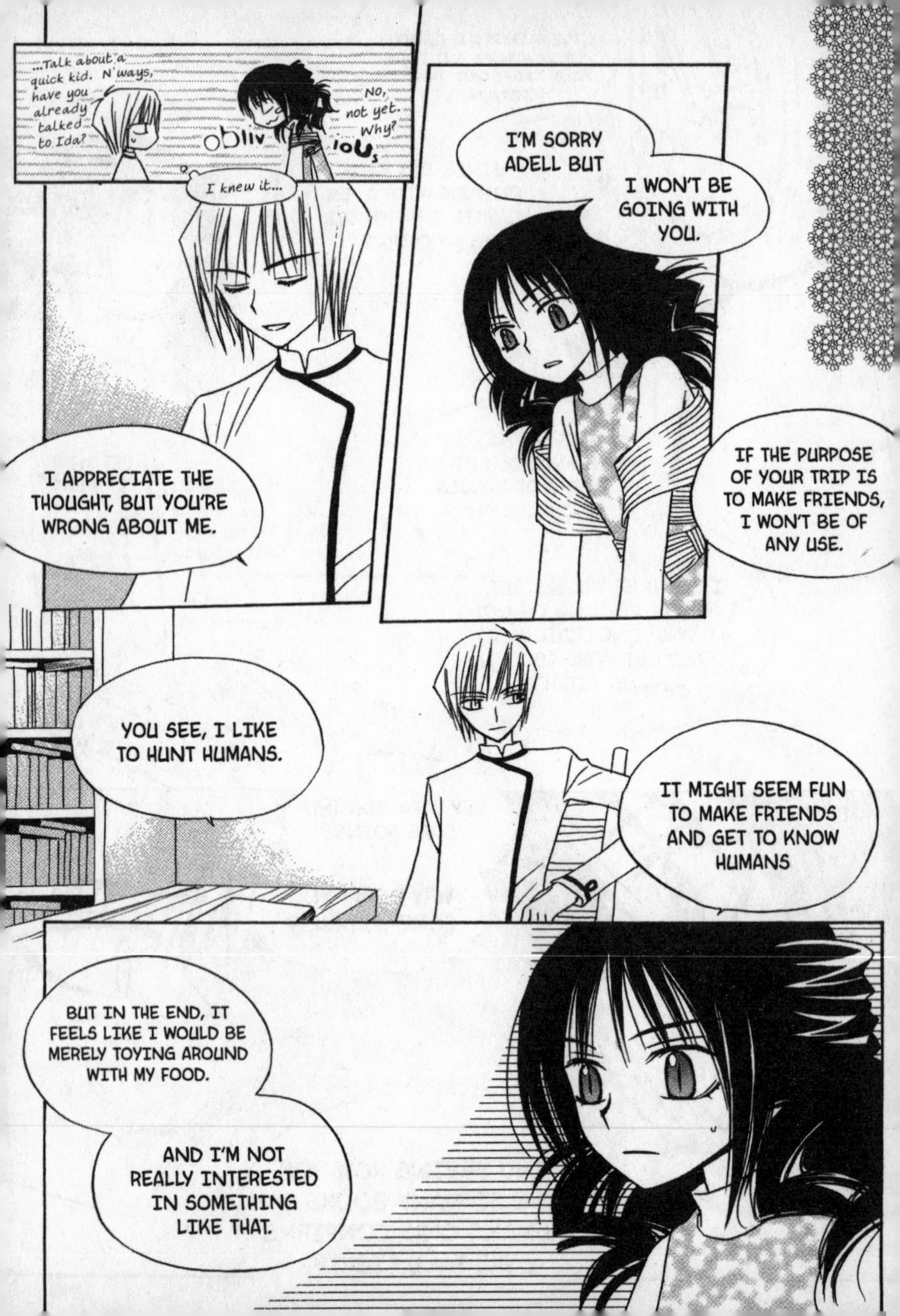
...Talk about a quick kid. N'ways, have you already talked to Ida?
No, not yet. Why?
oblivious
I knew it...
I APPRECIATE THE THOUGHT, BUT YOU'RE WRONG ABOUT ME.
I'M SORRY ADELL BUT
I WON'T BE GOING WITH YOU.
IF THE PURPOSE OF YOUR TRIP IS TO MAKE FRIENDS, I WON'T BE OF ANY USE.
YOU SEE, I LIKE TO HUNT HUMANS.
IT MIGHT SEEM FUN TO MAKE FRIENDS AND GET TO KNOW HUMANS
BUT IN THE END, IT FEELS LIKE I WOULD BE MERELY TOYING AROUND WITH MY FOOD.
AND I'M NOT REALLY INTERESTED IN SOMETHING LIKE THAT.

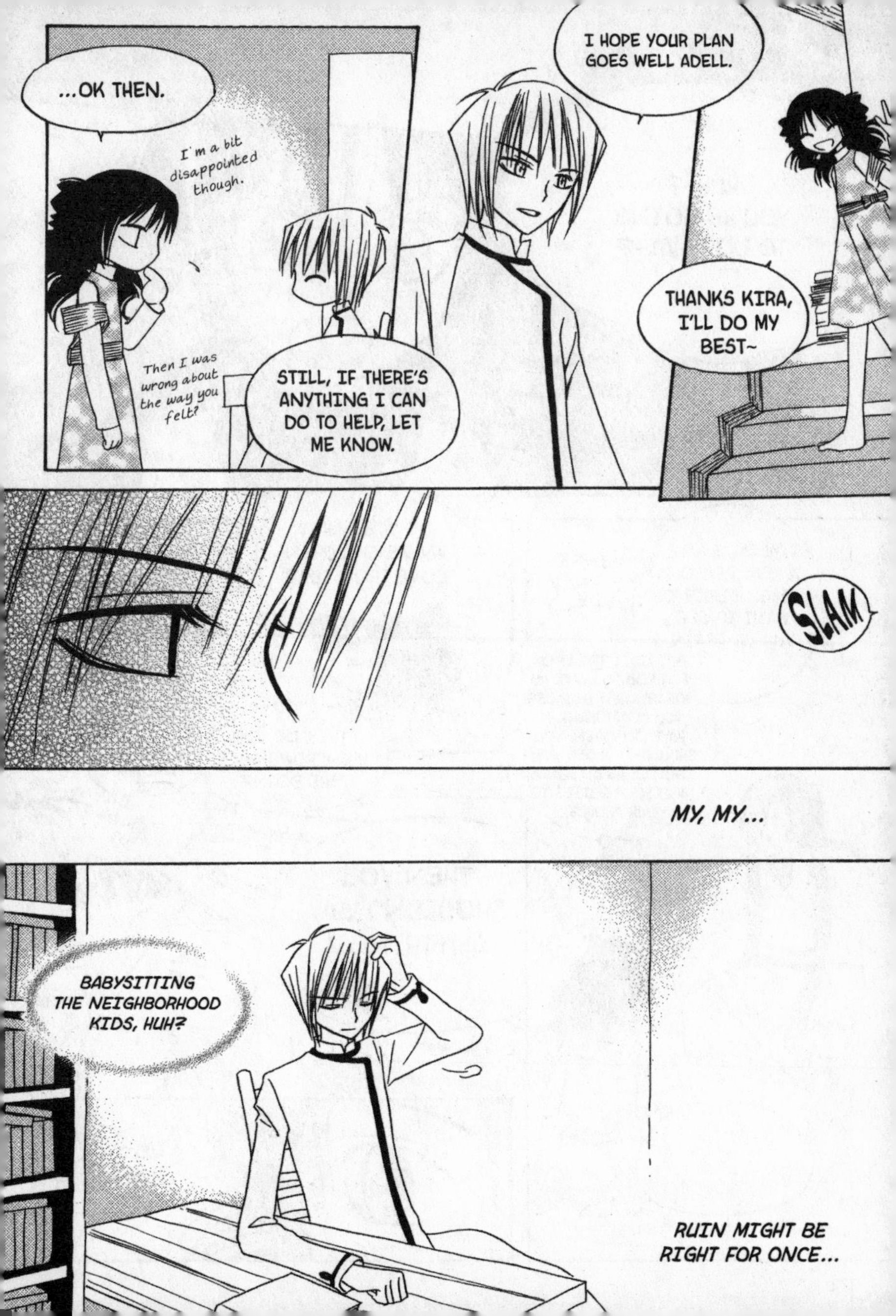
...OK THEN.
I'm a bit disappointed though.
Then I was wrong about the way you felt?
STILL, IF THERE'S ANYTHING I CAN DO TO HELP, LET ME KNOW.
I HOPE YOUR PLAN GOES WELL ADELL.
THANKS KIRA, I'LL DO MY BEST~
SLAM
MY, MY...
BABYSITTING THE NEIGHBORHOOD KIDS, HUH?
RUIN MIGHT BE RIGHT FOR ONCE...

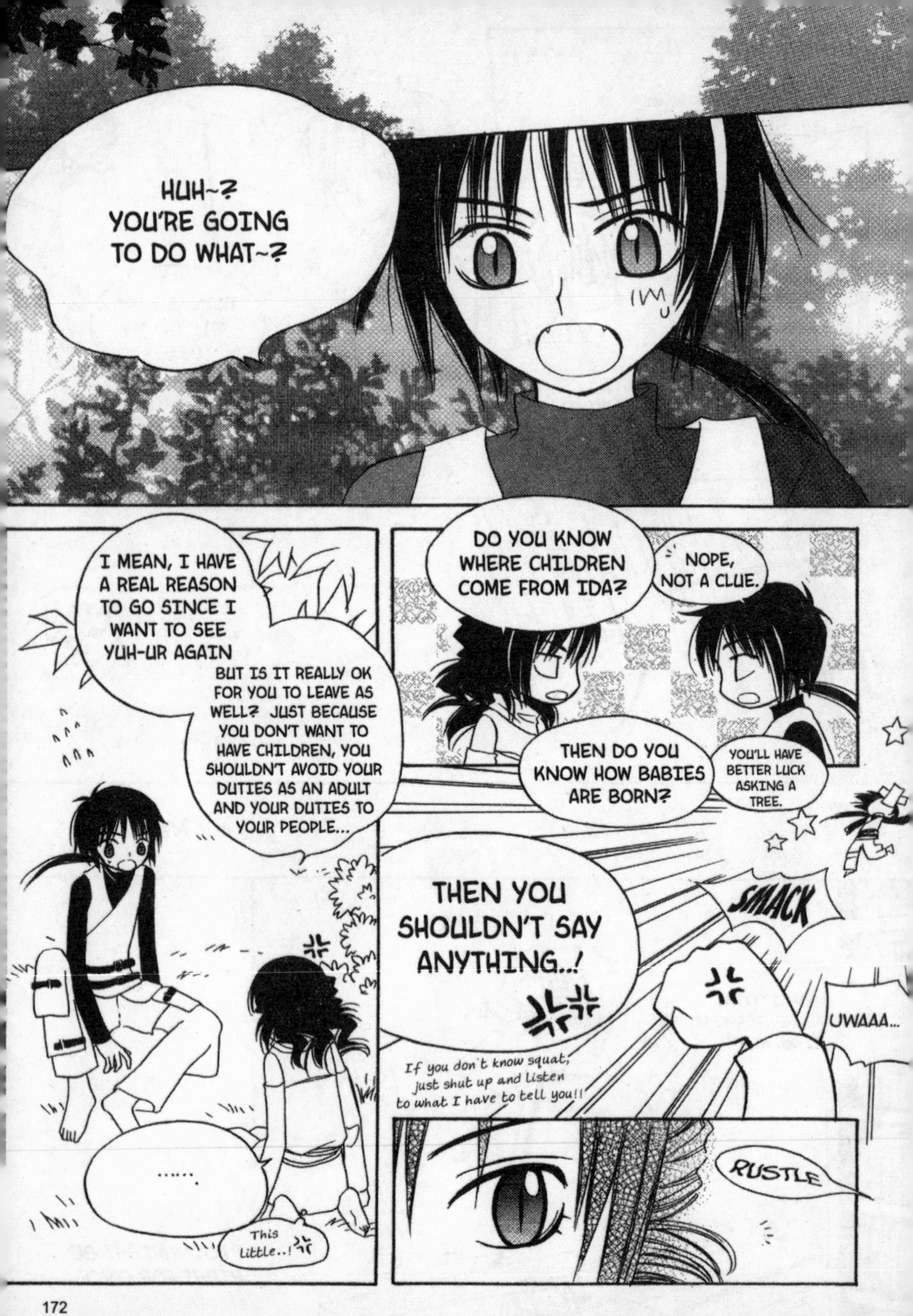
HUH~? YOU'RE GOING TO DO WHAT~?
I MEAN, I HAVE A REAL REASON TO GO SINCE I WANT TO SEE YUH-UR AGAIN
BUT IS IT REALLY OK FOR YOU TO LEAVE AS WELL? JUST BECAUSE YOU DON'T WANT TO HAVE CHILDREN, YOU SHOULDN'T AVOID YOUR DUTIES AS AN ADULT AND YOUR DUTIES TO YOUR PEOPLE...
......
This Little..!
DO YOU KNOW WHERE CHILDREN COME FROM IDA?
NOPE, NOT A CLUE.
THEN DO YOU KNOW HOW BABIES ARE BORN?
YOU'LL HAVE BETTER LUCK ASKING A TREE.
THEN YOU SHOULDN'T SAY ANYTHING..!
SMACK
UWAAA...
If you don't know squat, just shut up and listen to what I have to tell you!!
RUSTLE

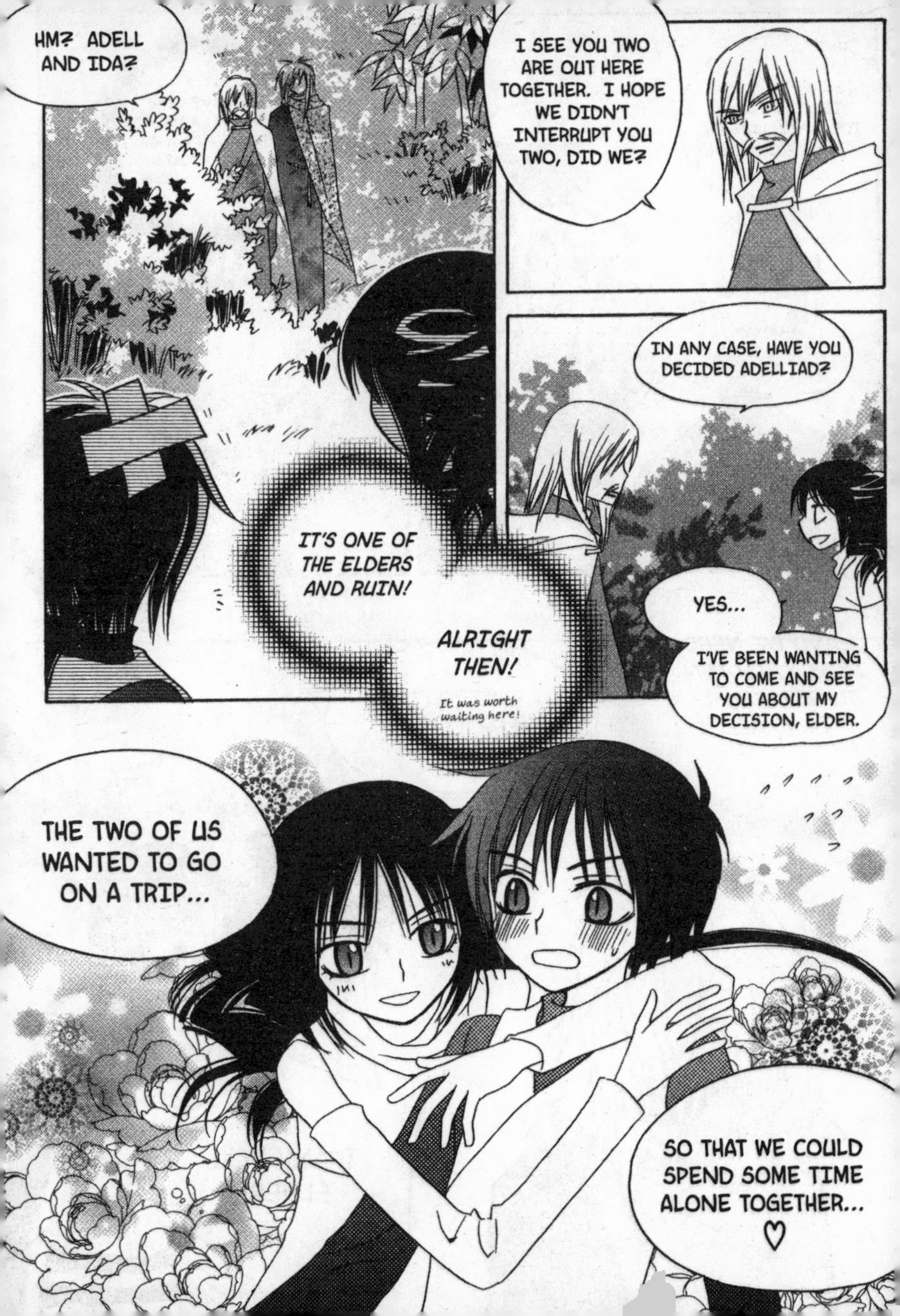
HM? ADELL AND IDA?
I SEE YOU TWO ARE OUT HERE TOGETHER. I HOPE WE DIDN'T INTERRUPT YOU TWO, DID WE?
IT'S ONE OF THE ELDERS AND RUIN!
ALRIGHT THEN!
It was worth waiting here!
IN ANY CASE, HAVE YOU DECIDED ADELLIAD?
YES...
I'VE BEEN WANTING TO COME AND SEE YOU ABOUT MY DECISION, ELDER.
THE TWO OF US WANTED TO GO ON A TRIP...
SO THAT WE COULD SPEND SOME TIME ALONE TOGETHER... ♡

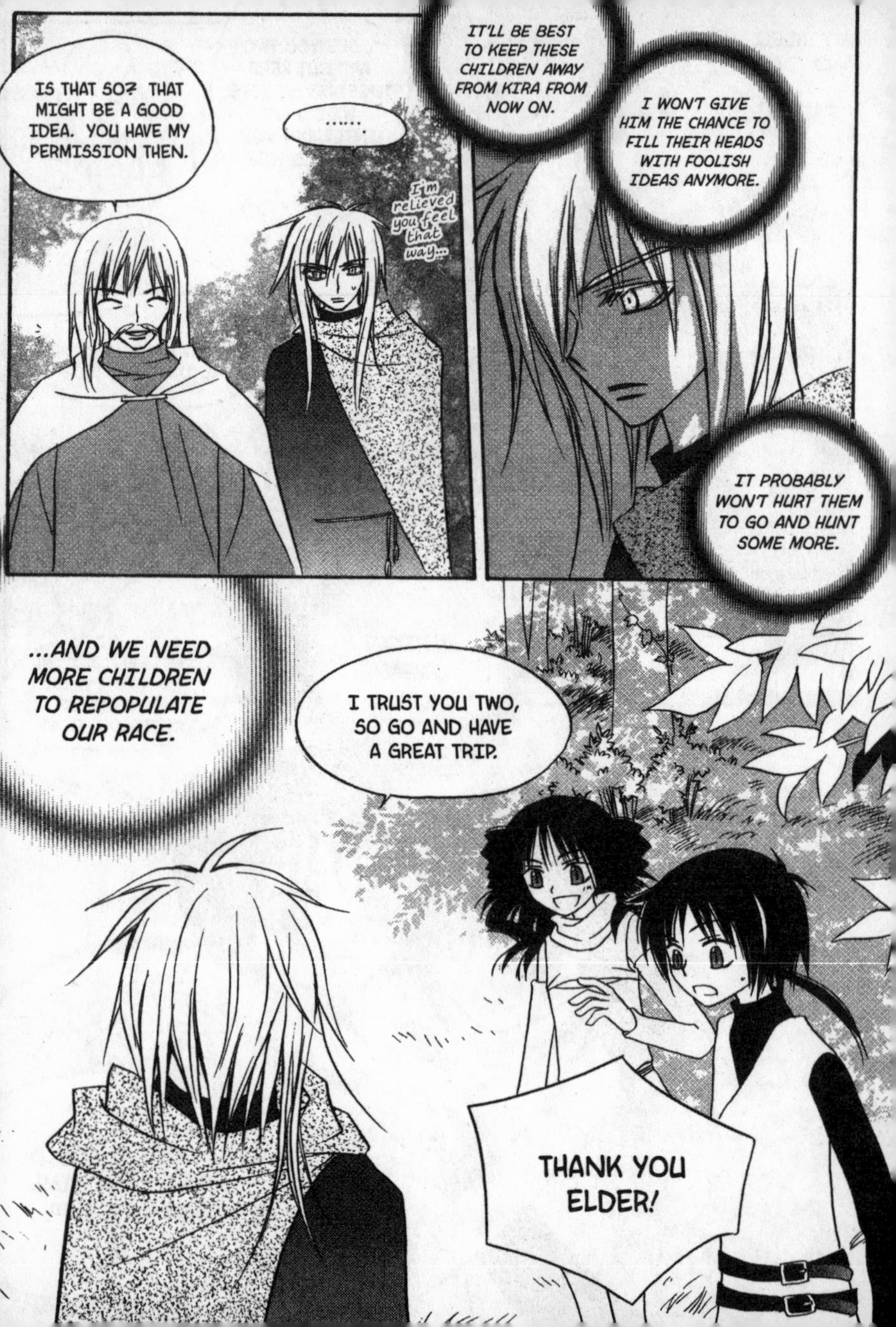
IS THAT SO? THAT MIGHT BE A GOOD IDEA. YOU HAVE MY PERMISSION THEN.
......
I'm relieved you feel that way...
IT'LL BE BEST TO KEEP THESE CHILDREN AWAY FROM KIRA FROM NOW ON.
I WON'T GIVE HIM THE CHANCE TO FILL THEIR HEADS WITH FOOLISH IDEAS ANYMORE.
IT PROBABLY WON'T HURT THEM TO GO AND HUNT SOME MORE.
...AND WE NEED MORE CHILDREN TO REPOPULATE OUR RACE.
I TRUST YOU TWO, SO GO AND HAVE A GREAT TRIP.
THANK YOU ELDER!

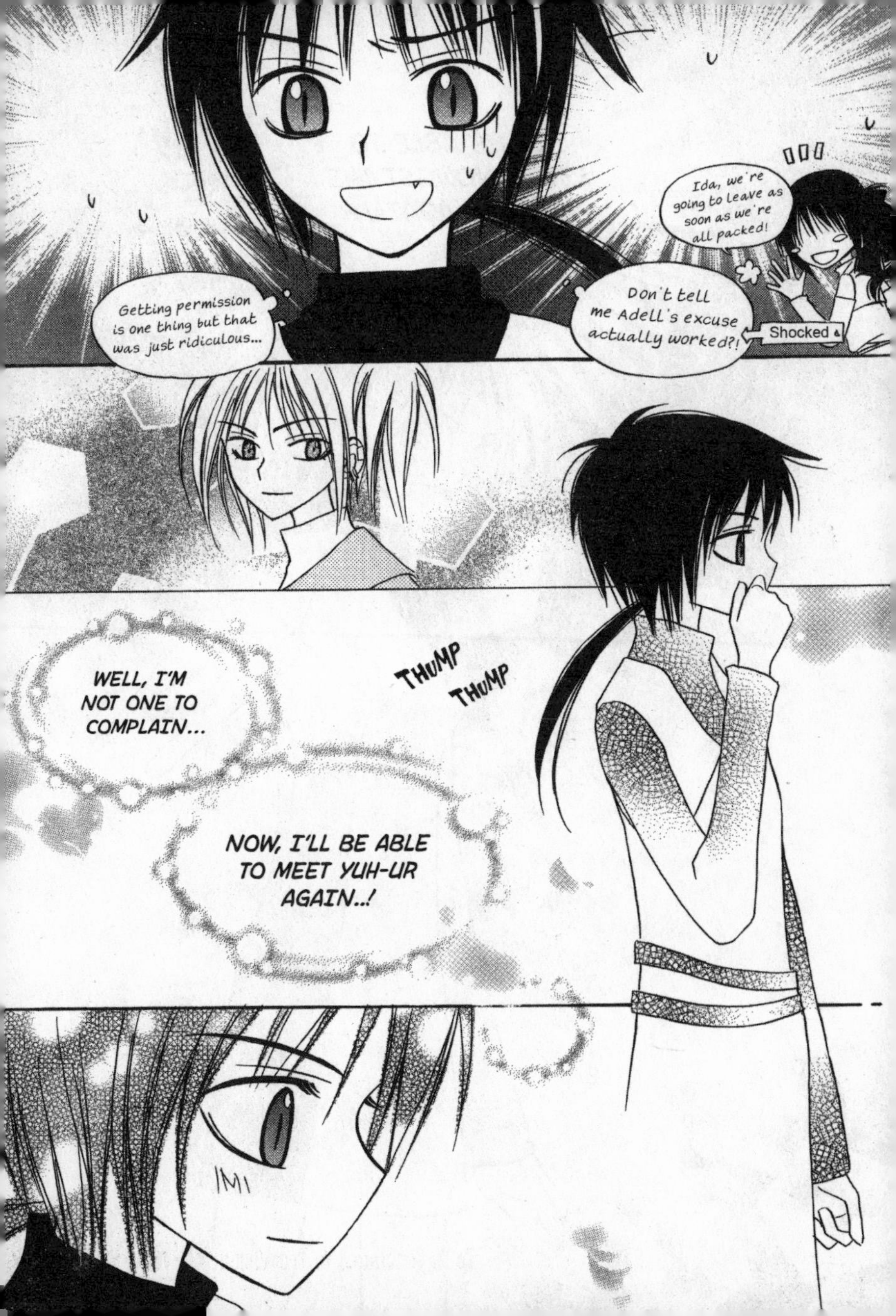
Getting permission is one thing but that was just ridiculous...
Don't tell me Adell's excuse actually worked?!
Shocked
Ida, we're going to leave as soon as we're all packed!
WELL, I'M NOT ONE TO COMPLAIN...
THUMP THUMP
NOW, I'LL BE ABLE TO MEET YUH-UR AGAIN..!

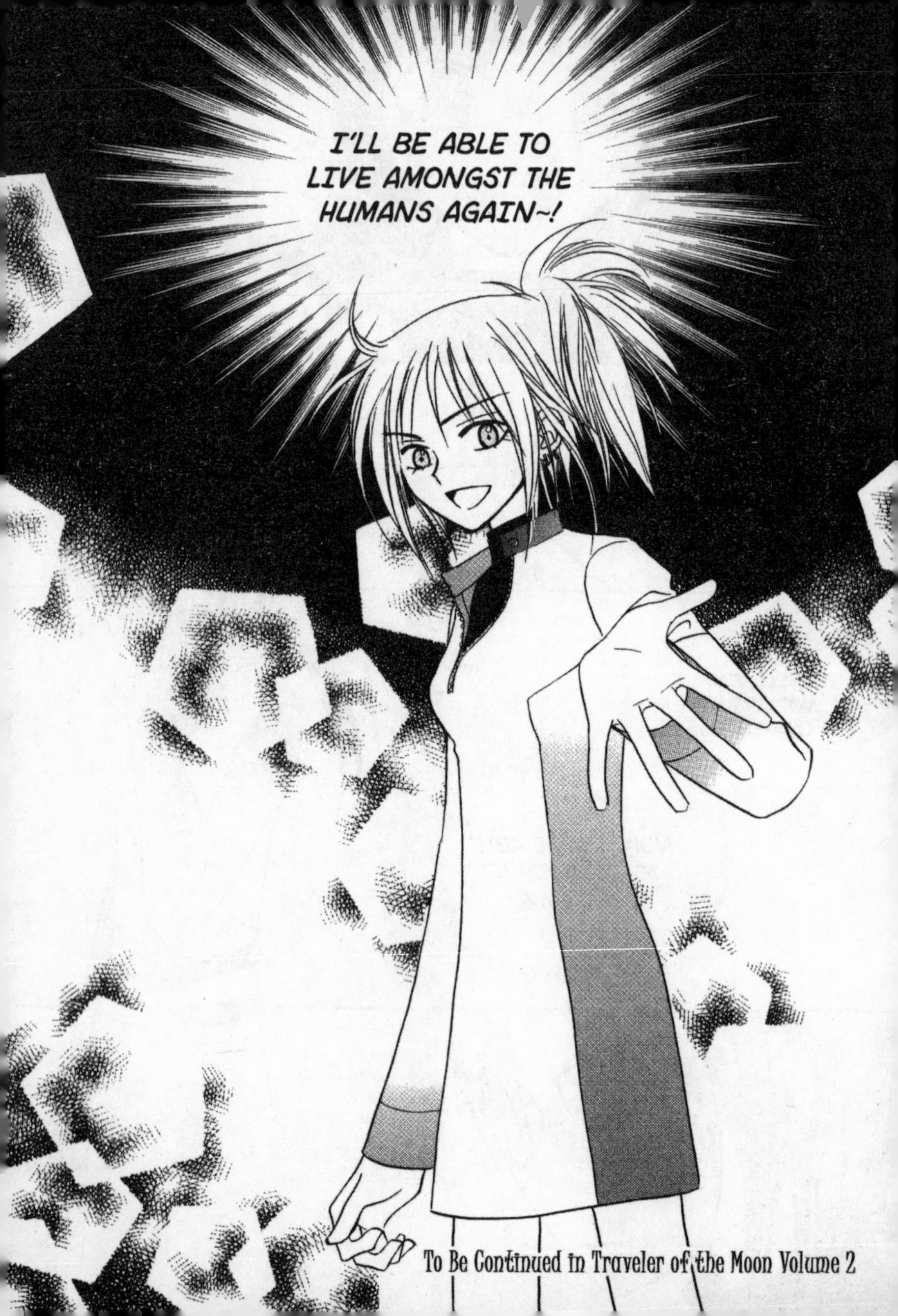
I'LL BE ABLE TO LIVE AMONGST THE HUMANS AGAIN~!

To Be Continued in Traveler of the Moon Volume 2

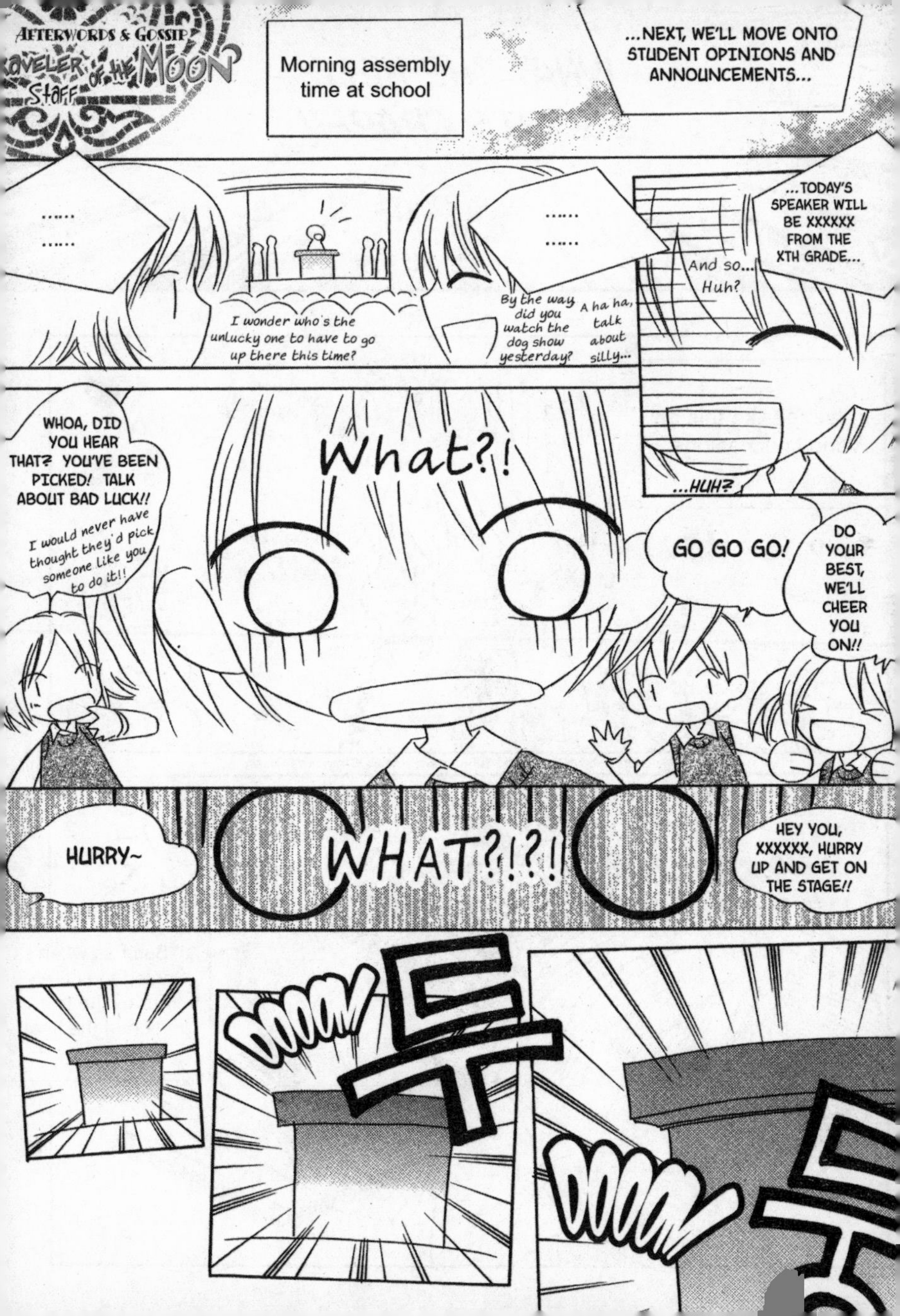
AFTERWORDS & GOSSIP
raveler of the MOON Staff
Morning assembly time at school
...NEXT, WE'LL MOVE ONTO STUDENT OPINIONS AND ANNOUNCEMENTS...
....
I wonder who's the unlucky one to have to go up there this time?
....
By the way did you watch the dog show yesterday?
A ha ha, talk about silly...
...TODAY'S SPEAKER WILL BE XXXXXX FROM THE XTH GRADE...
And so... Huh?
...HUH?
WHOA, DID YOU HEAR THAT? YOU'VE BEEN PICKED! TALK ABOUT BAD LUCK!!
I would never have thought they'd pick someone like you to do it!!
What?!
GO GO GO!
DO YOUR BEST, WE'LL CHEER YOU ON!!
HURRY~
WHAT?!?!
HEY YOU, XXXXXX, HURRY UP AND GET ON THE STAGE!!
DOOM!
DOOM

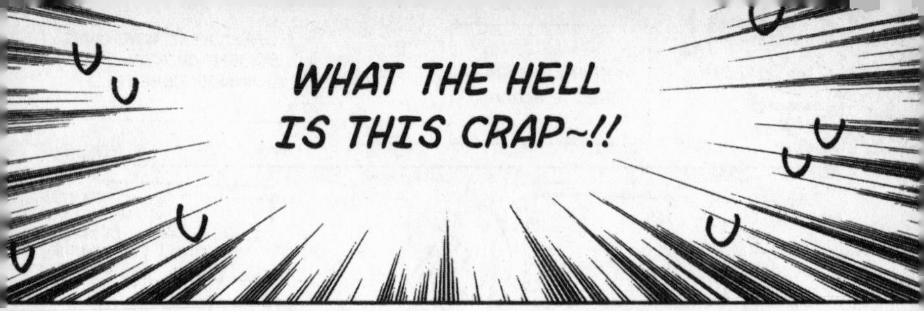
WHAT THE HELL
IS THIS CRAP~!!

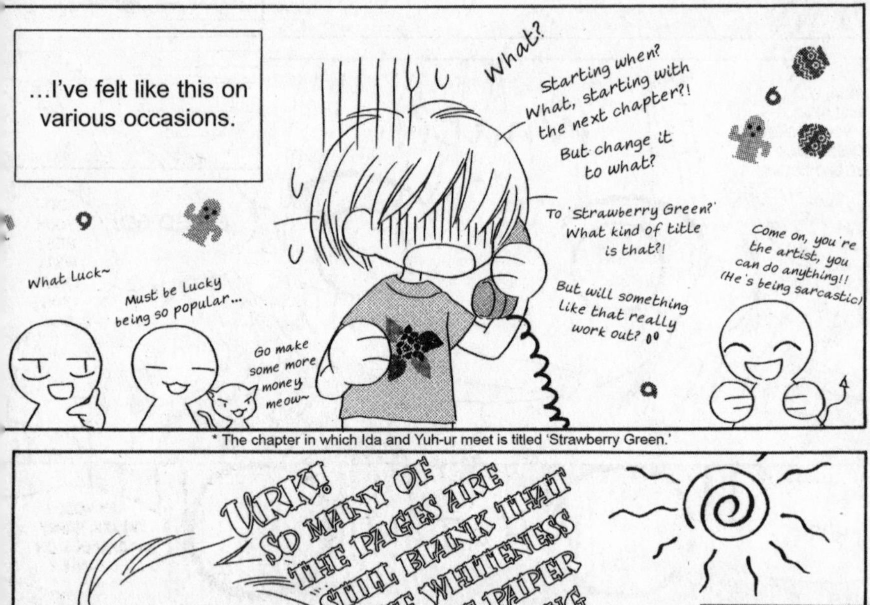
...I've felt like this on various occasions.
What?
Starting when? What, starting with the next chapter?!
But change it to what?
To 'Strawberry Green?' What kind of title is that?!
But will something like that really work out?
What luck~
Must be lucky being so popular...
Go make some more money meow~
Come on, you're the artist, you can do anything!! (He's being sarcastic)

* The chapter in which Ida and Yuh-ur meet is titled 'Strawberry Green.'

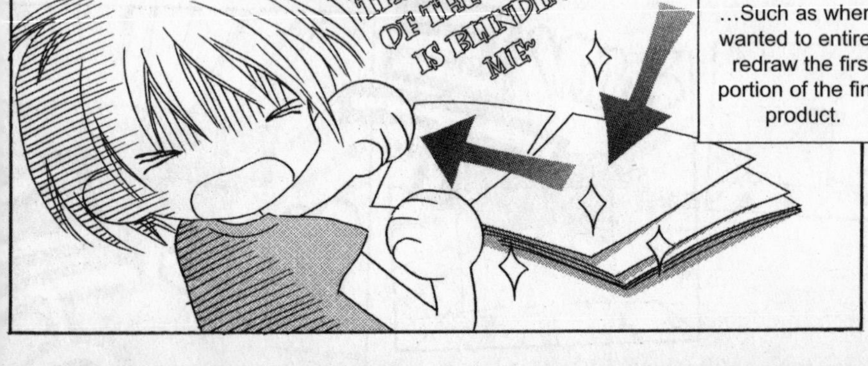
URK! SO MANY OF THE PAGES ARE STILL BLANK THAT THE WHITENESS OF THE PAPER IS BLINDING ME~
...Such as when I wanted to entirely redraw the first portion of the final product.

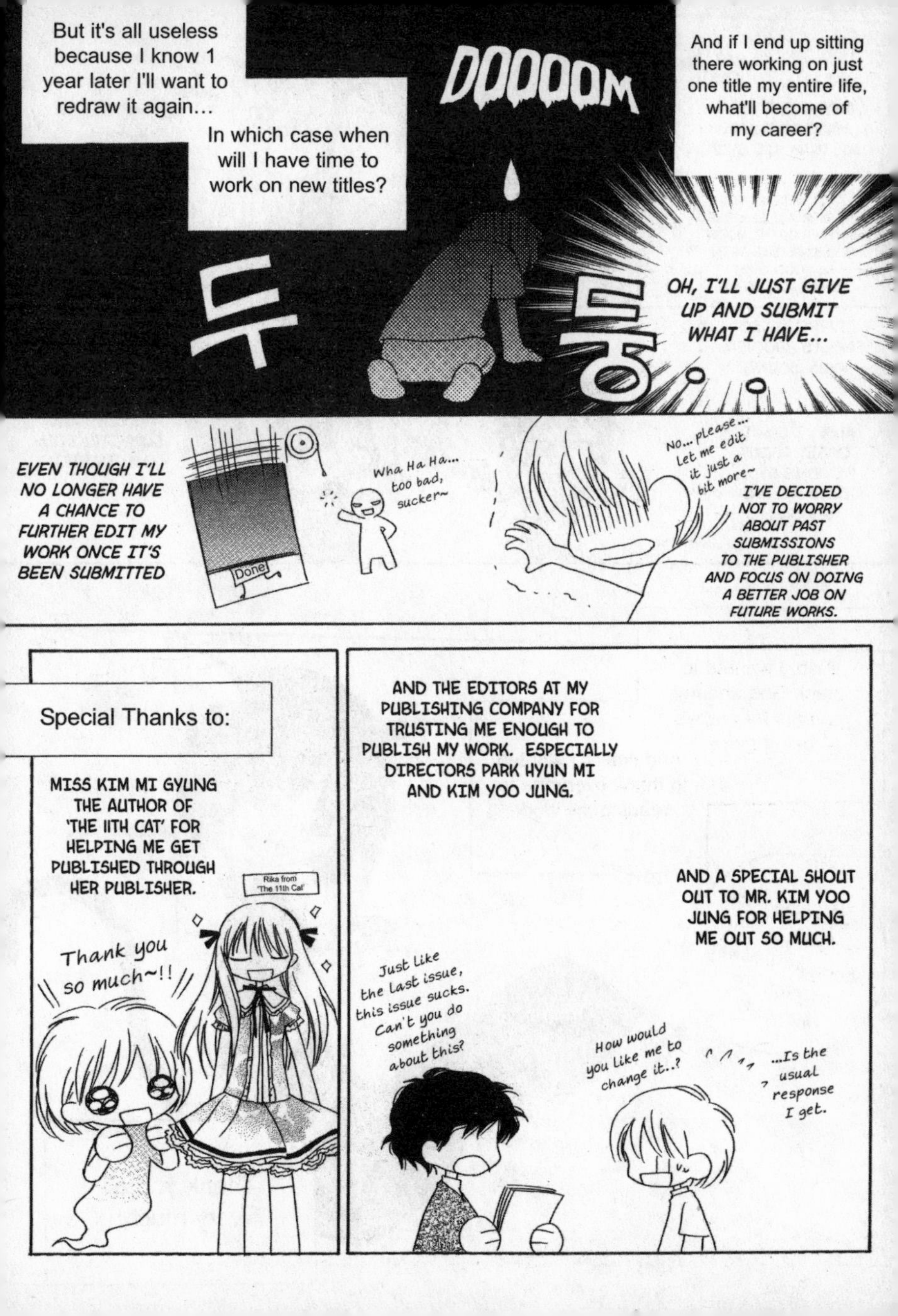
But it's all useless because I know 1 year later I'll want to redraw it again…
In which case when will I have time to work on new titles?
DOOOOM
And if I end up sitting there working on just one title my entire life, what'll become of my career?
두
둥
OH, I'LL JUST GIVE UP AND SUBMIT WHAT I HAVE...
EVEN THOUGH I'LL NO LONGER HAVE A CHANCE TO FURTHER EDIT MY WORK ONCE IT'S BEEN SUBMITTED
Done
Wha Ha Ha... too bad, sucker~
No... please... Let me edit it just a bit more~
I'VE DECIDED NOT TO WORRY ABOUT PAST SUBMISSIONS TO THE PUBLISHER AND FOCUS ON DOING A BETTER JOB ON FUTURE WORKS.
Special Thanks to:
MISS KIM MI GYUNG THE AUTHOR OF 'THE 11TH CAT' FOR HELPING ME GET PUBLISHED THROUGH HER PUBLISHER.
Rika from 'The 11th Cat'
Thank you so much~!!
AND THE EDITORS AT MY PUBLISHING COMPANY FOR TRUSTING ME ENOUGH TO PUBLISH MY WORK. ESPECIALLY DIRECTORS PARK HYUN MI AND KIM YOO JUNG.
AND A SPECIAL SHOUT OUT TO MR. KIM YOO JUNG FOR HELPING ME OUT SO MUCH.
Just like the last issue, this issue sucks. Can't you do something about this?
How would you like me to change it..?
...Is the usual response I get.

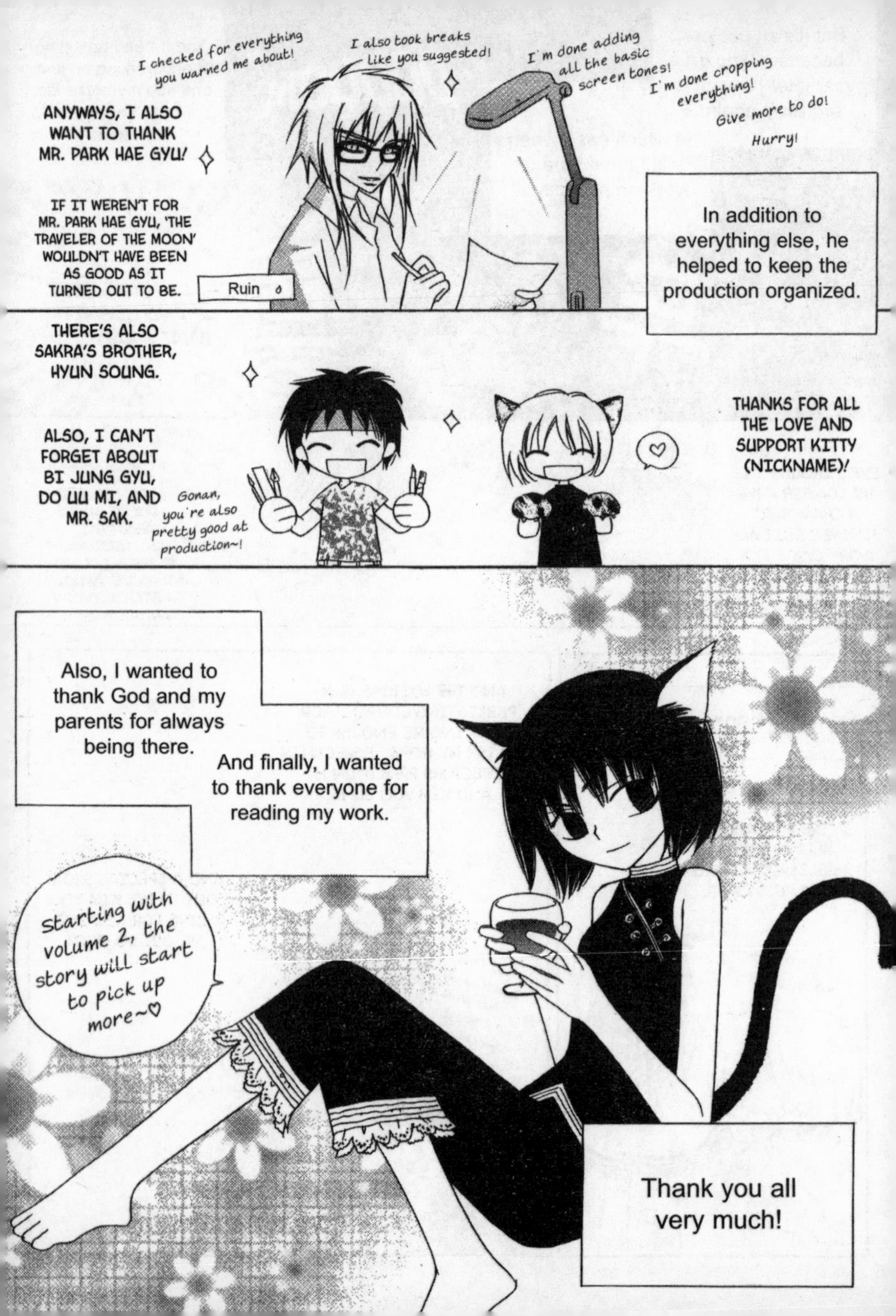
I checked for everything you warned me about!
I also took breaks like you suggested!
I'm done adding all the basic screen tones!
I'm done cropping everything!
Give more to do!
Hurry!
ANYWAYS, I ALSO WANT TO THANK MR. PARK HAE GYU!
IF IT WEREN'T FOR MR. PARK HAE GYU, 'THE TRAVELER OF THE MOON' WOULDN'T HAVE BEEN AS GOOD AS IT TURNED OUT TO BE.
Ruin
In addition to everything else, he helped to keep the production organized.
THERE'S ALSO SAKRA'S BROTHER, HYUN SOUNG.
ALSO, I CAN'T FORGET ABOUT BI JUNG GYU, DO UU MI, AND MR. SAK.
Gonan, you're also pretty good at production~!
THANKS FOR ALL THE LOVE AND SUPPORT KITTY (NICKNAME)!
Also, I wanted to thank God and my parents for always being there.
And finally, I wanted to thank everyone for reading my work.
Starting with volume 2, the story will start to pick up more~♡
Thank you all very much!

TRAVELER OF THE MOON

VOLUME 1

Art and Story by
Lee Na Hyeon

English Version First Print
February 2005

Produced By

Infinity Studios
www.infinitystudios.com

6331 Fairmount Ave Suite #1
El Cerrito, CA 94530

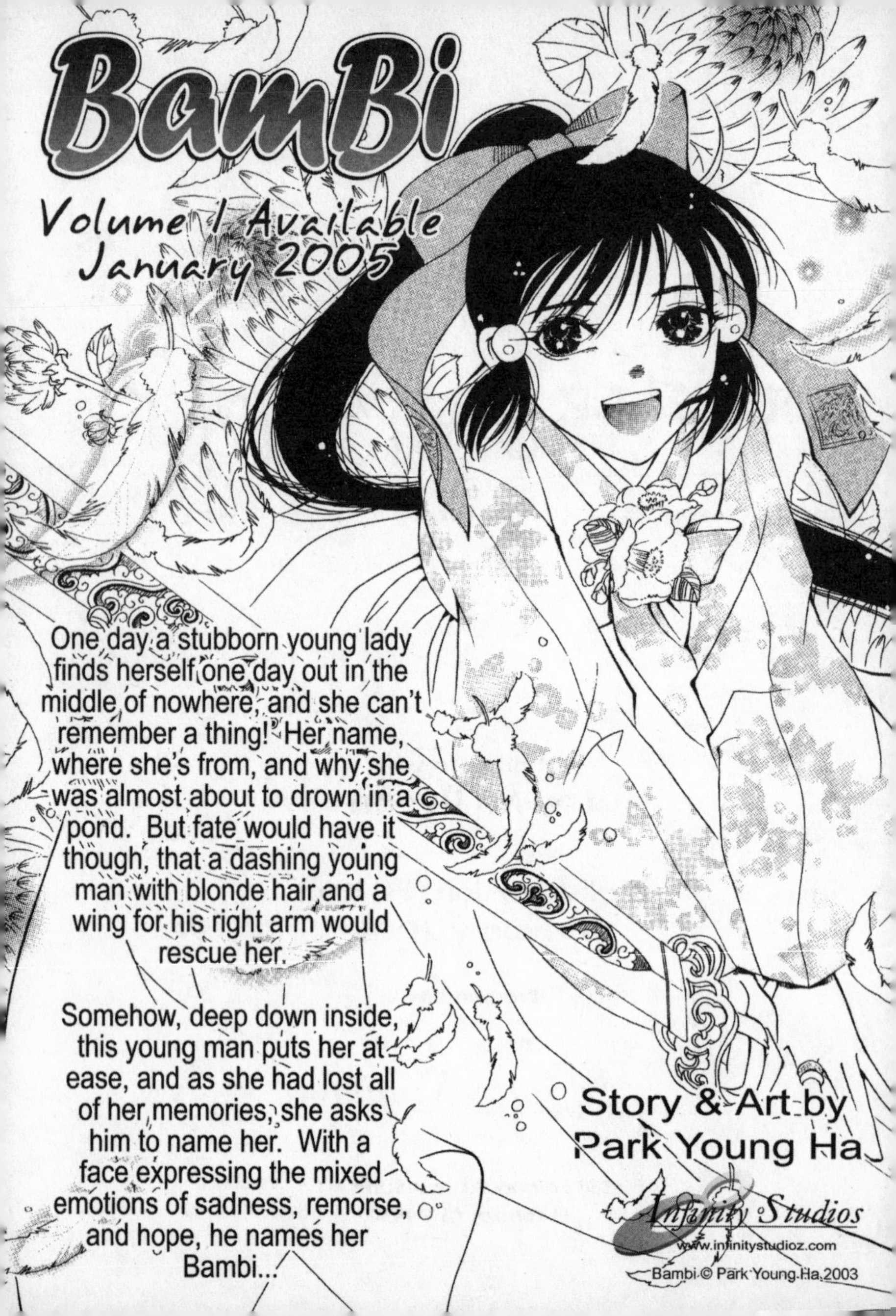
BamBi
Volume 1 Available
January 2005
One day a stubborn young lady finds herself one day out in the middle of nowhere, and she can't remember a thing! Her name, where she's from, and why she was almost about to drown in a pond. But fate would have it though, that a dashing young man with blonde hair and a wing for his right arm would rescue her.
Somehow, deep down inside, this young man puts her at ease, and as she had lost all of her memories, she asks him to name her. With a face expressing the mixed emotions of sadness, remorse, and hope, he names her Bambi...
Story & Art by
Park Young Ha
Infinity Studios
www.infinitystudioz.com
Bambi © Park Young Ha 2003

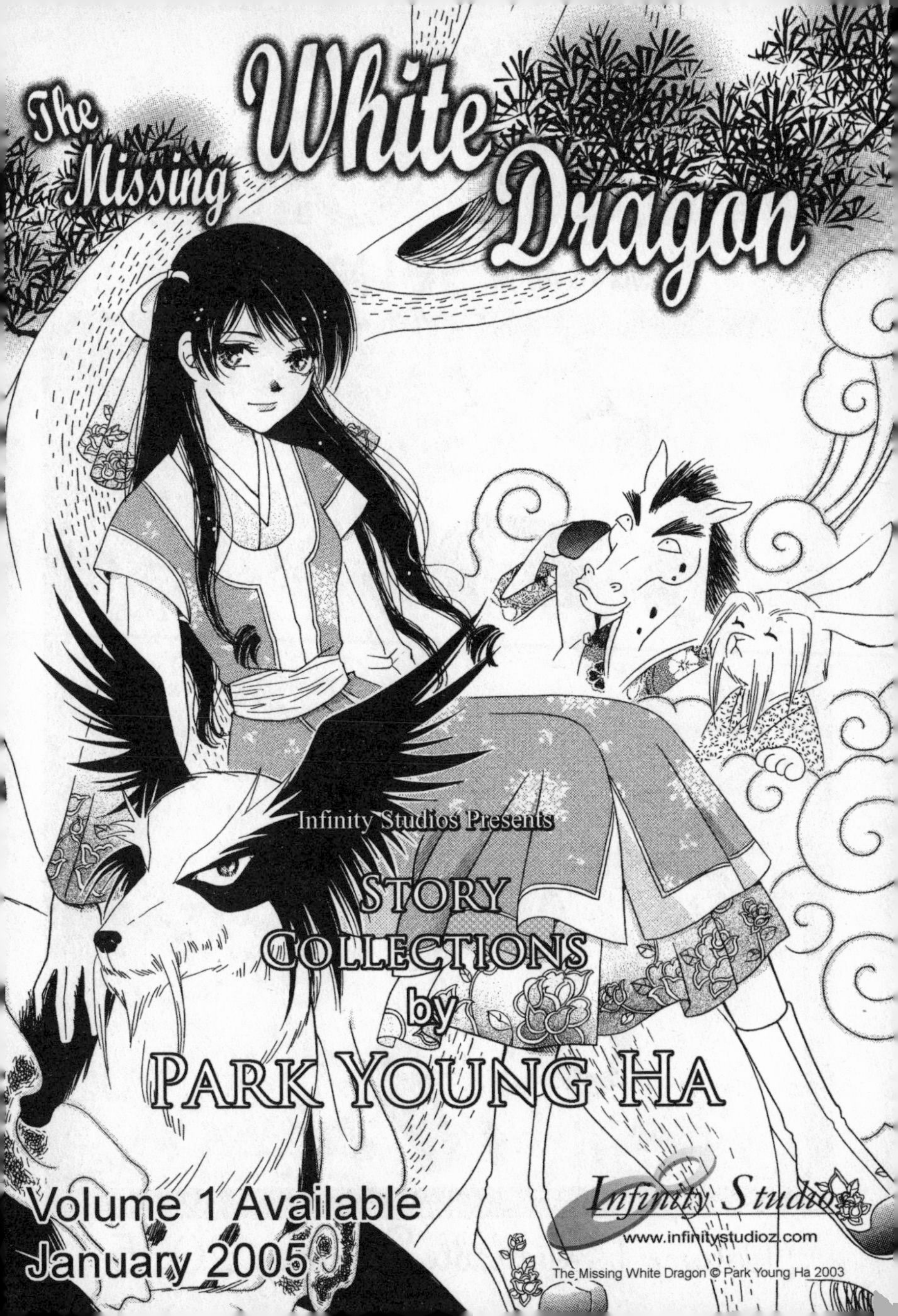
The Missing White Dragon
Infinity Studios Presents
STORY COLLECTIONS by
PARK YOUNG HA
Volume 1 Available
January 2005
Infinity Studios
www.infinitystudioz.com
The Missing White Dragon © Park Young Ha 2003

Infinity Studios Presents

Witch Class

Story & Art By ✽ Lee Ru

Name : Dorothy
Occupation : Student
Goal : "I want to become a witch to live out the romantic dream every girl wishes for... you know, like turning the world into a dark hellish cauldron, making everyone bow to me, and summoning cute zombies, tee hee hee~!

Volume 1 Available January 2005

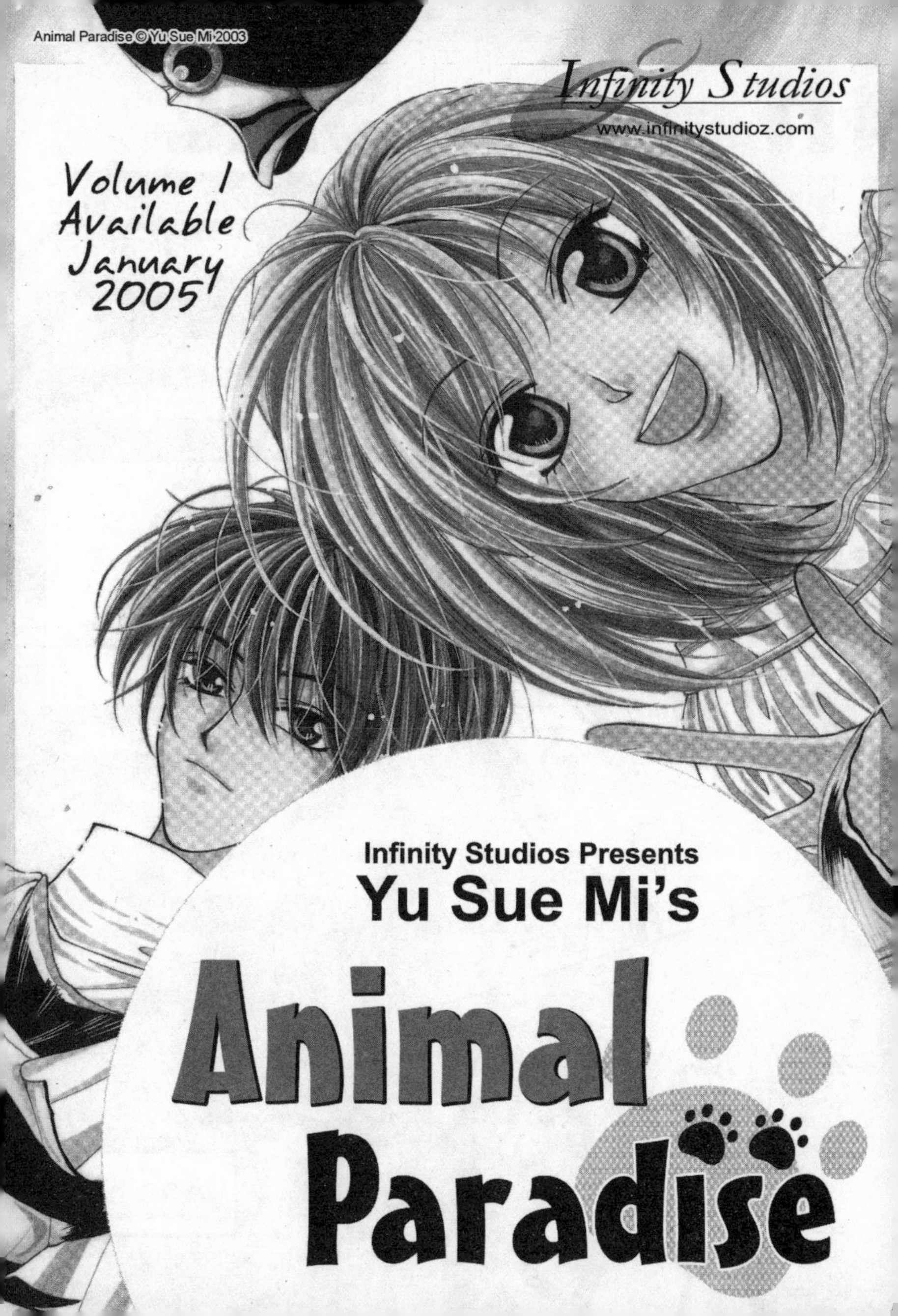
Animal Paradise © Yu Sue Mi 2003
Infinity Studios
www.infinitystudioz.com
Volume 1
Available
January
2005
Infinity Studios Presents
Yu Sue Mi's
Animal
Paradise

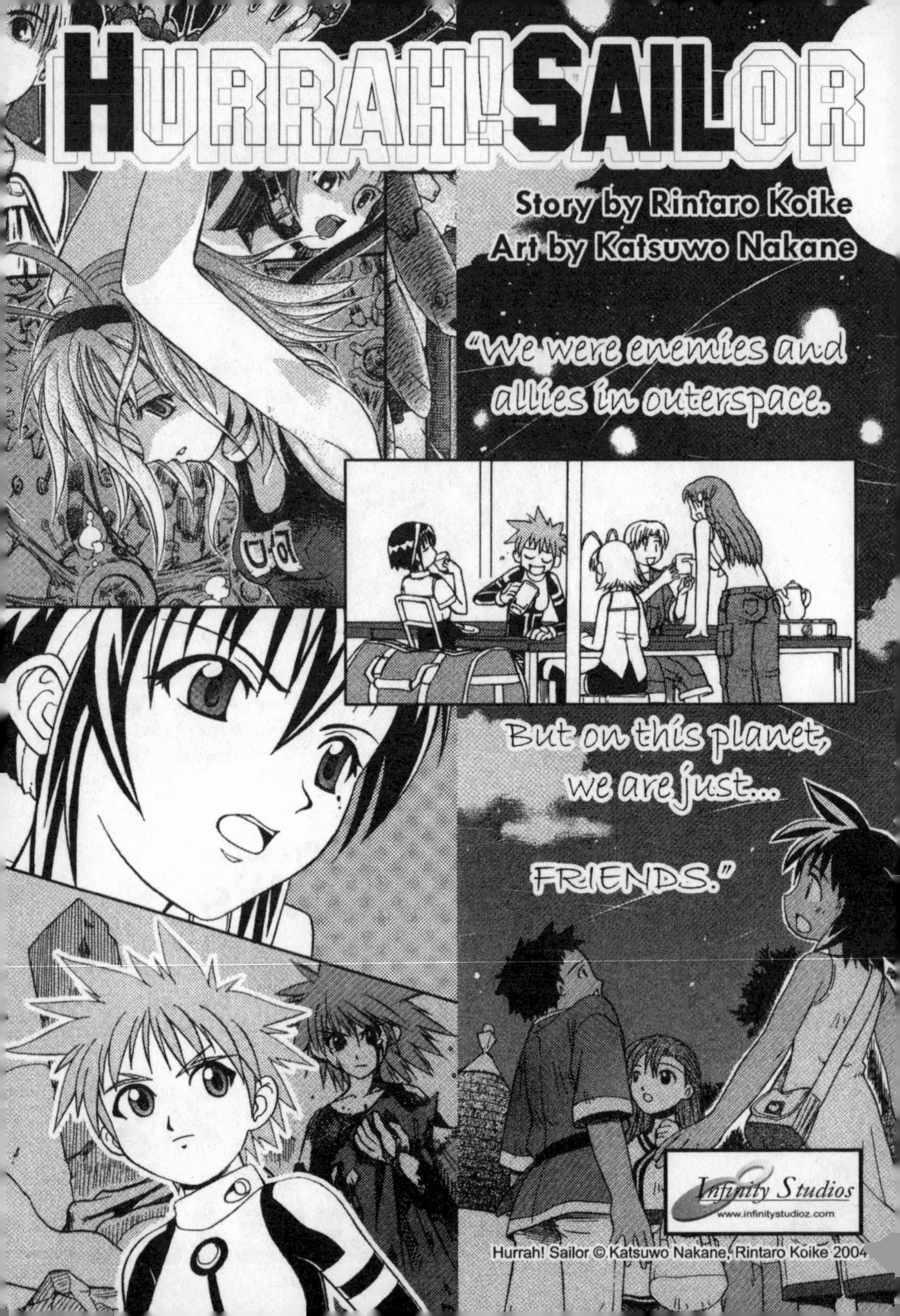
HURRAH! SAILOR
Story by Rintaro Koike
Art by Katsuwo Nakane
"We were enemies and allies in outerspace.
But on this planet, we are just...
FRIENDS."
Infinity Studios
www.infinitystudioz.com
Hurrah! Sailor © Katsuwo Nakane, Rintaro Koike 2004

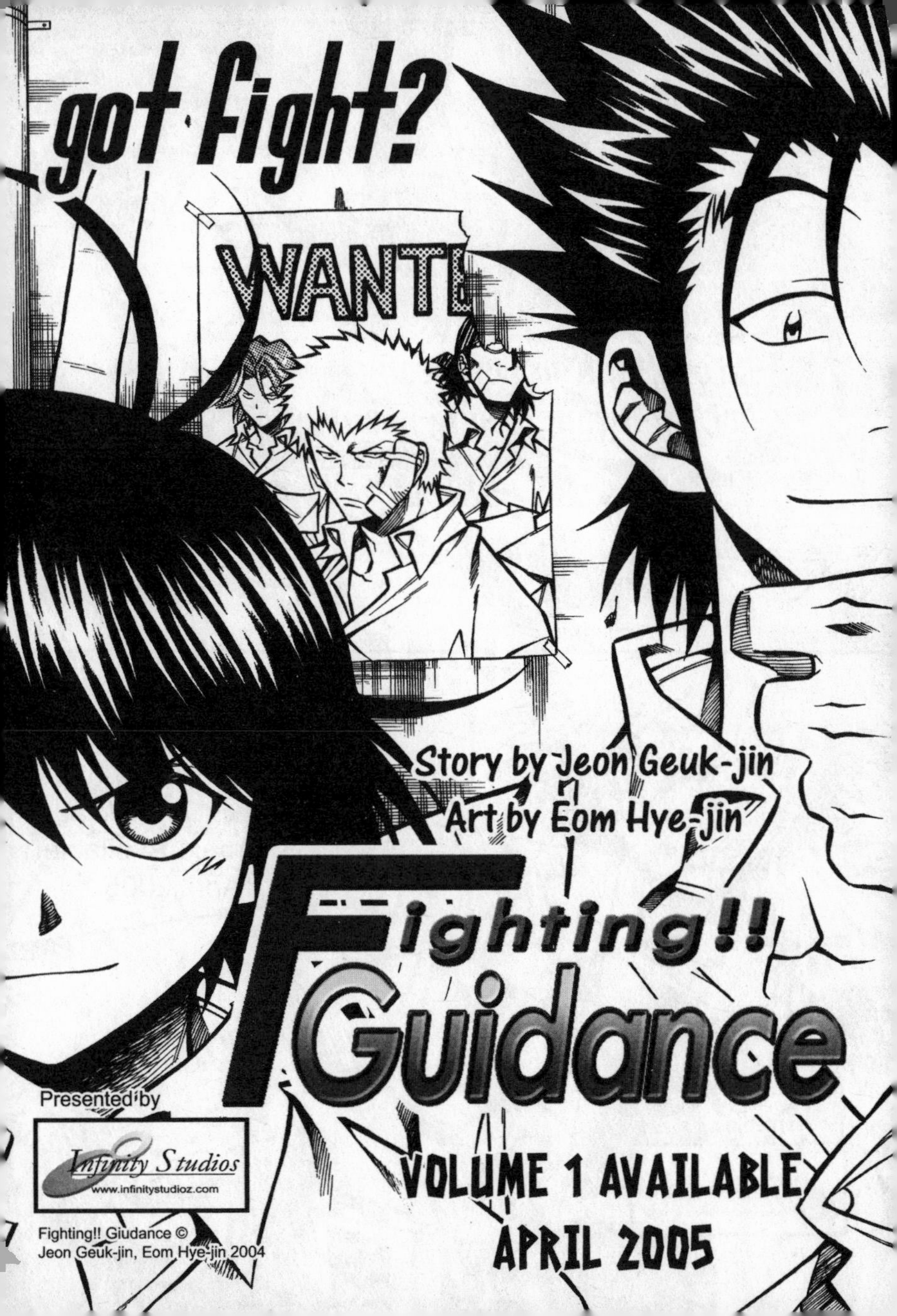
got fight?
WANTE
Story by Jeon Geuk-jin
Art by Eom Hye-jin
Fighting!!
Guidance
Presented by
Infinity Studios
www.infinitystudioz.com
VOLUME 1 AVAILABLE
APRIL 2005
Fighting!! Giudance ©
Jeon Geuk-jin, Eom Hye-jin 2004

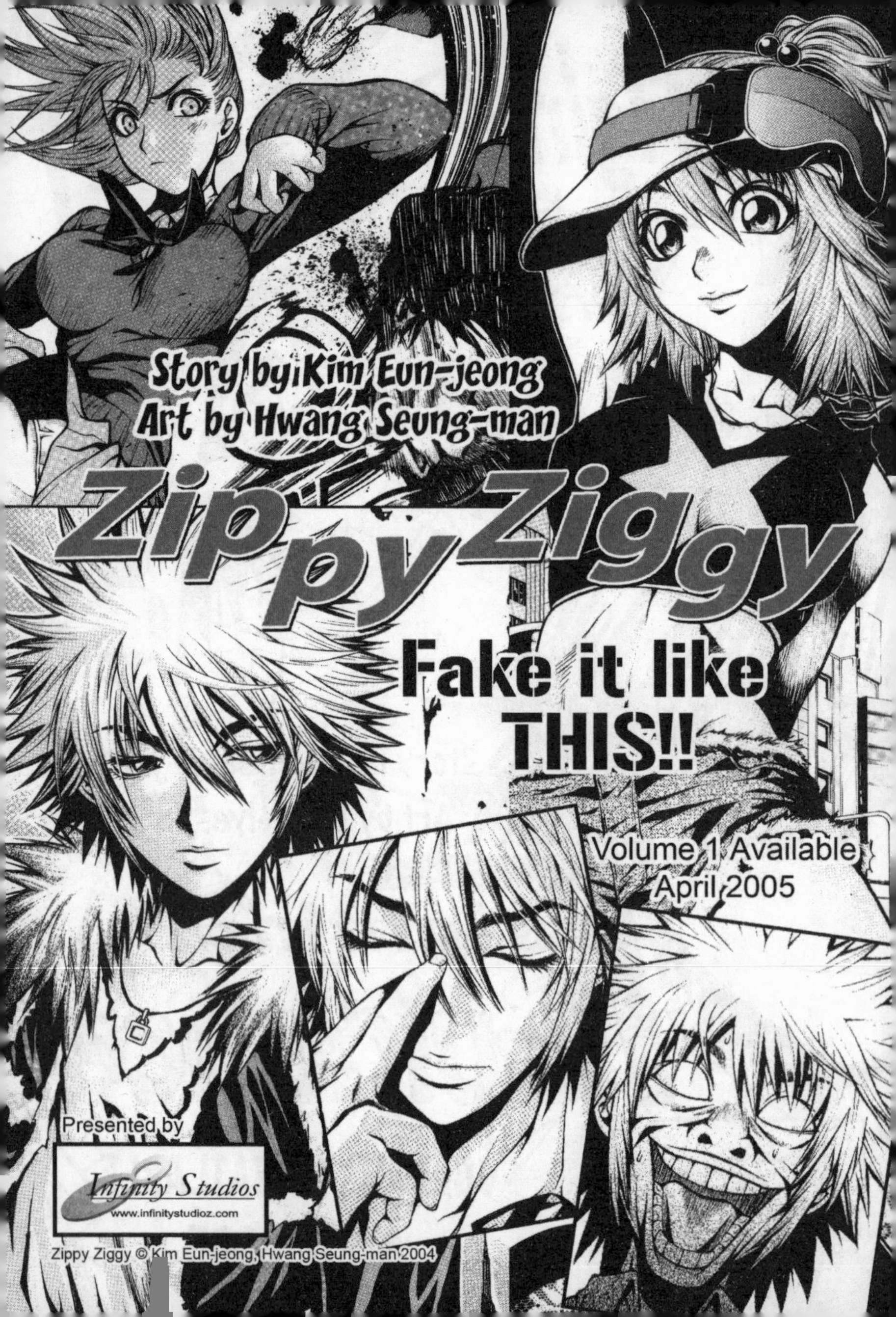
Story by Kim Eun-jeong
Art by Hwang Seung-man
Zippy Ziggy
Fake it like THIS!!
Volume 1 Available April 2005
Presented by
Infinity Studios
www.infinitystudioz.com
Zippy Ziggy © Kim Eun-jeong, Hwang Seung-man 2004

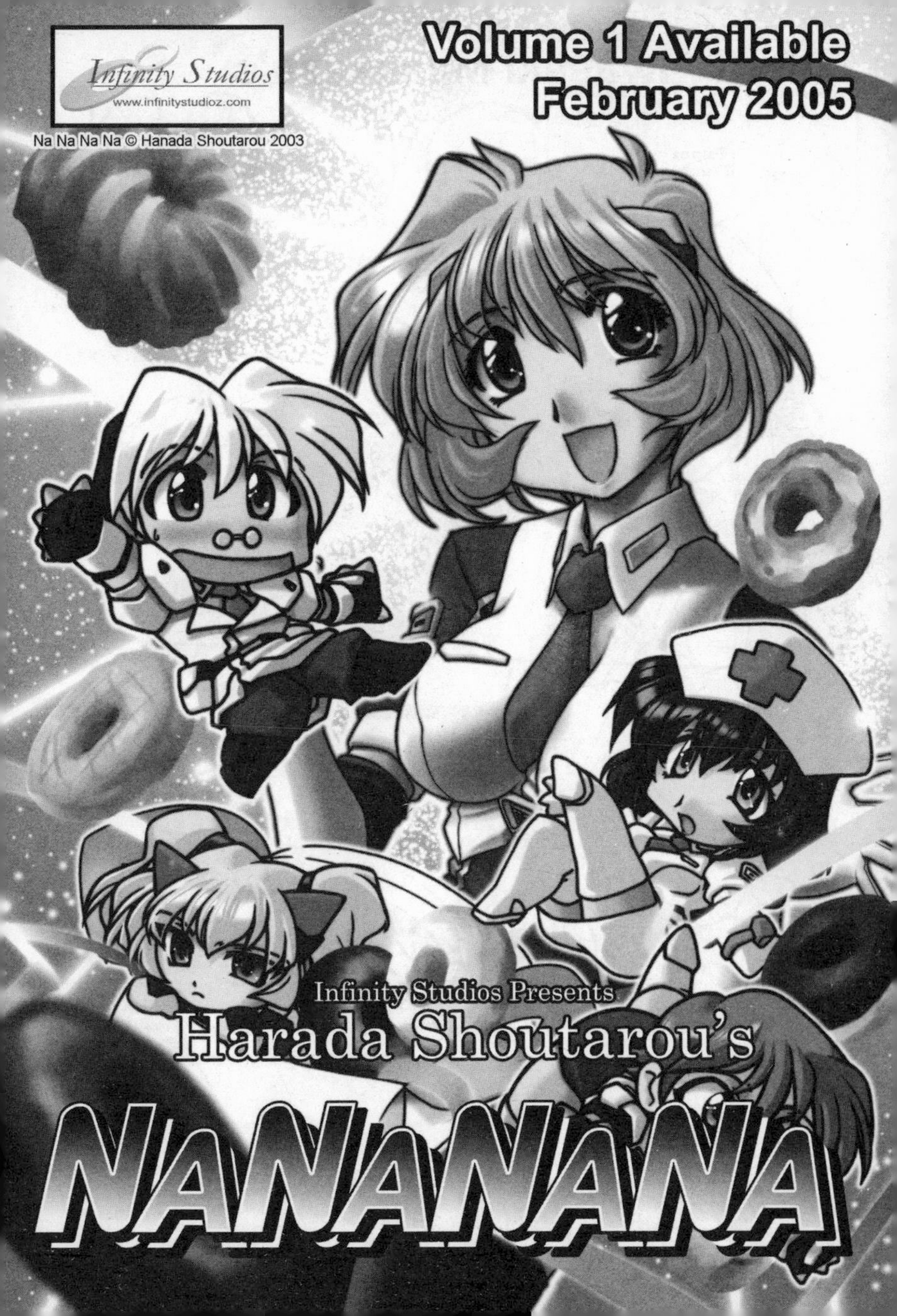
Infinity Studios
www.infinitystudioz.com
Na Na Na Na © Hanada Shoutarou 2003
Volume 1 Available
February 2005
Infinity Studios Presents
Harada Shoutarou's
NANANANA

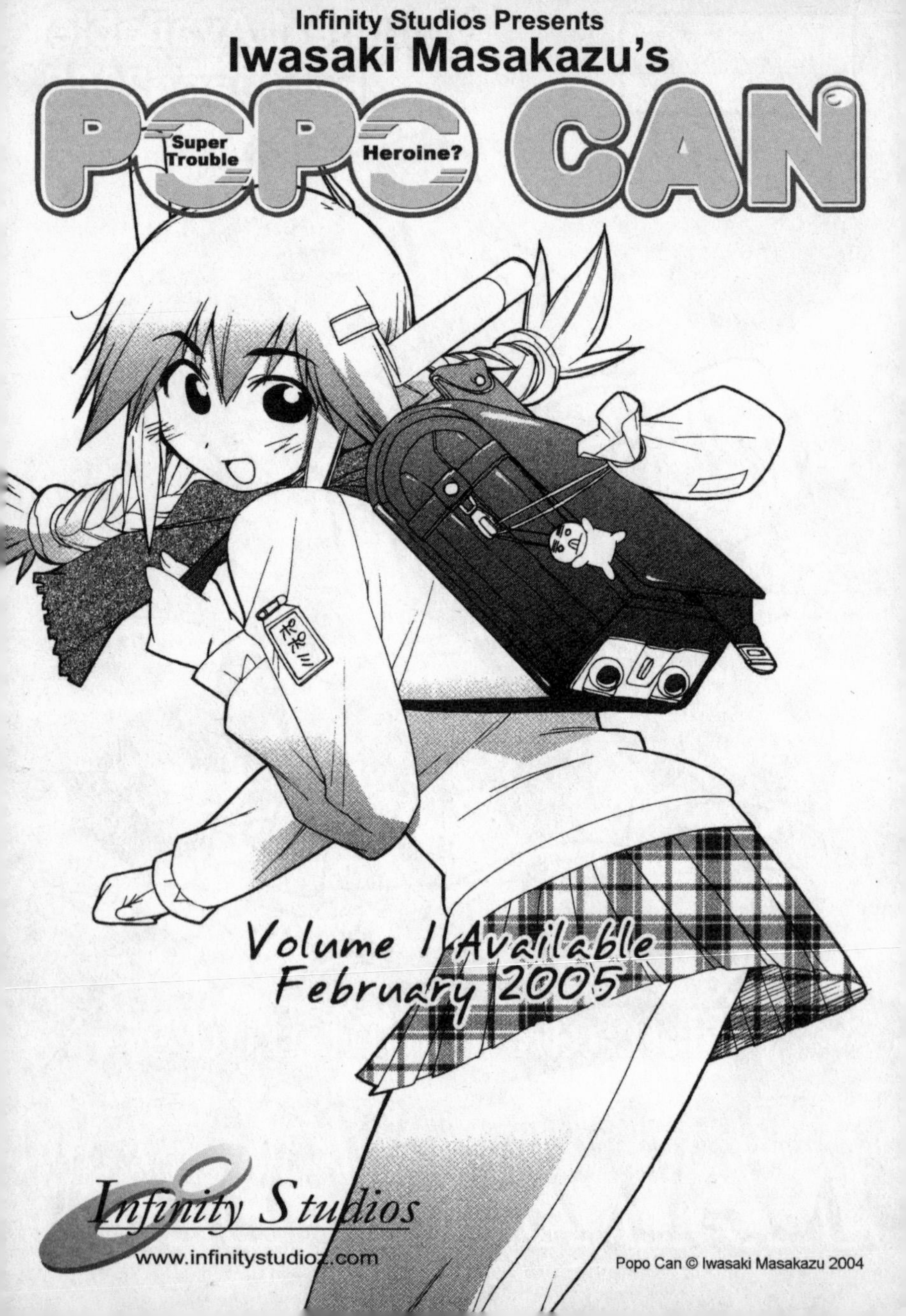
Infinity Studios Presents
Iwasaki Masakazu's
POPO CAN
Super Trouble Heroine?
Volume 1 Available
February 2005
Infinity Studios
www.infinitystudioz.com
Popo Can © Iwasaki Masakazu 2004